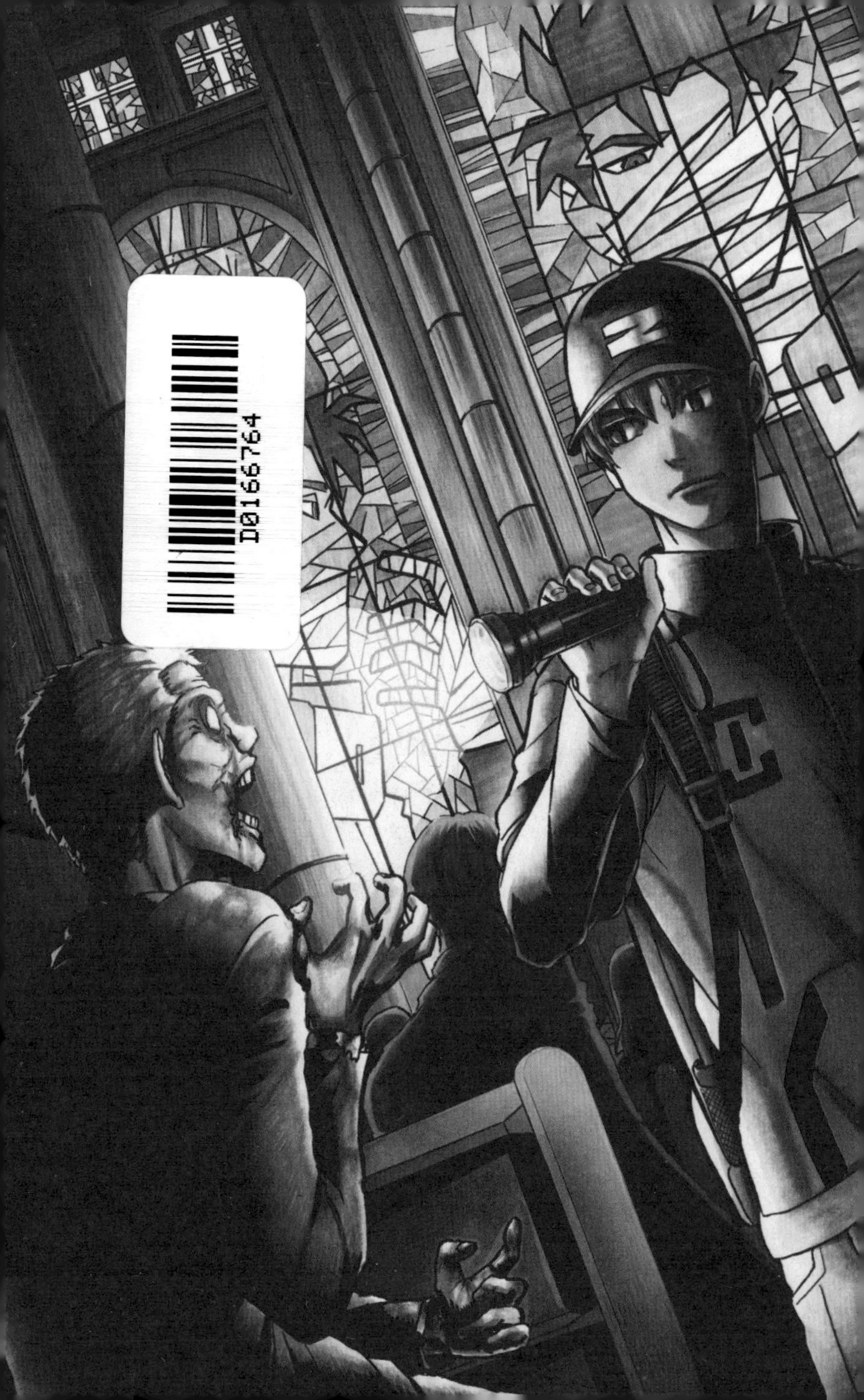

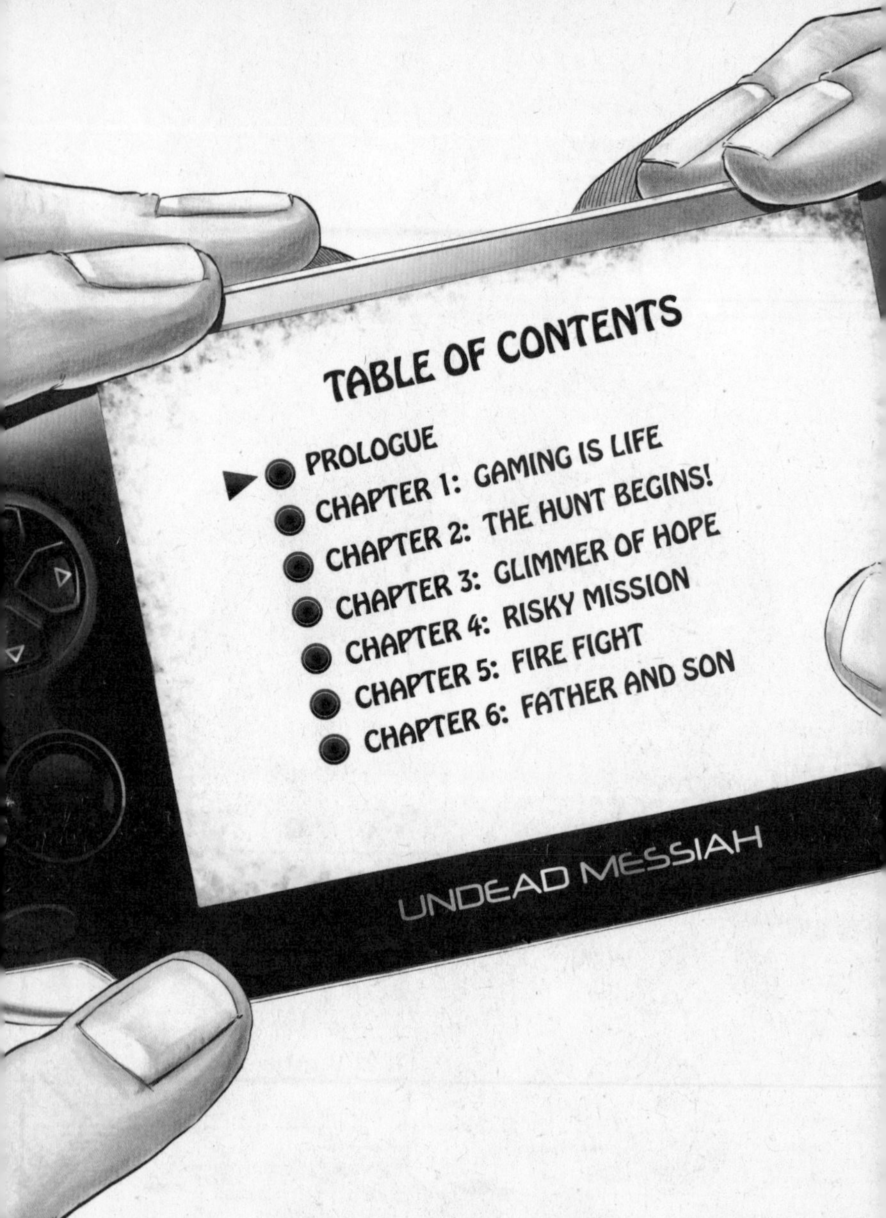
TABLE OF CONTENTS
PROLOGUE
CHAPTER 1: GAMING IS LIFE
CHAPTER 2: THE HUNT BEGINS!
CHAPTER 3: GLIMMER OF HOPE
CHAPTER 4: RISKY MISSION
CHAPTER 5: FIRE FIGHT
CHAPTER 6: FATHER AND SON
UNDEAD MESSIAH

UNDEAD MESSIAH 1

Gin Zarbo

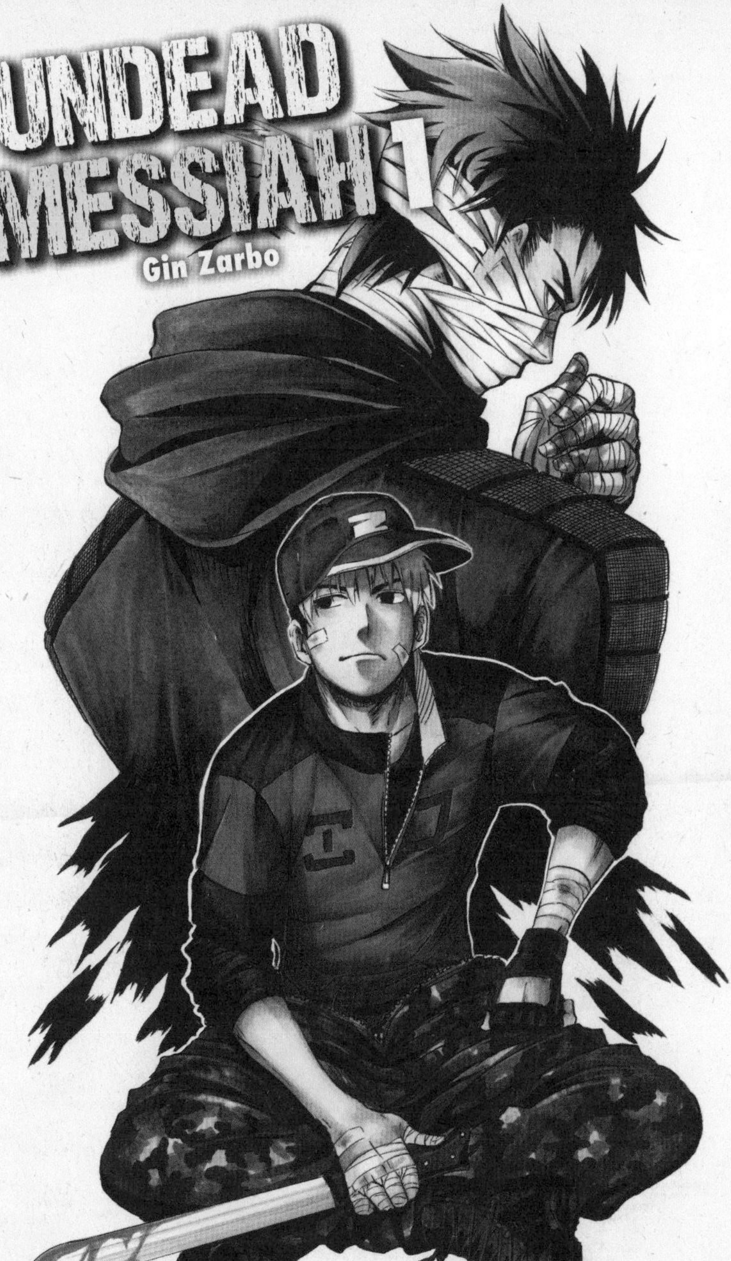

TOKYOPOP

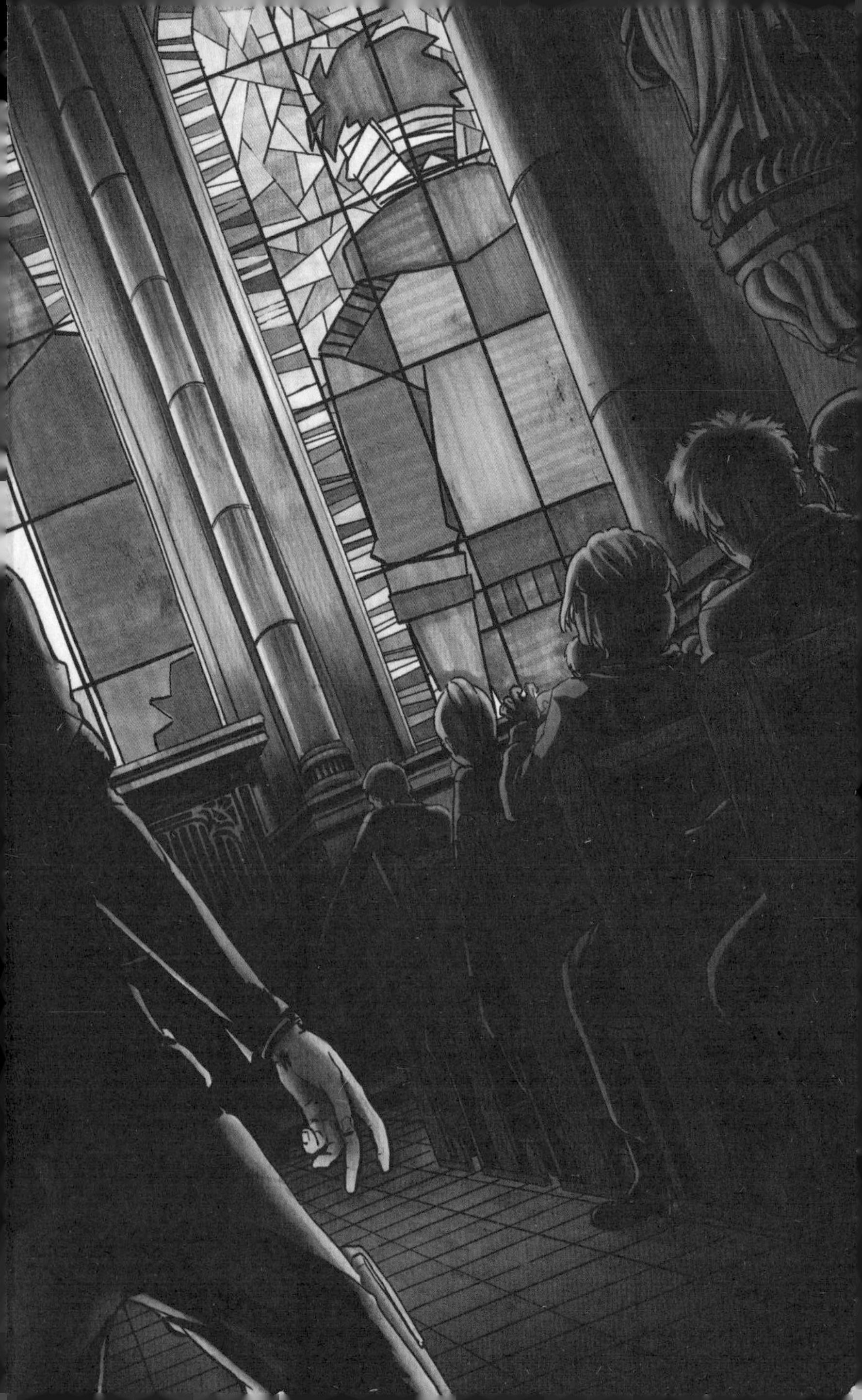

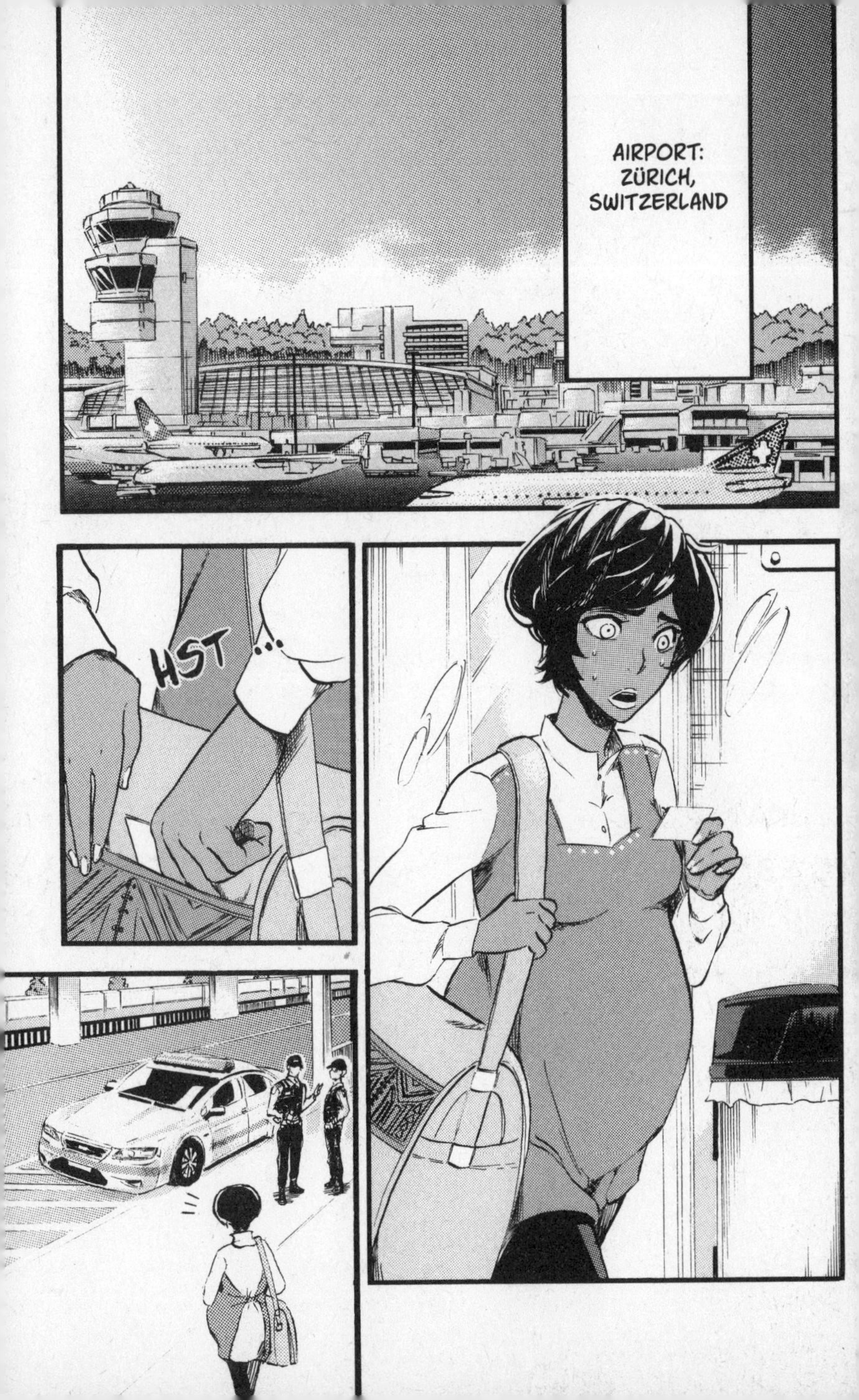
AIRPORT: ZÜRICH, SWITZERLAND
HST ..

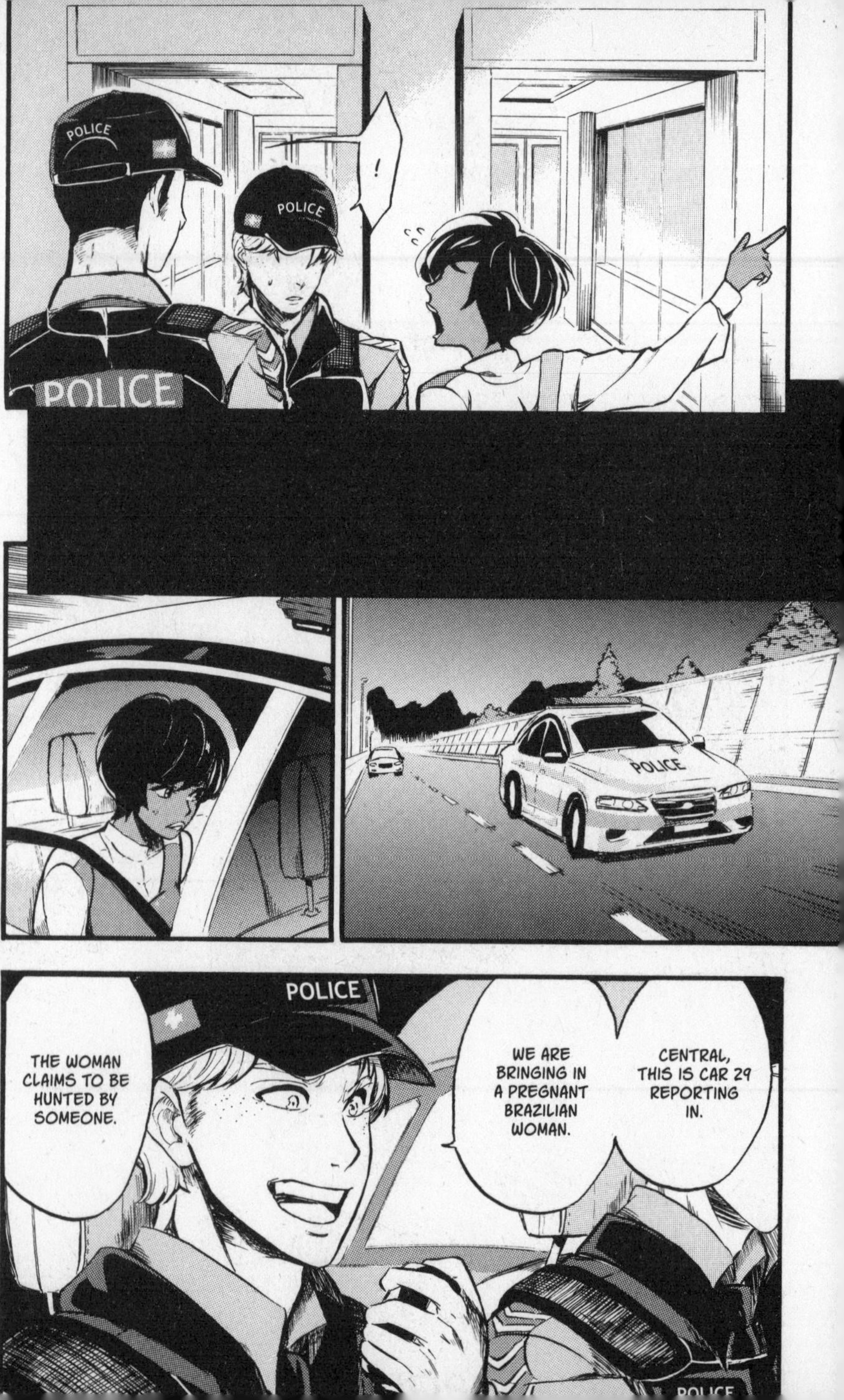
!
CENTRAL, THIS IS CAR 29 REPORTING IN.
WE ARE BRINGING IN A PREGNANT BRAZILIAN WOMAN.
THE WOMAN CLAIMS TO BE HUNTED BY SOMEONE.

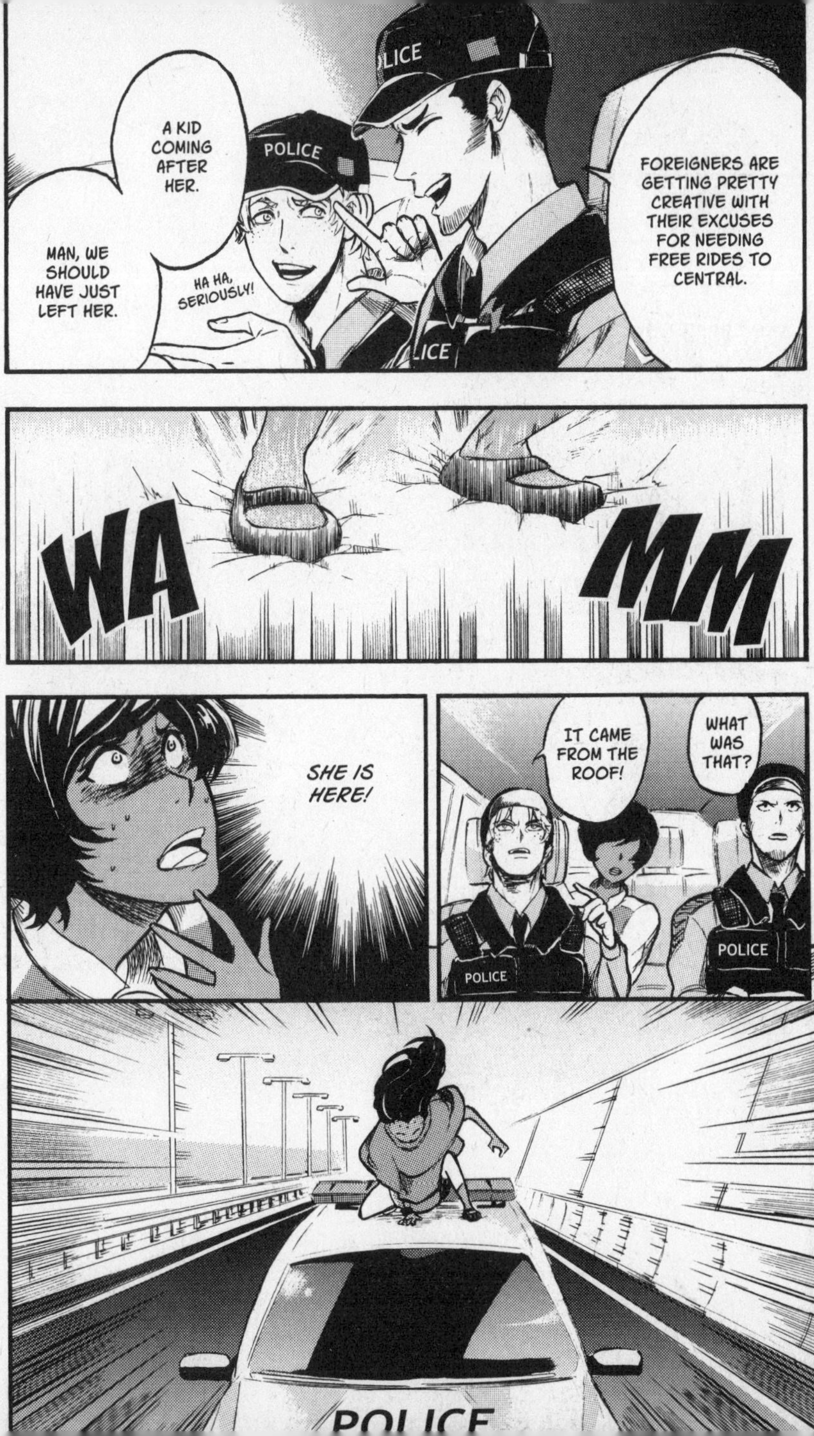
FOREIGNERS ARE GETTING PRETTY CREATIVE WITH THEIR EXCUSES FOR NEEDING FREE RIDES TO CENTRAL.
A KID COMING AFTER HER.
HA HA, SERIOUSLY!
MAN, WE SHOULD HAVE JUST LEFT HER.
WAMM
WHAT WAS THAT?
IT CAME FROM THE ROOF!
SHE IS HERE!
POLICE

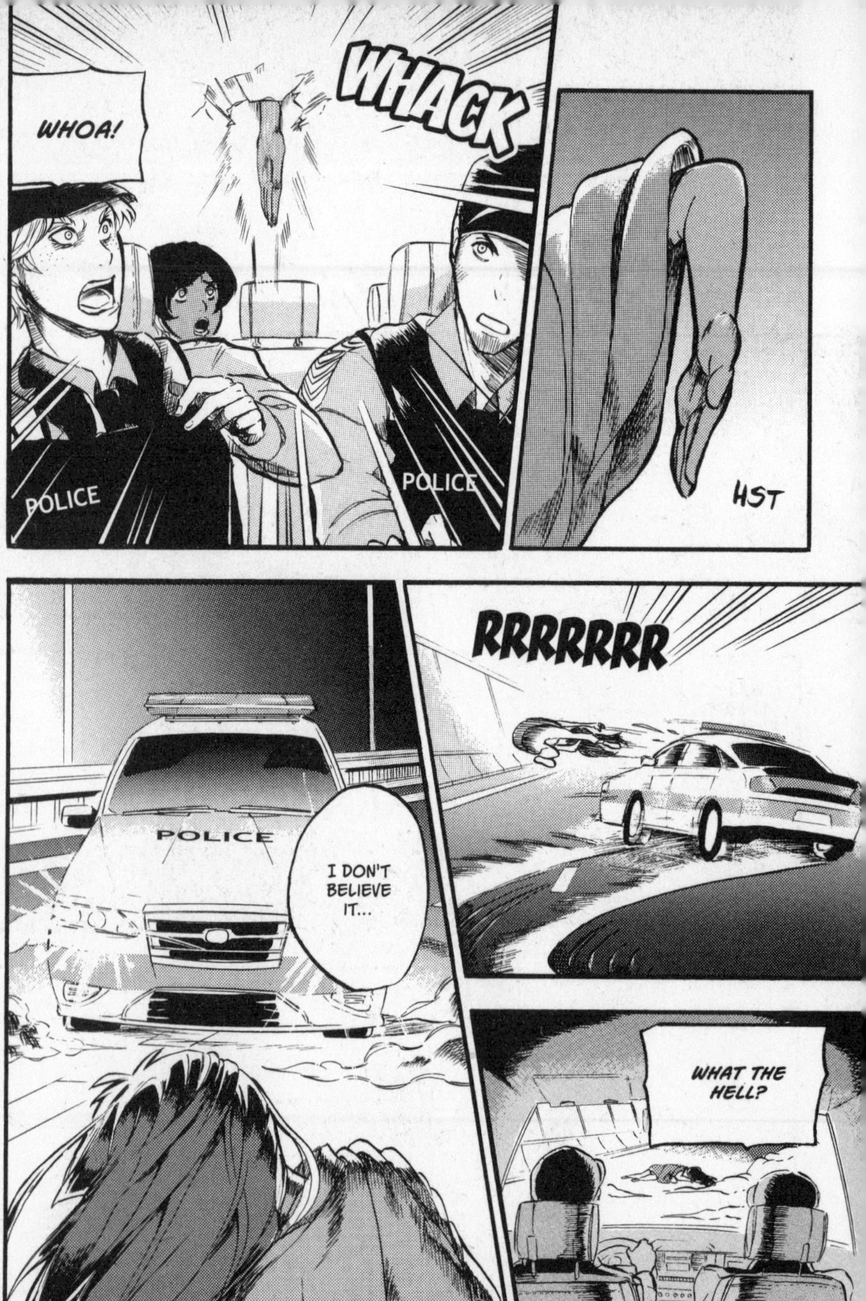
HST
WHACK
WHOA!
POLICE
POLICE
RRRRRRR
WHAT THE HELL?
POLICE
I DON'T BELIEVE IT...

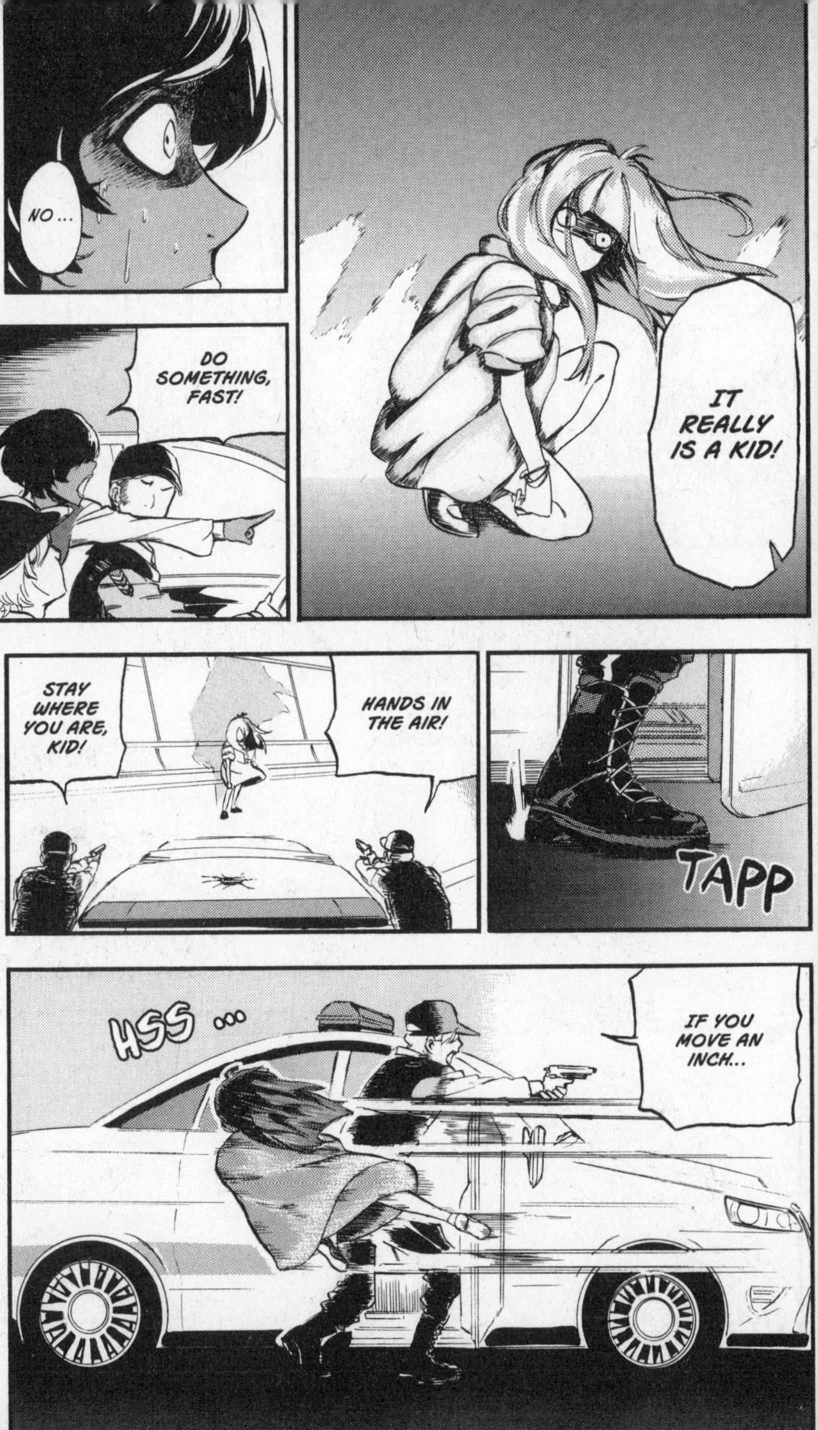
IT REALLY IS A KID!
NO...
DO SOMETHING, FAST!
TAPP
HANDS IN THE AIR!
STAY WHERE YOU ARE, KID!
IF YOU MOVE AN INCH...
HSS ...

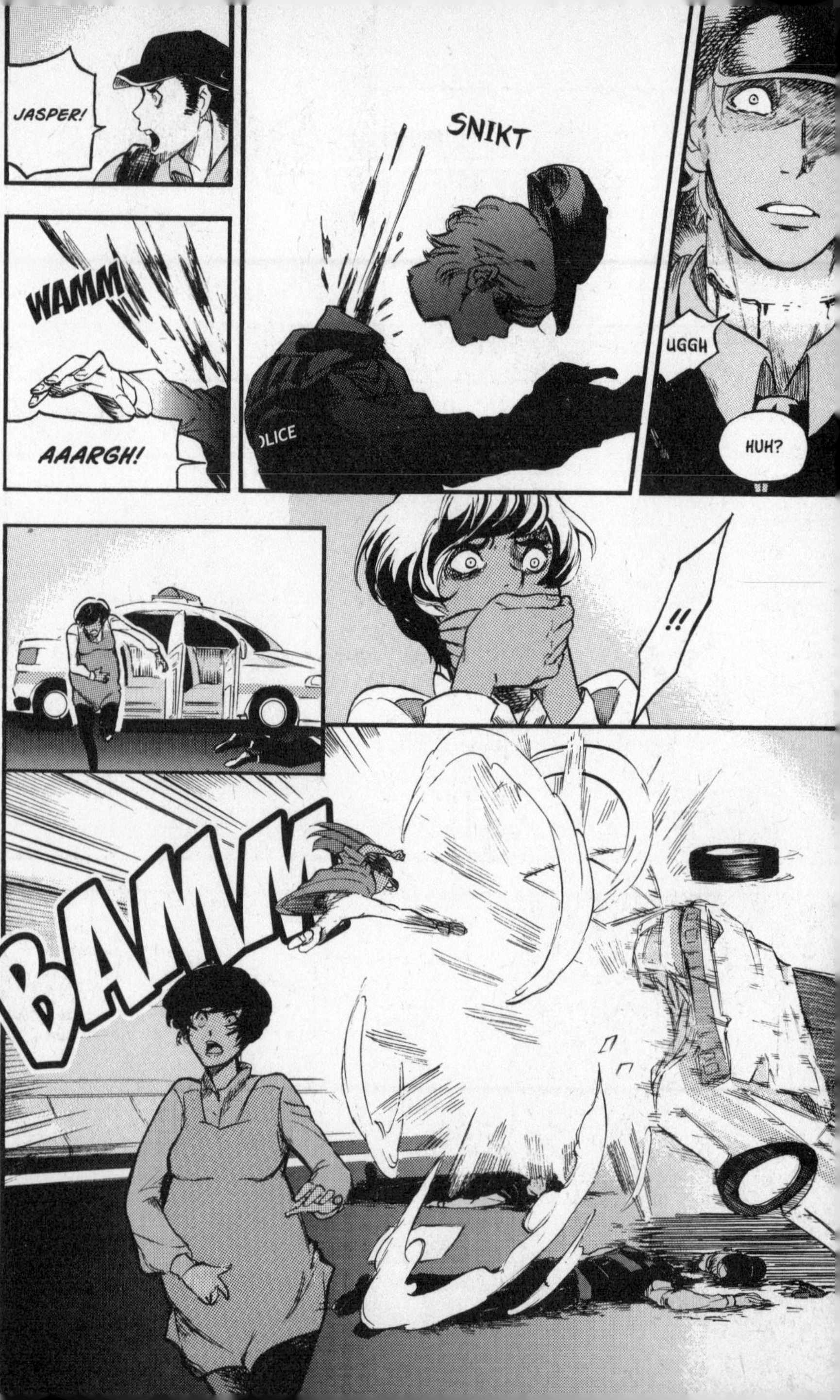
UGGH
HUH?
SNIKT
JASPER!
WAMM
AAARGH!
!!
BAMM

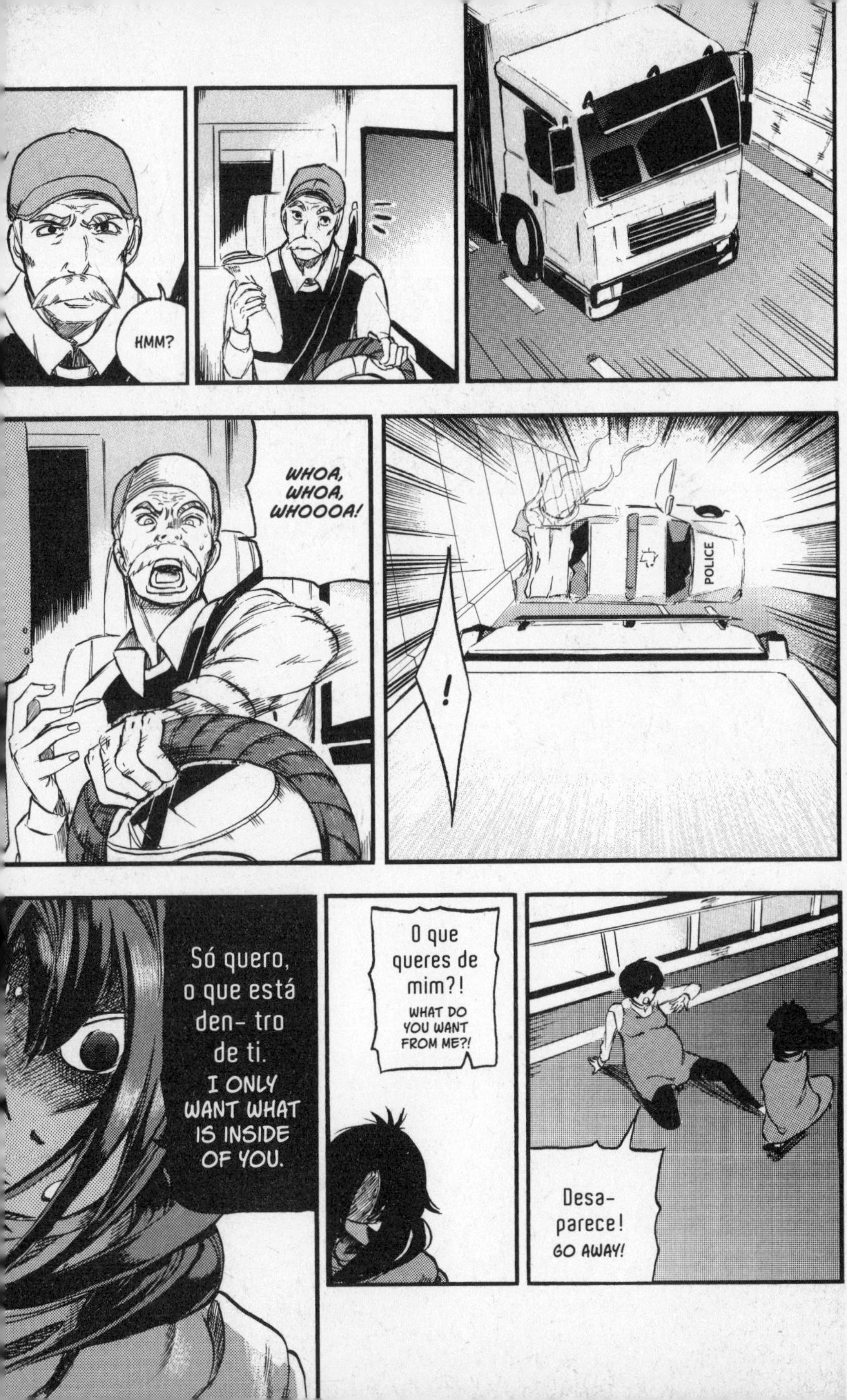
HMM?
!
WHOA, WHOA, WHOOOA!
Desa- parece!
GO AWAY!
O que queres de mim?!
WHAT DO YOU WANT FROM ME?!
Só quero, o que está den- tro de ti.
I ONLY WANT WHAT IS INSIDE OF YOU.

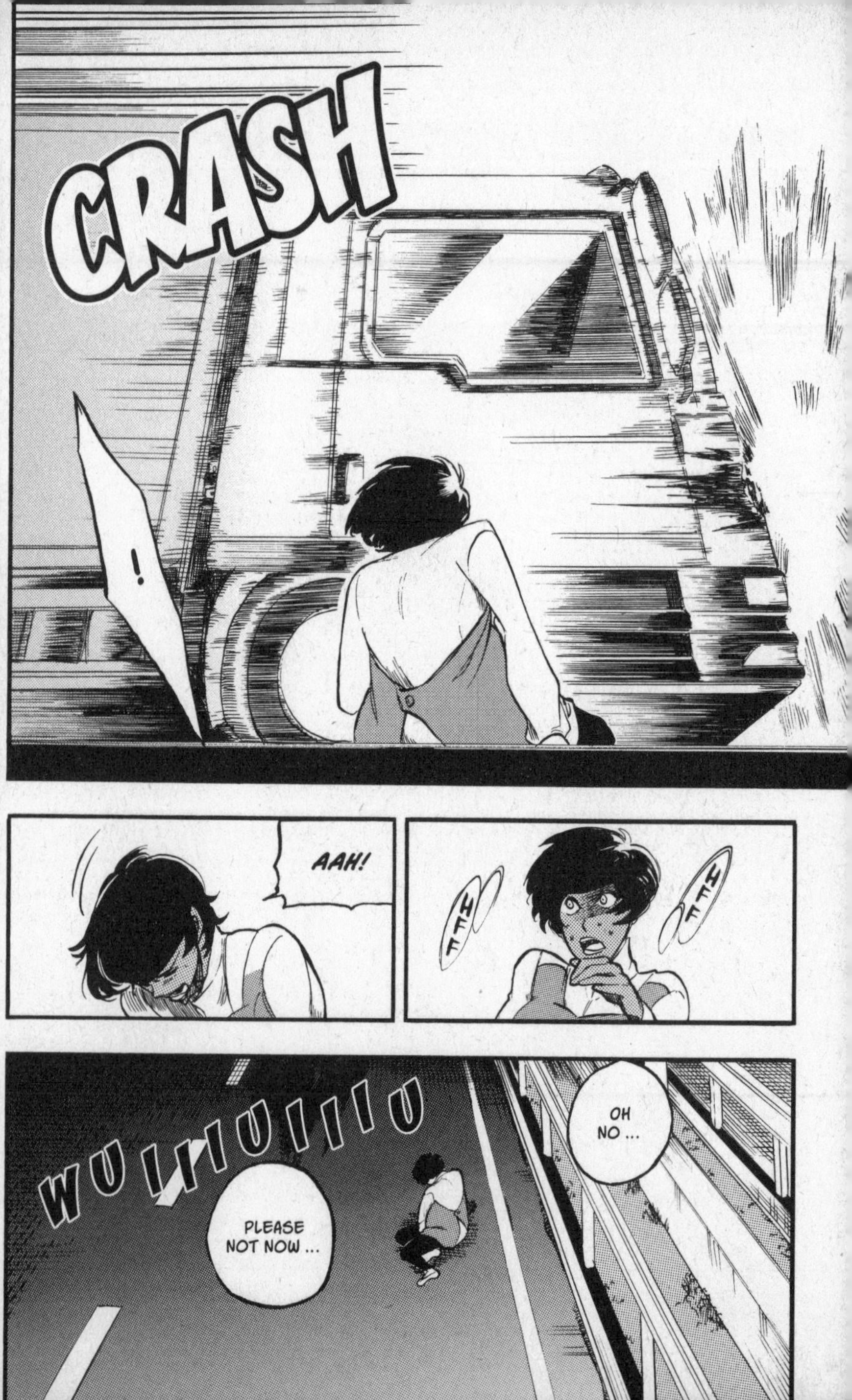
CRASH
!
HFF
HFF
AAH!
OH NO ...
WUIIIUIIIU
PLEASE NOT NOW ...

CHAPTER 1: GAMING IS LIFE

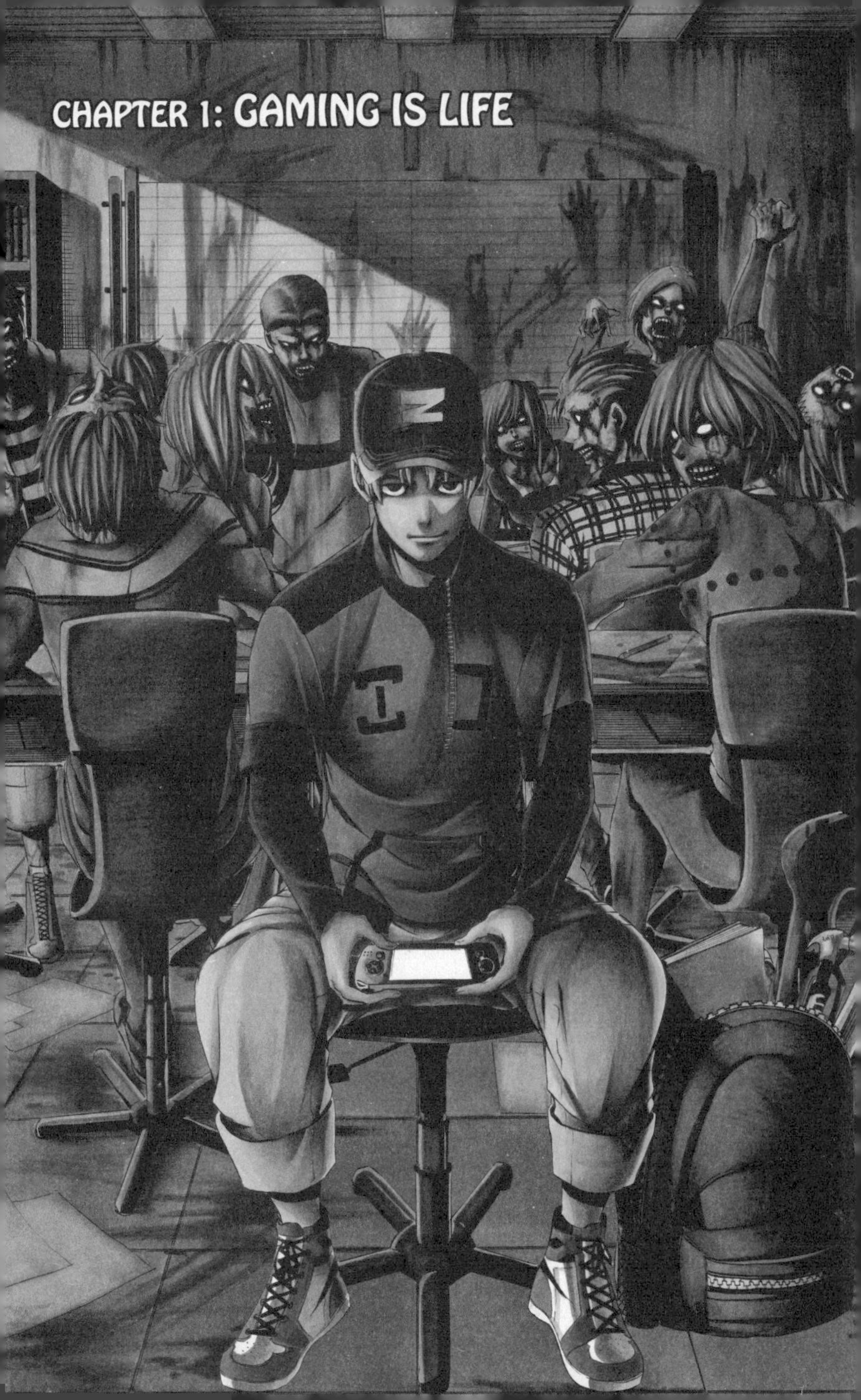

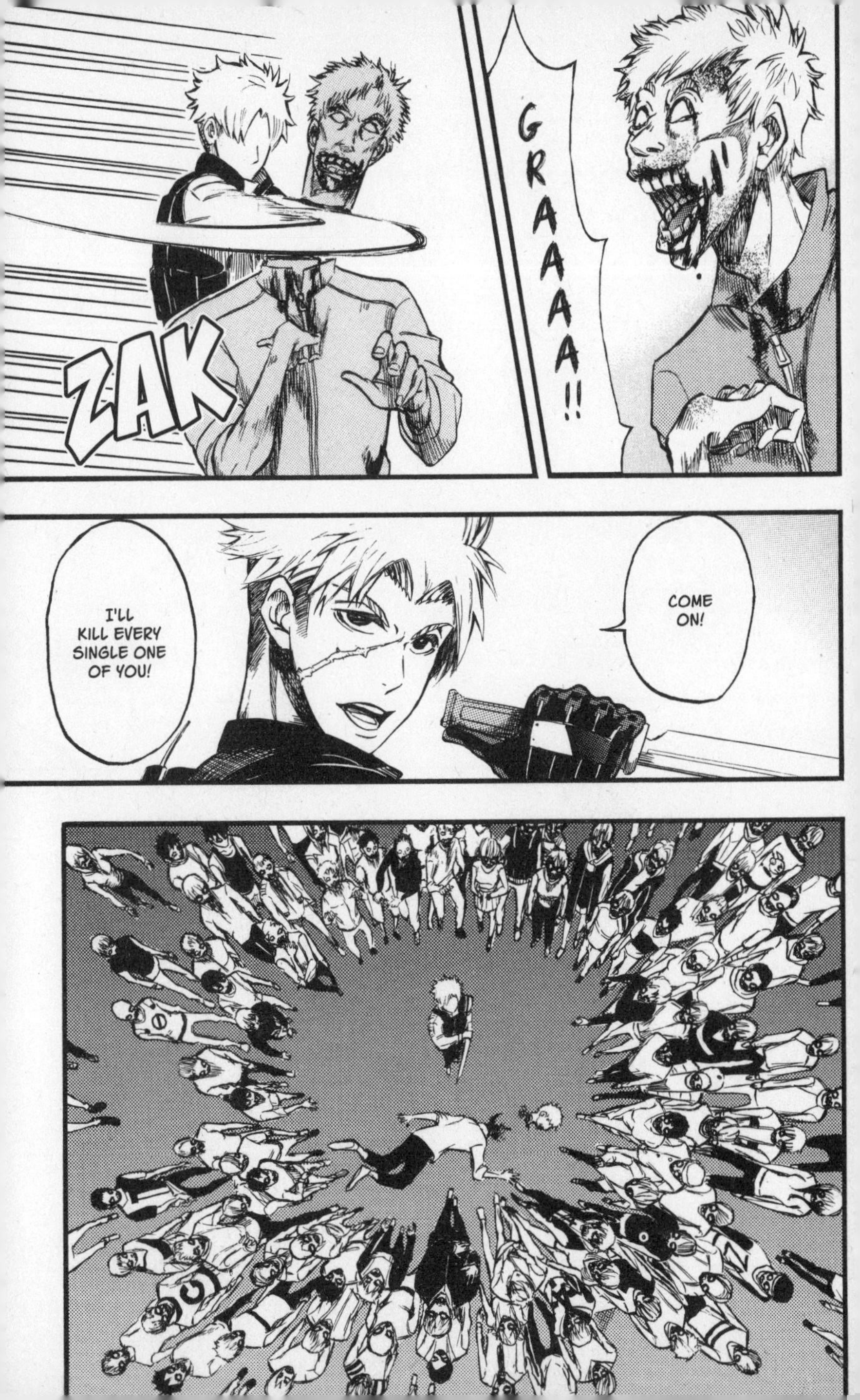
GRAAAAA!!
ZAK
COME ON!
I'LL KILL EVERY SINGLE ONE OF YOU!

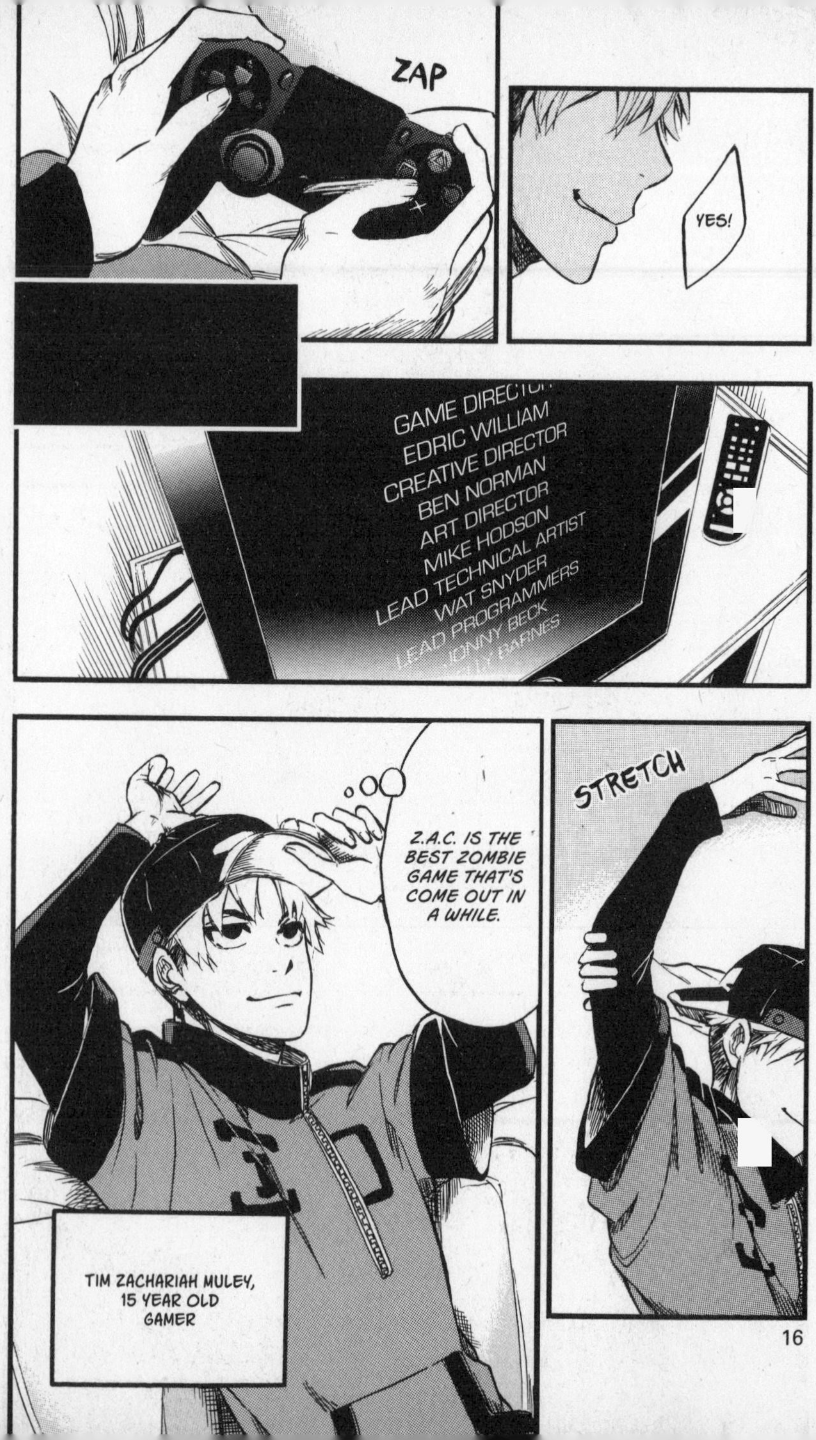
YES!
ZAP
GAME DIRECTOR
EDRIC WILLIAM
CREATIVE DIRECTOR
BEN NORMAN
ART DIRECTOR
MIKE HODSON
LEAD TECHNICAL ARTIST
WAT SNYDER
LEAD PROGRAMMERS
JONNY BECK
STRETCH
Z.A.C. IS THE BEST ZOMBIE GAME THAT'S COME OUT IN A WHILE.
TIM ZACHARIAH MULEY, 15 YEAR OLD GAMER

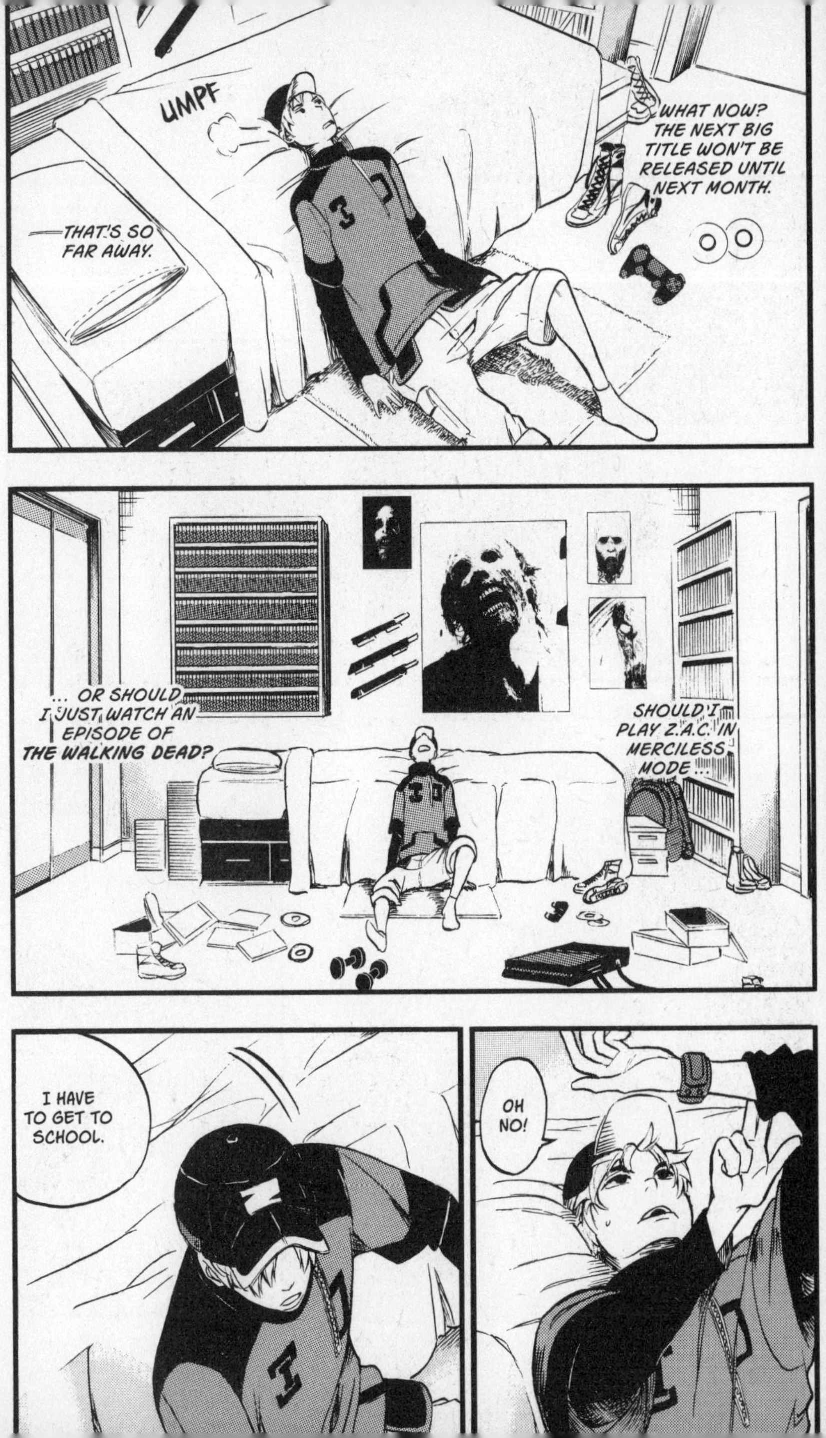
WHAT NOW? THE NEXT BIG TITLE WON'T BE RELEASED UNTIL NEXT MONTH.
UMPF
THAT'S SO FAR AWAY.
SHOULD I PLAY Z.A.C. IN MERCILESS MODE ...
... OR SHOULD I JUST WATCH AN EPISODE OF THE WALKING DEAD?
OH NO!
I HAVE TO GET TO SCHOOL.

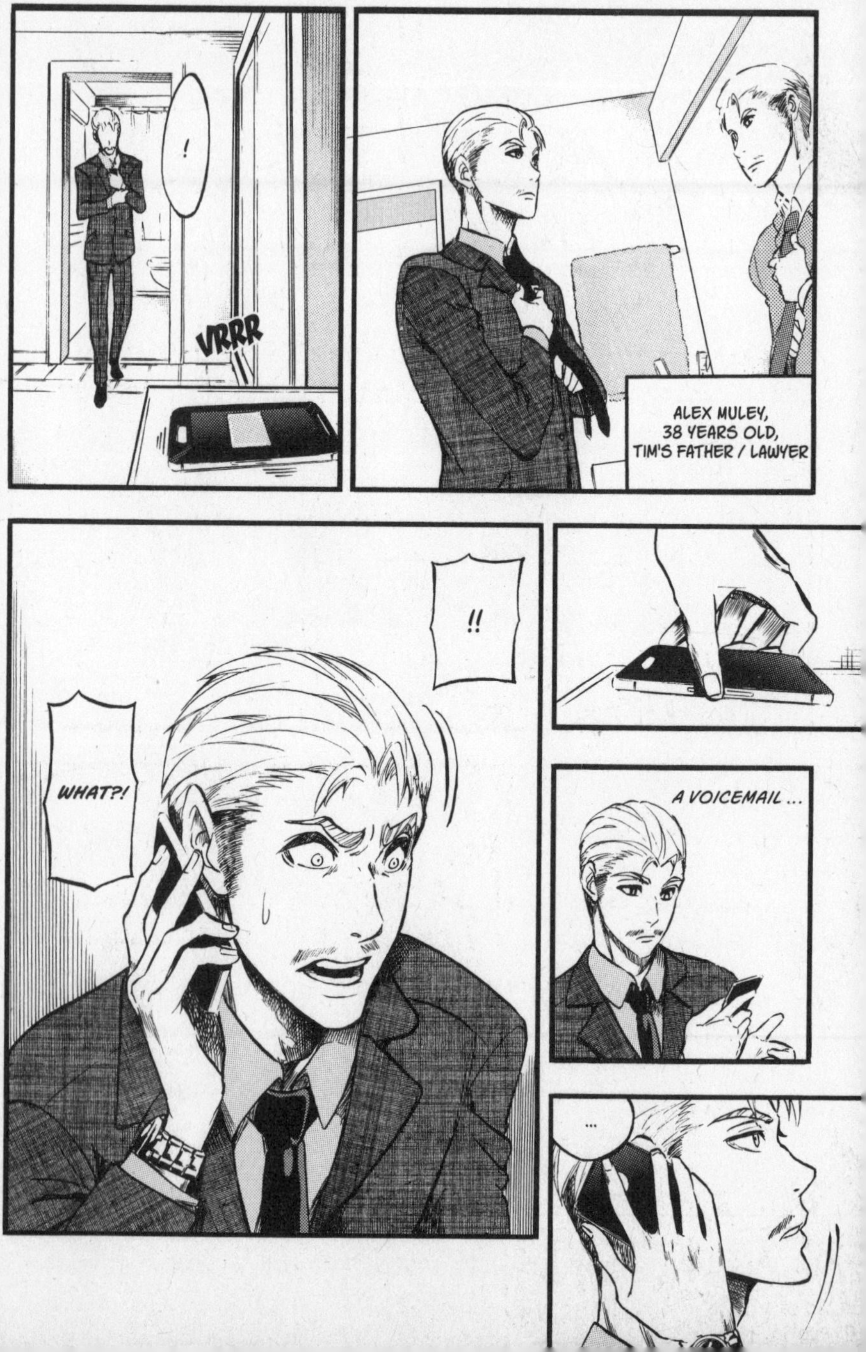
ALEX MULEY,
38 YEARS OLD,
TIM'S FATHER / LAWYER
!
VRRR
A VOICEMAIL ...
...
!!
WHAT?!

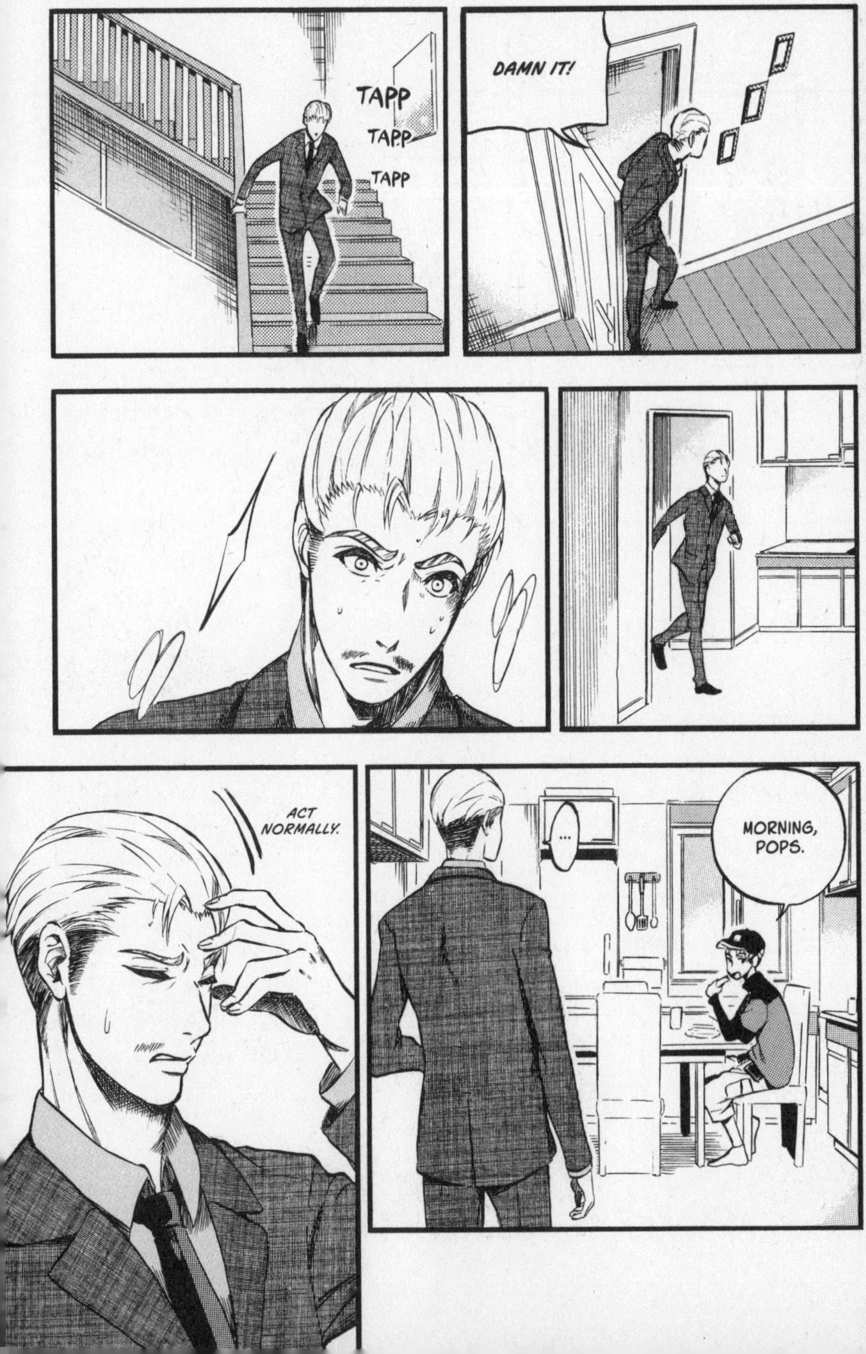
DAMN IT!
TAPP
TAPP
TAPP
MORNING, POPS.
...
ACT NORMALLY.

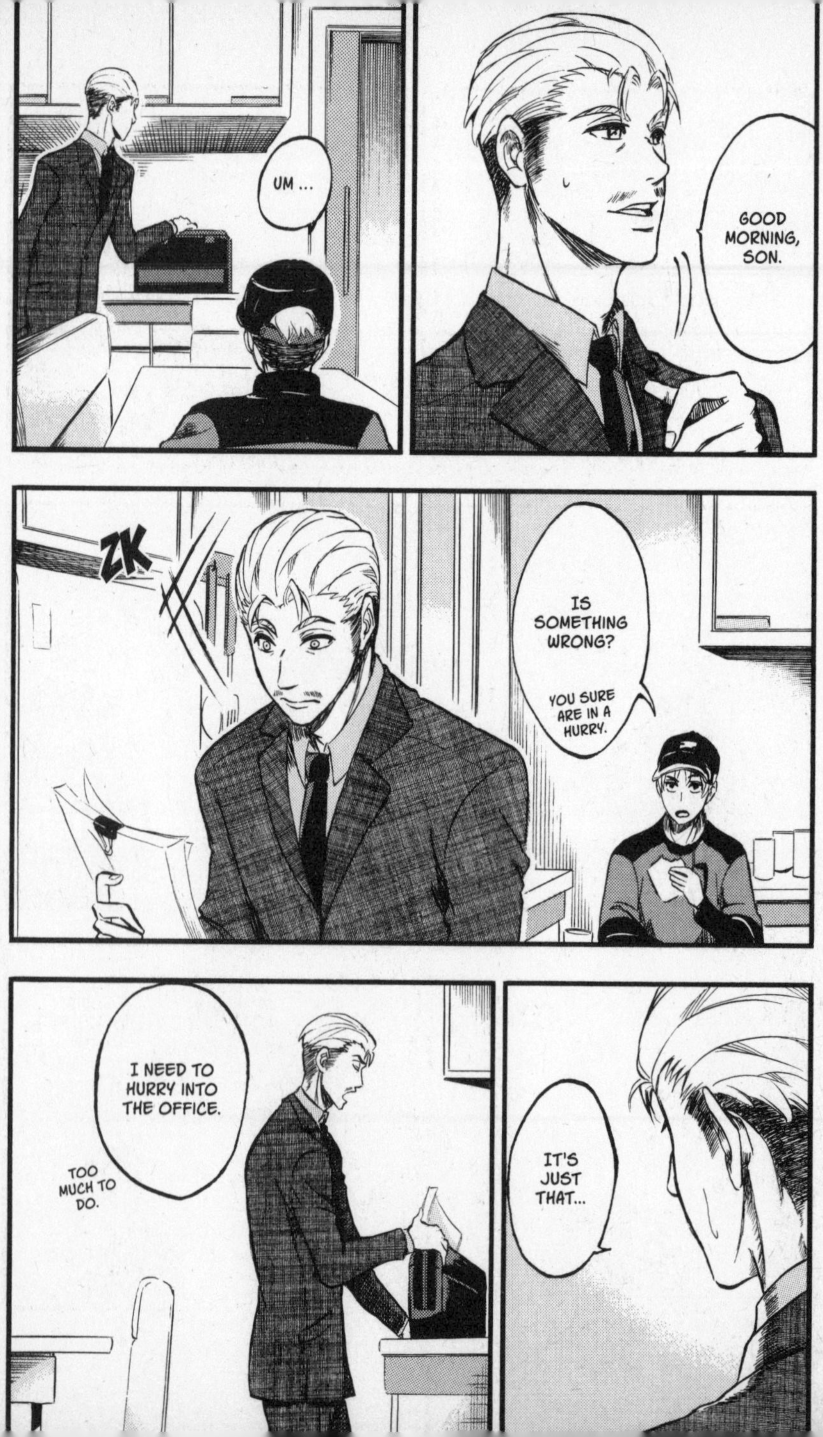
GOOD MORNING, SON.
UM ...
IS SOMETHING WRONG?
YOU SURE ARE IN A HURRY.
ZK
IT'S JUST THAT...
I NEED TO HURRY INTO THE OFFICE.
TOO MUCH TO DO.

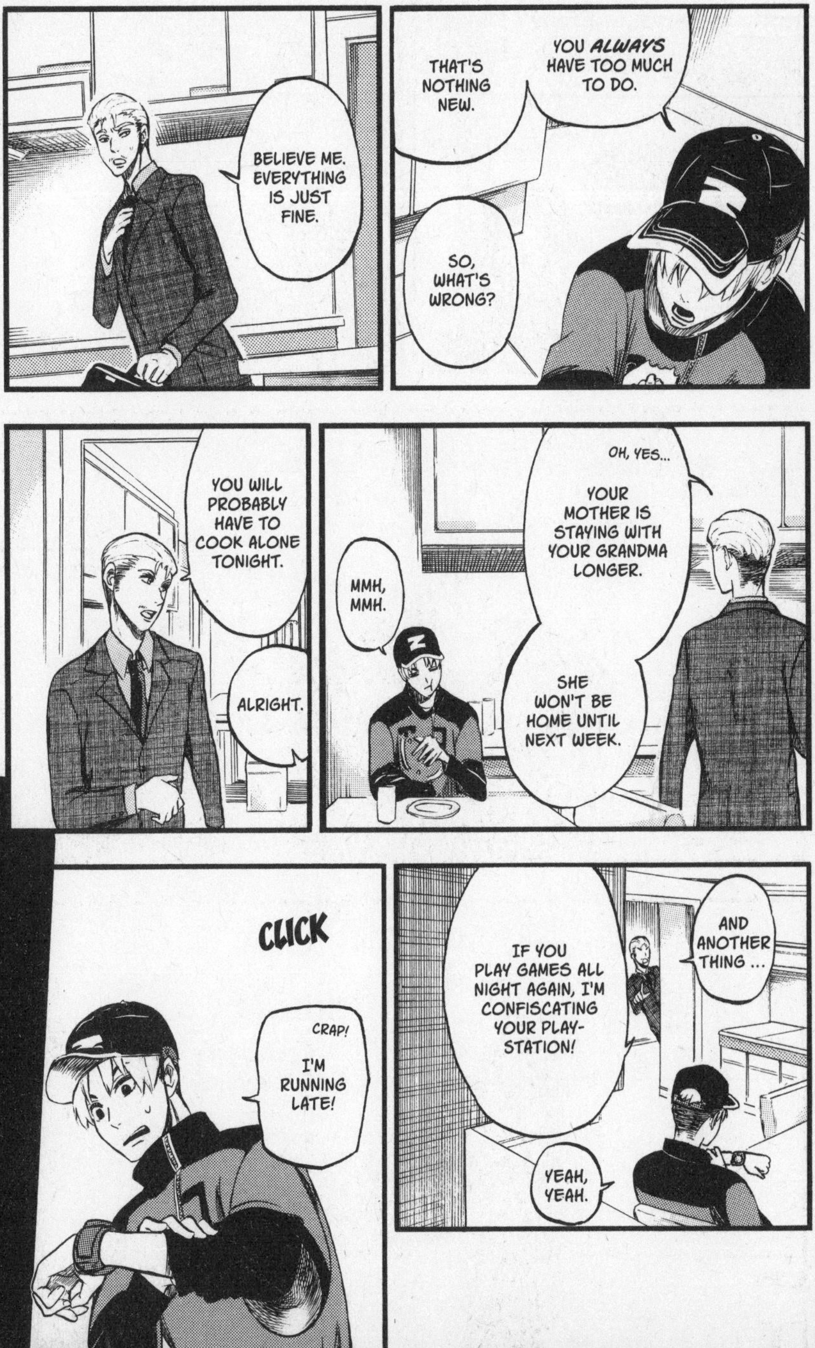

YOU *ALWAYS* HAVE TOO MUCH TO DO.
THAT'S NOTHING NEW.
SO, WHAT'S WRONG?
BELIEVE ME. EVERYTHING IS JUST FINE.
OH, YES...
YOUR MOTHER IS STAYING WITH YOUR GRANDMA LONGER.
SHE WON'T BE HOME UNTIL NEXT WEEK.
MMH, MMH.
YOU WILL PROBABLY HAVE TO COOK ALONE TONIGHT.
ALRIGHT.
AND ANOTHER THING ...
IF YOU PLAY GAMES ALL NIGHT AGAIN, I'M CONFISCATING YOUR PLAY-STATION!
YEAH, YEAH.
CLICK
CRAP!
I'M RUNNING LATE!

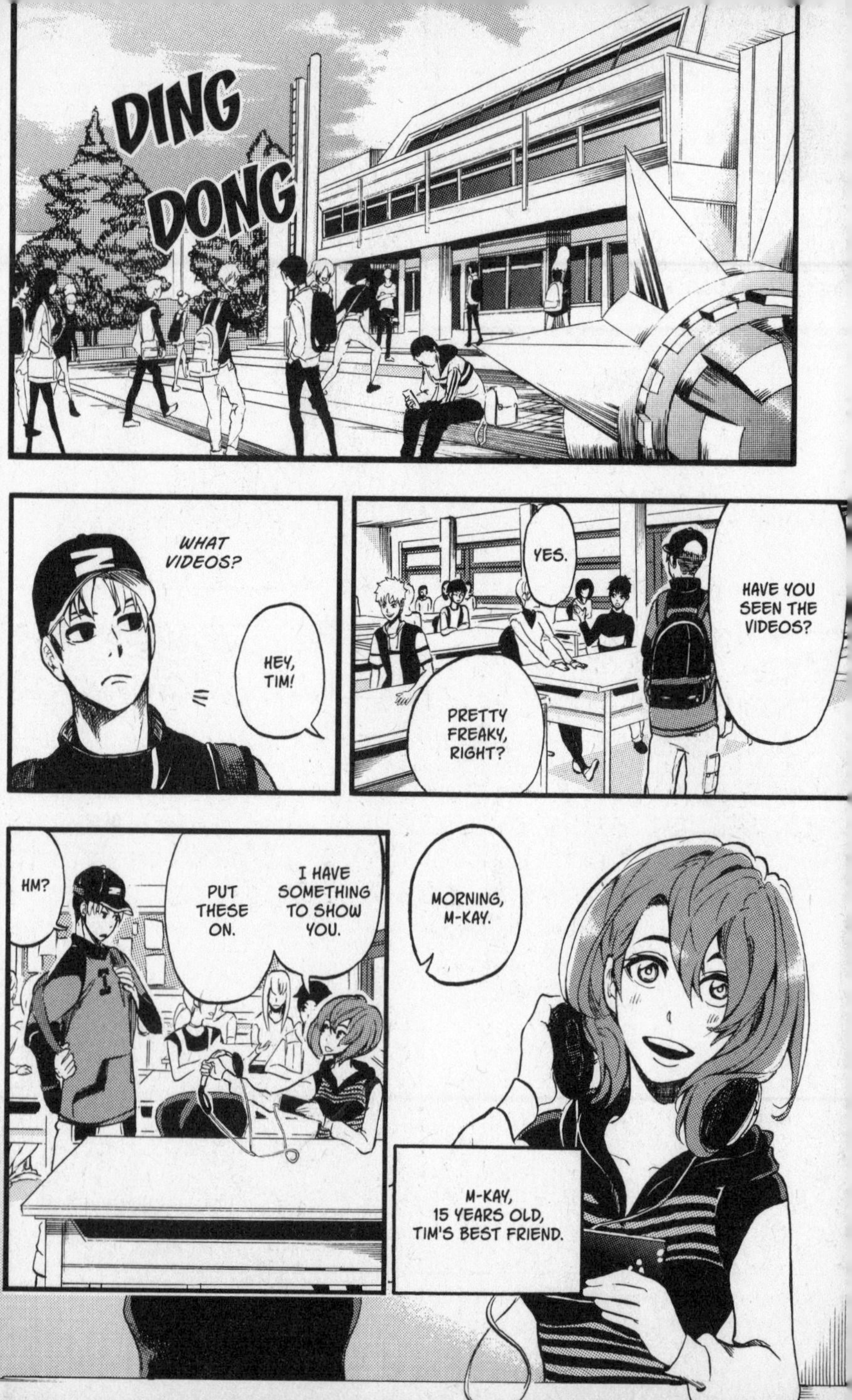
DING DONG
HAVE YOU SEEN THE VIDEOS?
YES.
PRETTY FREAKY, RIGHT?
WHAT VIDEOS?
HEY, TIM!
MORNING, M-KAY.
M-KAY, 15 YEARS OLD, TIM'S BEST FRIEND.
I HAVE SOMETHING TO SHOW YOU.
PUT THESE ON.
HM?

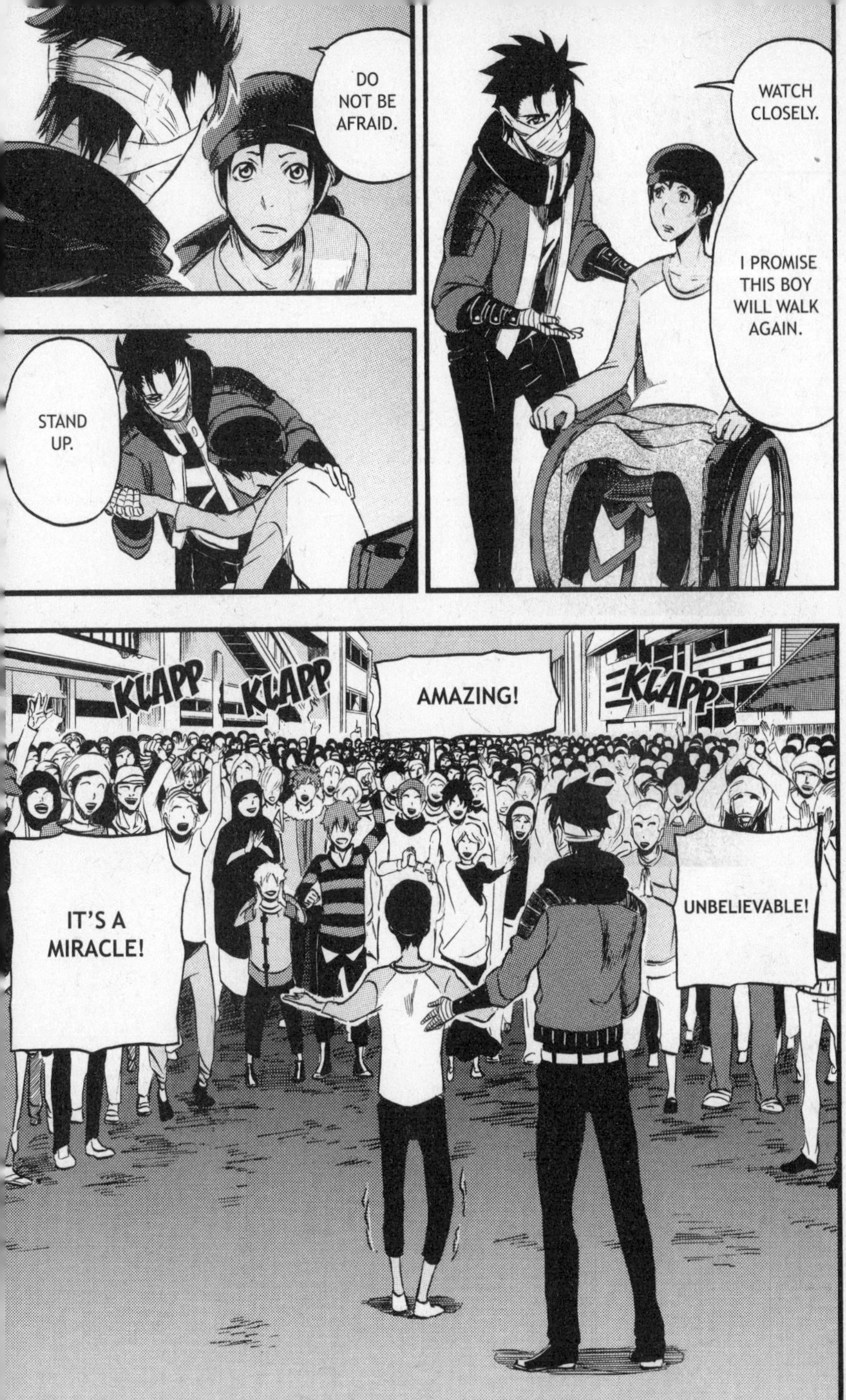
WATCH CLOSELY.
I PROMISE THIS BOY WILL WALK AGAIN.
DO NOT BE AFRAID.
STAND UP.
KLAPP
AMAZING!
KLAPP
KLAPP
UNBELIEVABLE!
IT'S A MIRACLE!

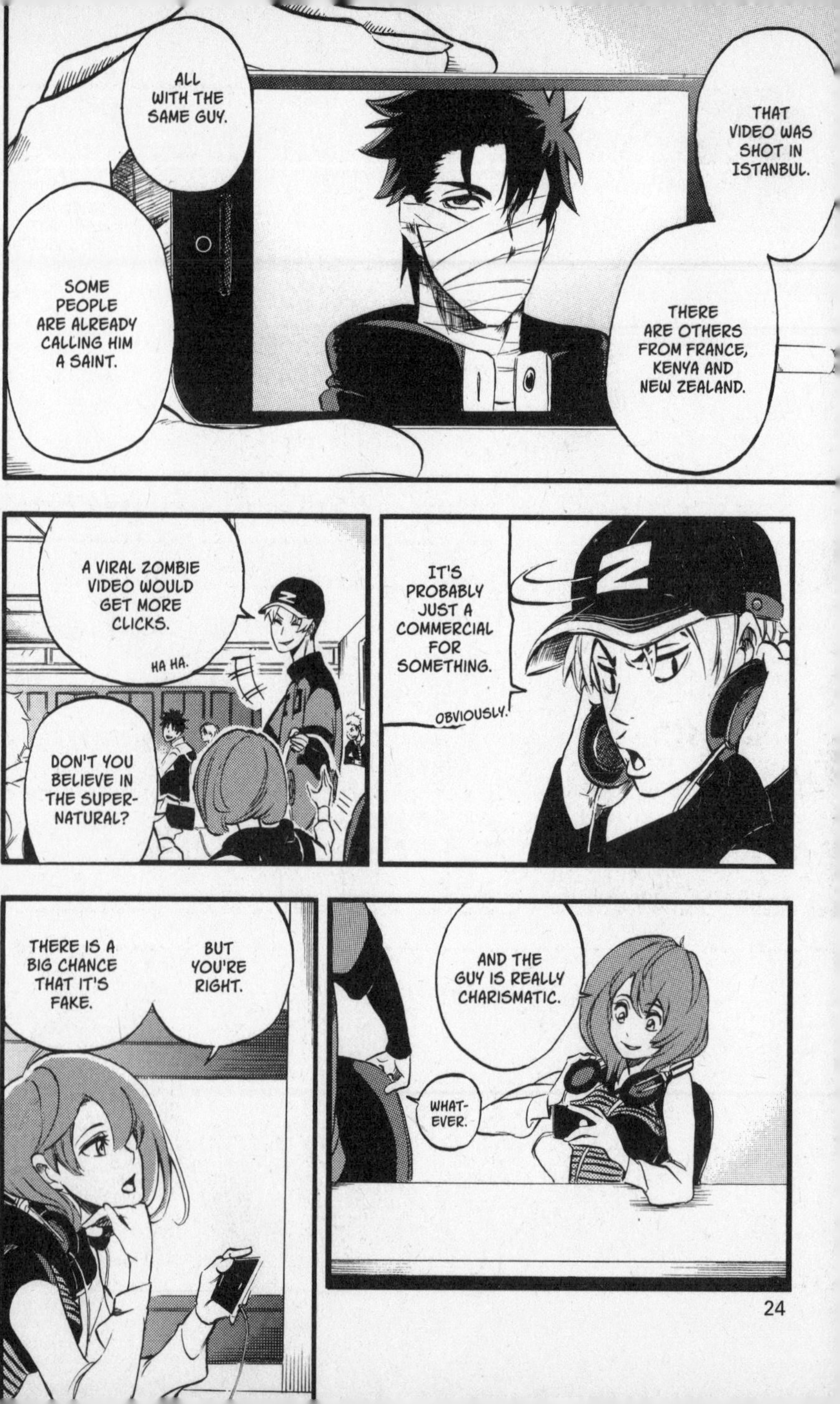
THAT VIDEO WAS SHOT IN ISTANBUL.
THERE ARE OTHERS FROM FRANCE, KENYA AND NEW ZEALAND.
ALL WITH THE SAME GUY.
SOME PEOPLE ARE ALREADY CALLING HIM A SAINT.
IT'S PROBABLY JUST A COMMERCIAL FOR SOMETHING.
OBVIOUSLY.
A VIRAL ZOMBIE VIDEO WOULD GET MORE CLICKS.
HA HA.
DON'T YOU BELIEVE IN THE SUPER-NATURAL?
AND THE GUY IS REALLY CHARISMATIC.
WHAT-EVER.
BUT YOU'RE RIGHT.
THERE IS A BIG CHANCE THAT IT'S FAKE.

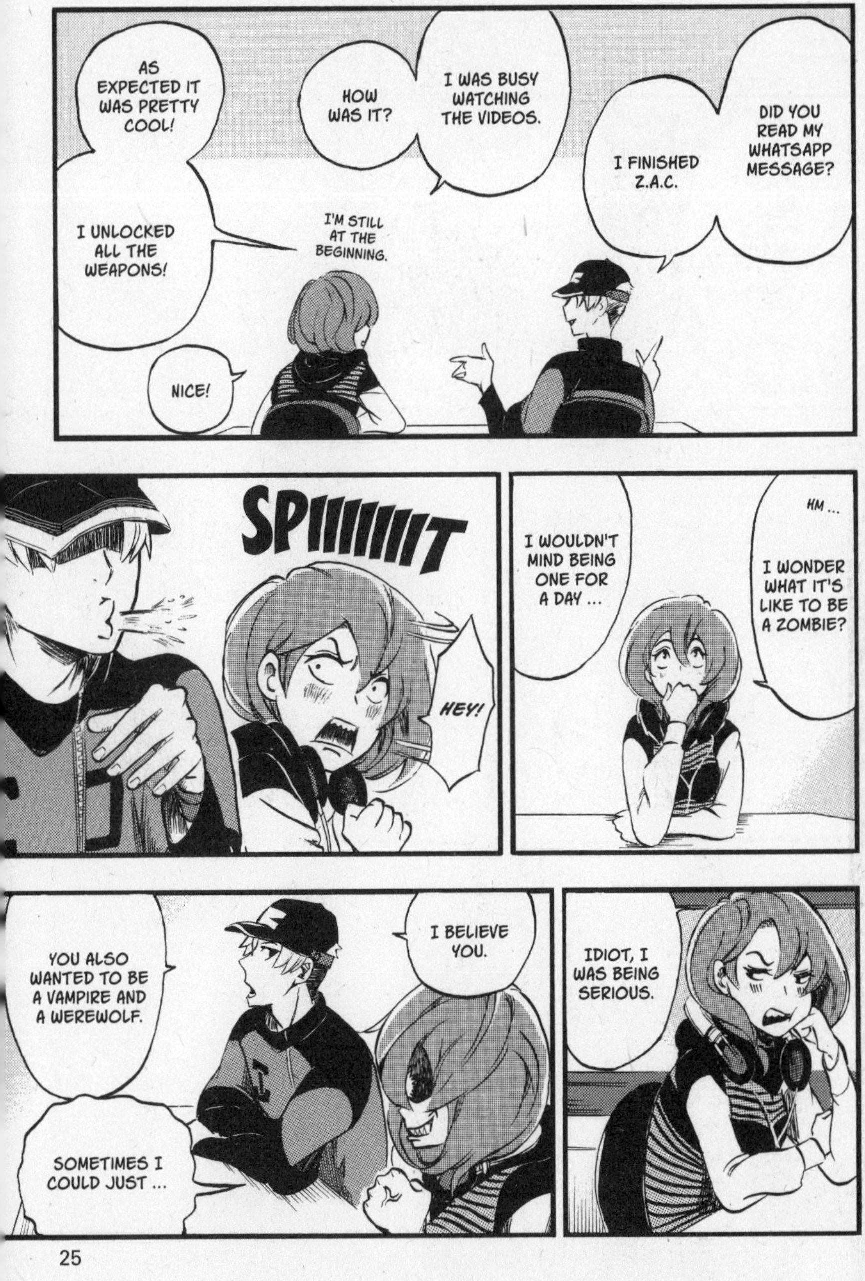
DID YOU READ MY WHATSAPP MESSAGE?
I FINISHED Z.A.C.
I WAS BUSY WATCHING THE VIDEOS.
HOW WAS IT?
AS EXPECTED IT WAS PRETTY COOL!
I'M STILL AT THE BEGINNING.
I UNLOCKED ALL THE WEAPONS!
NICE!
HM ...
I WONDER WHAT IT'S LIKE TO BE A ZOMBIE?
I WOULDN'T MIND BEING ONE FOR A DAY ...
SPIIIIIIT
HEY!
IDIOT, I WAS BEING SERIOUS.
I BELIEVE YOU.
YOU ALSO WANTED TO BE A VAMPIRE AND A WEREWOLF.
SOMETIMES I COULD JUST ...

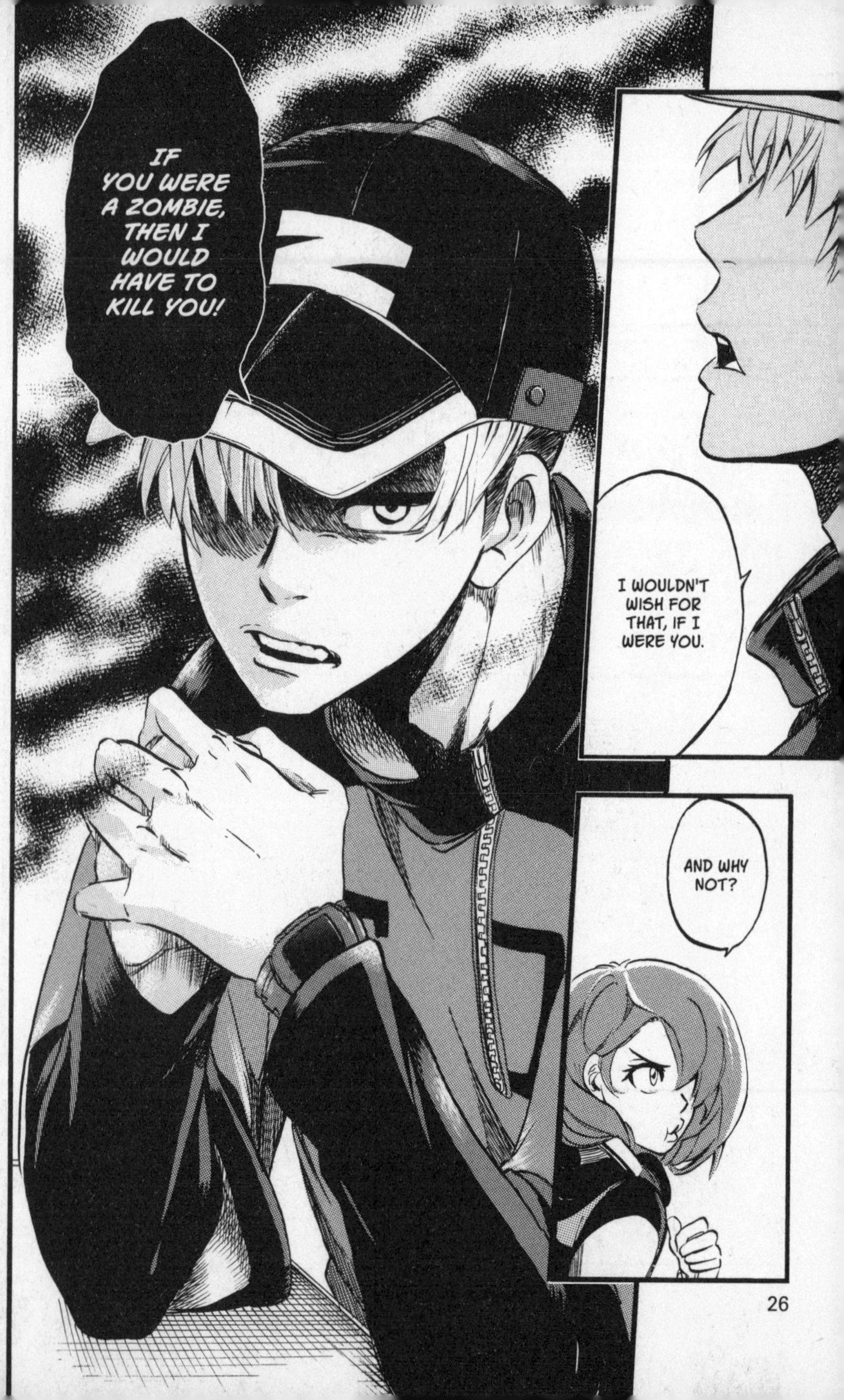
IF YOU WERE A ZOMBIE, THEN I WOULD HAVE TO KILL YOU!
I WOULDN'T WISH FOR THAT, IF I WERE YOU.
AND WHY NOT?

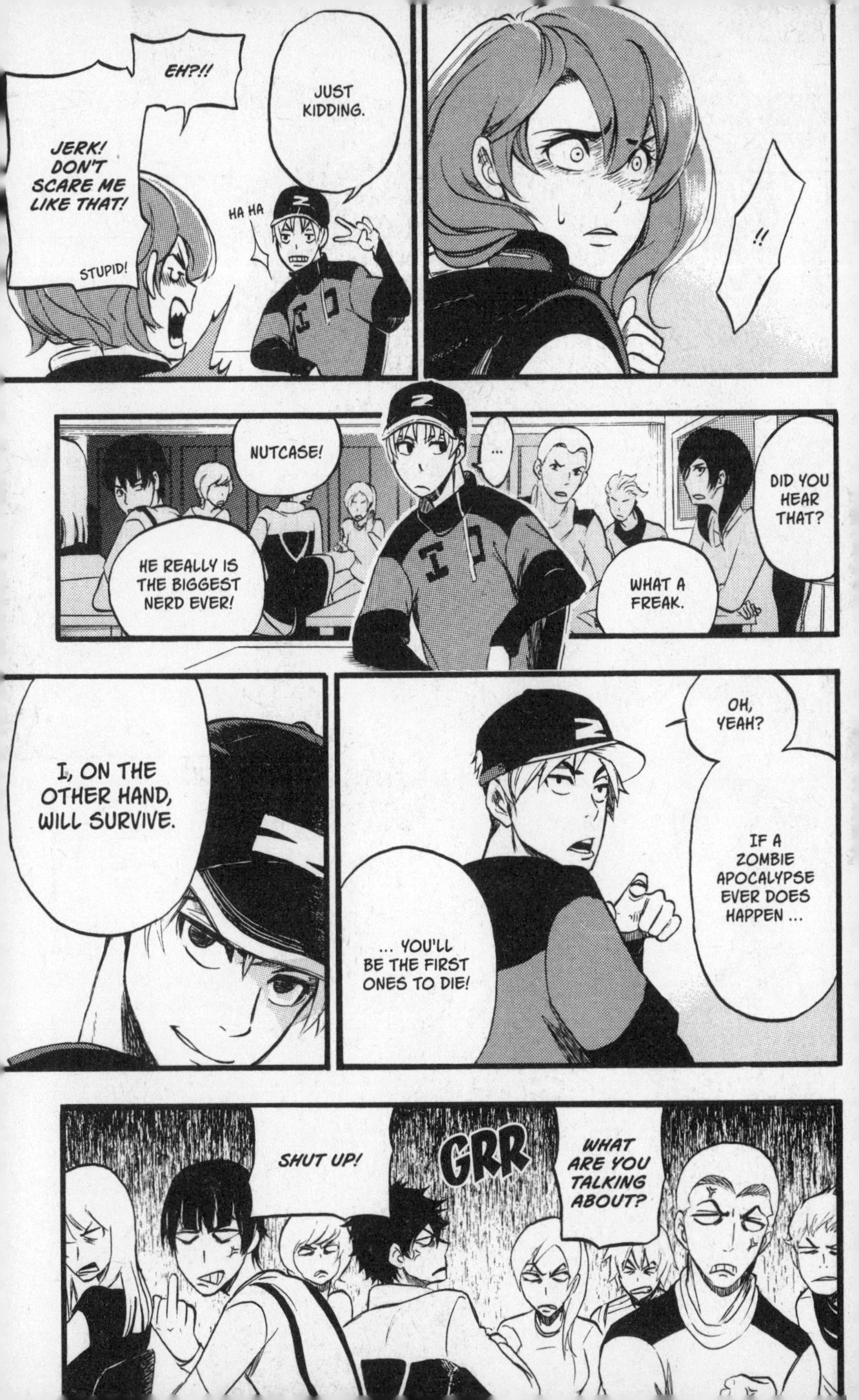
!!
JUST KIDDING.
EH?!!
HA HA
JERK! DON'T SCARE ME LIKE THAT!
STUPID!
DID YOU HEAR THAT?
WHAT A FREAK.
...
NUTCASE!
HE REALLY IS THE BIGGEST NERD EVER!
OH, YEAH?
IF A ZOMBIE APOCALYPSE EVER DOES HAPPEN ...
... YOU'LL BE THE FIRST ONES TO DIE!
I, ON THE OTHER HAND, WILL SURVIVE.
WHAT ARE YOU TALKING ABOUT?
GRR
SHUT UP!

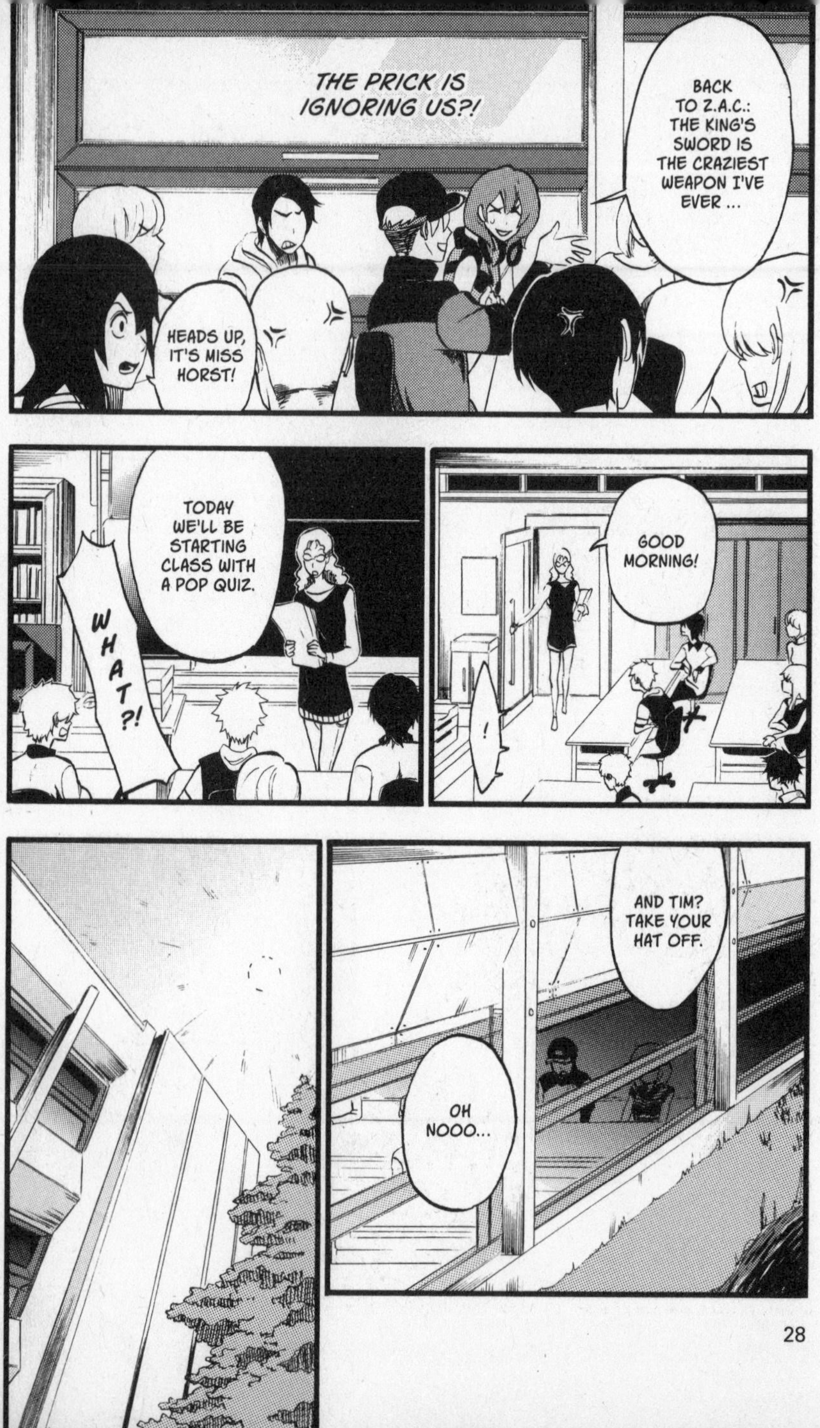
BACK TO Z.A.C.: THE KING'S SWORD IS THE CRAZIEST WEAPON I'VE EVER ...
THE PRICK IS IGNORING US?!
HEADS UP, IT'S MISS HORST!
GOOD MORNING!
!
TODAY WE'LL BE STARTING CLASS WITH A POP QUIZ.
WHAT?!
AND TIM? TAKE YOUR HAT OFF.
OH NOOO...

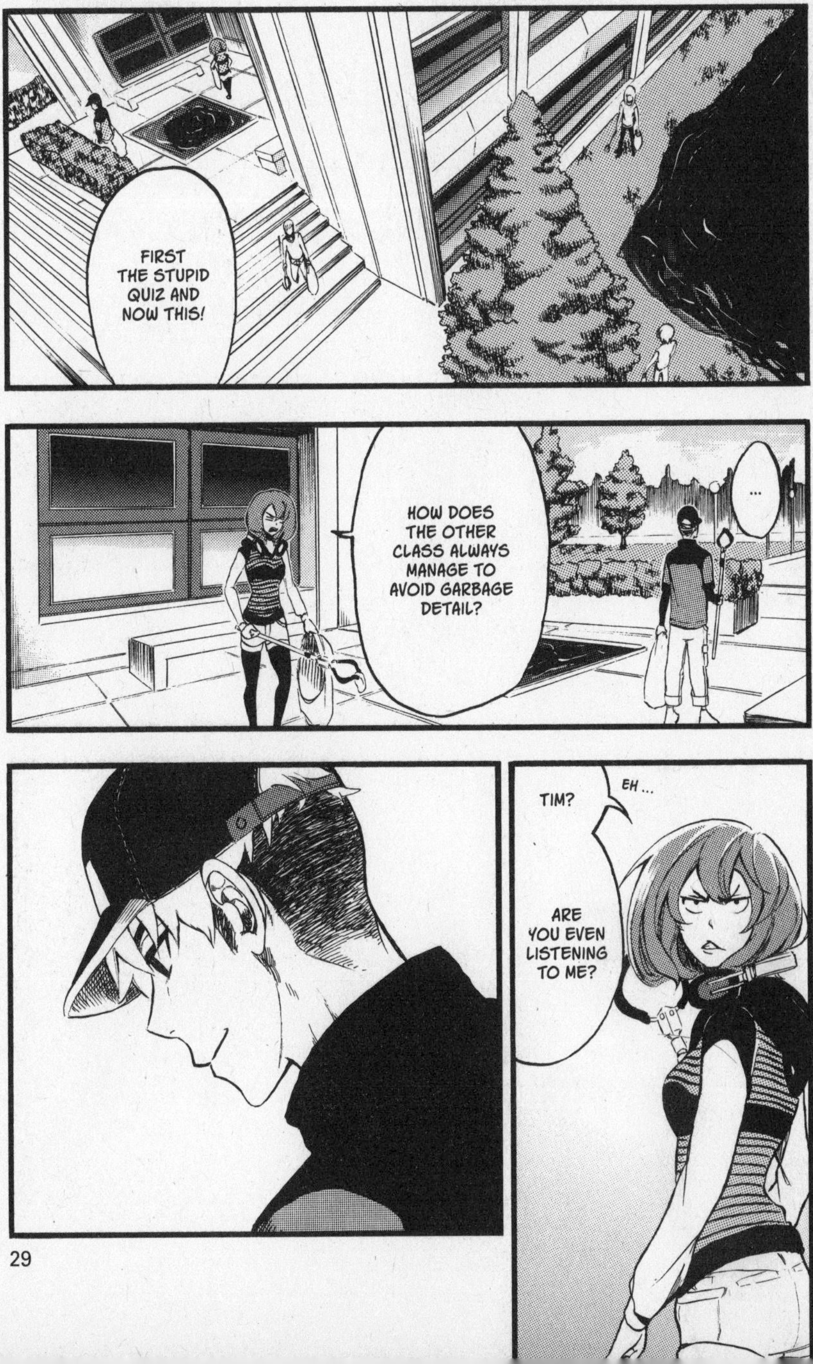
FIRST THE STUPID QUIZ AND NOW THIS!
...
HOW DOES THE OTHER CLASS ALWAYS MANAGE TO AVOID GARBAGE DETAIL?
EH ...
TIM?
ARE YOU EVEN LISTENING TO ME?

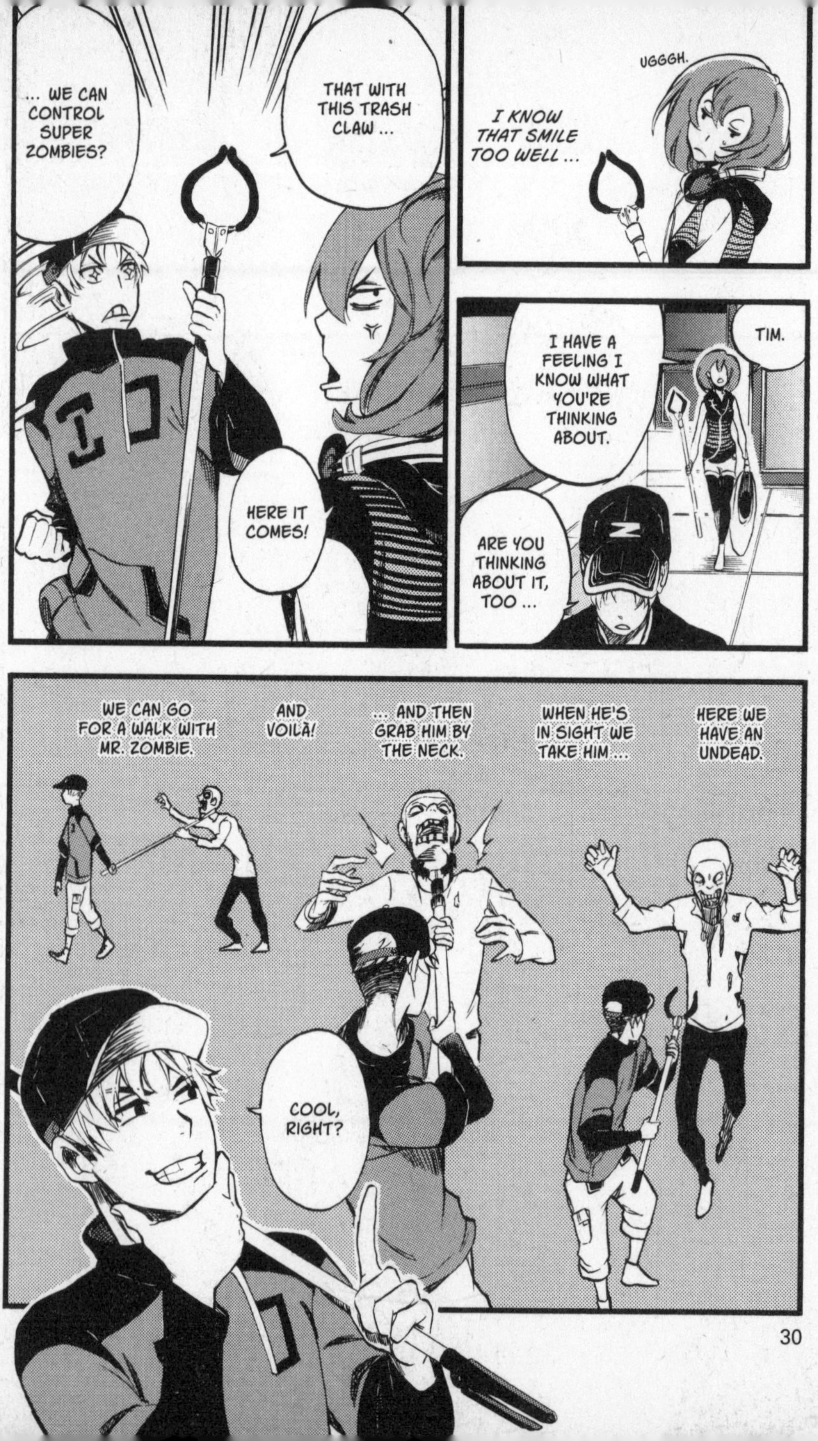
UGGGH.
I KNOW THAT SMILE TOO WELL ...
TIM.
I HAVE A FEELING I KNOW WHAT YOU'RE THINKING ABOUT.
ARE YOU THINKING ABOUT IT, TOO ...
THAT WITH THIS TRASH CLAW ...
... WE CAN CONTROL SUPER ZOMBIES?
HERE IT COMES!
HERE WE HAVE AN UNDEAD.
WHEN HE'S IN SIGHT WE TAKE HIM ...
... AND THEN GRAB HIM BY THE NECK.
AND VOILÀ!
WE CAN GO FOR A WALK WITH MR. ZOMBIE.
COOL, RIGHT?

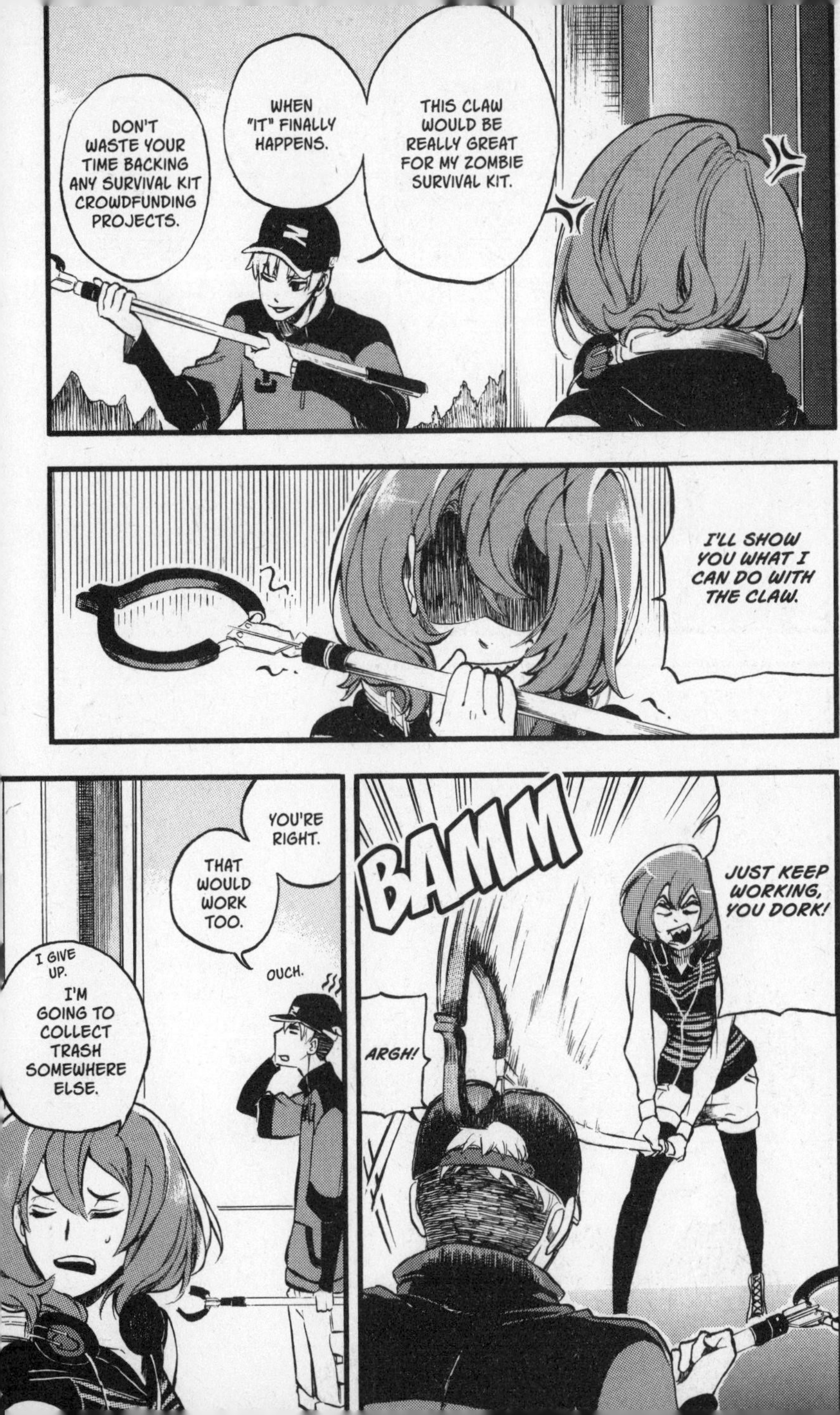
THIS CLAW WOULD BE REALLY GREAT FOR MY ZOMBIE SURVIVAL KIT.
WHEN "IT" FINALLY HAPPENS.
DON'T WASTE YOUR TIME BACKING ANY SURVIVAL KIT CROWDFUNDING PROJECTS.
I'LL SHOW YOU WHAT I CAN DO WITH THE CLAW.
BAMM
JUST KEEP WORKING, YOU DORK!
ARGH!
YOU'RE RIGHT.
THAT WOULD WORK TOO.
OUCH.
I GIVE UP.
I'M GOING TO COLLECT TRASH SOMEWHERE ELSE.

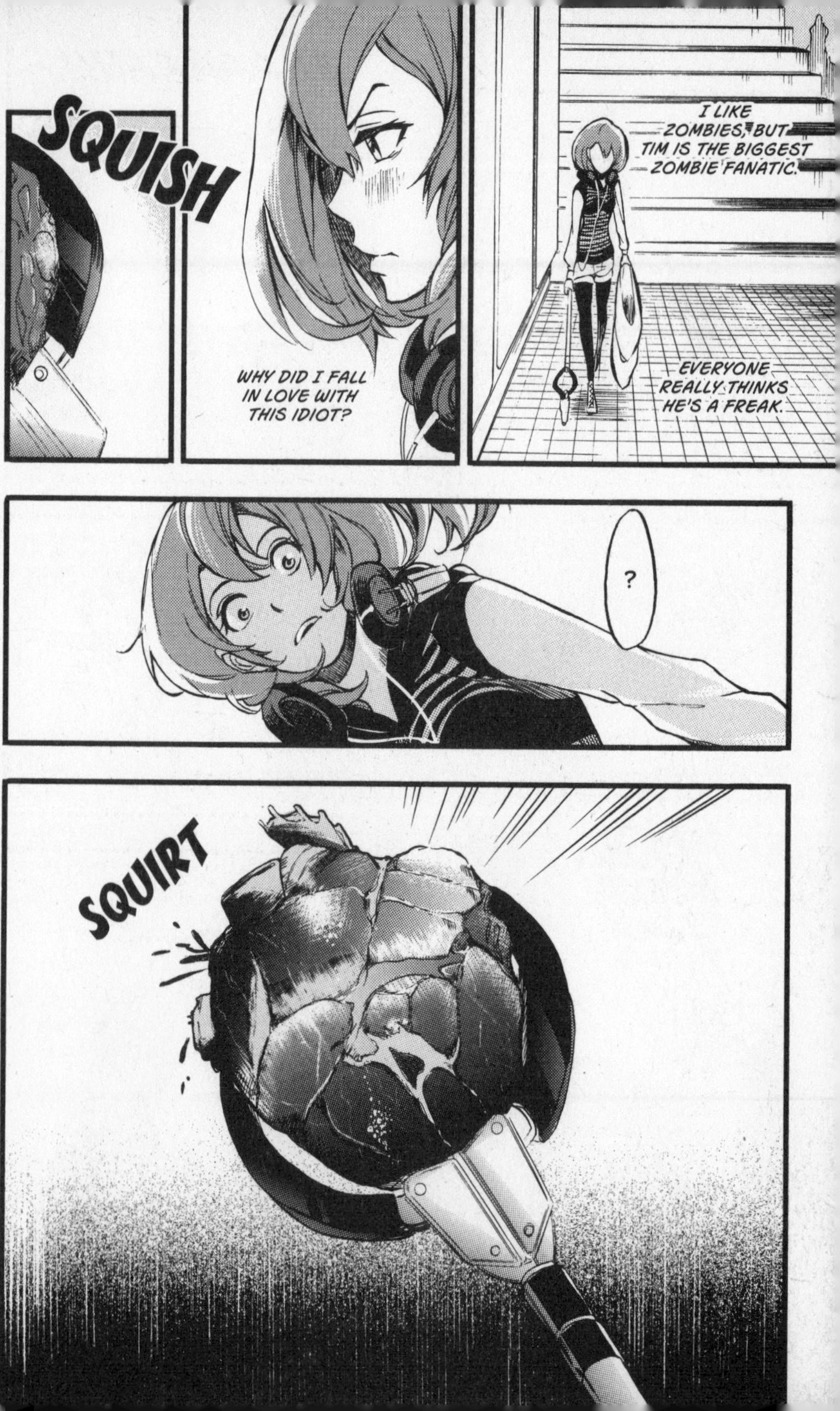
I LIKE ZOMBIES, BUT TIM IS THE BIGGEST ZOMBIE FANATIC.
EVERYONE REALLY THINKS HE'S A FREAK.
WHY DID I FALL IN LOVE WITH THIS IDIOT?
SQUISH
?
SQUIRT

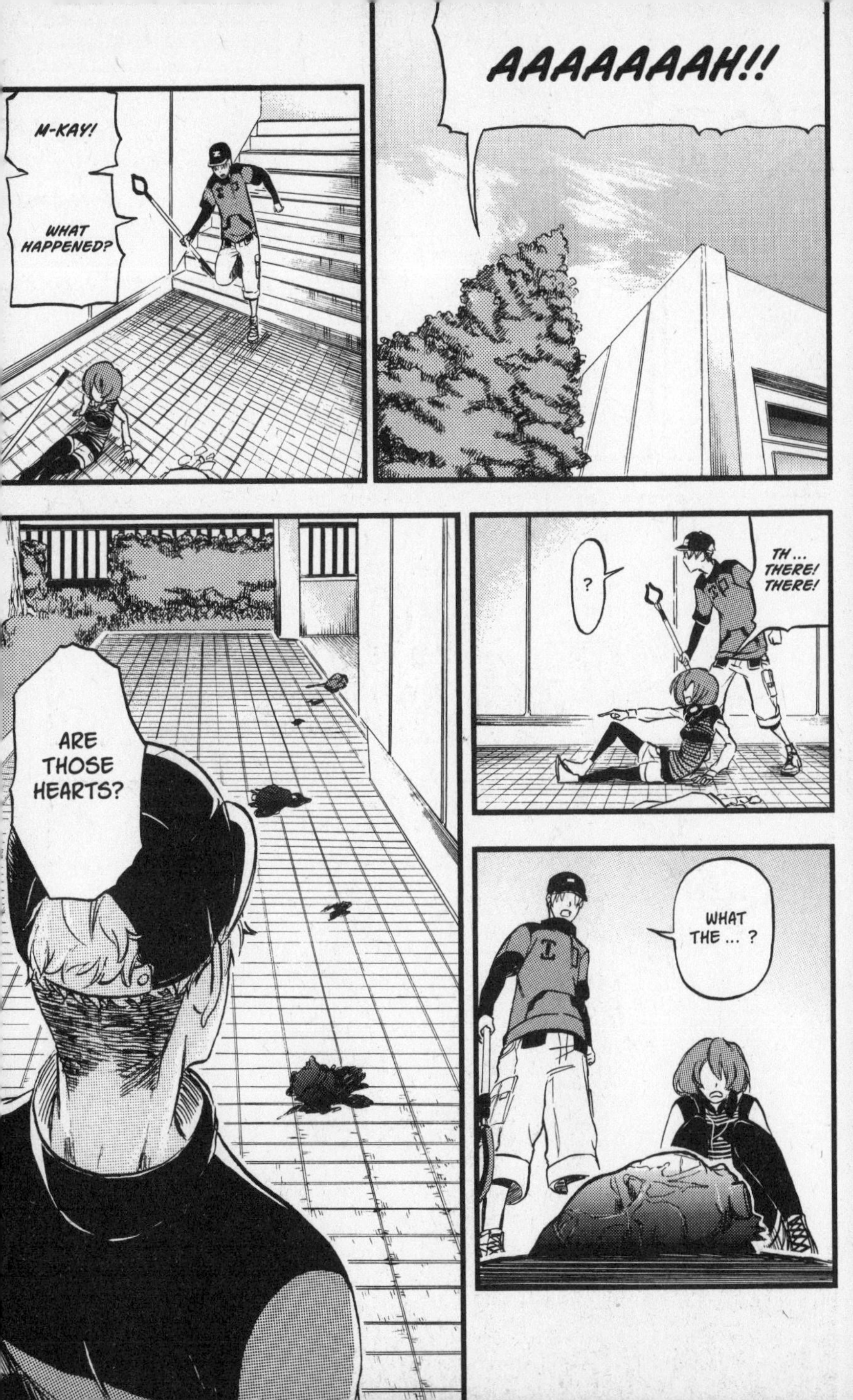
AAAAAAAH!!
M-KAY!
WHAT HAPPENED?
TH ... THERE! THERE!
?
WHAT THE ... ?
ARE THOSE HEARTS?

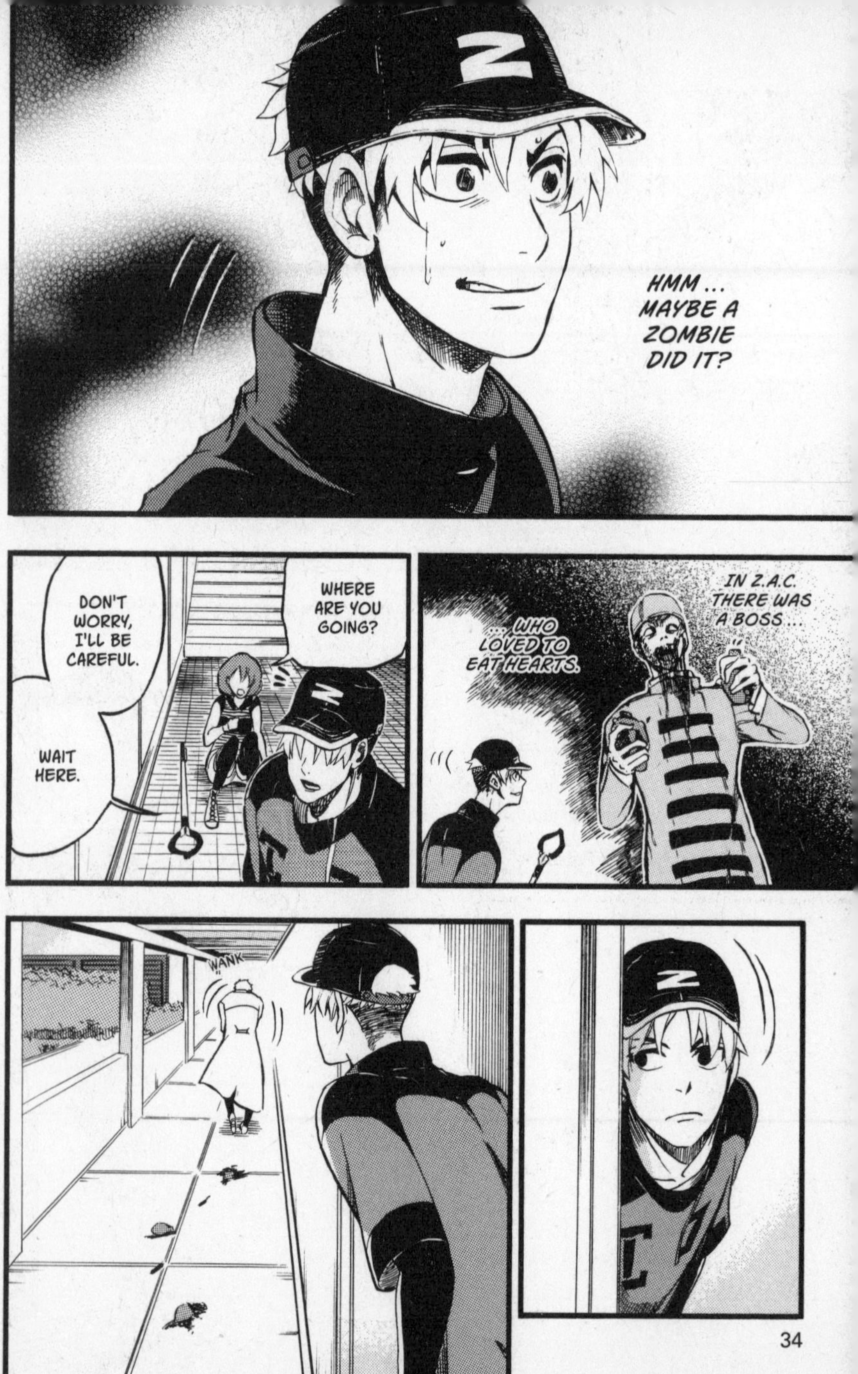
HMM ... MAYBE A ZOMBIE DID IT?
IN Z.A.C. THERE WAS A BOSS ...
... WHO LOVED TO EAT HEARTS.
WHERE ARE YOU GOING?
DON'T WORRY, I'LL BE CAREFUL.
WAIT HERE.
WANK

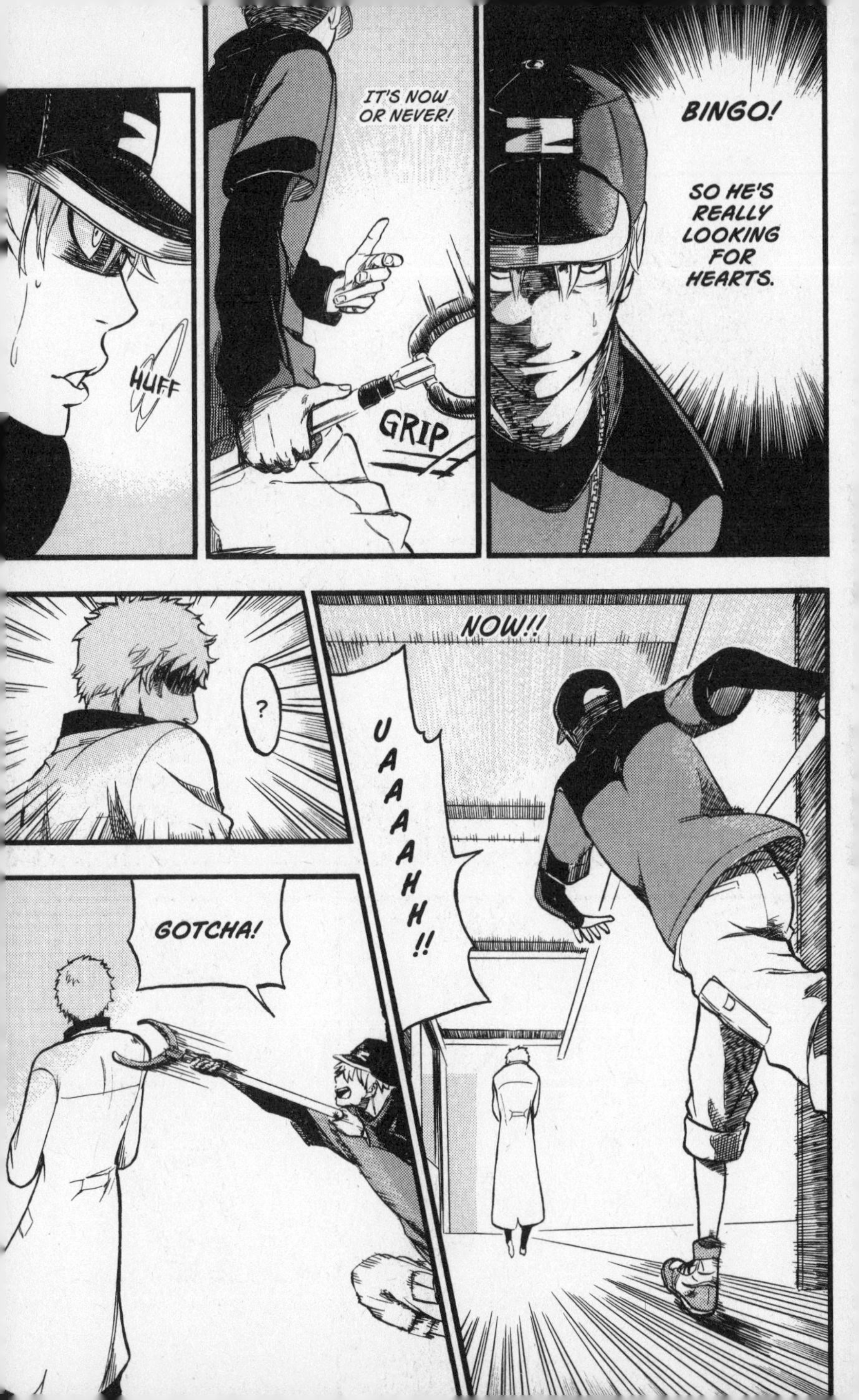
BINGO!
SO HE'S REALLY LOOKING FOR HEARTS.
IT'S NOW OR NEVER!
GRIP
HUFF
NOW!!
?
UAAAAHH!!
GOTCHA!

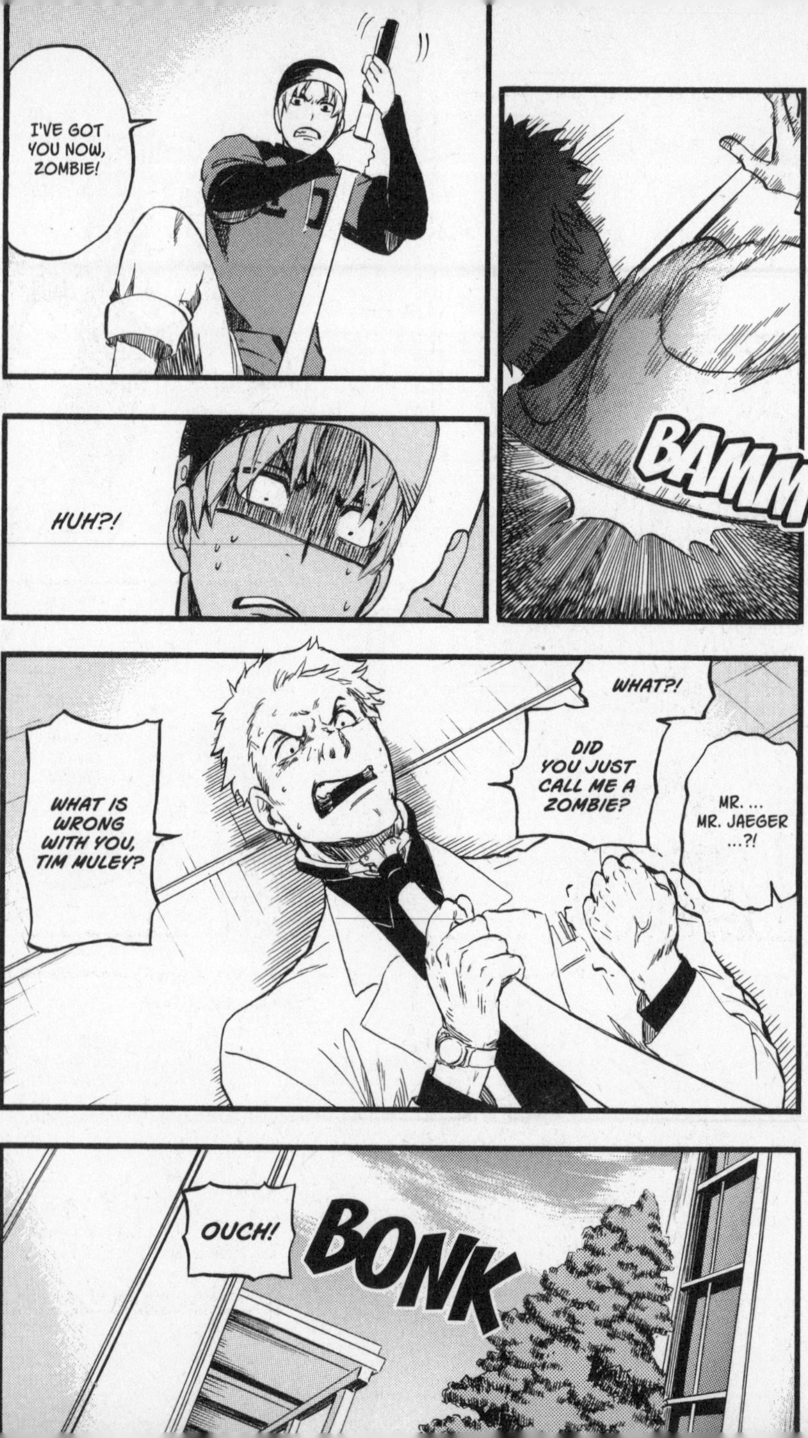
BAMM
I'VE GOT YOU NOW, ZOMBIE!
HUH?!
MR. ... MR. JAEGER ...?!
WHAT?!
DID YOU JUST CALL ME A ZOMBIE?
WHAT IS WRONG WITH YOU, TIM MULEY?
BONK
OUCH!

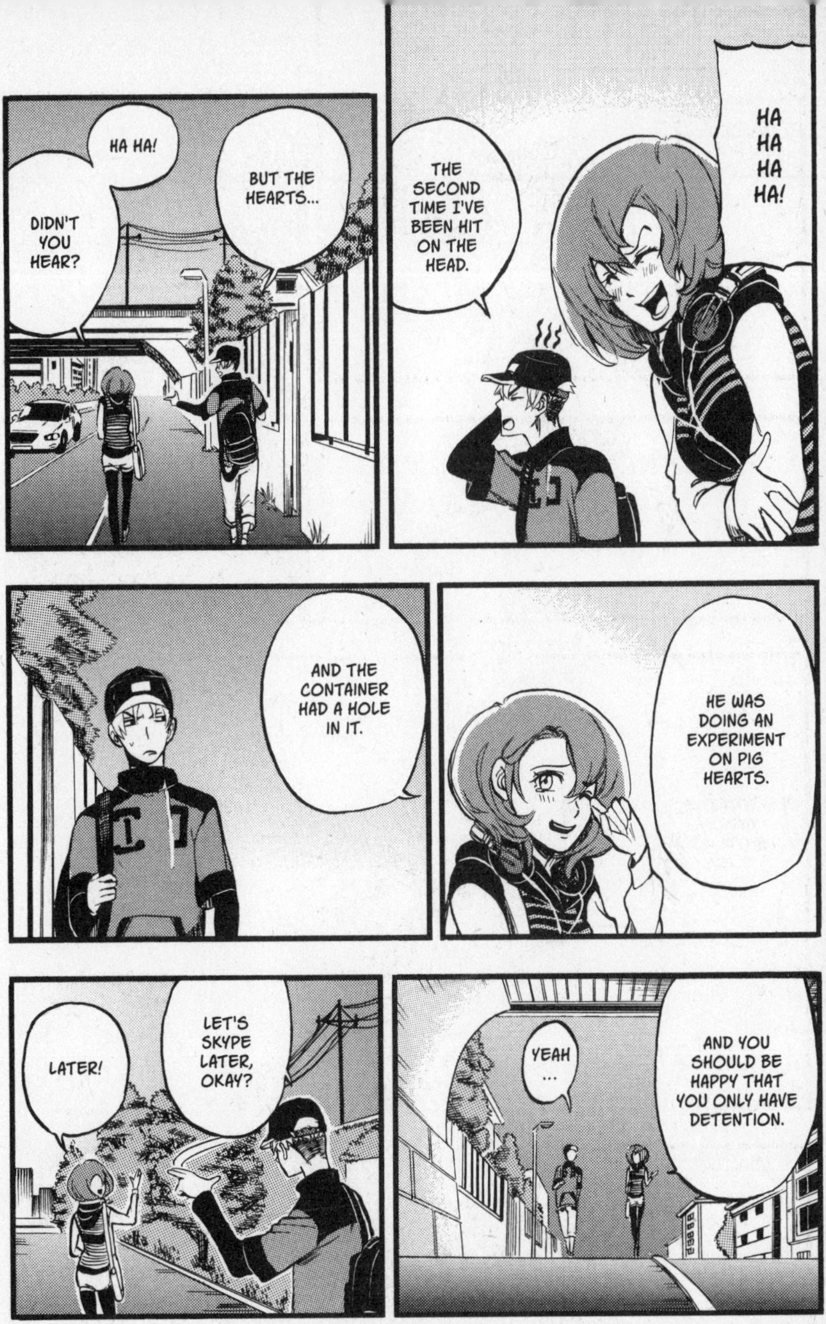

HA HA HA HA!
THE SECOND TIME I'VE BEEN HIT ON THE HEAD.
BUT THE HEARTS...
HA HA!
DIDN'T YOU HEAR?
HE WAS DOING AN EXPERIMENT ON PIG HEARTS.
AND THE CONTAINER HAD A HOLE IN IT.
AND YOU SHOULD BE HAPPY THAT YOU ONLY HAVE DETENTION.
YEAH ...
LET'S SKYPE LATER, OKAY?
LATER!

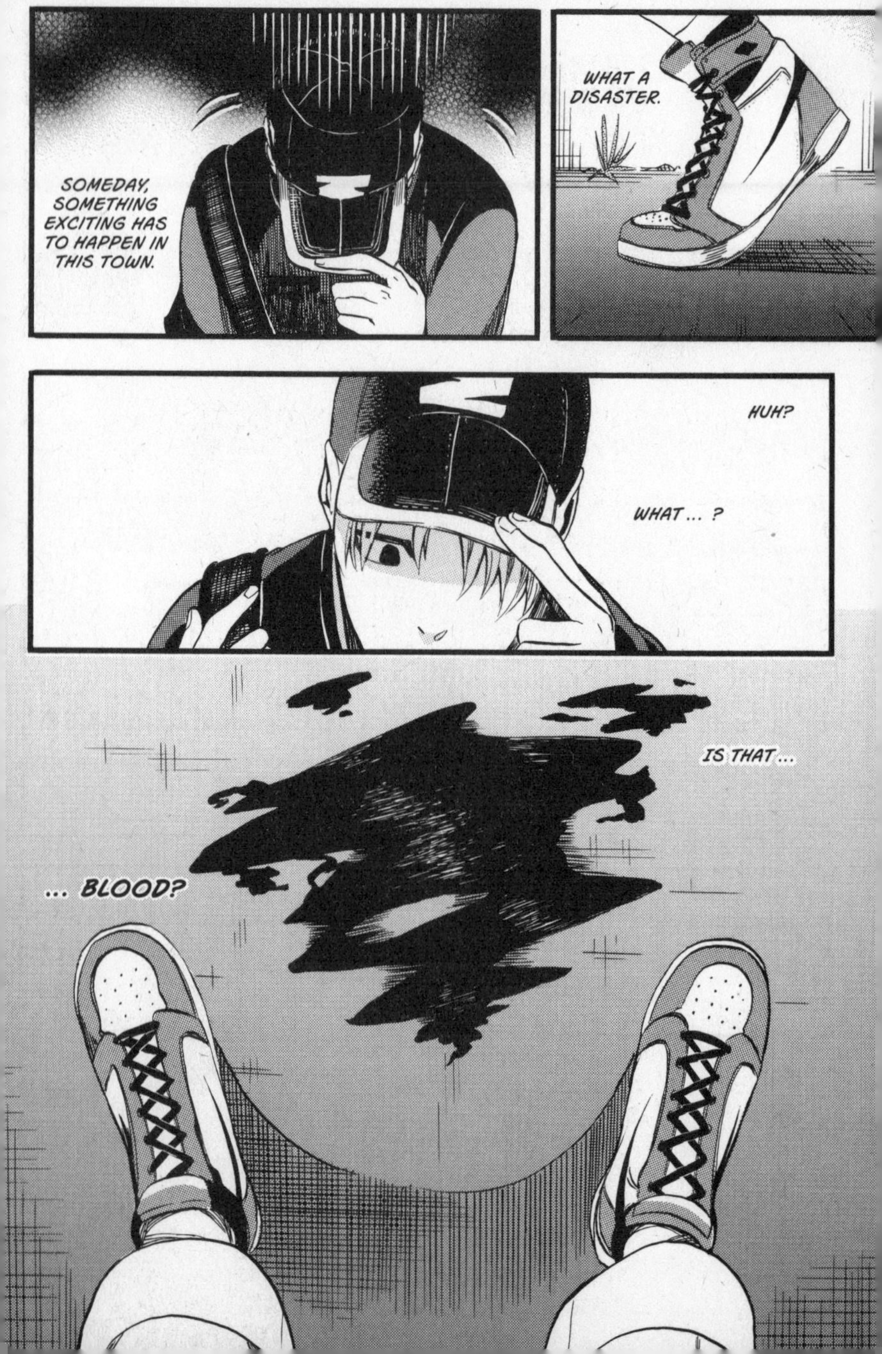
WHAT A DISASTER.
SOMEDAY, SOMETHING EXCITING HAS TO HAPPEN IN THIS TOWN.
HUH?
WHAT... ?
IS THAT...
... BLOOD?

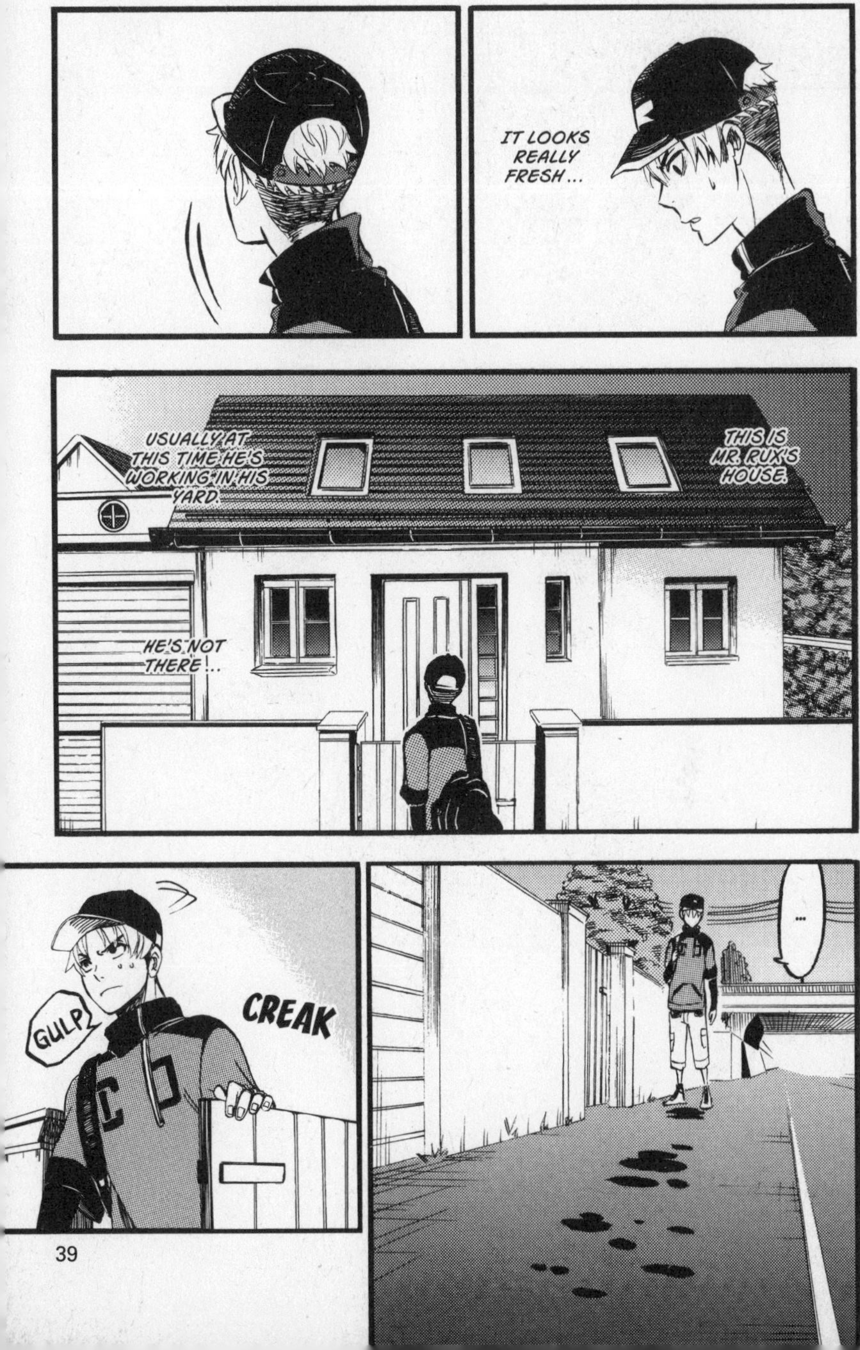
IT LOOKS REALLY FRESH...
THIS IS MR. RUX'S HOUSE.
USUALLY AT THIS TIME HE'S WORKING IN HIS YARD.
HE'S NOT THERE...
...
CREAK
GULP

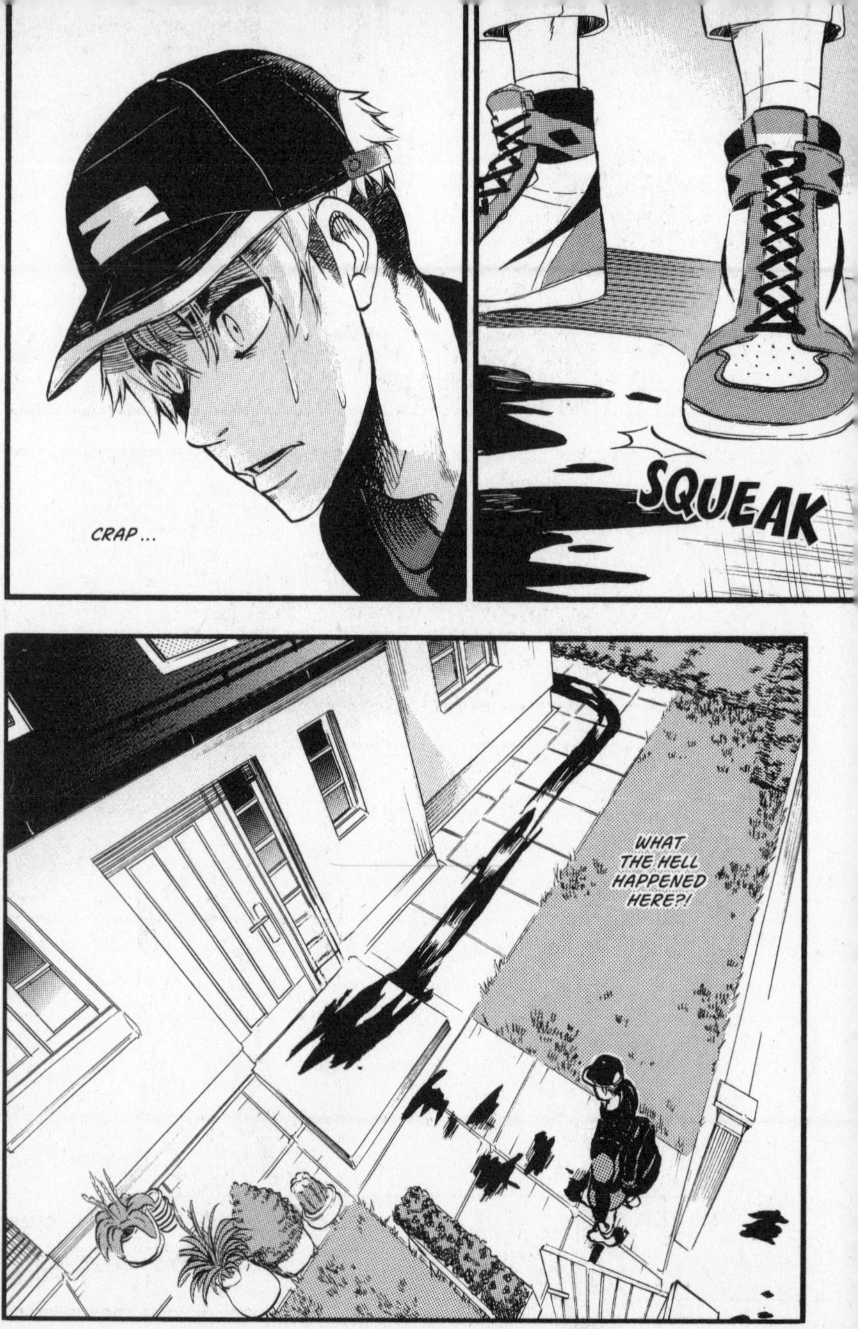
SQUEAK
CRAP...
WHAT THE HELL HAPPENED HERE?!

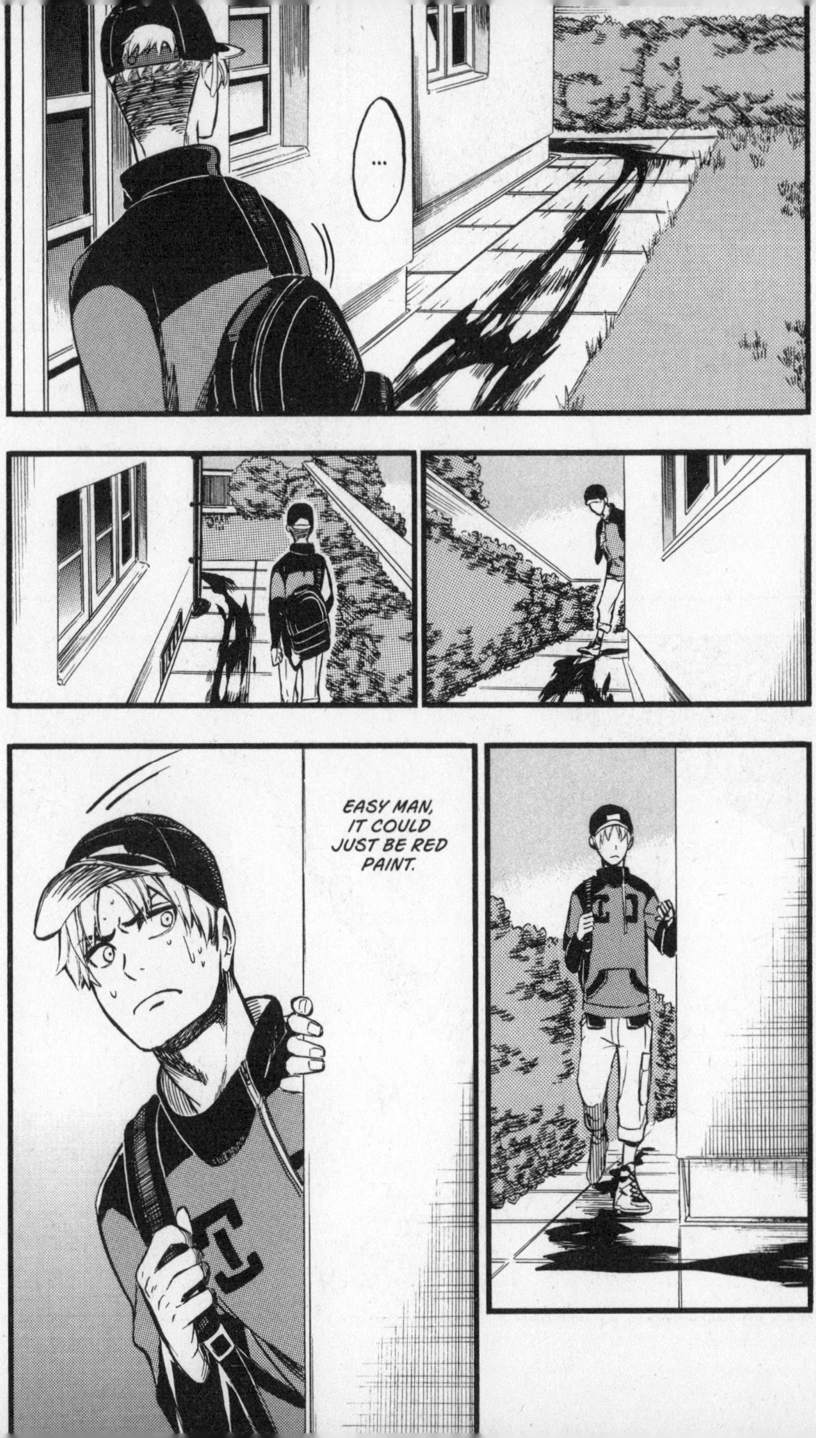
...
EASY MAN, IT COULD JUST BE RED PAINT.

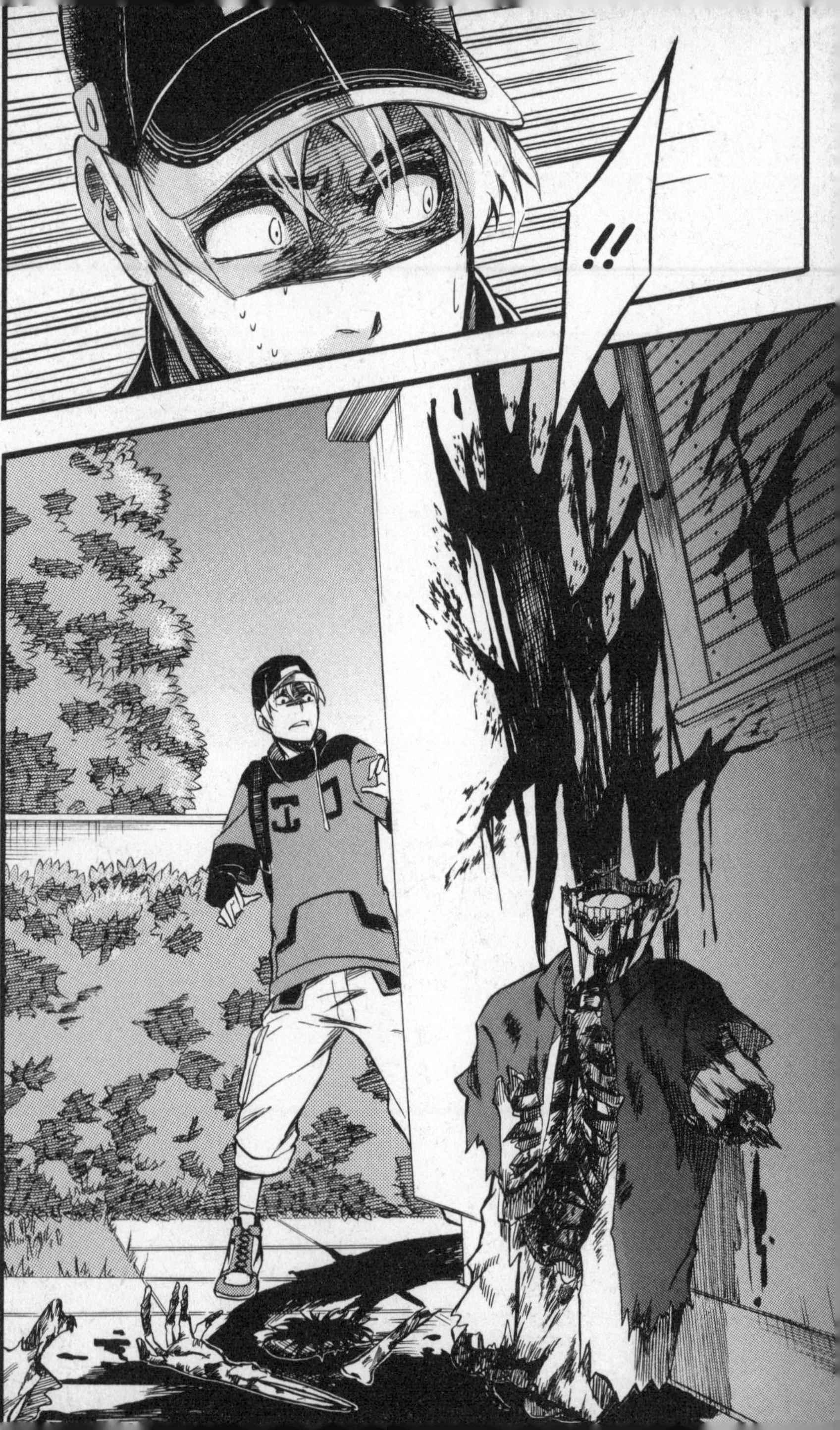
!!

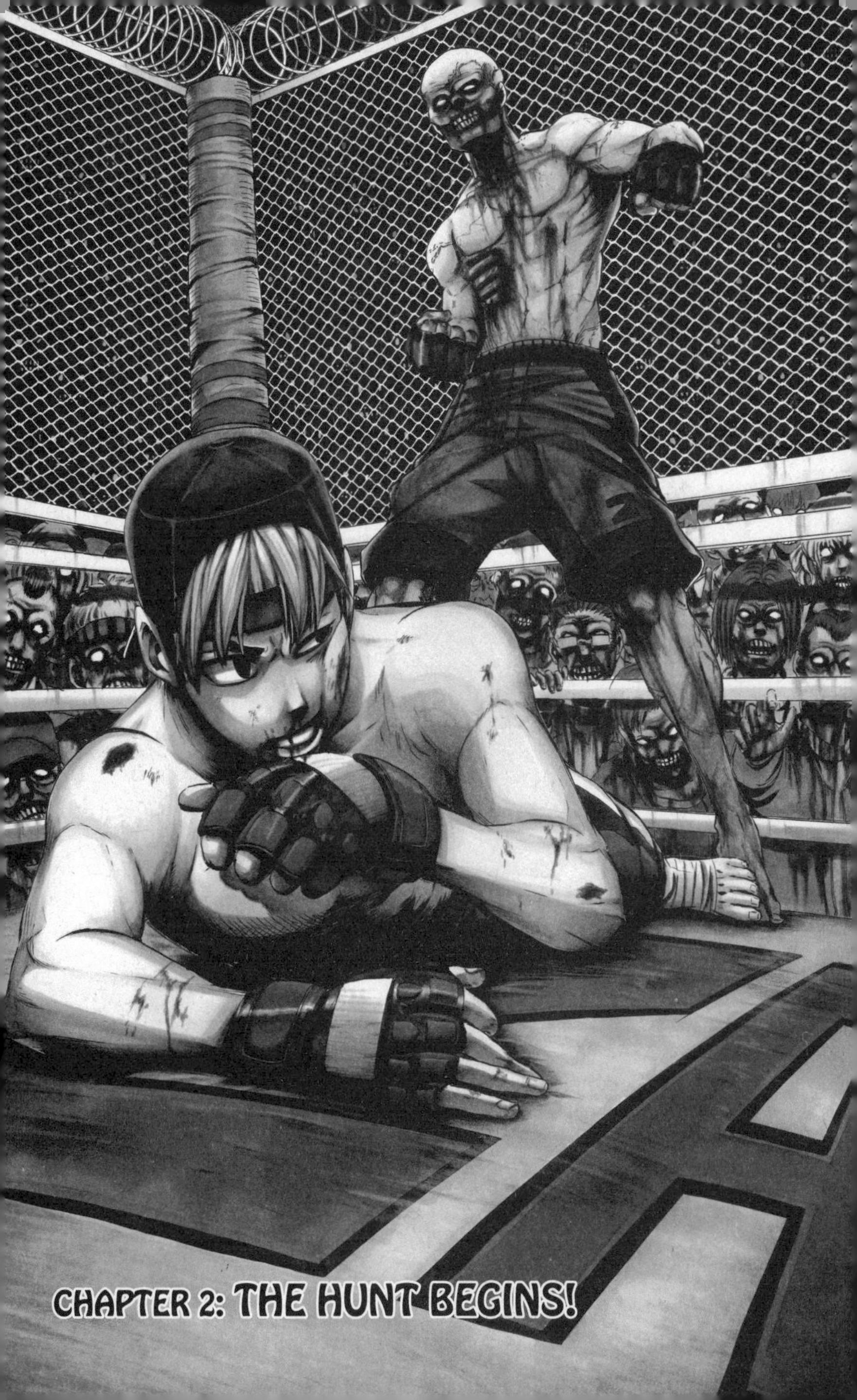
CHAPTER 2: THE HUNT BEGINS!

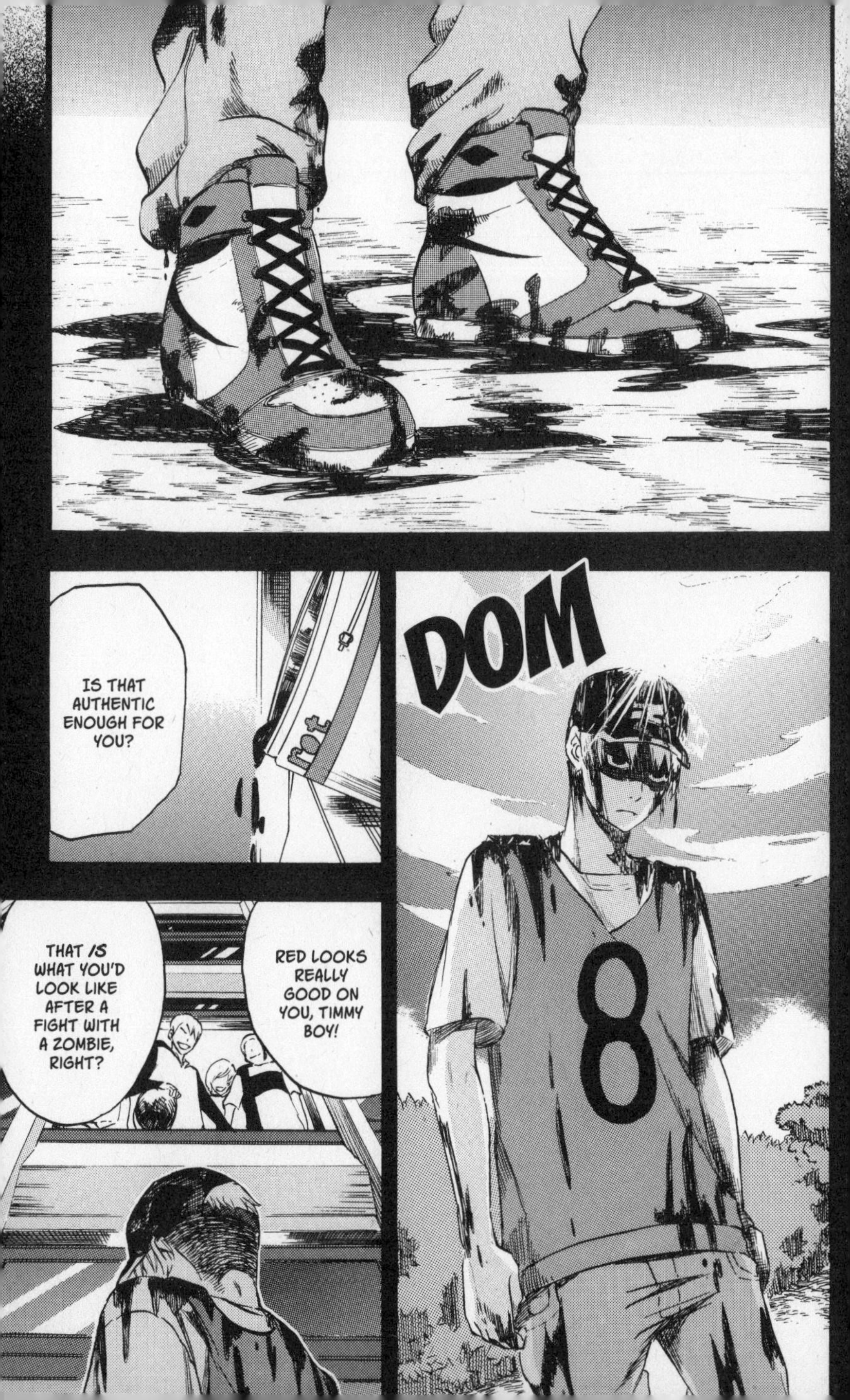
DOM
IS THAT AUTHENTIC ENOUGH FOR YOU?
RED LOOKS REALLY GOOD ON YOU, TIMMY BOY!
THAT IS WHAT YOU'D LOOK LIKE AFTER A FIGHT WITH A ZOMBIE, RIGHT?

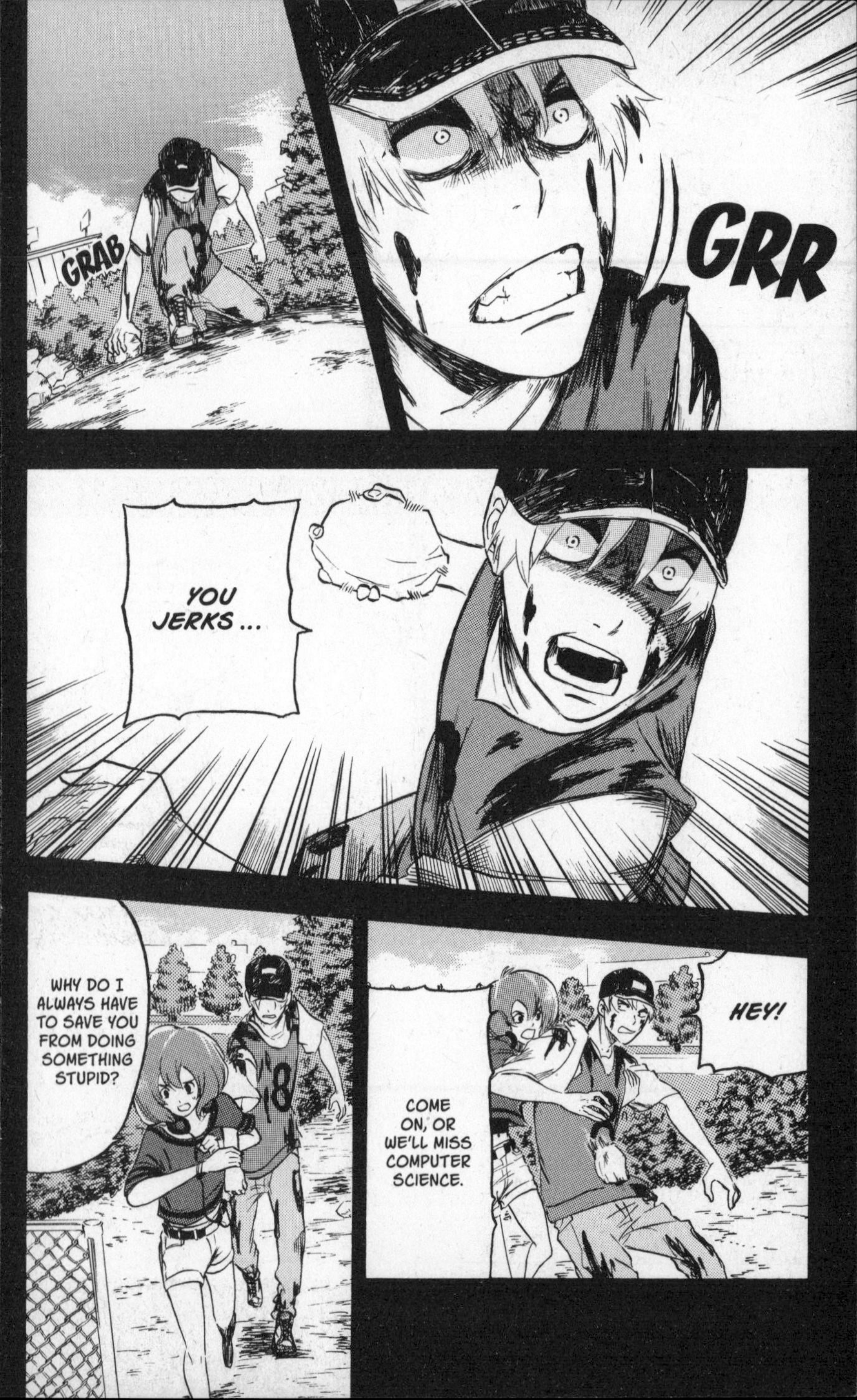
GRR
GRAB
YOU JERKS ...
HEY!
COME ON, OR WE'LL MISS COMPUTER SCIENCE.
WHY DO I ALWAYS HAVE TO SAVE YOU FROM DOING SOMETHING STUPID?

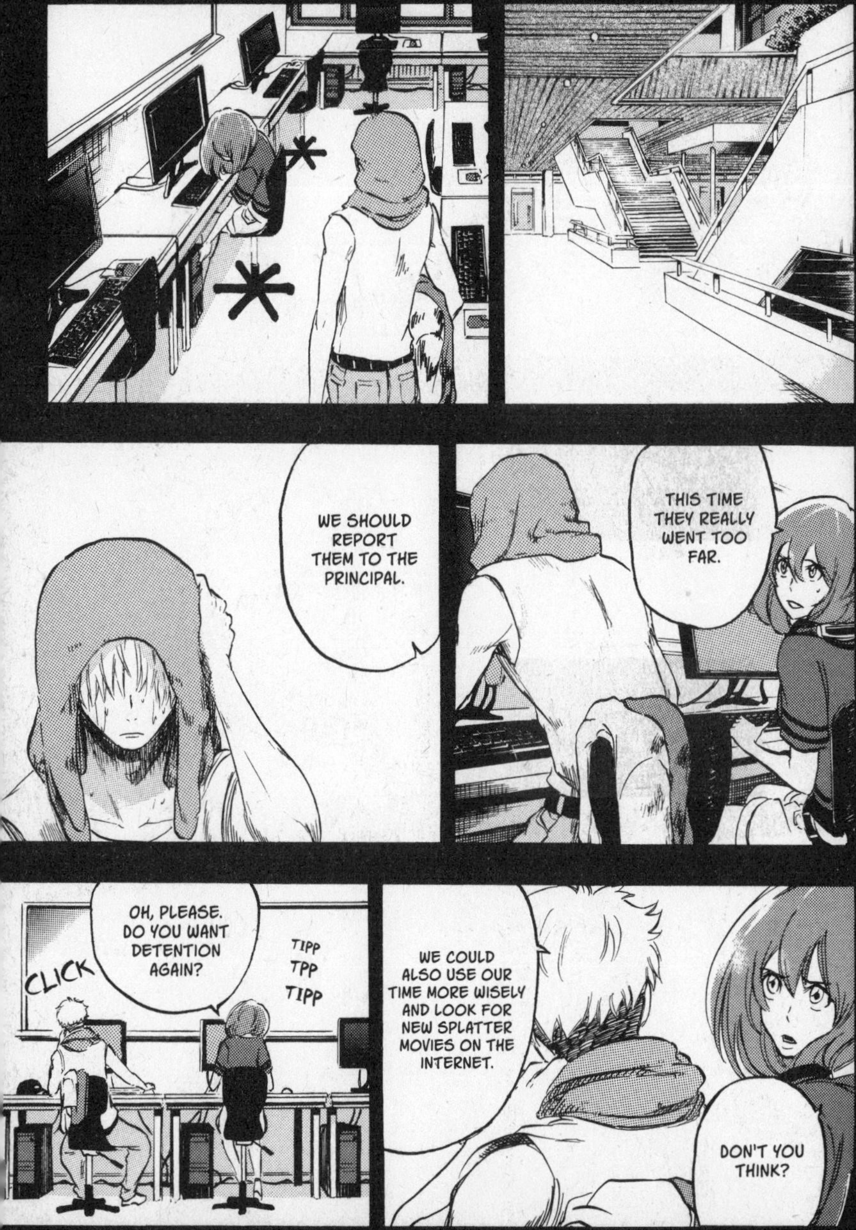
THIS TIME THEY REALLY WENT TOO FAR.
WE SHOULD REPORT THEM TO THE PRINCIPAL.
WE COULD ALSO USE OUR TIME MORE WISELY AND LOOK FOR NEW SPLATTER MOVIES ON THE INTERNET.
DON'T YOU THINK?
OH, PLEASE. DO YOU WANT DETENTION AGAIN?
TIPP TPP TIPP
CLICK

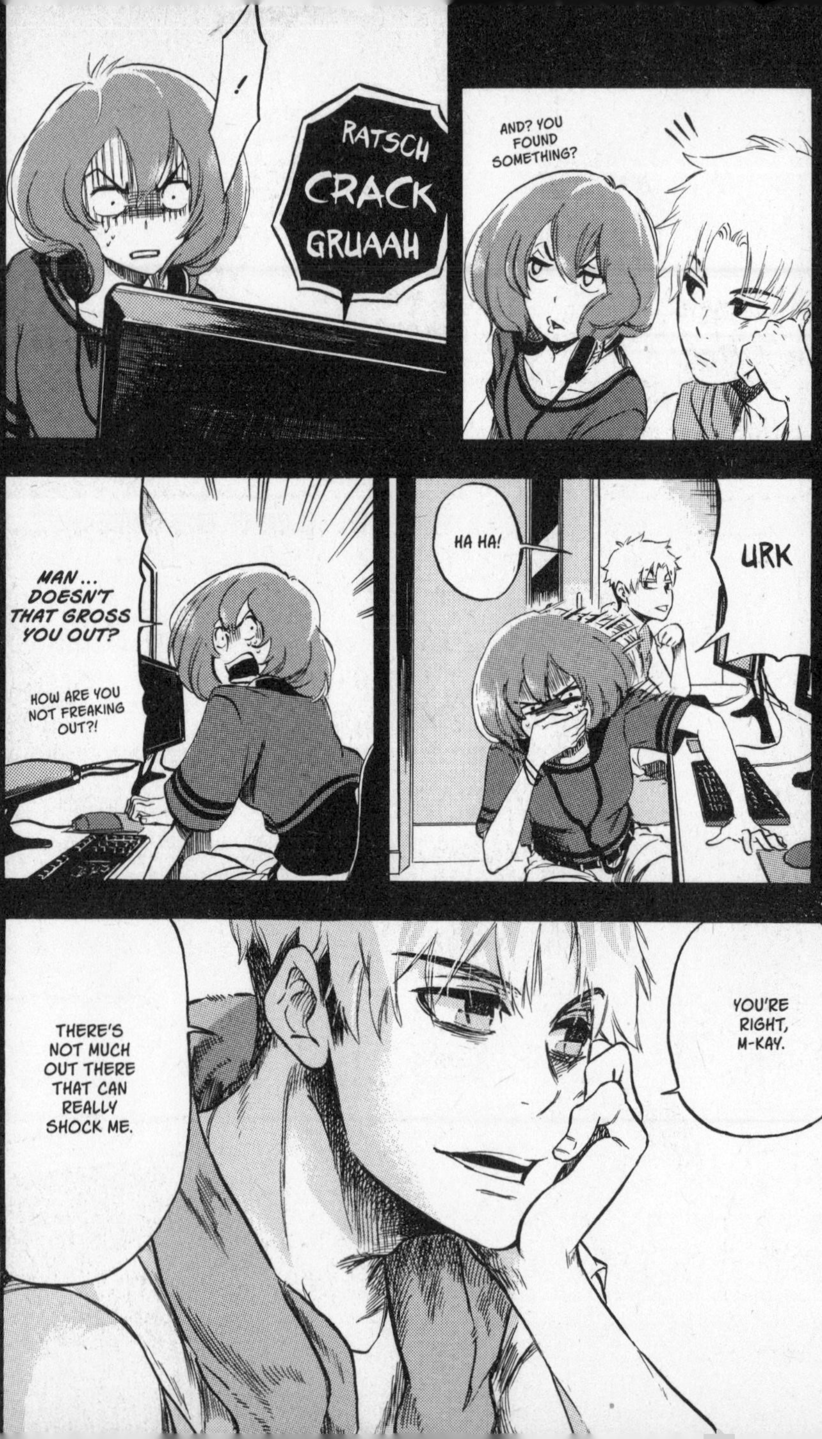
AND? YOU FOUND SOMETHING?
!
RATSCH
CRACK
GRUAAH
URK
HA HA!
MAN ... DOESN'T THAT GROSS YOU OUT?
HOW ARE YOU NOT FREAKING OUT?!
YOU'RE RIGHT, M-KAY.
THERE'S NOT MUCH OUT THERE THAT CAN REALLY SHOCK ME.

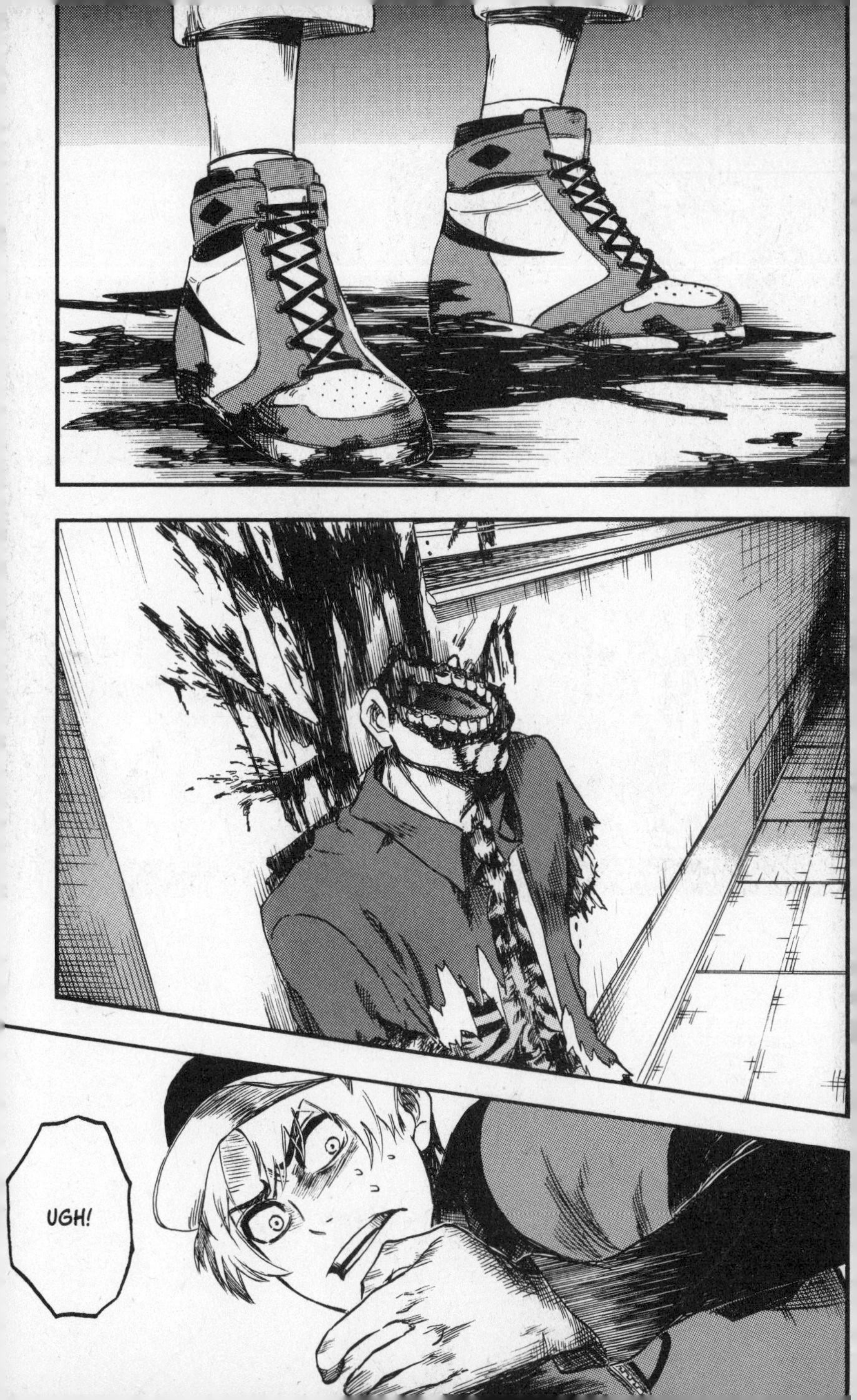
UGH!

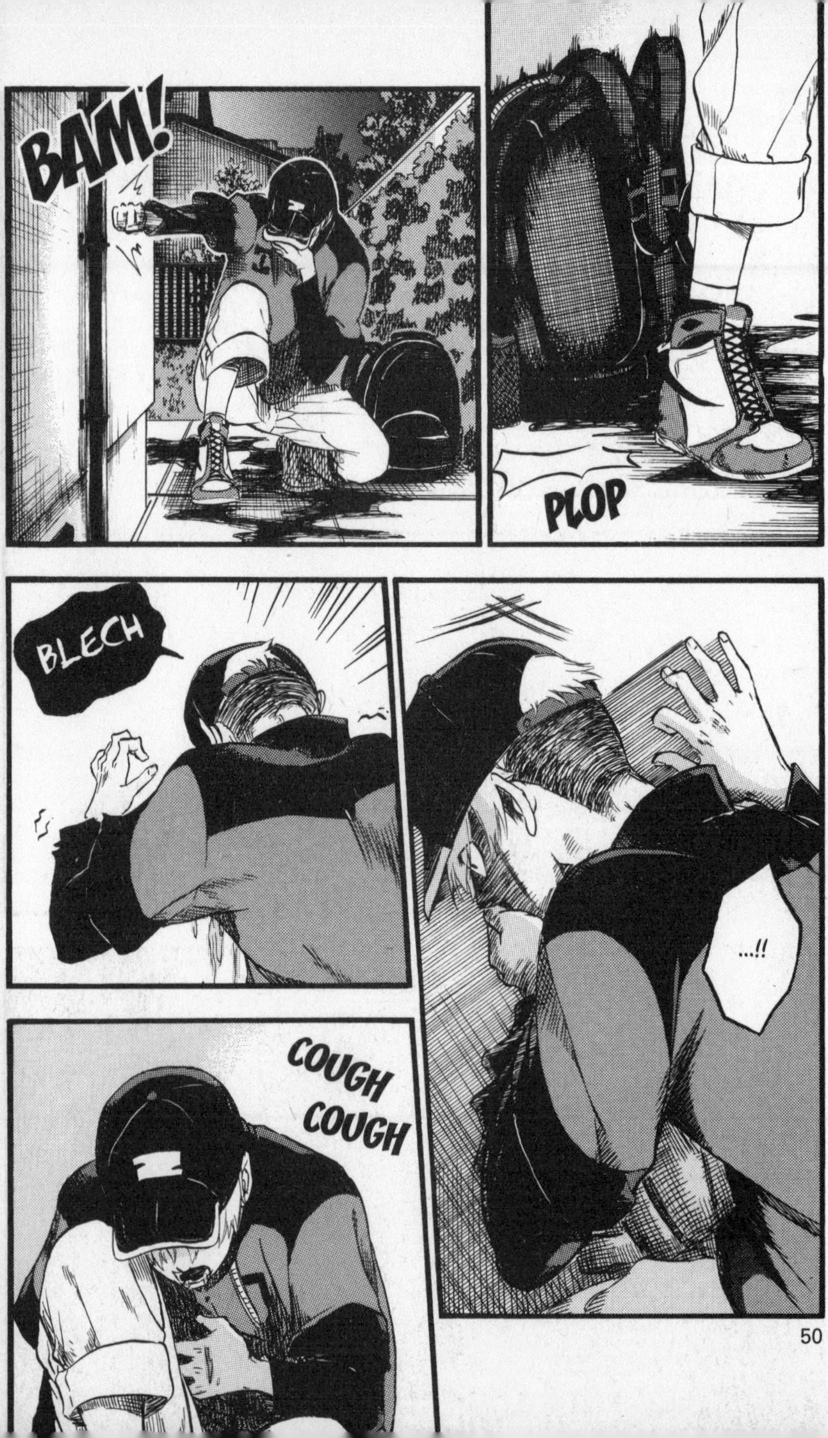
PLOP
BAM!
...!!
BLECH
COUGH COUGH

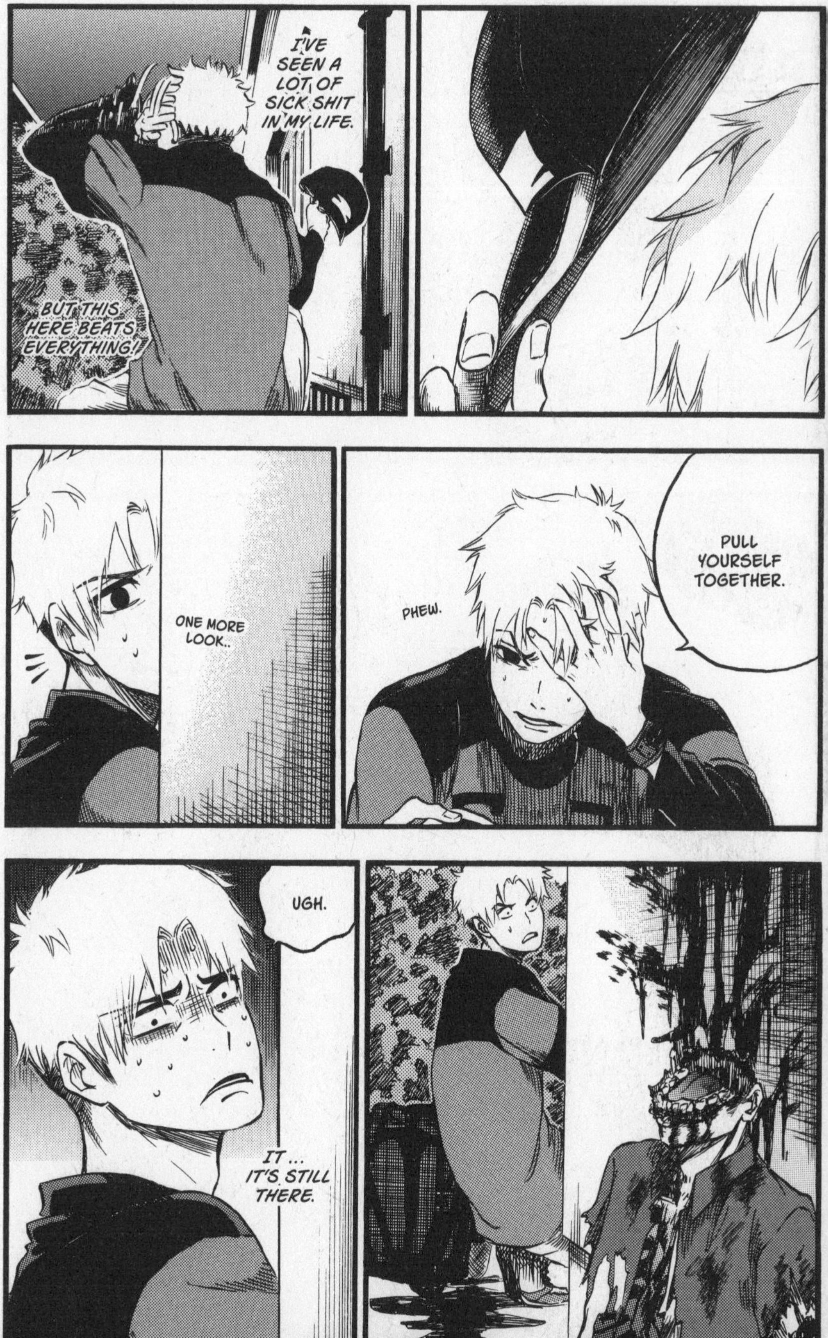
I'VE SEEN A LOT OF SICK SHIT IN MY LIFE.
BUT THIS HERE BEATS EVERYTHING!
PULL YOURSELF TOGETHER.
PHEW.
ONE MORE LOOK..
UGH.
IT... IT'S STILL THERE.

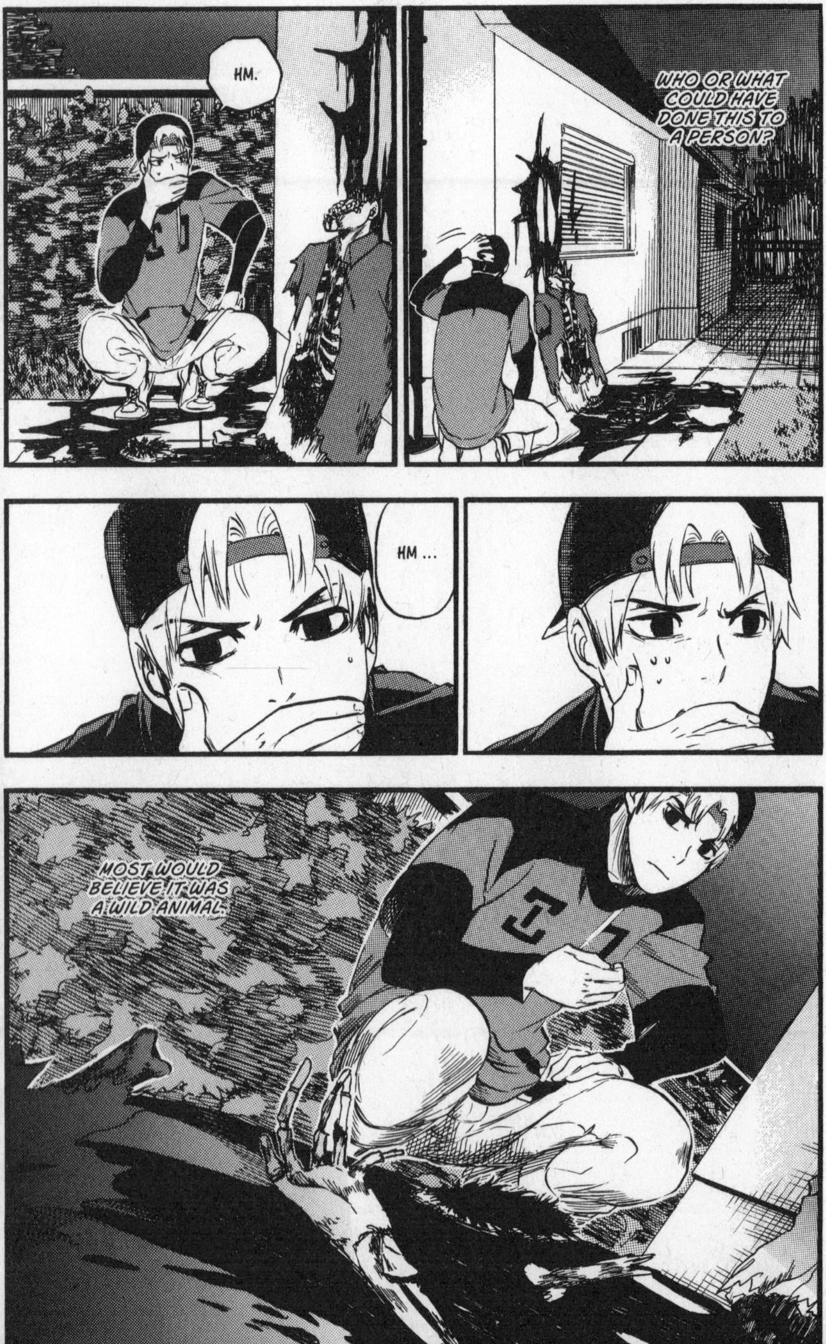
WHO OR WHAT COULD HAVE DONE THIS TO A PERSON?
HM.
HM ...
MOST WOULD BELIEVE IT WAS A WILD ANIMAL.

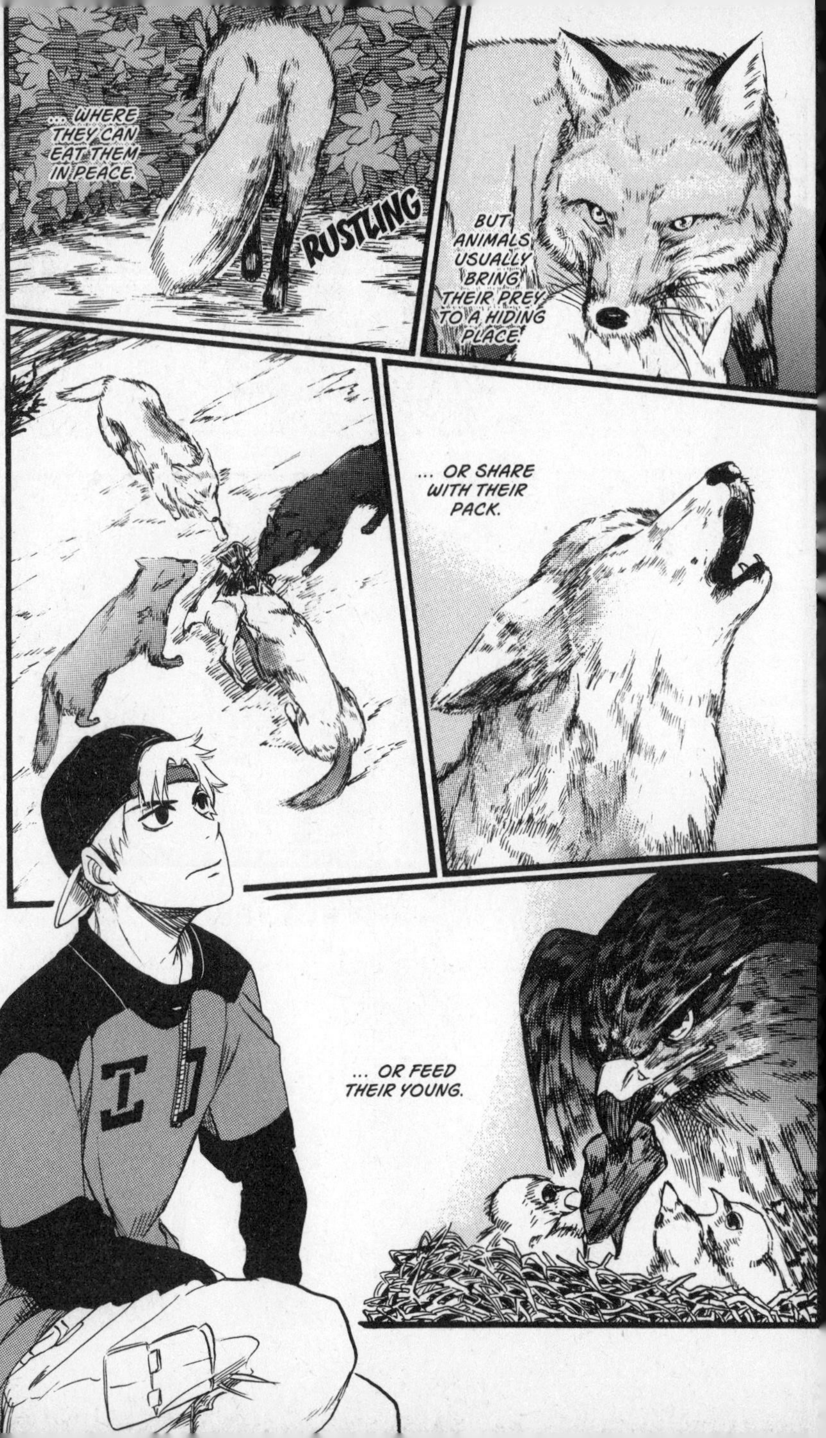
BUT ANIMALS USUALLY BRING THEIR PREY TO A HIDING PLACE.
... WHERE THEY CAN EAT THEM IN PEACE.
RUSTLING
... OR SHARE WITH THEIR PACK.
... OR FEED THEIR YOUNG.

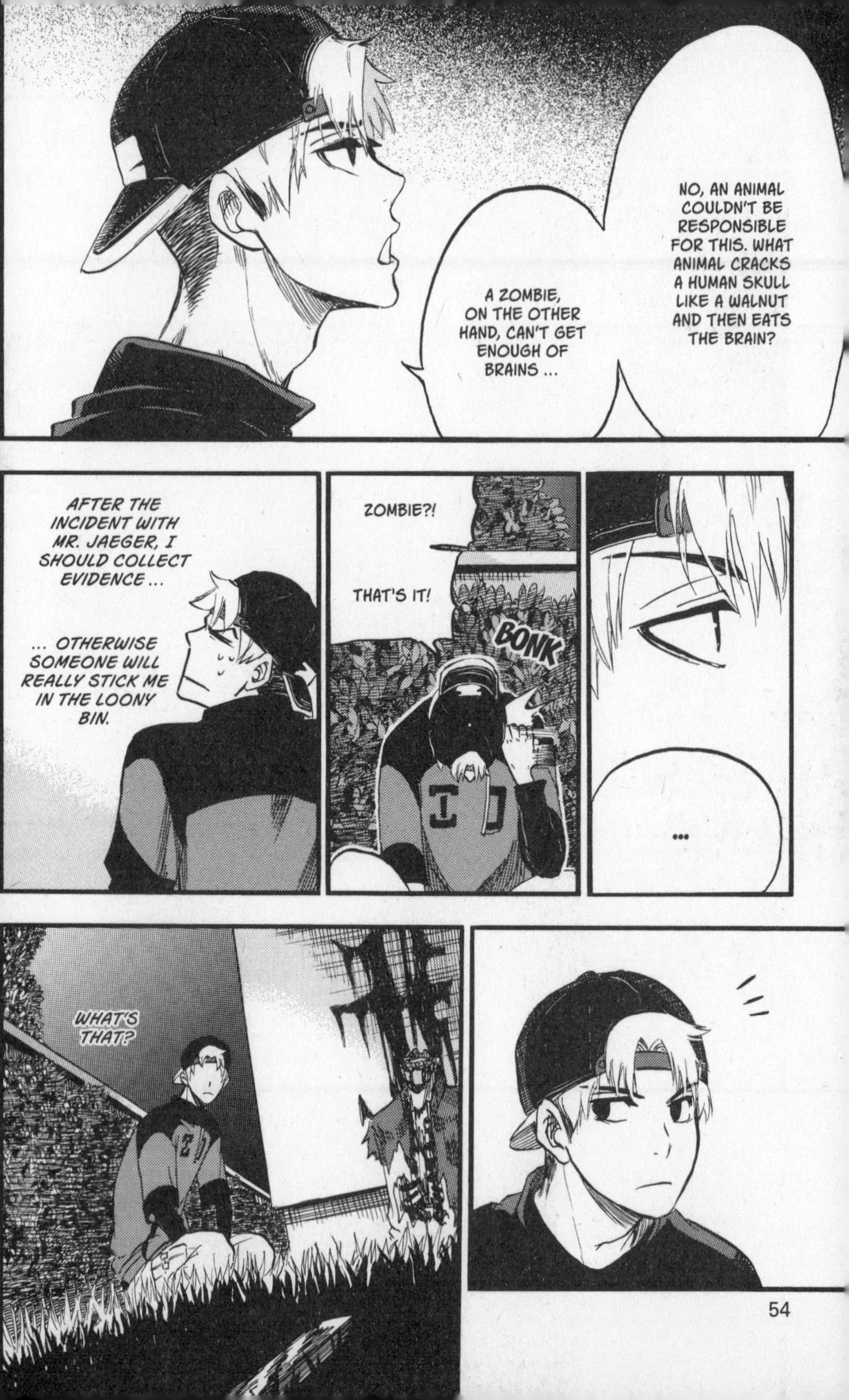
NO, AN ANIMAL COULDN'T BE RESPONSIBLE FOR THIS. WHAT ANIMAL CRACKS A HUMAN SKULL LIKE A WALNUT AND THEN EATS THE BRAIN?
A ZOMBIE, ON THE OTHER HAND, CAN'T GET ENOUGH OF BRAINS ...
...
ZOMBIE?!
THAT'S IT!
BONK
AFTER THE INCIDENT WITH MR. JAEGER, I SHOULD COLLECT EVIDENCE ...
... OTHERWISE SOMEONE WILL REALLY STICK ME IN THE LOONY BIN.
WHAT'S THAT?

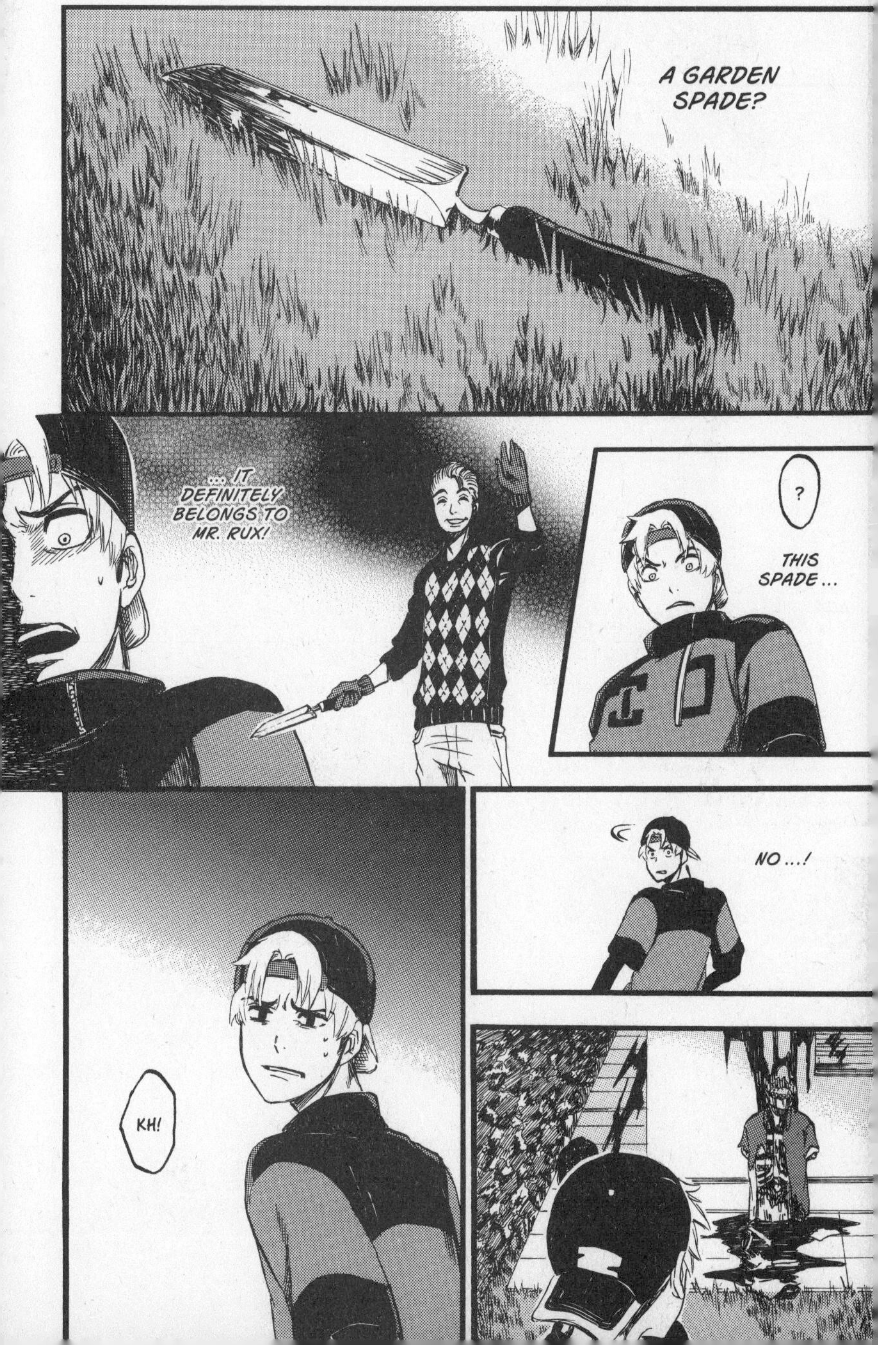
A GARDEN SPADE?
?
THIS SPADE...
... IT DEFINITELY BELONGS TO MR. RUX!
NO...!
KH!

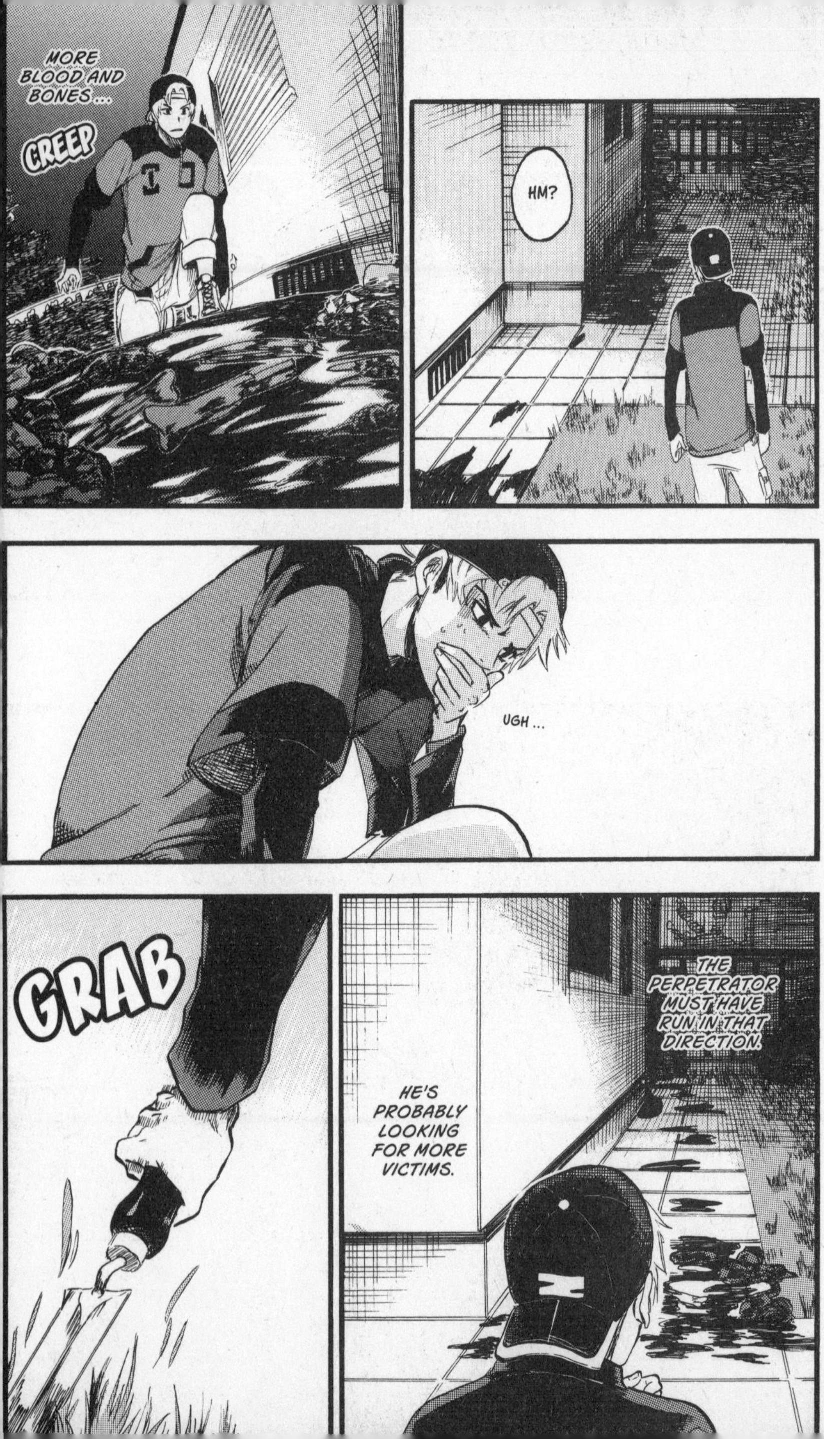
HM?
MORE BLOOD AND BONES...
CREEP
UGH ...
THE PERPETRATOR MUST HAVE RUN IN THAT DIRECTION.
HE'S PROBABLY LOOKING FOR MORE VICTIMS.
GRAB

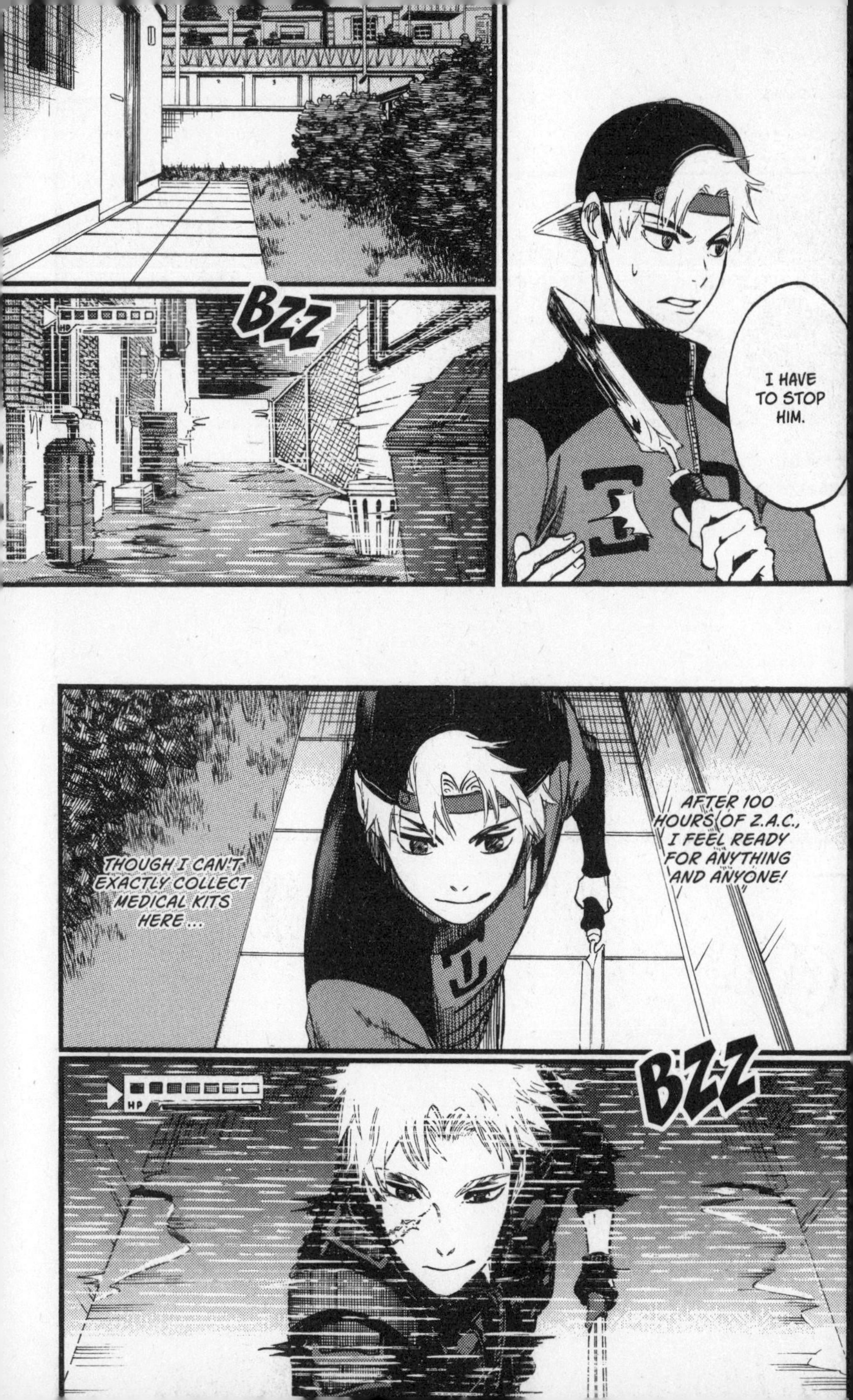
I HAVE TO STOP HIM.
BZZ
AFTER 100 HOURS OF Z.A.C., I FEEL READY FOR ANYTHING AND ANYONE!
THOUGH I CAN'T EXACTLY COLLECT MEDICAL KITS HERE ...
HP
BZZ

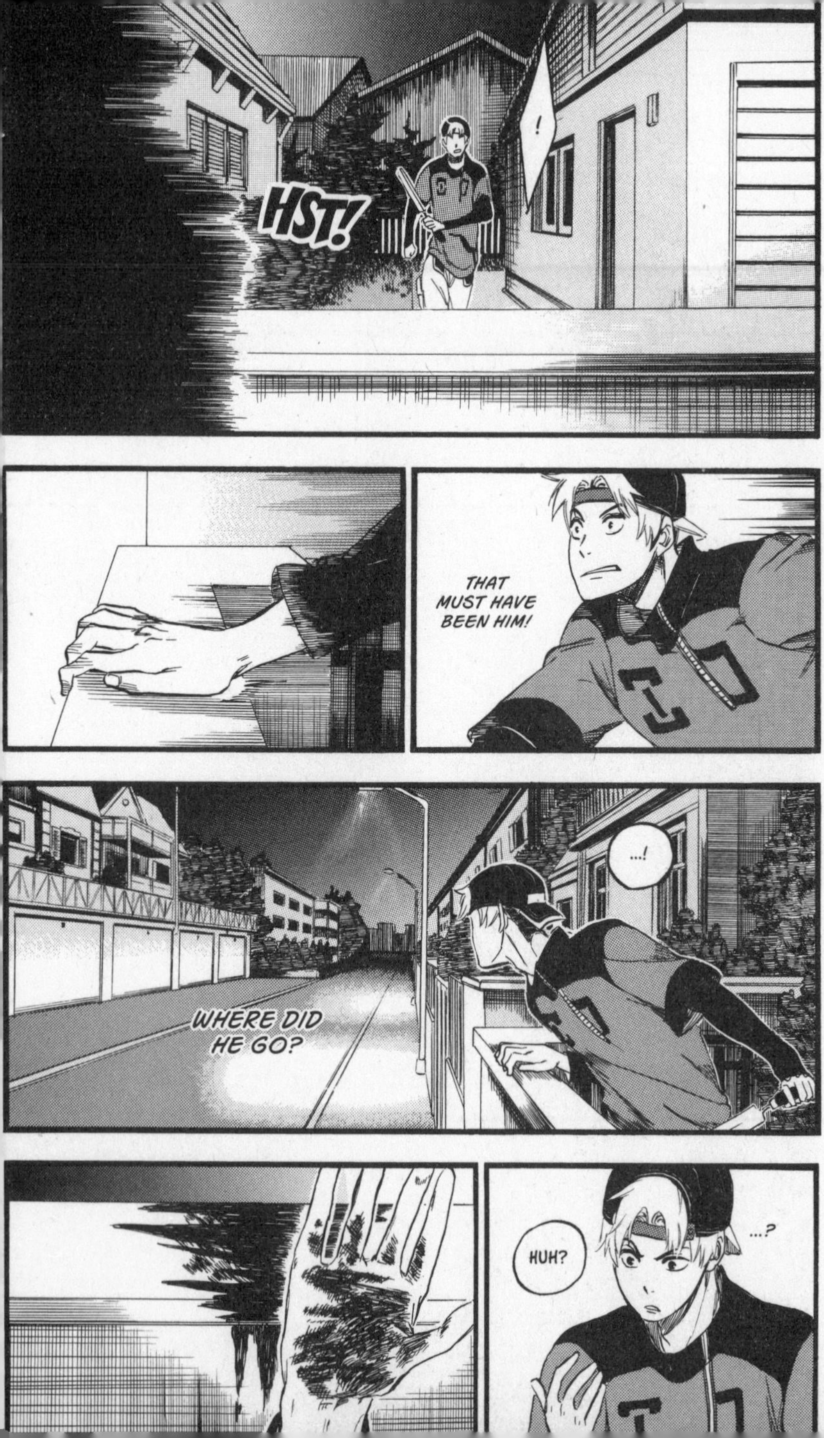
!
HST!
THAT MUST HAVE BEEN HIM!
...!
WHERE DID HE GO?
...?
HUH?

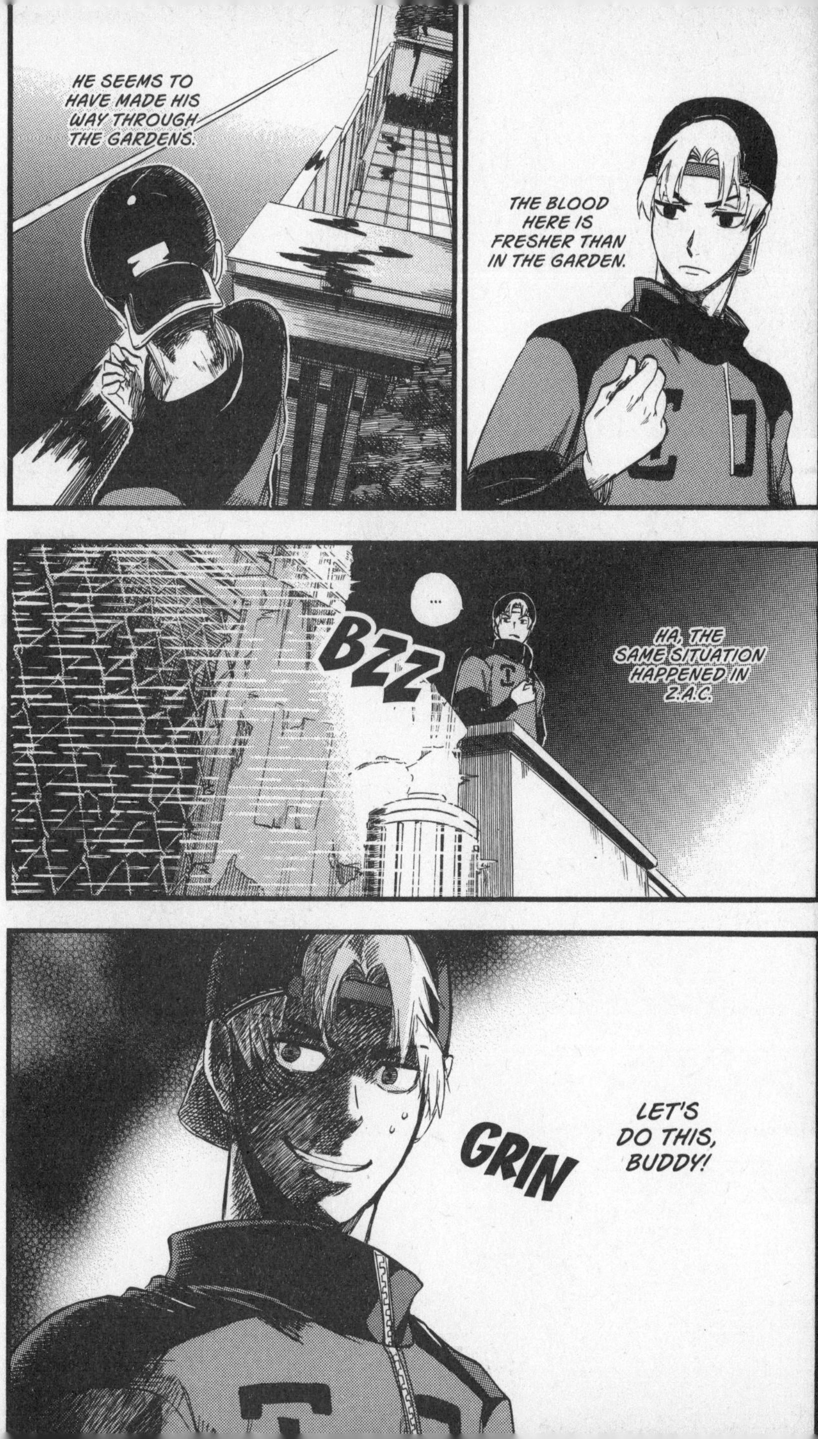
THE BLOOD HERE IS FRESHER THAN IN THE GARDEN.
HE SEEMS TO HAVE MADE HIS WAY THROUGH THE GARDENS.
...
BZZ
HA, THE SAME SITUATION HAPPENED IN Z.A.C.
LET'S DO THIS, BUDDY!
GRIN

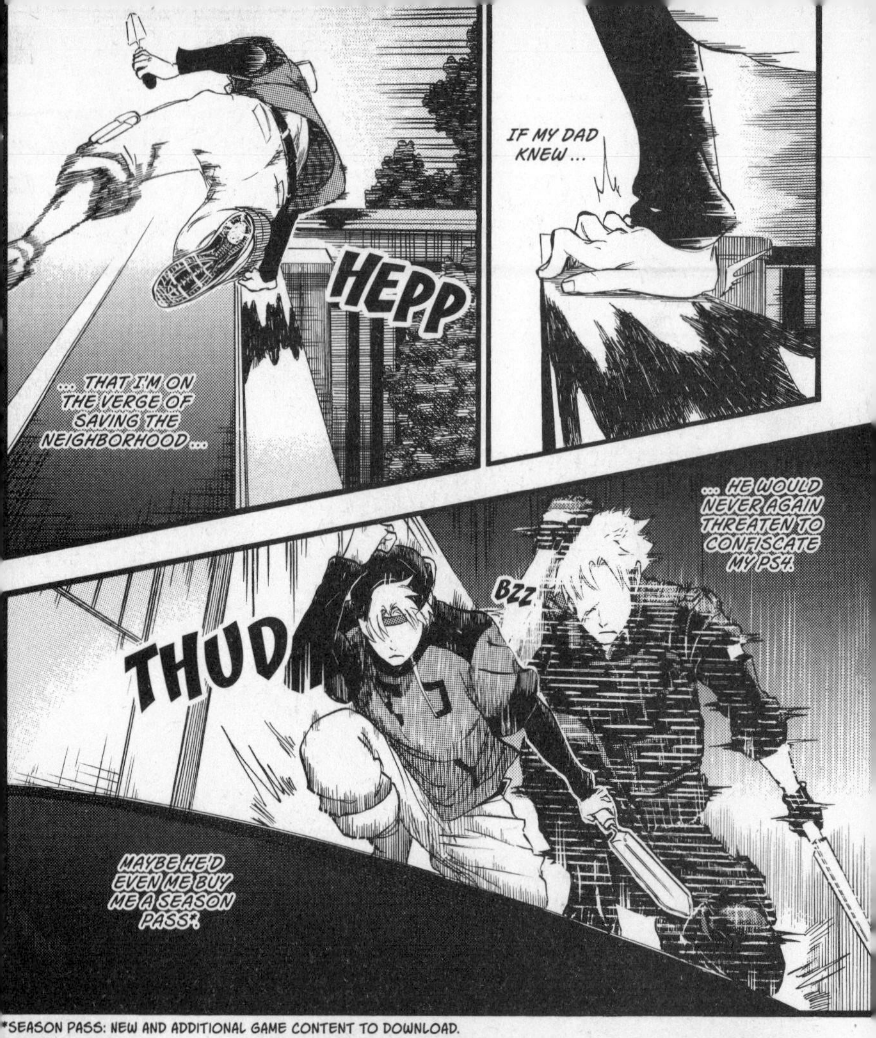
IF MY DAD KNEW...
HEPP
... THAT I'M ON THE VERGE OF SAVING THE NEIGHBORHOOD...
... HE WOULD NEVER AGAIN THREATEN TO CONFISCATE MY PS4.
BZZ
THUD
MAYBE HE'D EVEN ME BUY ME A SEASON PASS*.

*SEASON PASS: NEW AND ADDITIONAL GAME CONTENT TO DOWNLOAD.

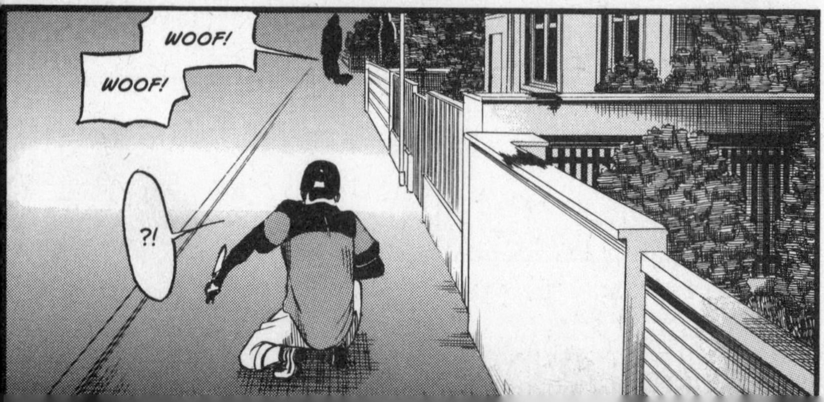
WOOF!
WOOF!
?!

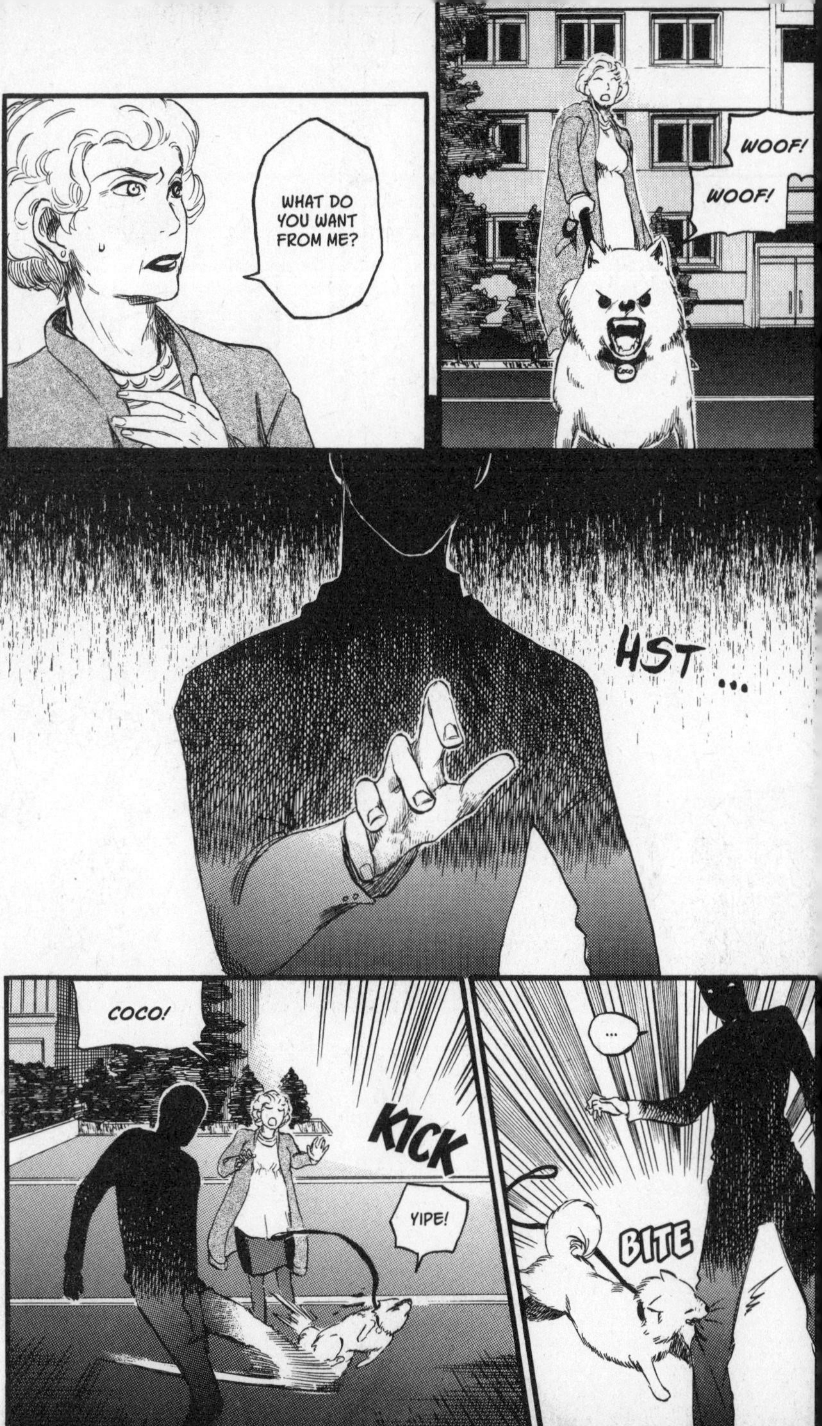
WOOF!
WOOF!
WHAT DO YOU WANT FROM ME?
HST ...
...
BITE
COCO!
KICK
YIPE!

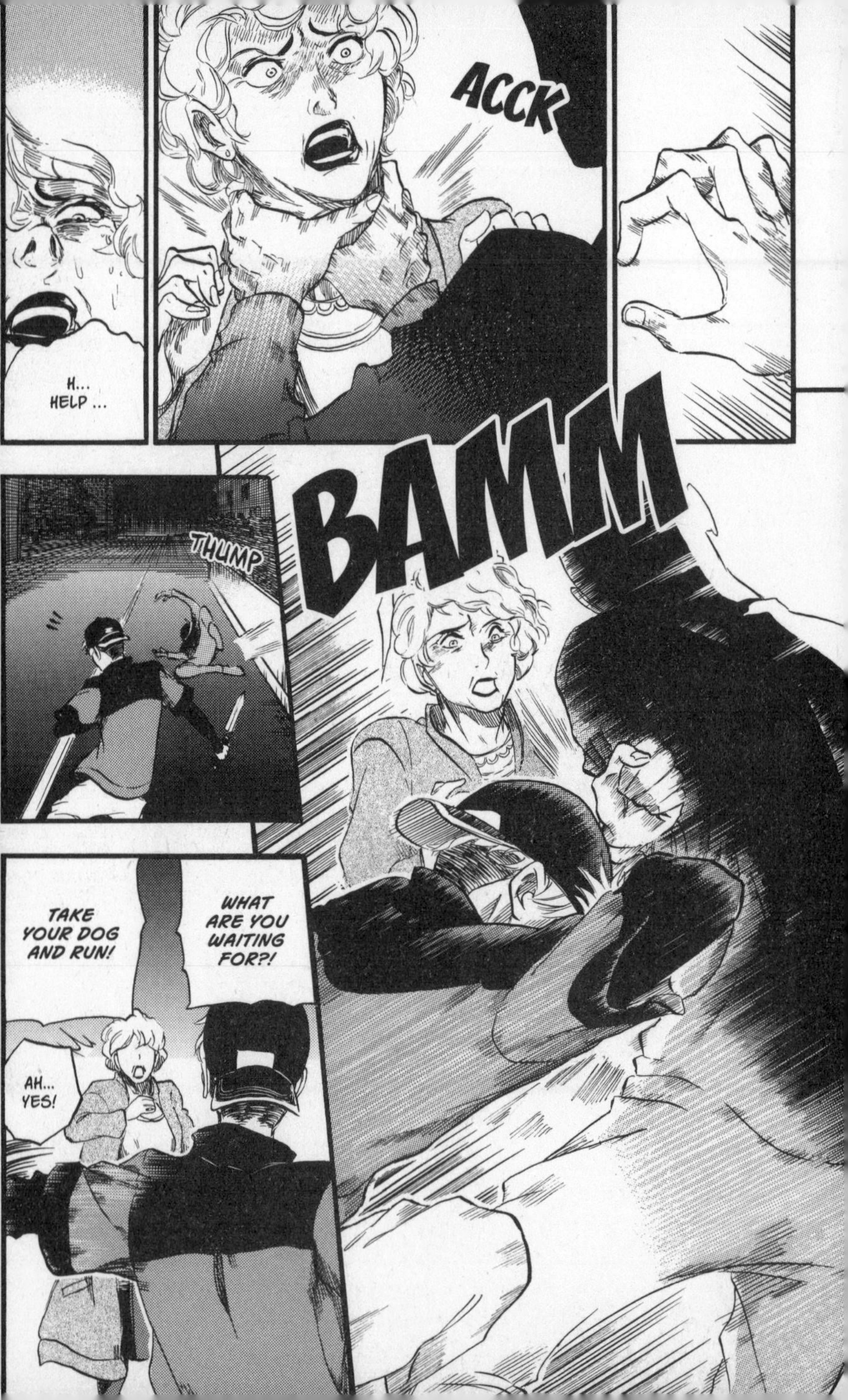
ACCK
H... HELP ...
BAMM
THUMP
WHAT ARE YOU WAITING FOR?!
TAKE YOUR DOG AND RUN!
AH... YES!

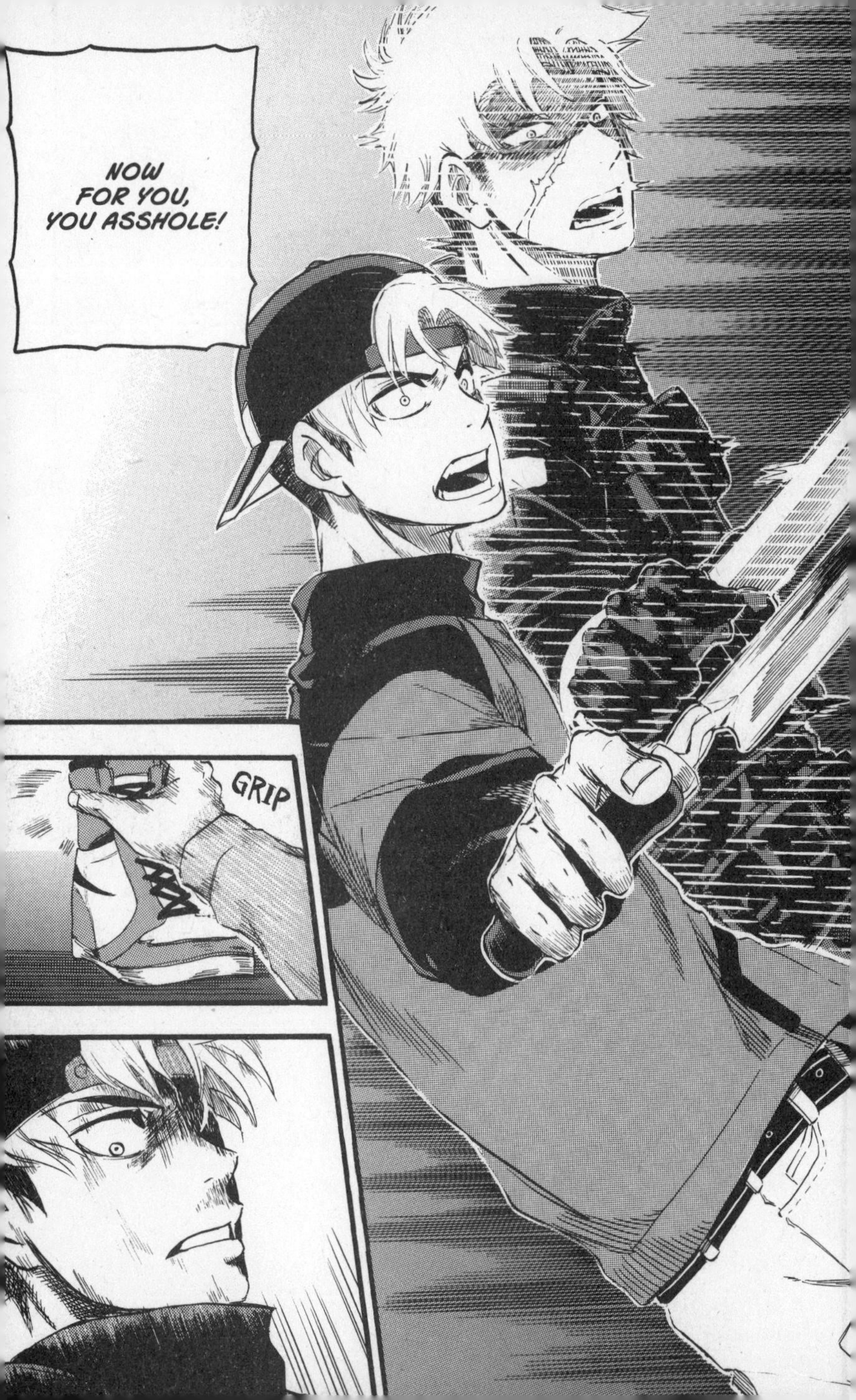
NOW FOR YOU, YOU ASSHOLE!
GRIP

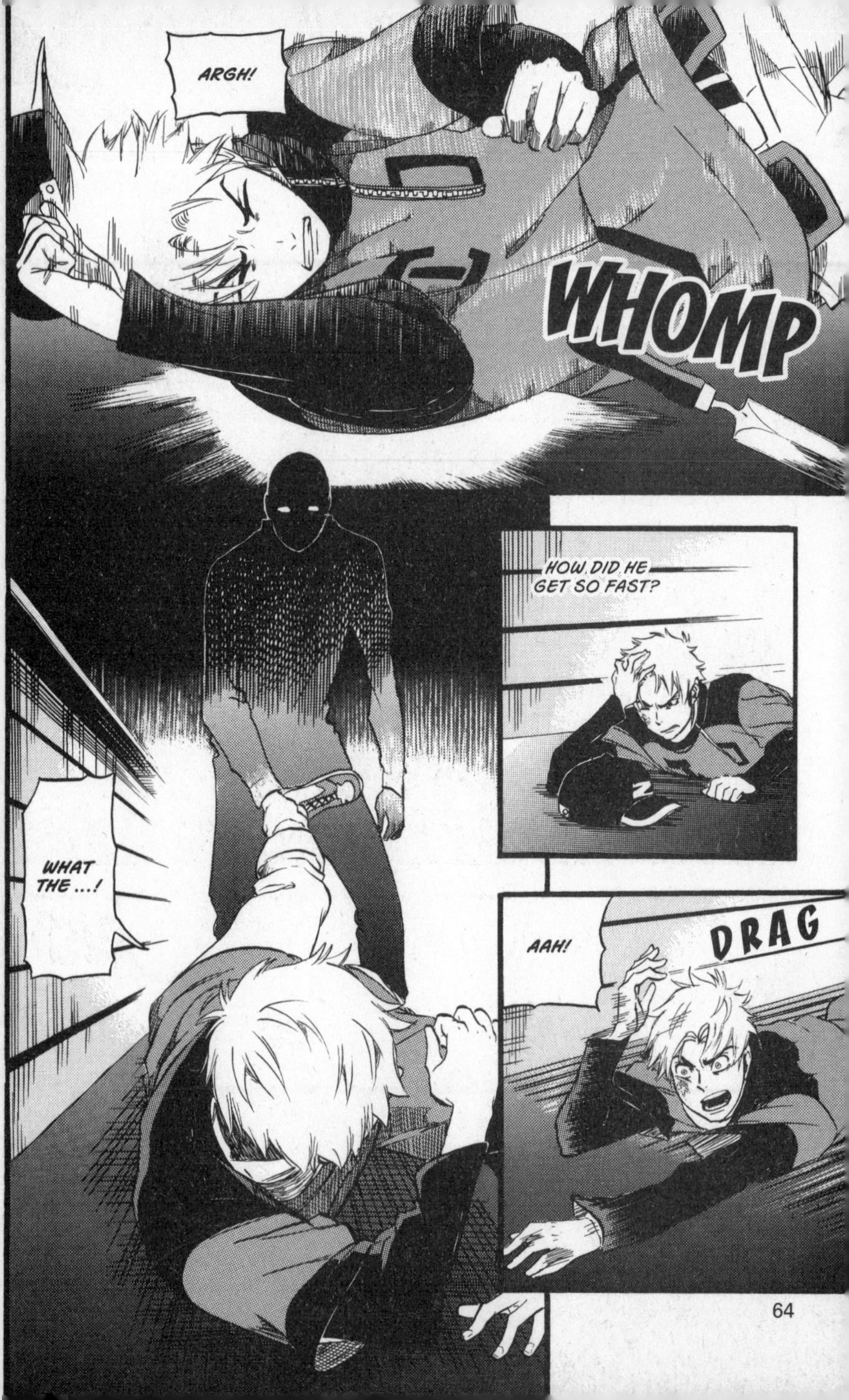
ARGH!
WHOMP
HOW DID HE GET SO FAST?
AAH!
DRAG
WHAT THE ...!

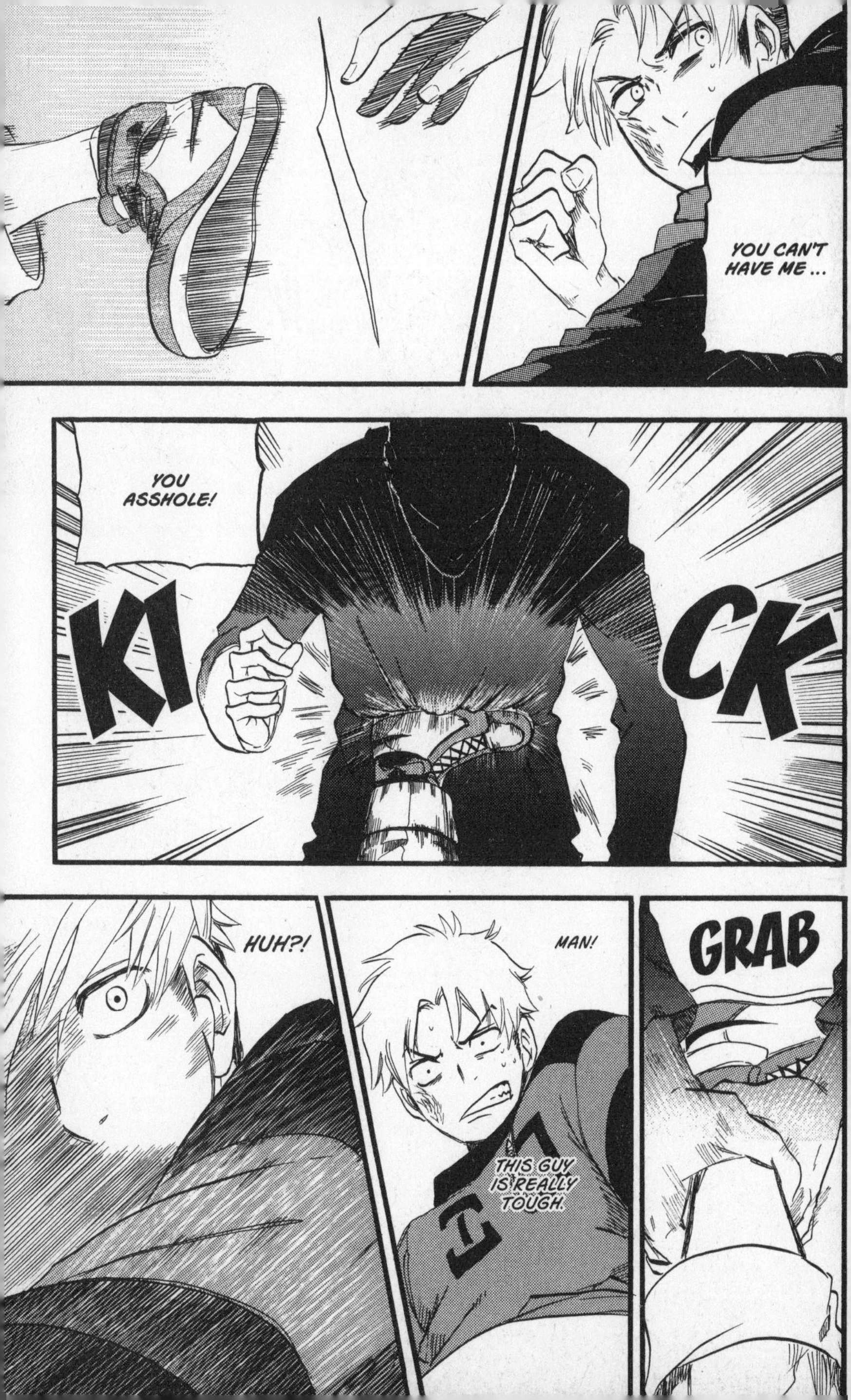
YOU CAN'T HAVE ME ...
YOU ASSHOLE!
KICK
GRAB
MAN!
THIS GUY IS REALLY TOUGH.
HUH?!

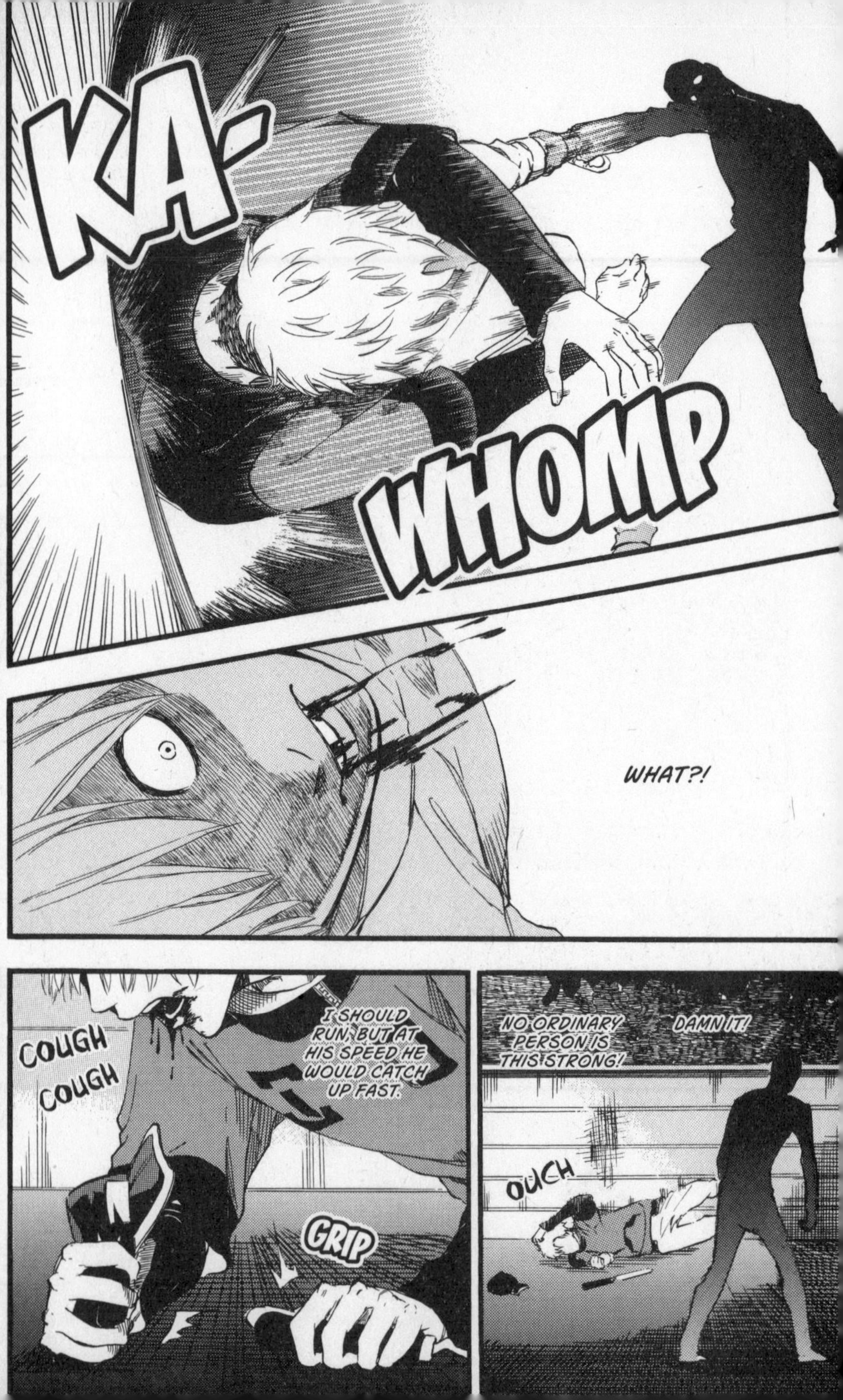
KA-
WHOMP
WHAT?!
NO ORDINARY PERSON IS THIS STRONG!
DAMN IT!
OUCH
I SHOULD RUN, BUT AT HIS SPEED HE WOULD CATCH UP FAST.
COUGH COUGH
GRIP

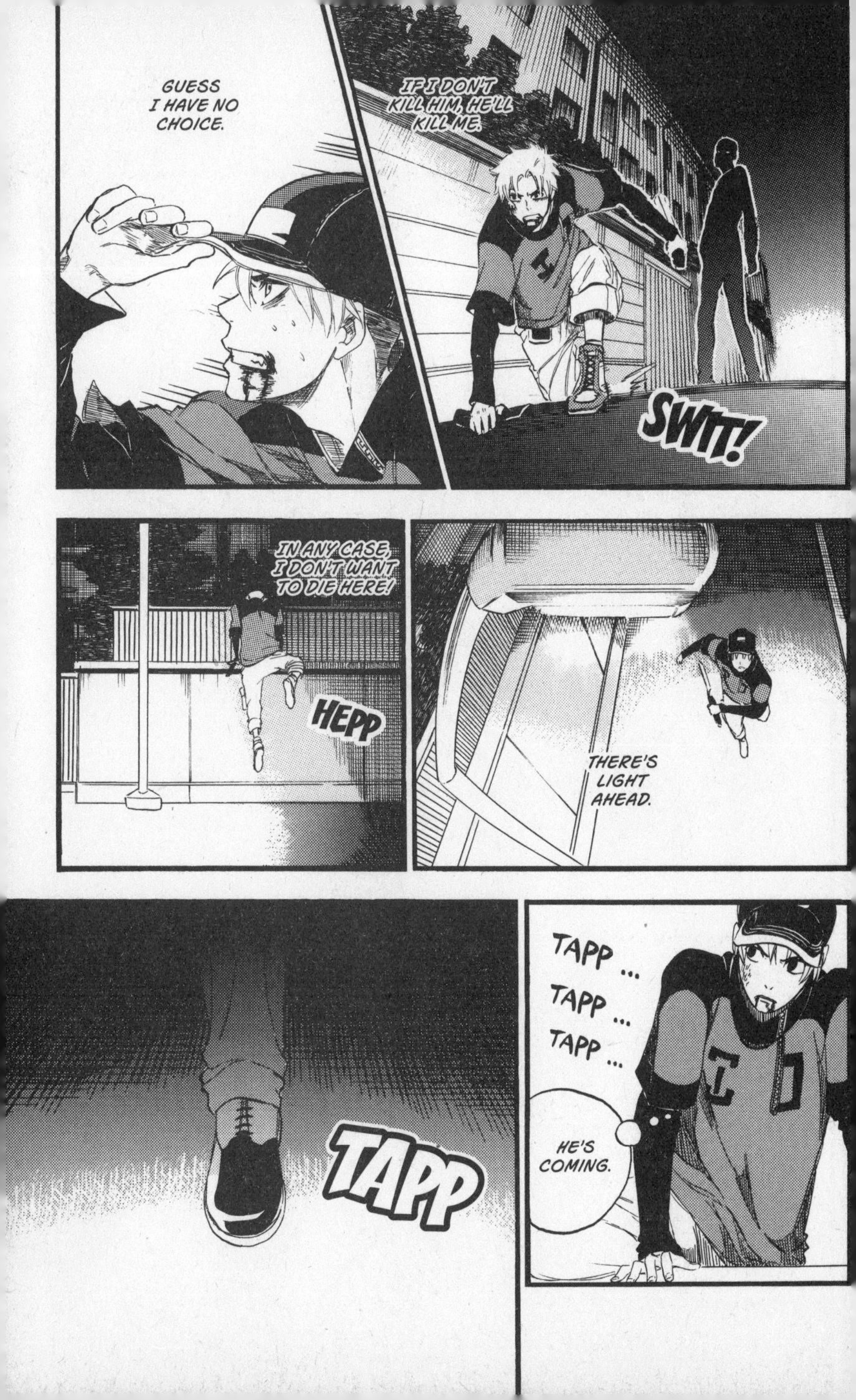
IF I DON'T KILL HIM, HE'LL KILL ME.
SWITT!
GUESS I HAVE NO CHOICE.
THERE'S LIGHT AHEAD.
IN ANY CASE, I DON'T WANT TO DIE HERE!
HEPP
TAPP ... TAPP ... TAPP ...
HE'S COMING.
TAPP

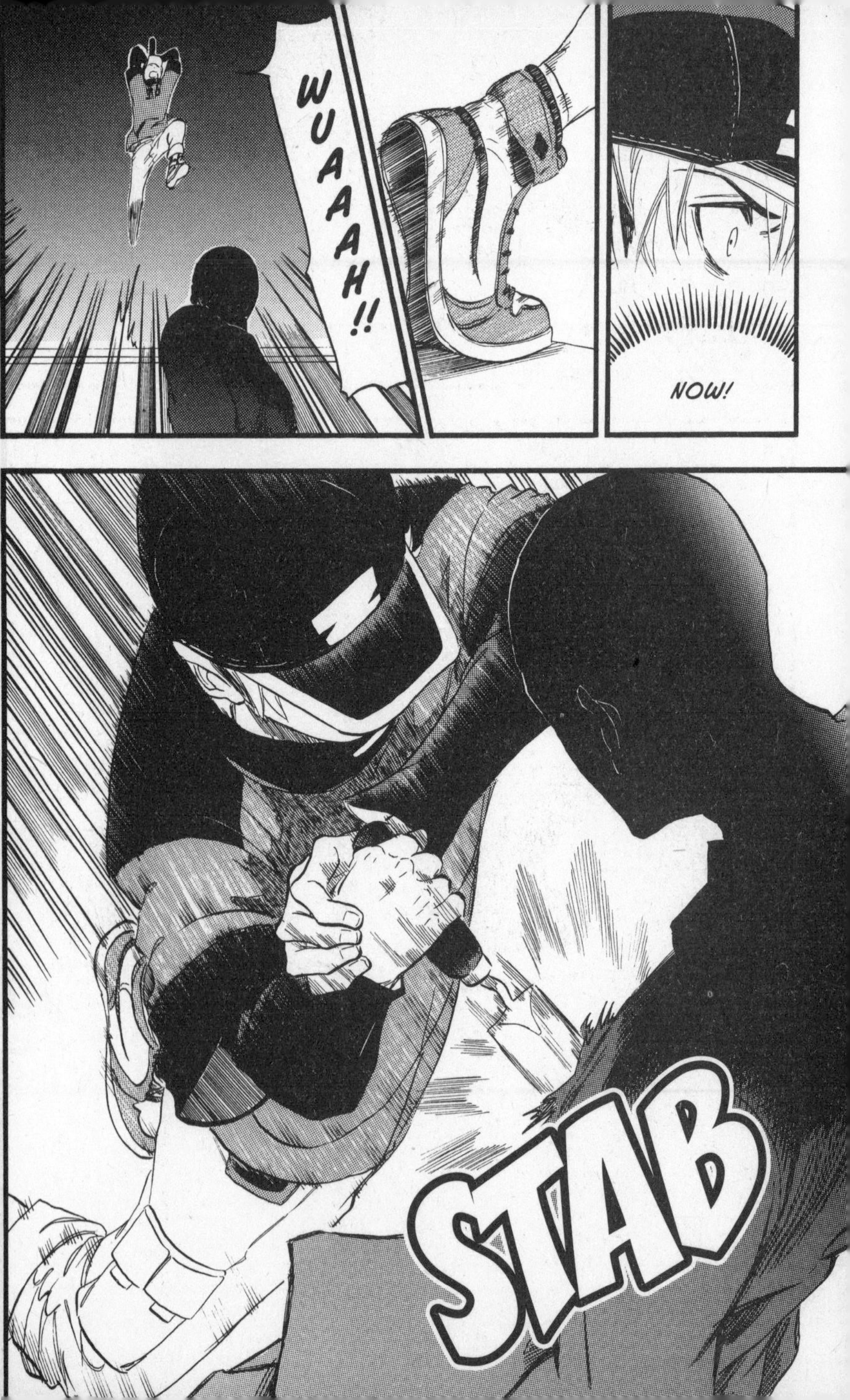
NOW!
WUAAAAH!!
STAB

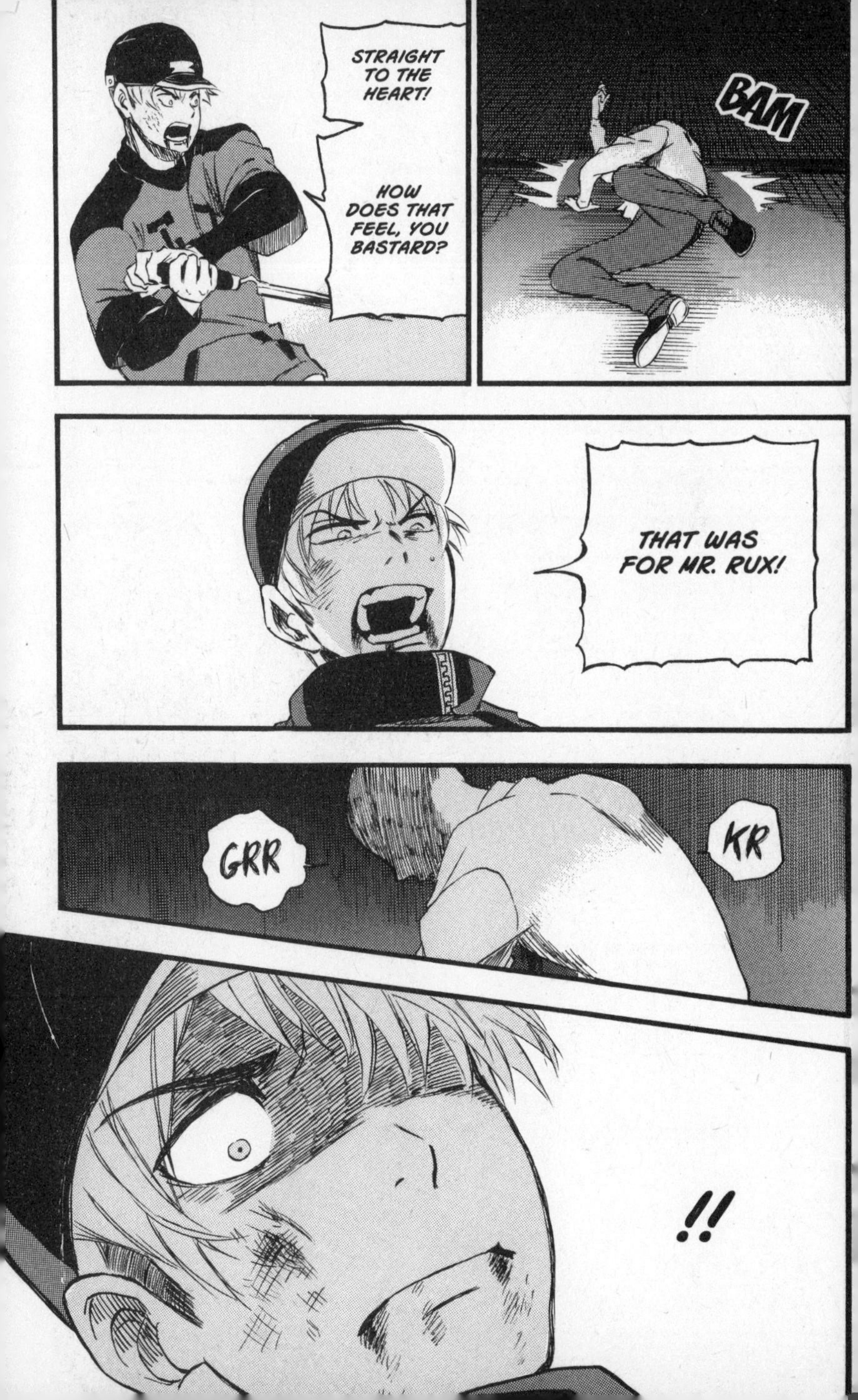
BAM
STRAIGHT TO THE HEART!
HOW DOES THAT FEEL, YOU BASTARD?
THAT WAS FOR MR. RUX!
KR
GRR
!!

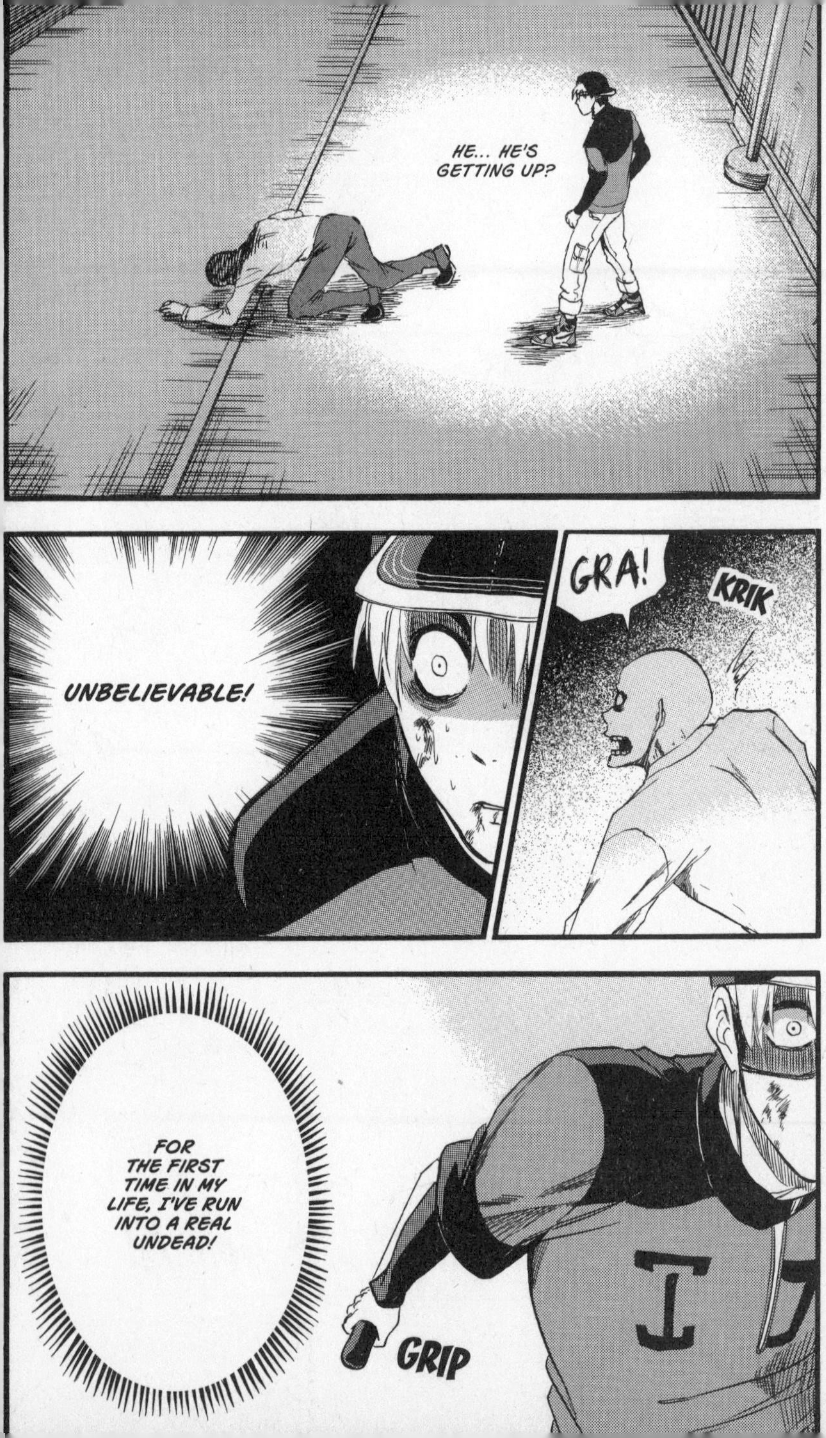
HE... HE'S GETTING UP?
GRA!
KRIK
UNBELIEVABLE!
FOR THE FIRST TIME IN MY LIFE, I'VE RUN INTO A REAL UNDEAD!
GRIP

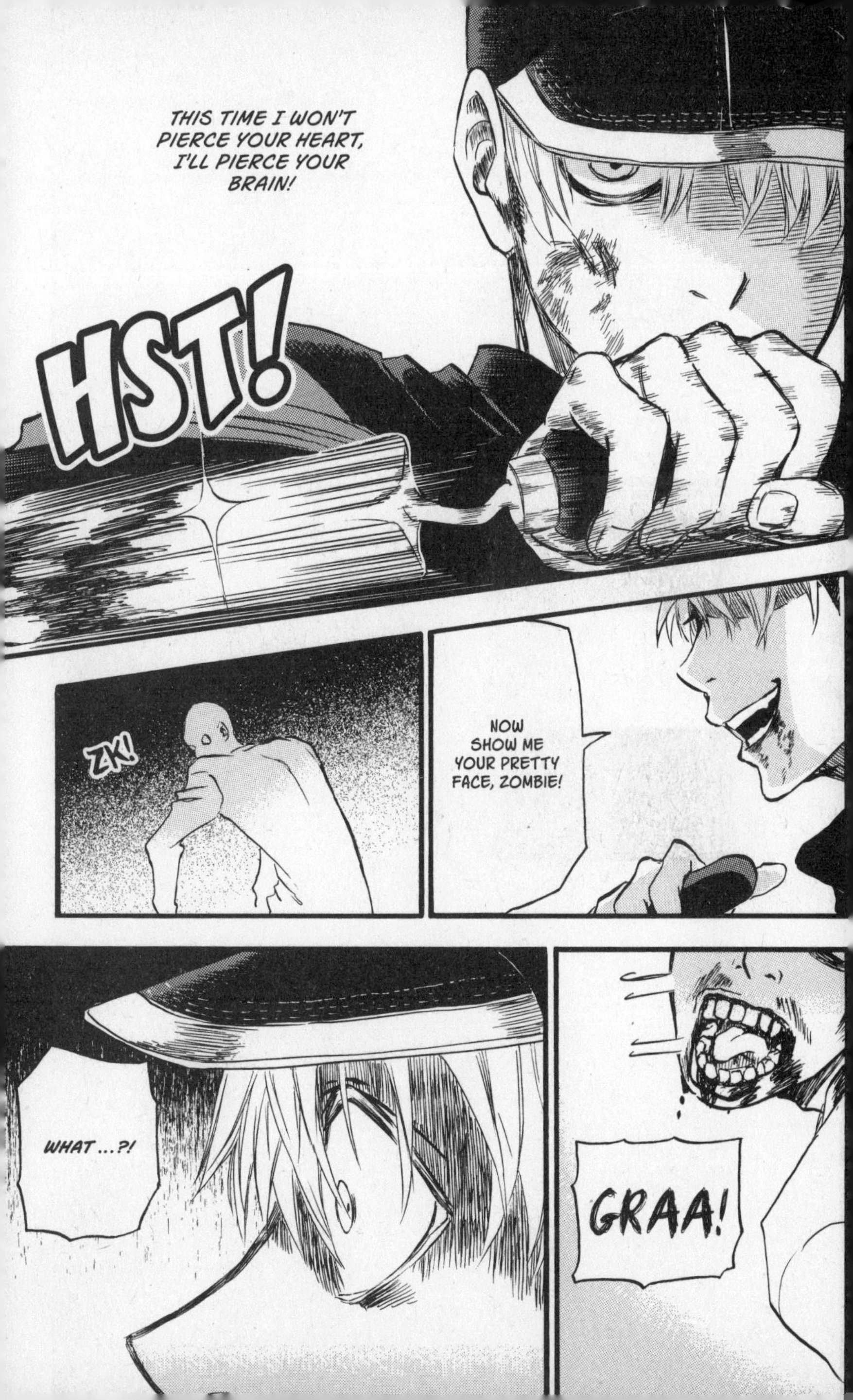
THIS TIME I WON'T PIERCE YOUR HEART, I'LL PIERCE YOUR BRAIN!
HST!
NOW SHOW ME YOUR PRETTY FACE, ZOMBIE!
ZK!
GRAA!
WHAT ...?!

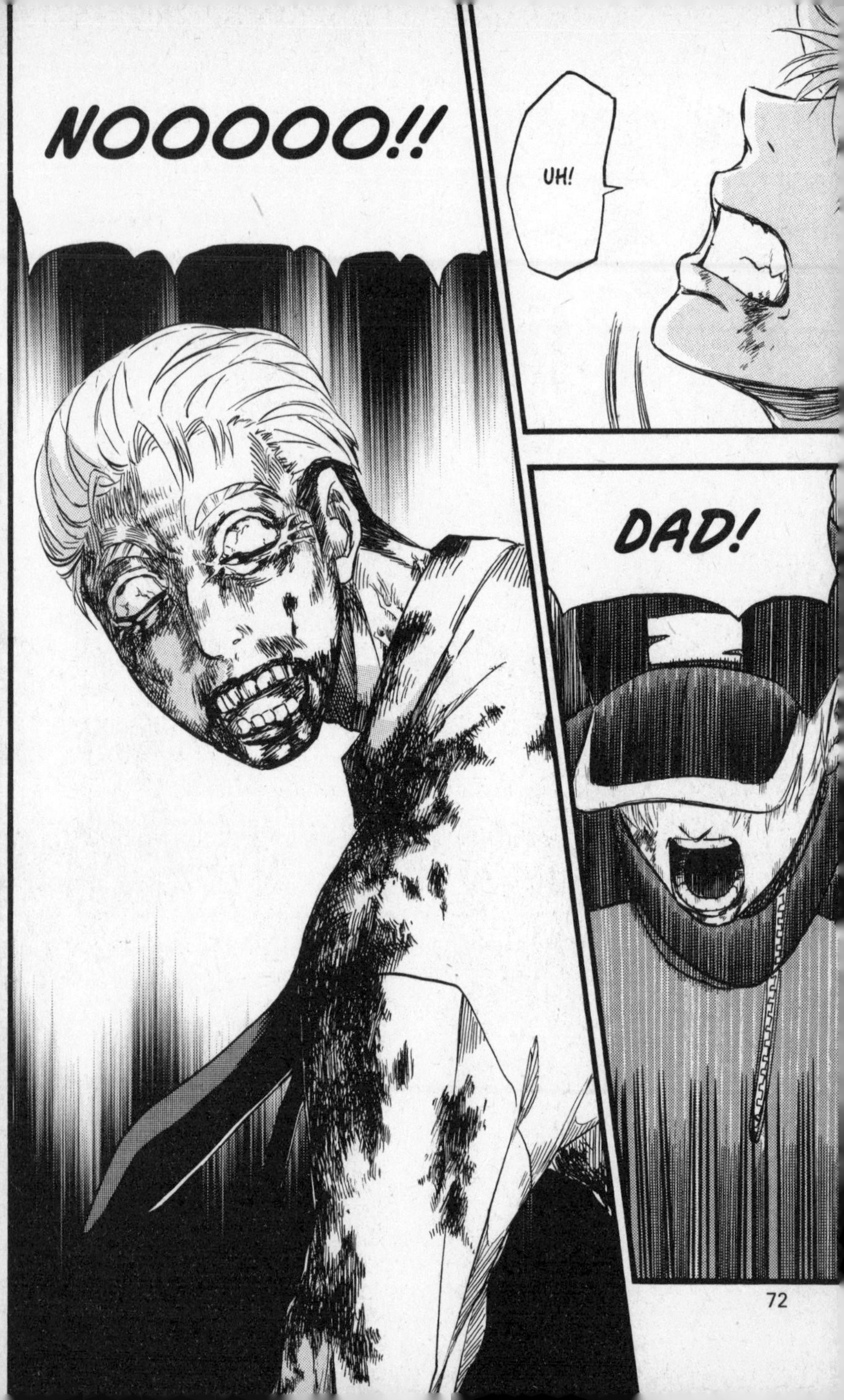
UH!
DAD!
NOOOOO!!

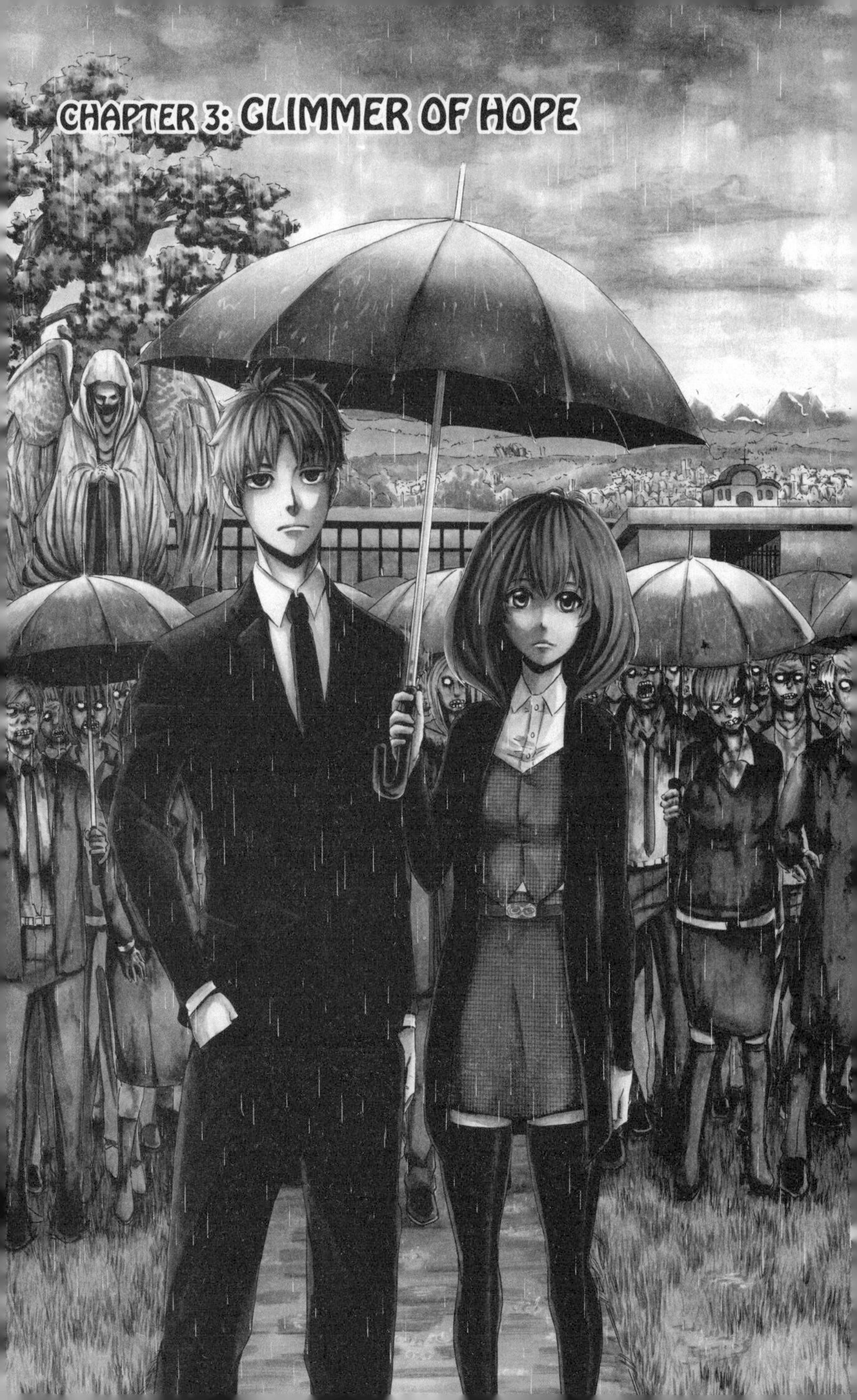
CHAPTER 3: GLIMMER OF HOPE

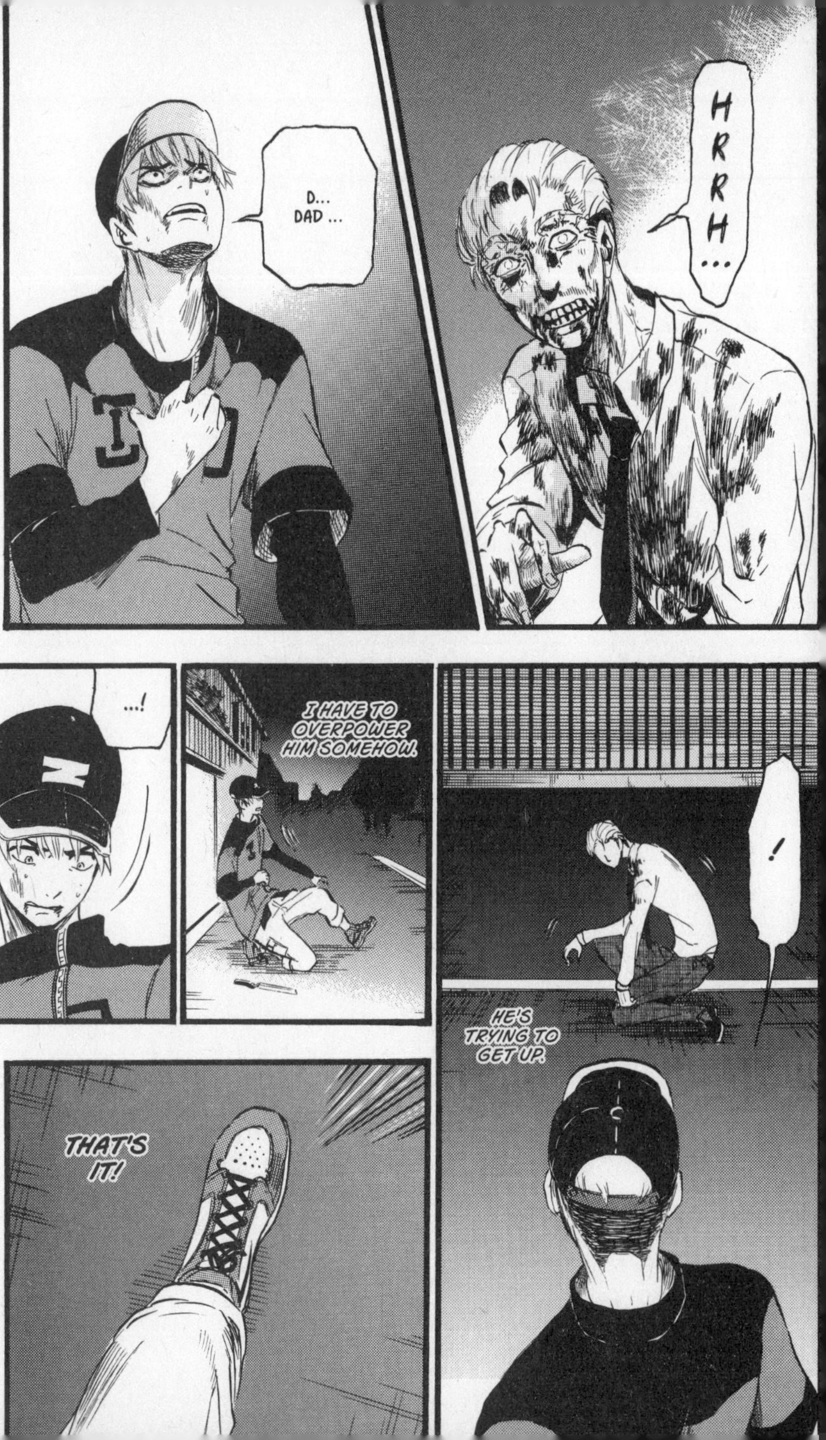
HRRH...
D... DAD ...
!
I HAVE TO OVERPOWER HIM SOMEHOW.
...!
HE'S TRYING TO GET UP.
THAT'S IT!

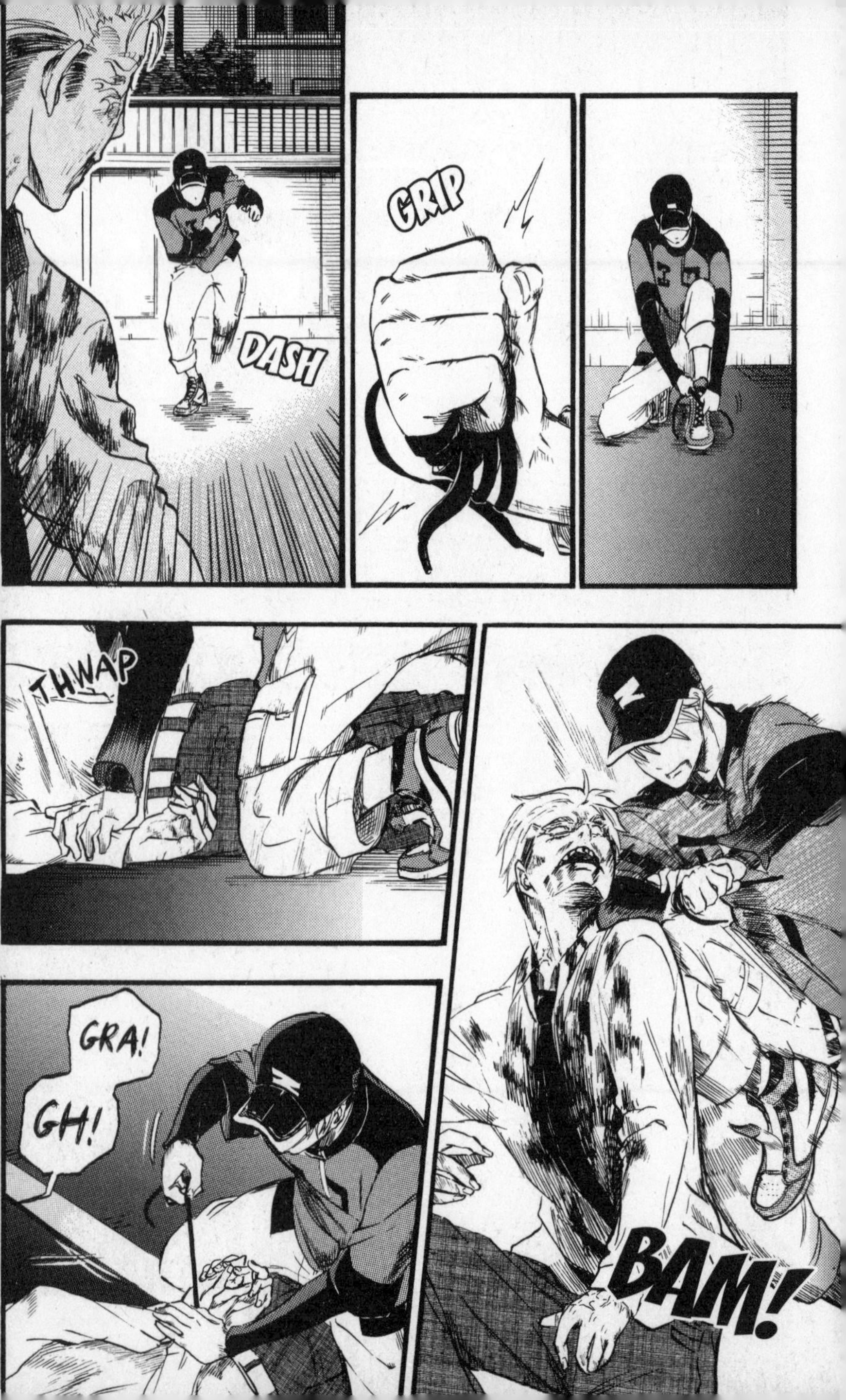
GRIP
DASH
BAM!
THWAP
GRA!
GH!

THOSE, TOO...

BIND

BIND

KICK!

ARGH!

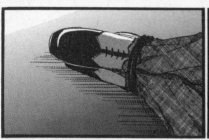

I'M TAKING YOU HOME, DAD!

GRA!

RAHH!

TAPP

TAPP

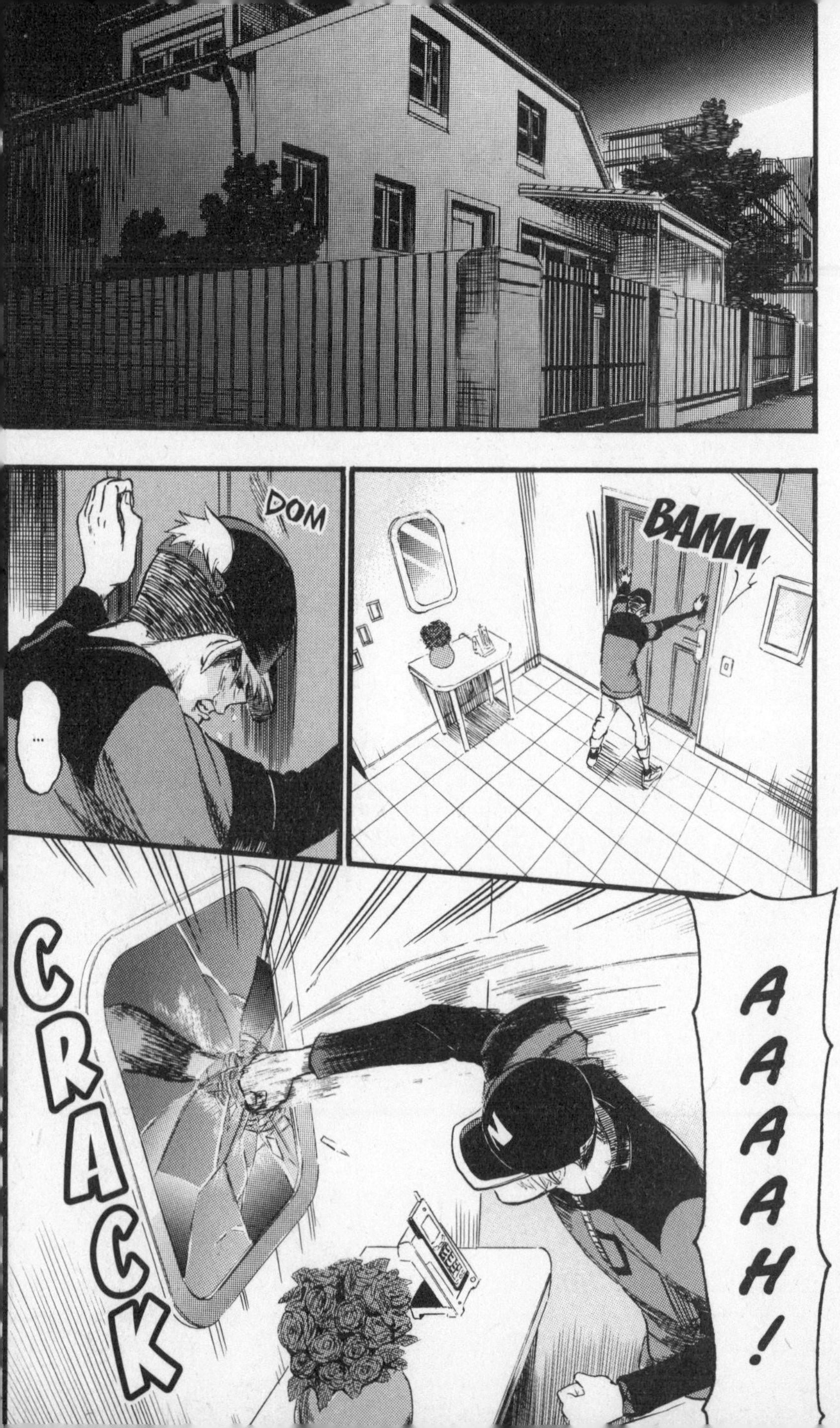
BAMM
DOM
...
AAAAAH!
CRACK

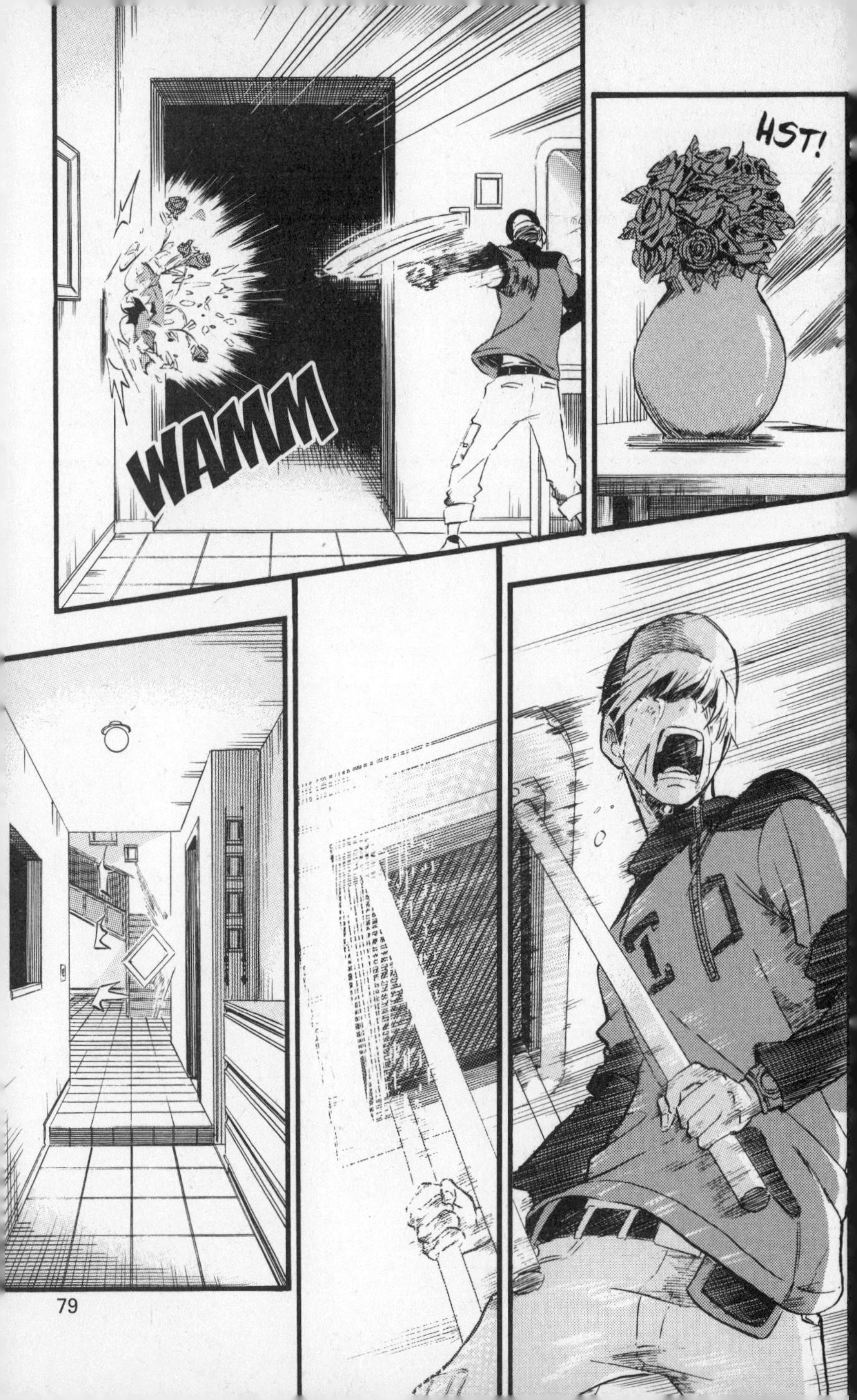
HST!
WAMM

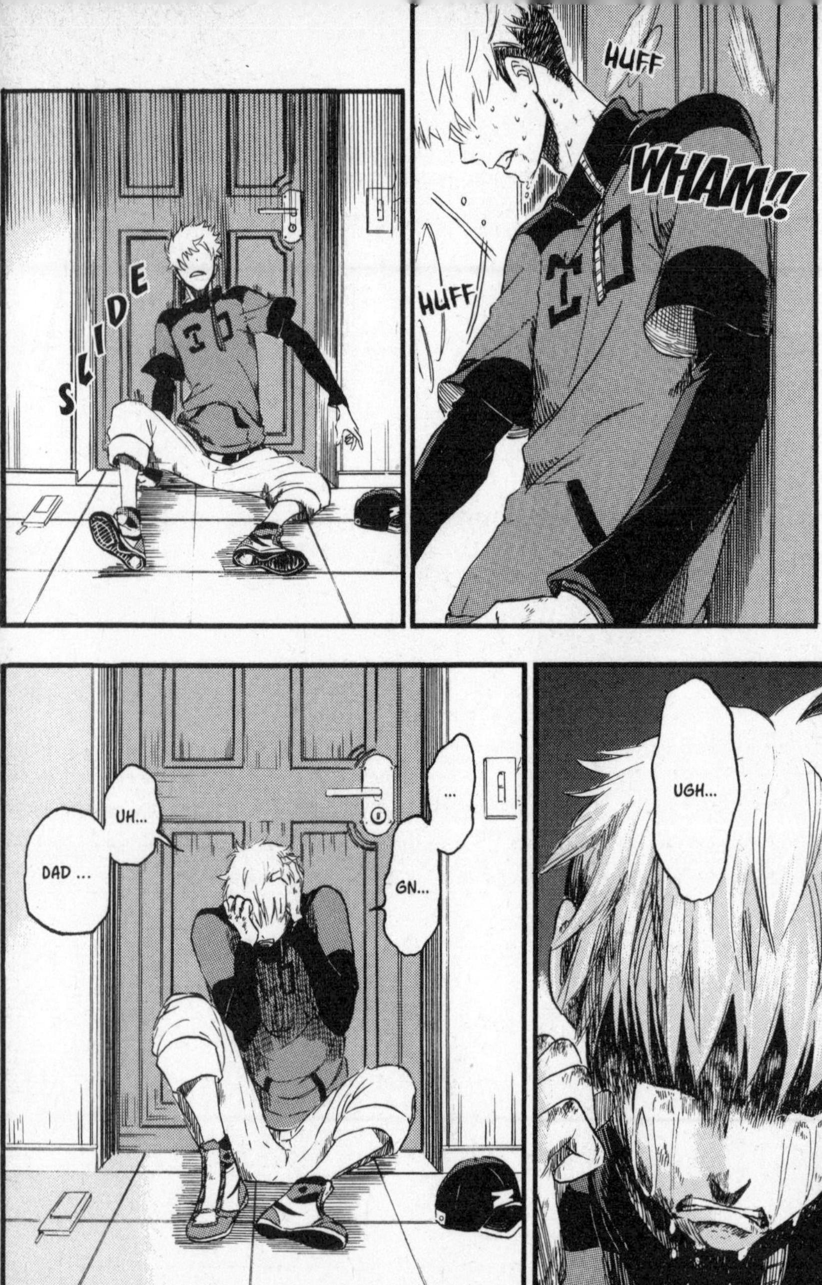
HUFF
WHAM!!
HUFF
SLIDE
UGH...
...
GN...
UH...
DAD ...

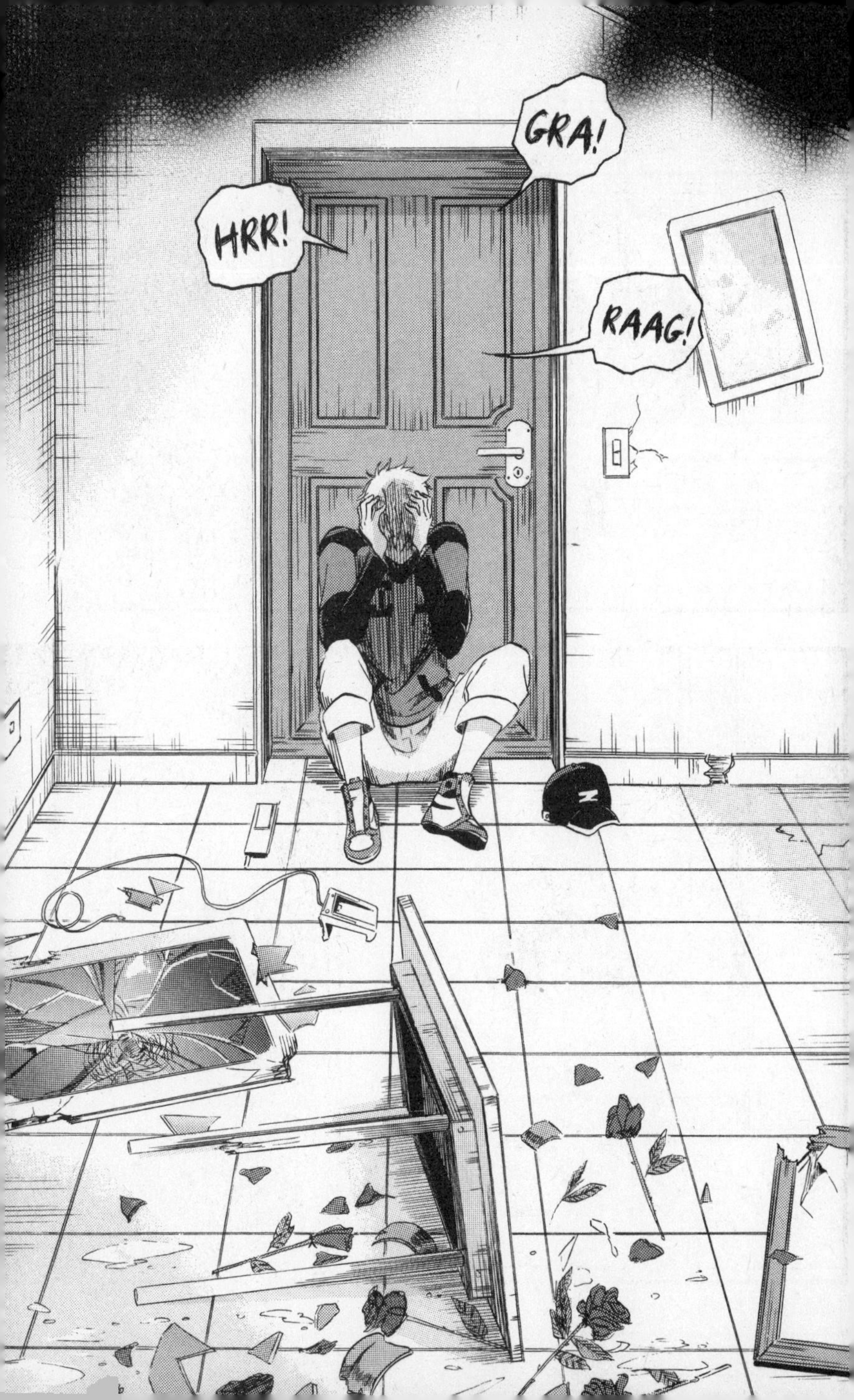
GRA!
HRR!
RAAG!

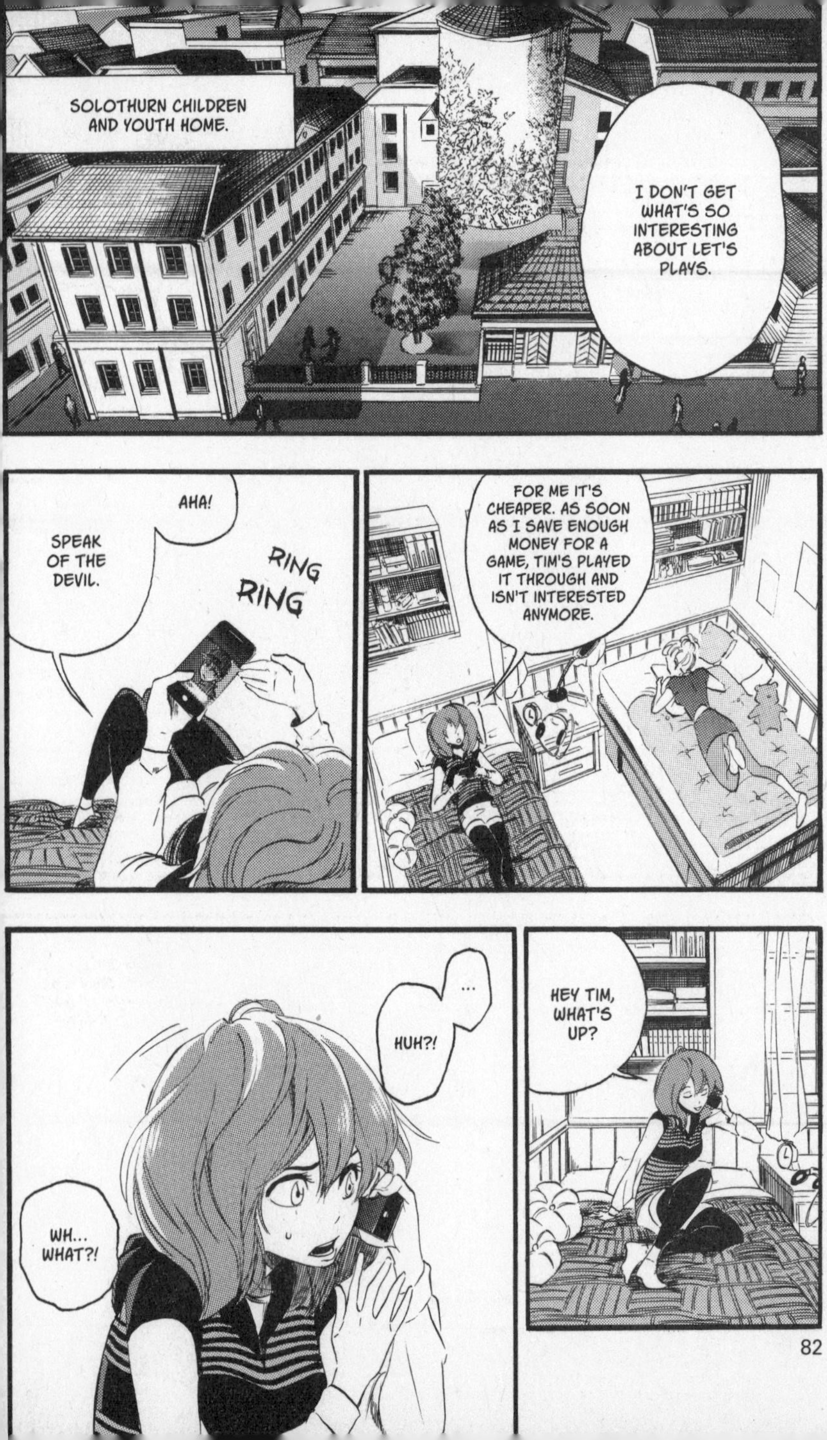
SOLOTHURN CHILDREN AND YOUTH HOME.
I DON'T GET WHAT'S SO INTERESTING ABOUT LET'S PLAYS.
FOR ME IT'S CHEAPER. AS SOON AS I SAVE ENOUGH MONEY FOR A GAME, TIM'S PLAYED IT THROUGH AND ISN'T INTERESTED ANYMORE.
RING RING
AHA!
SPEAK OF THE DEVIL.
HEY TIM, WHAT'S UP?
... HUH?!
WH... WHAT?!

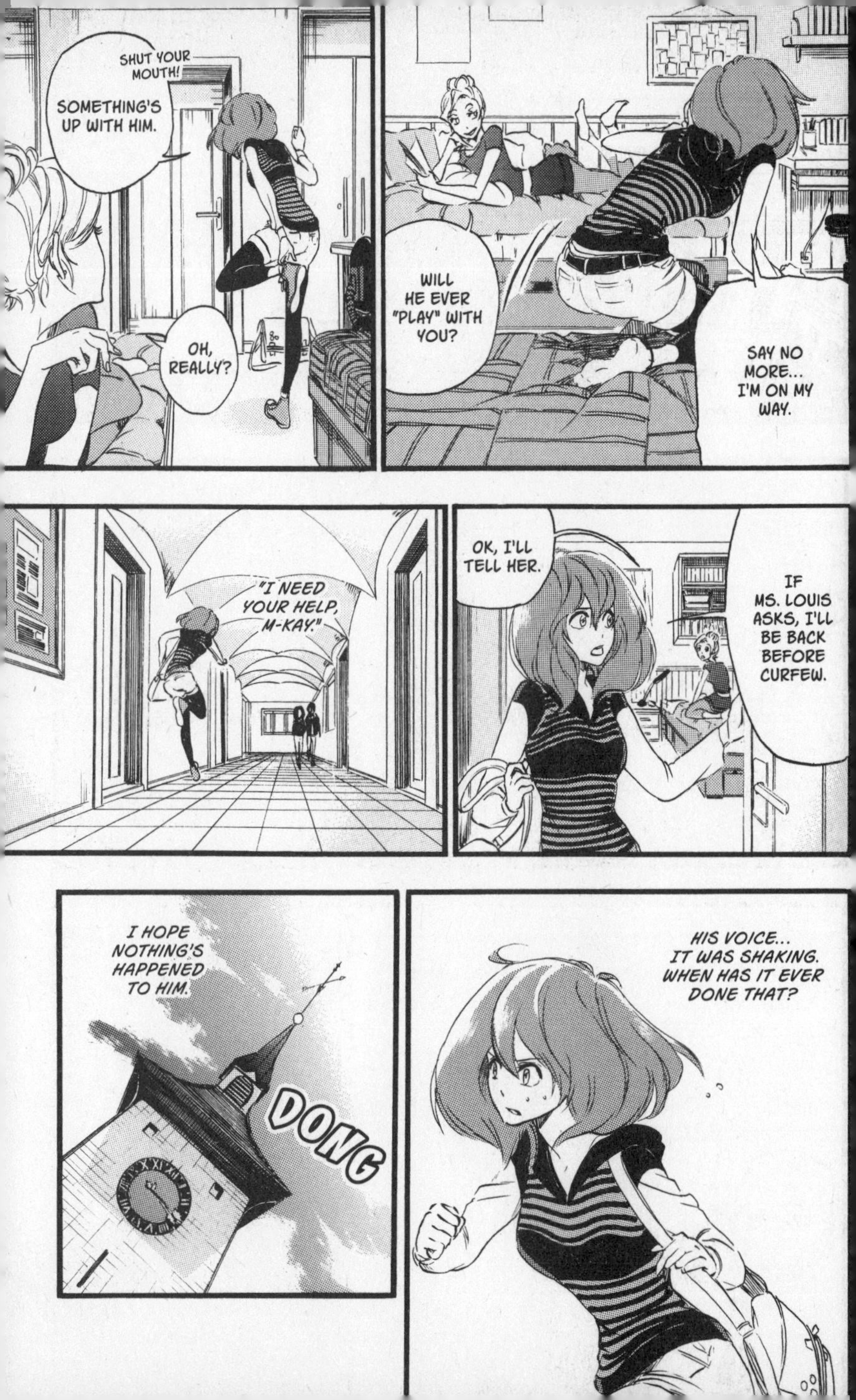
WILL HE EVER "PLAY" WITH YOU?
SAY NO MORE... I'M ON MY WAY.
SHUT YOUR MOUTH!
SOMETHING'S UP WITH HIM.
OH, REALLY?
IF MS. LOUIS ASKS, I'LL BE BACK BEFORE CURFEW.
OK, I'LL TELL HER.
"I NEED YOUR HELP, M-KAY."
HIS VOICE... IT WAS SHAKING. WHEN HAS IT EVER DONE THAT?
I HOPE NOTHING'S HAPPENED TO HIM.
DONG

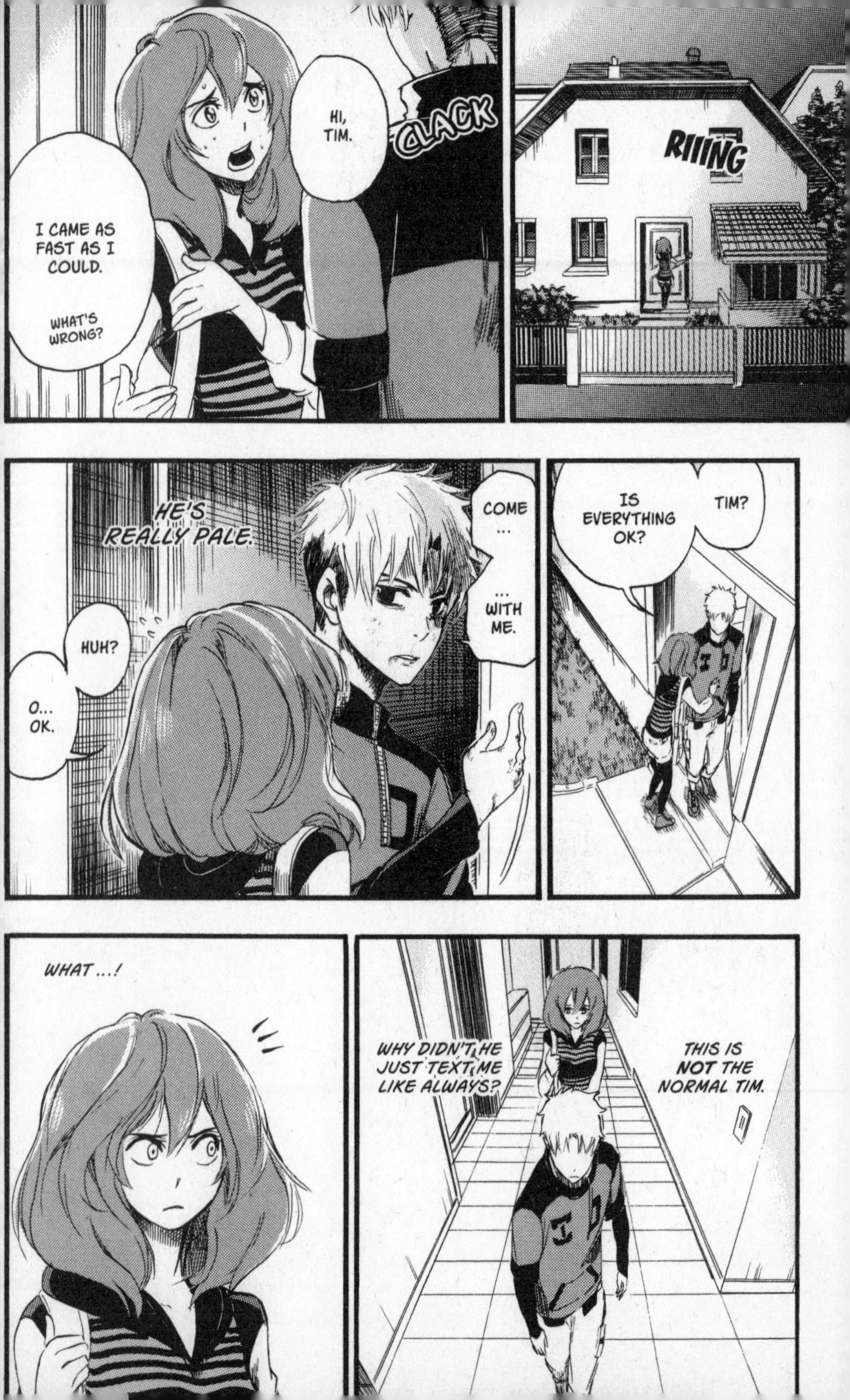
RIIING
CLACK
HI, TIM.
I CAME AS FAST AS I COULD.
WHAT'S WRONG?
TIM?
IS EVERYTHING OK?
COME ...
... WITH ME.
HE'S REALLY PALE.
HUH?
O... OK.
THIS IS NOT THE NORMAL TIM.
WHY DIDN'T HE JUST TEXT ME LIKE ALWAYS?
WHAT ...!

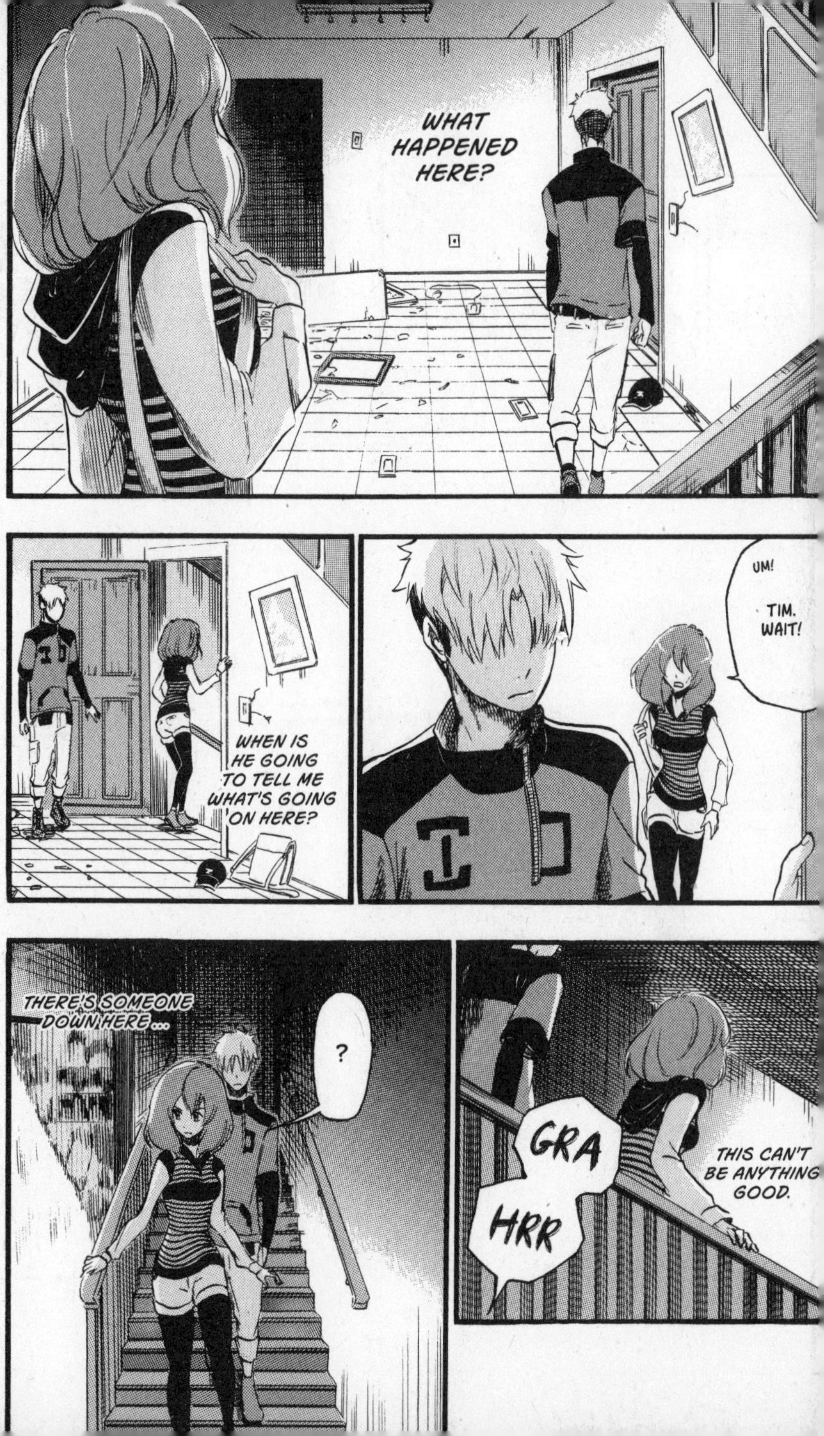
WHAT HAPPENED HERE?
UM!
TIM. WAIT!
WHEN IS HE GOING TO TELL ME WHAT'S GOING ON HERE?
THIS CAN'T BE ANYTHING GOOD.
GRA
HRR
THERE'S SOMEONE DOWN HERE...
?

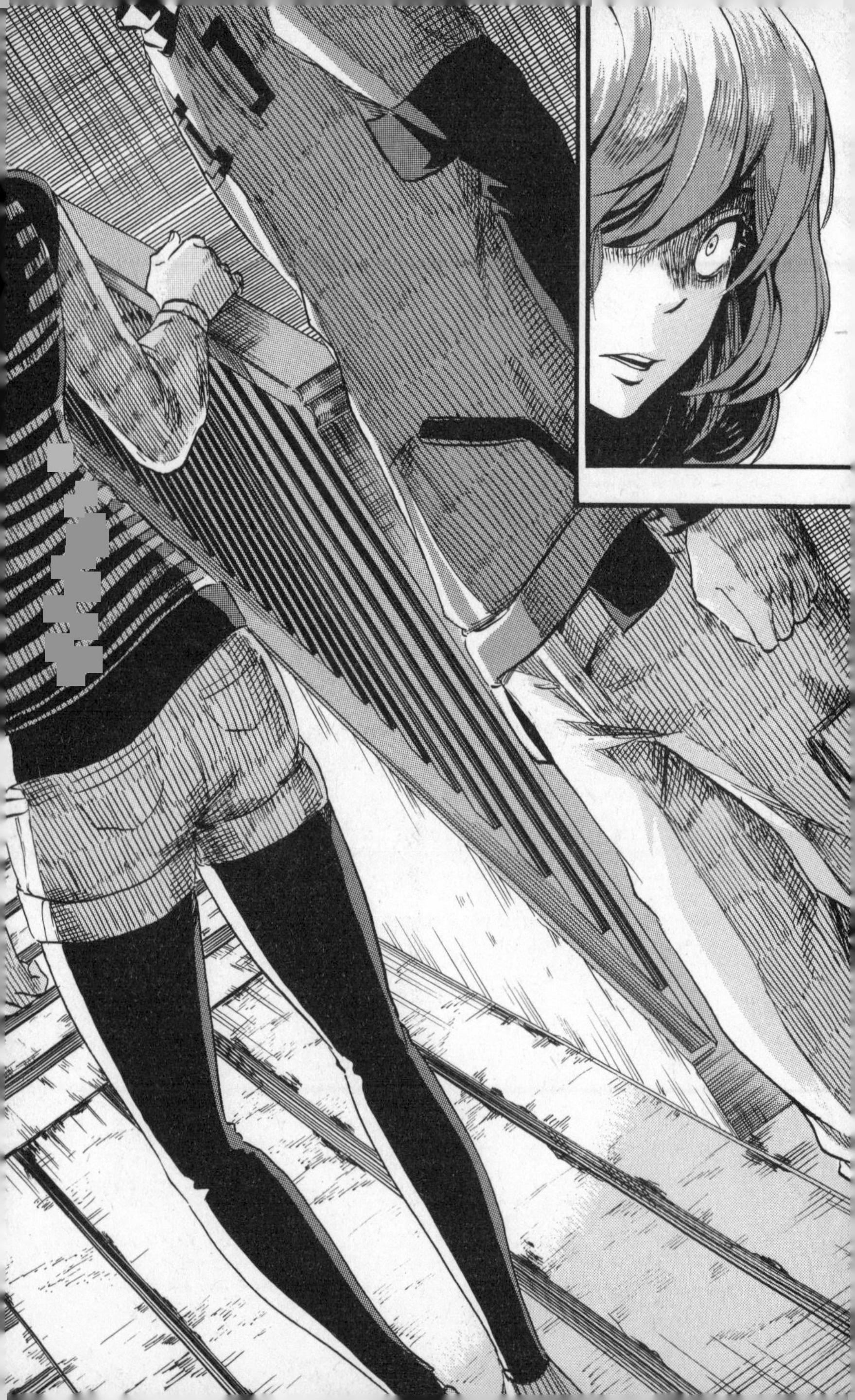

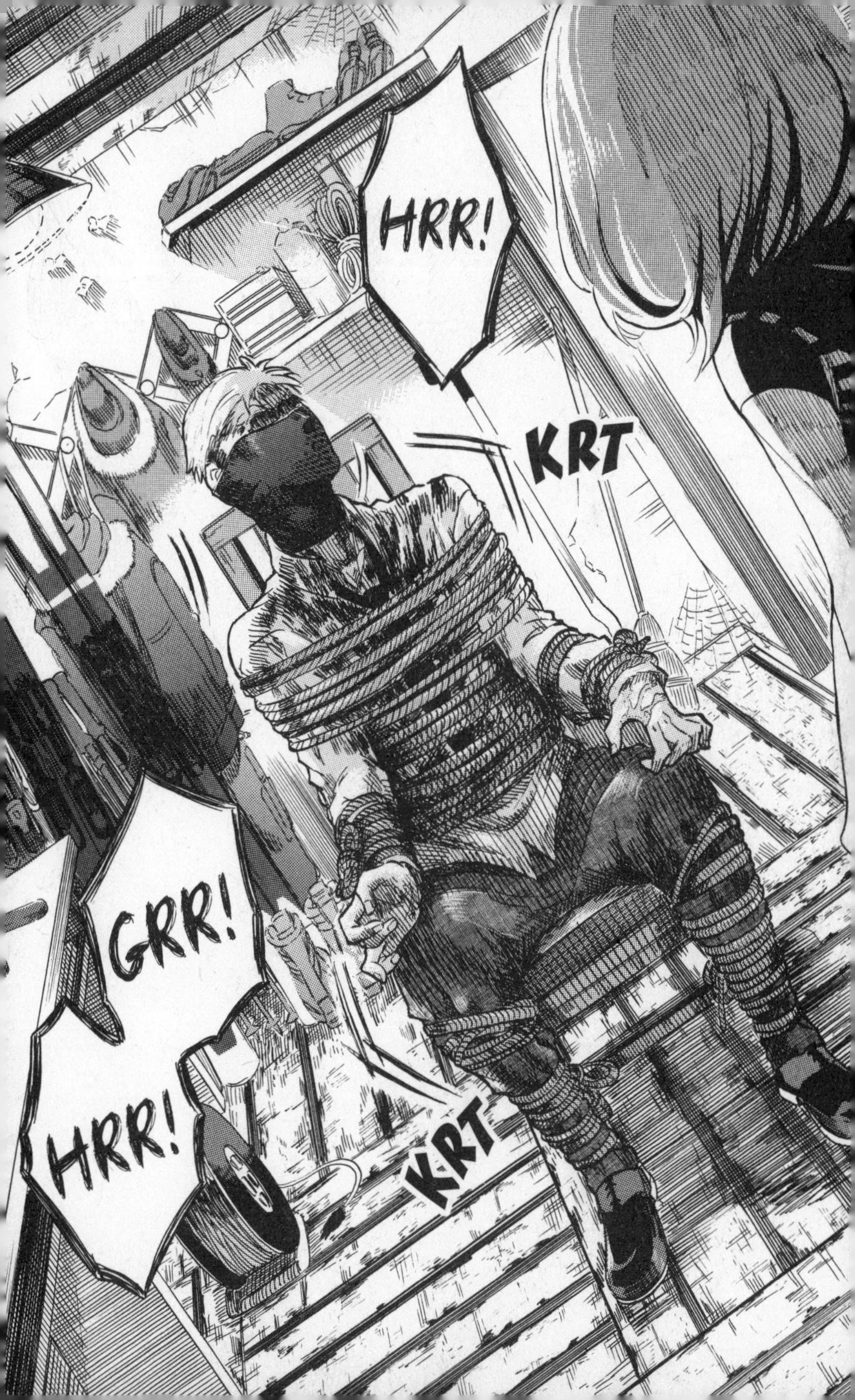
HRR!
KRT
GRR!
KRT
HRR!

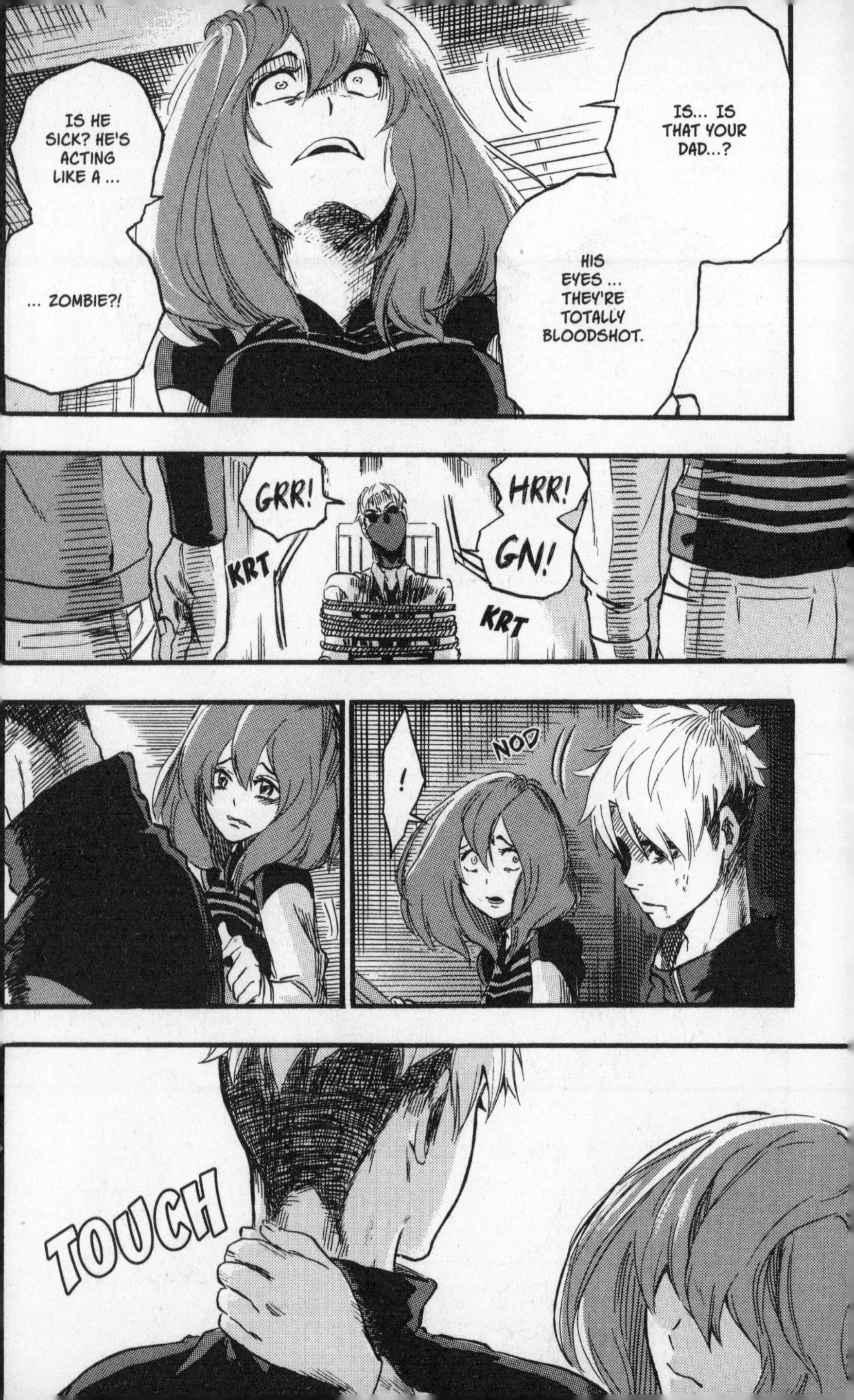
IS... IS THAT YOUR DAD...?
HIS EYES ... THEY'RE TOTALLY BLOODSHOT.
IS HE SICK? HE'S ACTING LIKE A ...
... ZOMBIE?!
HRR!
GN!
KRT
GRR!
KRT
!
NOD
TOUCH

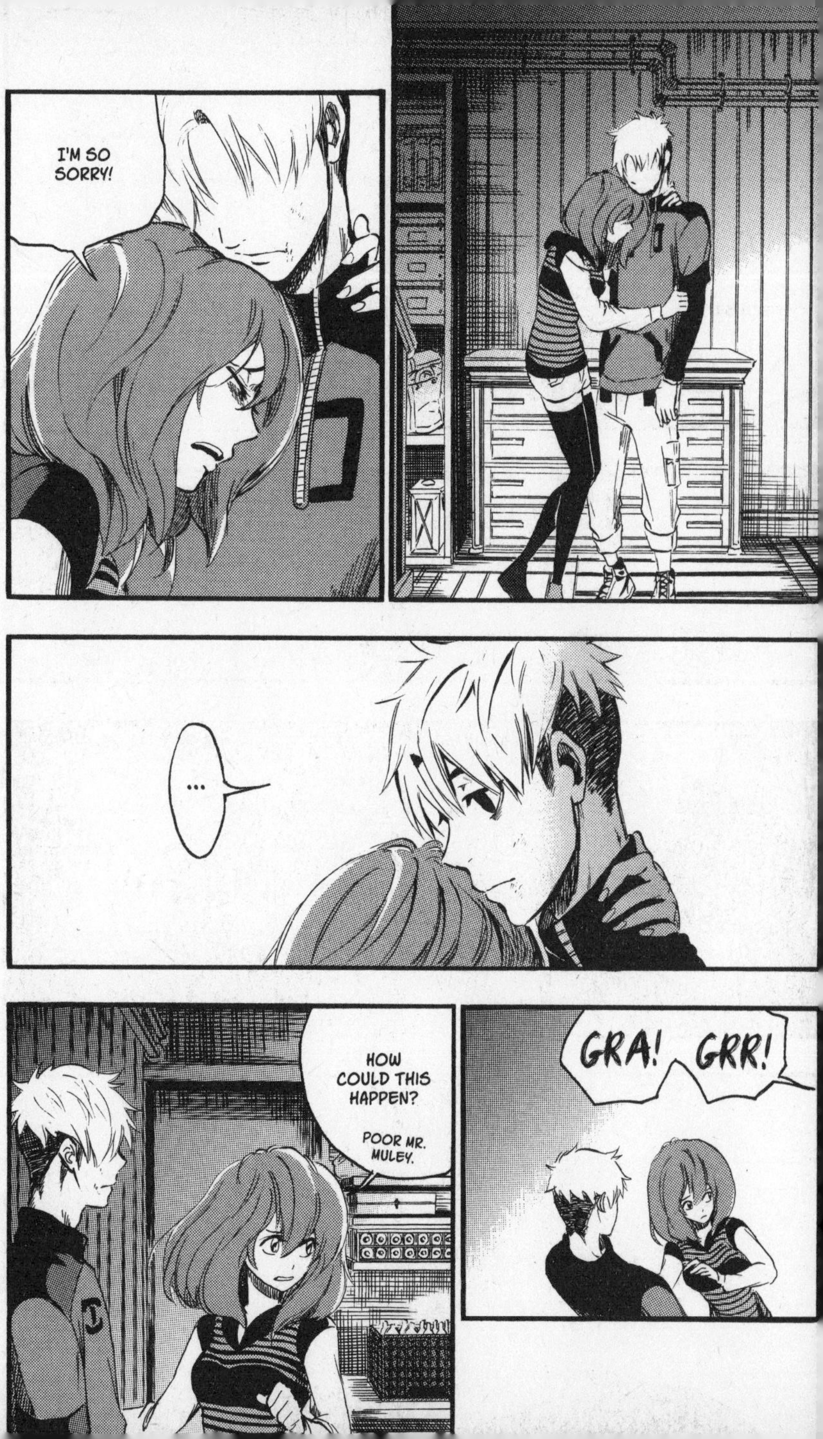
I'M SO SORRY!
...
GRA! GRR!
HOW COULD THIS HAPPEN?
POOR MR. MULEY.

WOW...

HRR!

GN!

...

AM I STUPID?

ST

ST

WHAT IS WRONG WITH ME?

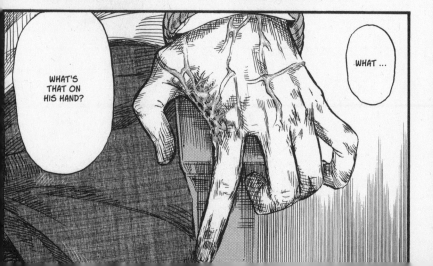

WHAT'S THAT ON HIS HAND?

WHAT ...

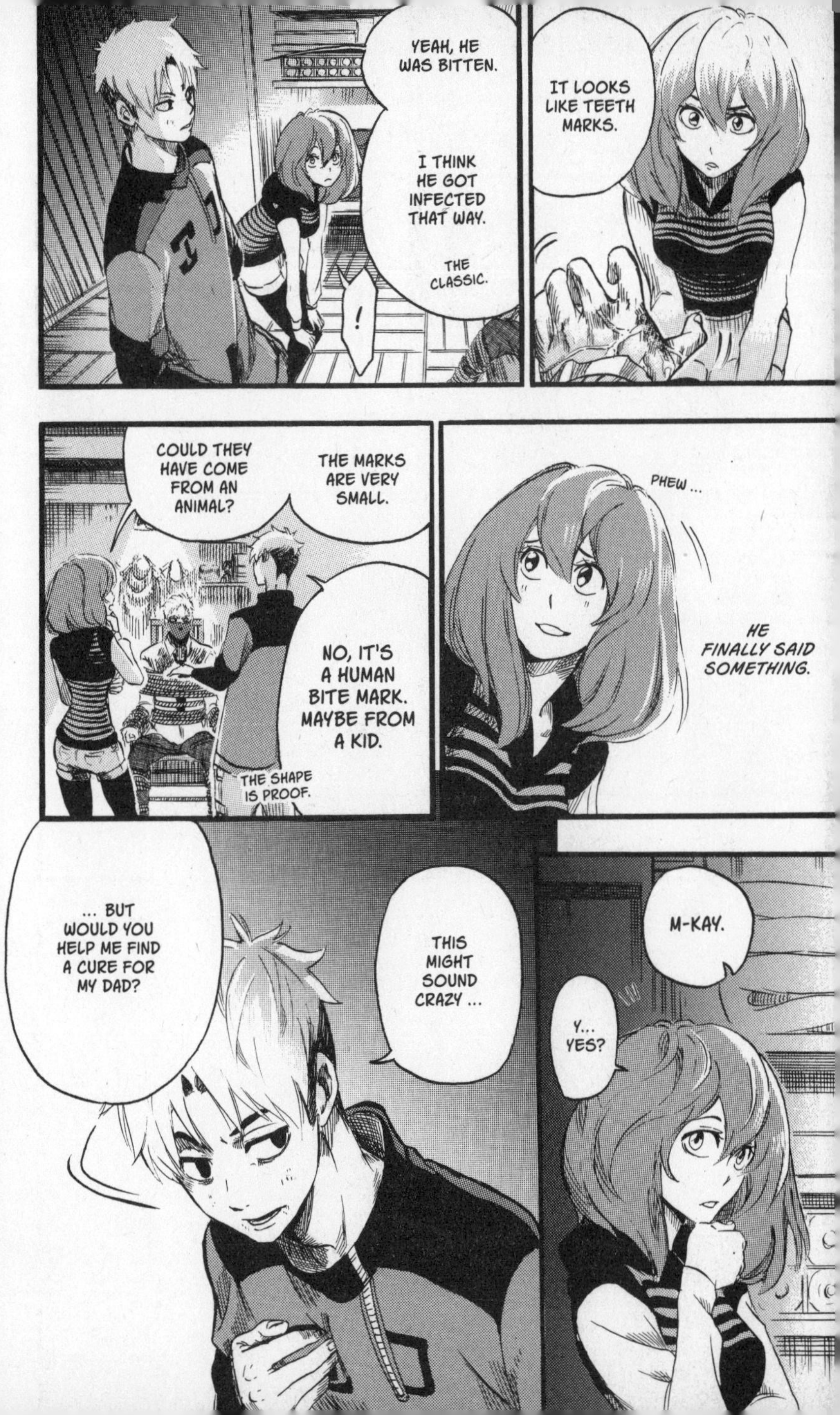

IT LOOKS LIKE TEETH MARKS.
YEAH, HE WAS BITTEN.
I THINK HE GOT INFECTED THAT WAY.
THE CLASSIC.
!
PHEW ...
HE FINALLY SAID SOMETHING.
THE MARKS ARE VERY SMALL.
COULD THEY HAVE COME FROM AN ANIMAL?
NO, IT'S A HUMAN BITE MARK. MAYBE FROM A KID.
THE SHAPE IS PROOF.
M-KAY.
Y... YES?
THIS MIGHT SOUND CRAZY ...
... BUT WOULD YOU HELP ME FIND A CURE FOR MY DAD?

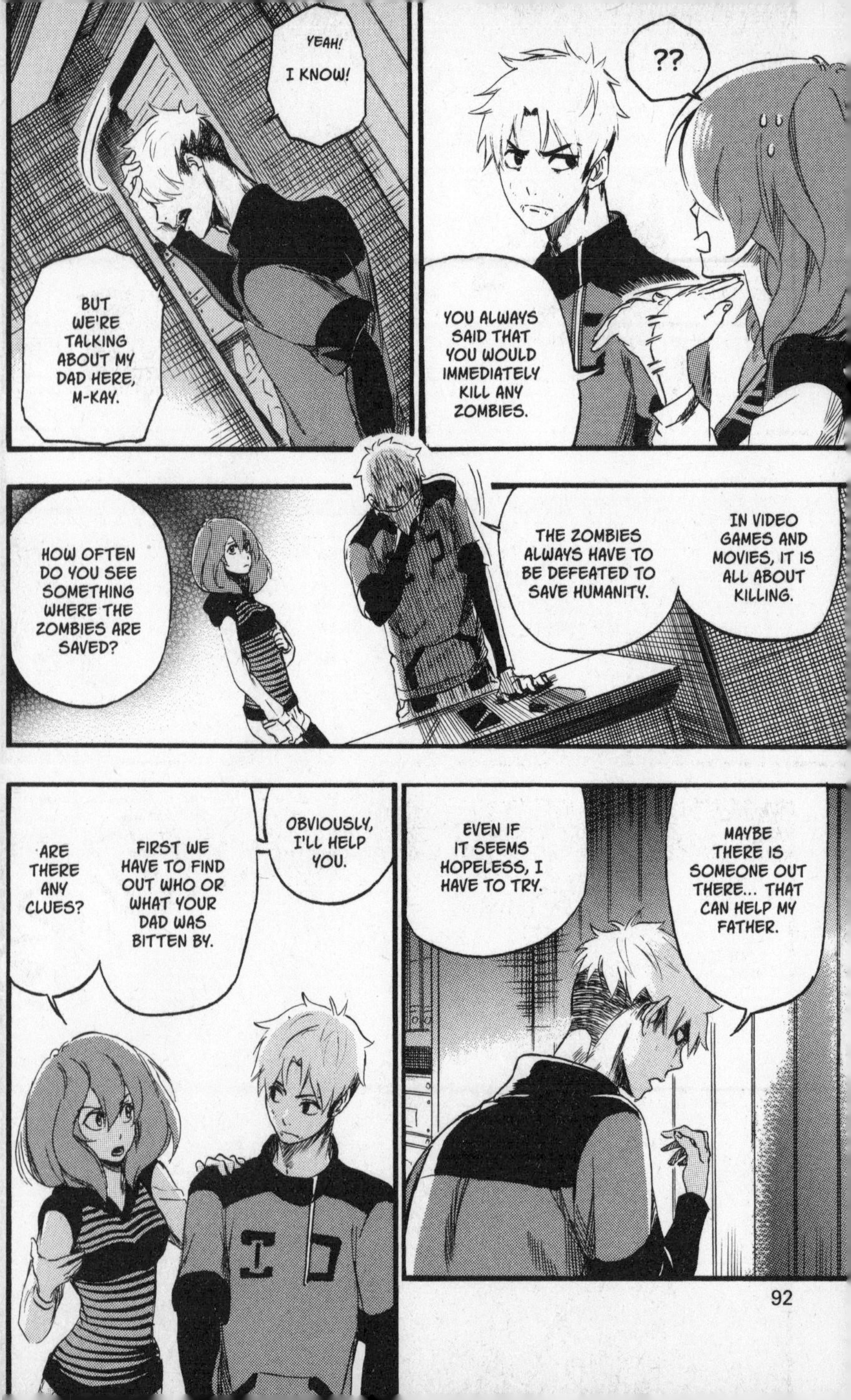
??
YOU ALWAYS SAID THAT YOU WOULD IMMEDIATELY KILL ANY ZOMBIES.
YEAH! I KNOW!
BUT WE'RE TALKING ABOUT MY DAD HERE, M-KAY.
IN VIDEO GAMES AND MOVIES, IT IS ALL ABOUT KILLING.
THE ZOMBIES ALWAYS HAVE TO BE DEFEATED TO SAVE HUMANITY.
HOW OFTEN DO YOU SEE SOMETHING WHERE THE ZOMBIES ARE SAVED?
MAYBE THERE IS SOMEONE OUT THERE... THAT CAN HELP MY FATHER.
EVEN IF IT SEEMS HOPELESS, I HAVE TO TRY.
OBVIOUSLY, I'LL HELP YOU.
FIRST WE HAVE TO FIND OUT WHO OR WHAT YOUR DAD WAS BITTEN BY.
ARE THERE ANY CLUES?

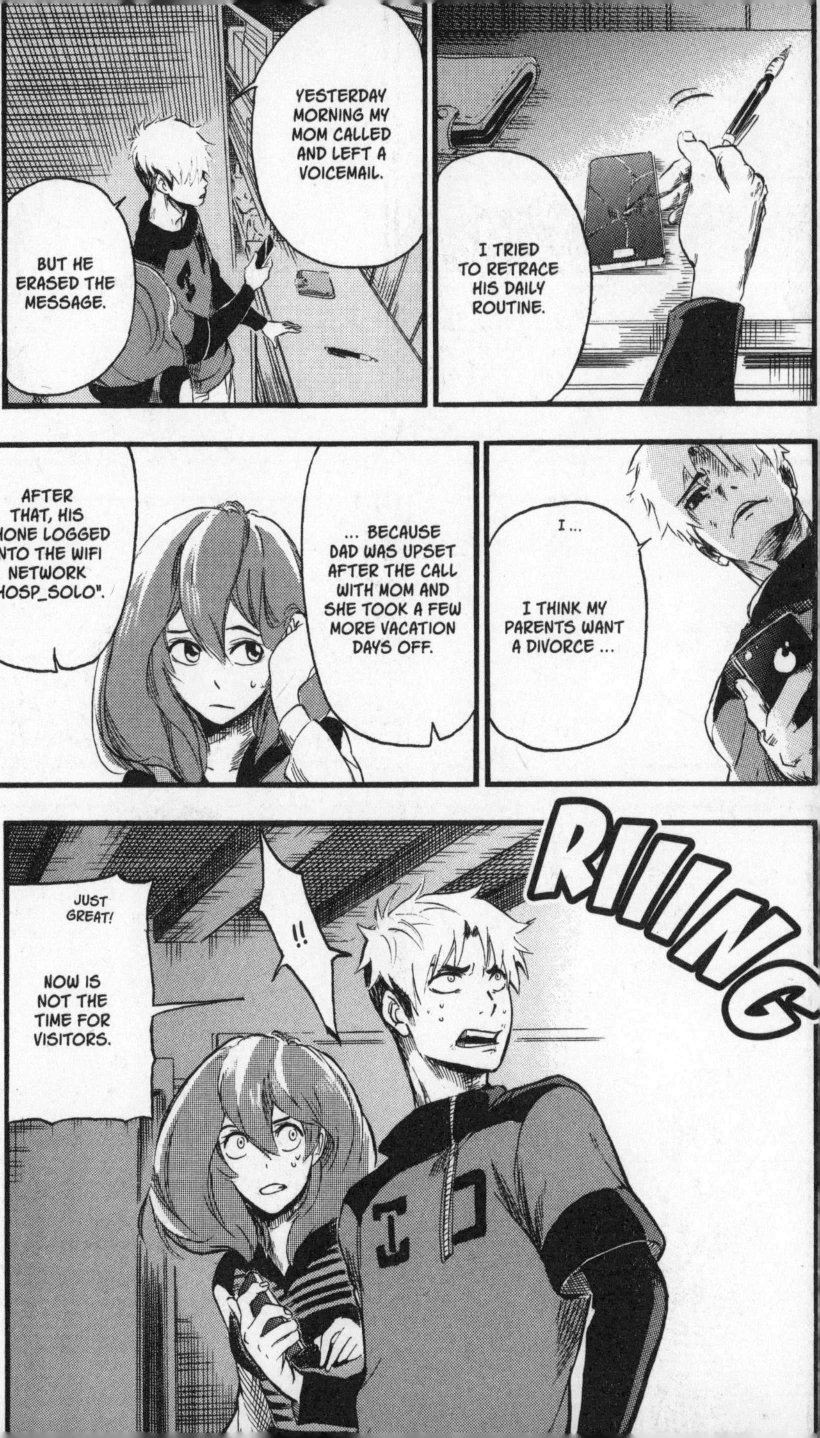
I TRIED TO RETRACE HIS DAILY ROUTINE.
YESTERDAY MORNING MY MOM CALLED AND LEFT A VOICEMAIL.
BUT HE ERASED THE MESSAGE.
I ...
I THINK MY PARENTS WANT A DIVORCE ...
... BECAUSE DAD WAS UPSET AFTER THE CALL WITH MOM AND SHE TOOK A FEW MORE VACATION DAYS OFF.
AFTER THAT, HIS PHONE LOGGED INTO THE WIFI NETWORK "HOSP_SOLO".
RIIING
!!
JUST GREAT!
NOW IS NOT THE TIME FOR VISITORS.

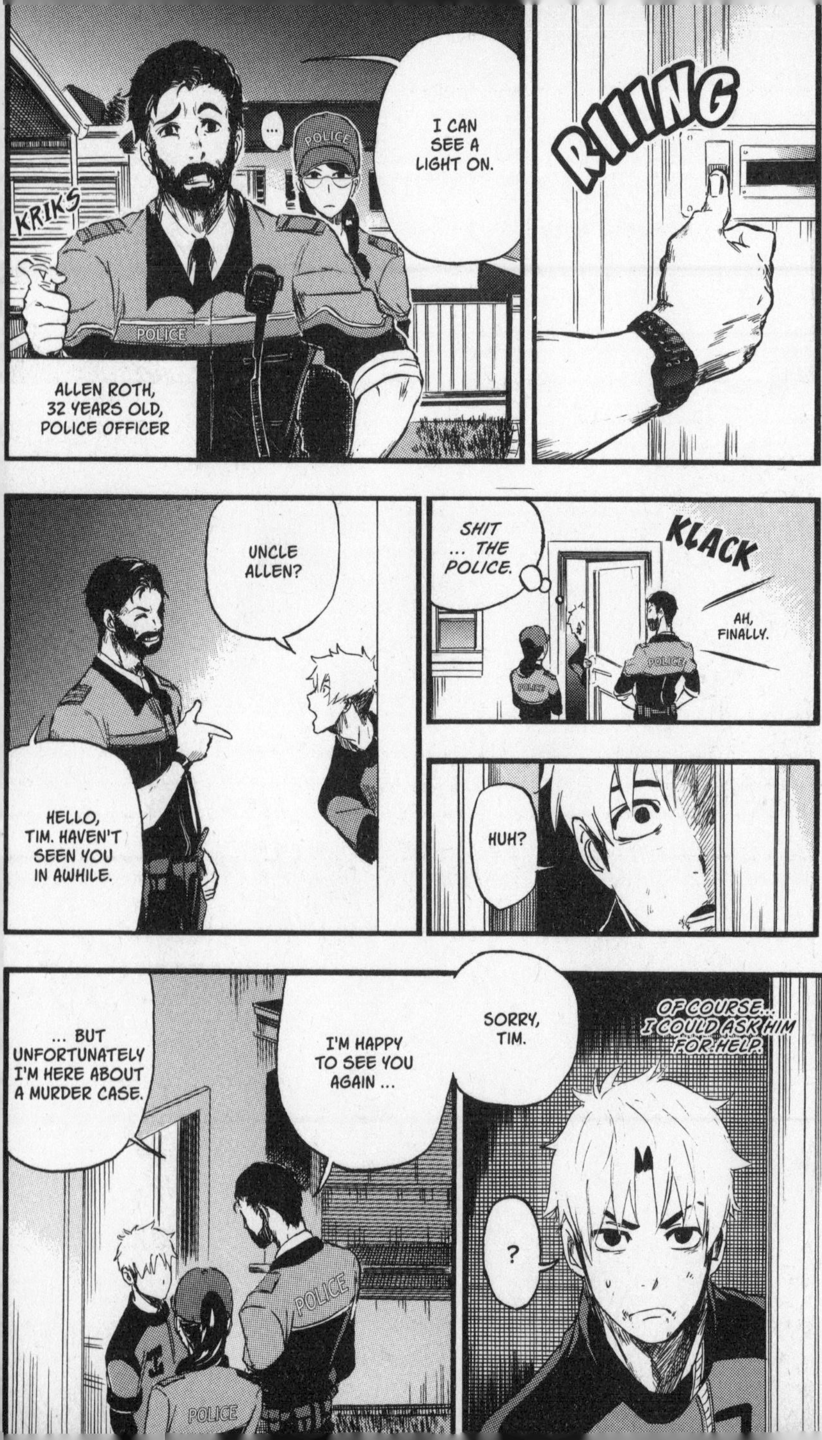
RIIING
I CAN SEE A LIGHT ON.
...
KRIKS
ALLEN ROTH, 32 YEARS OLD, POLICE OFFICER
KLACK
AH, FINALLY.
SHIT ... THE POLICE.
HUH?
UNCLE ALLEN?
HELLO, TIM. HAVEN'T SEEN YOU IN AWHILE.
OF COURSE... I COULD ASK HIM FOR HELP.
?
SORRY, TIM.
I'M HAPPY TO SEE YOU AGAIN ...
... BUT UNFORTUNATELY I'M HERE ABOUT A MURDER CASE.

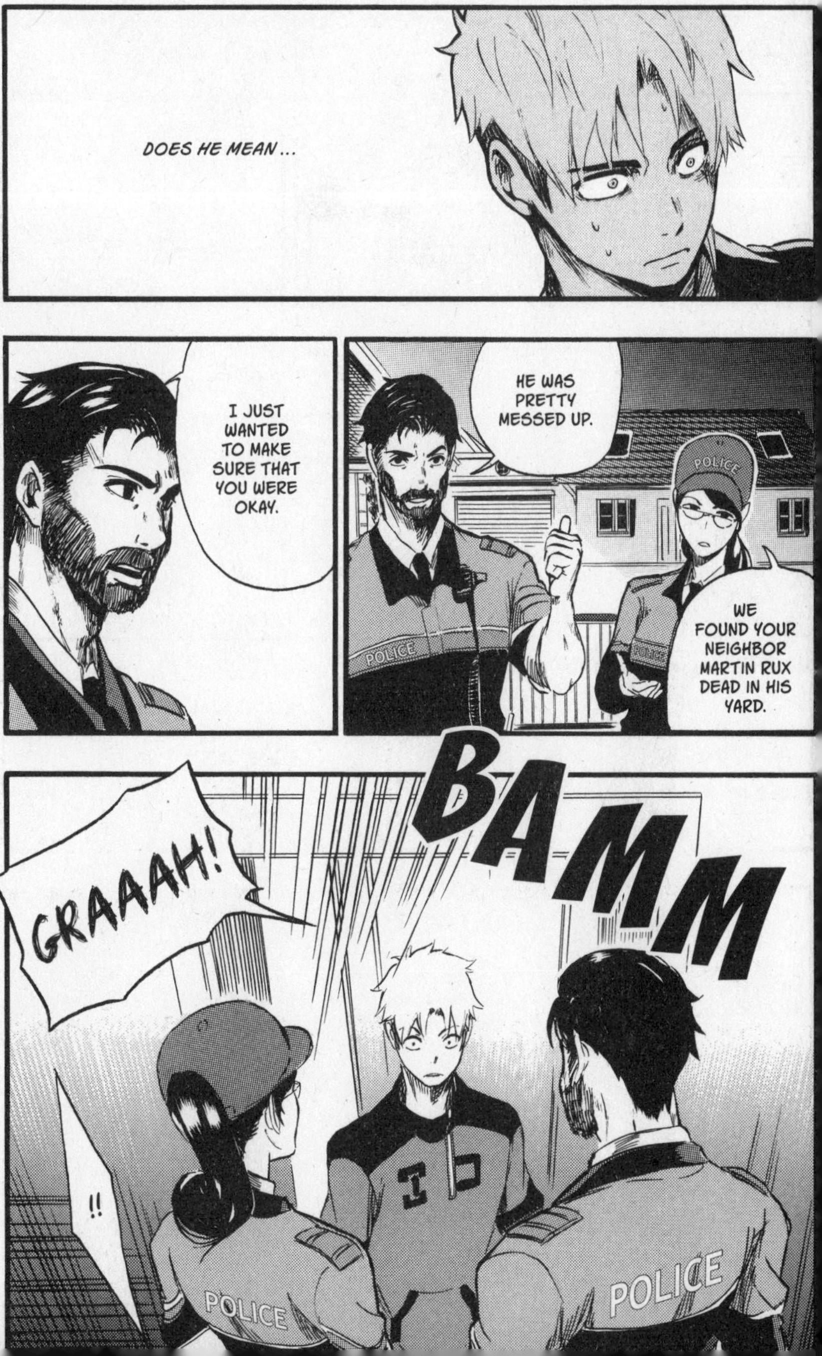
DOES HE MEAN ...
HE WAS PRETTY MESSED UP.
WE FOUND YOUR NEIGHBOR MARTIN RUX DEAD IN HIS YARD.
I JUST WANTED TO MAKE SURE THAT YOU WERE OKAY.
BAMM
GRAAAH!
!!

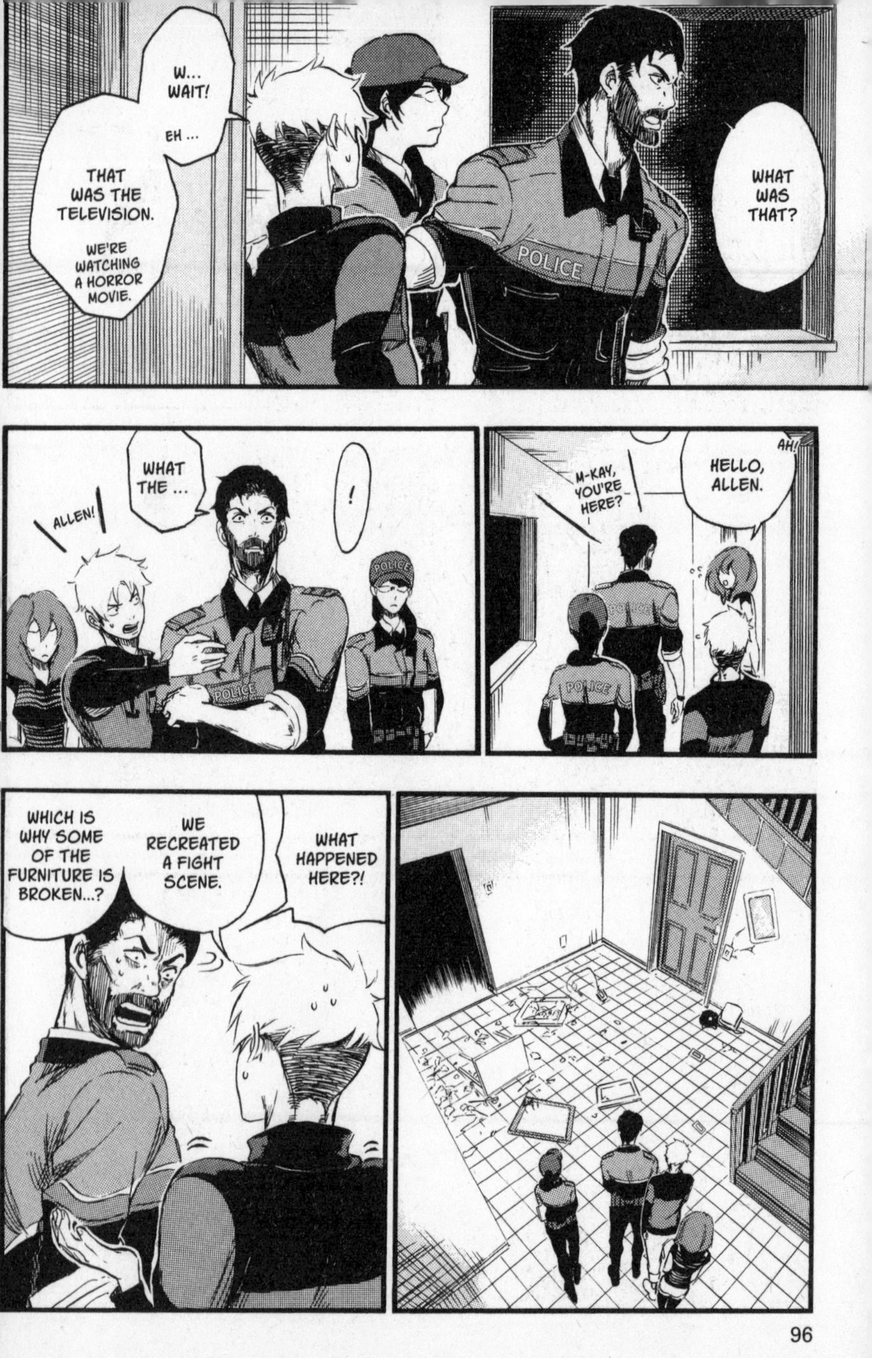
WHAT WAS THAT?
W... WAIT!
EH ...
THAT WAS THE TELEVISION.
WE'RE WATCHING A HORROR MOVIE.
AH!
HELLO, ALLEN.
M-KAY, YOU'RE HERE?
!
WHAT THE ...
ALLEN!
WHAT HAPPENED HERE?!
WE RECREATED A FIGHT SCENE.
WHICH IS WHY SOME OF THE FURNITURE IS BROKEN...?

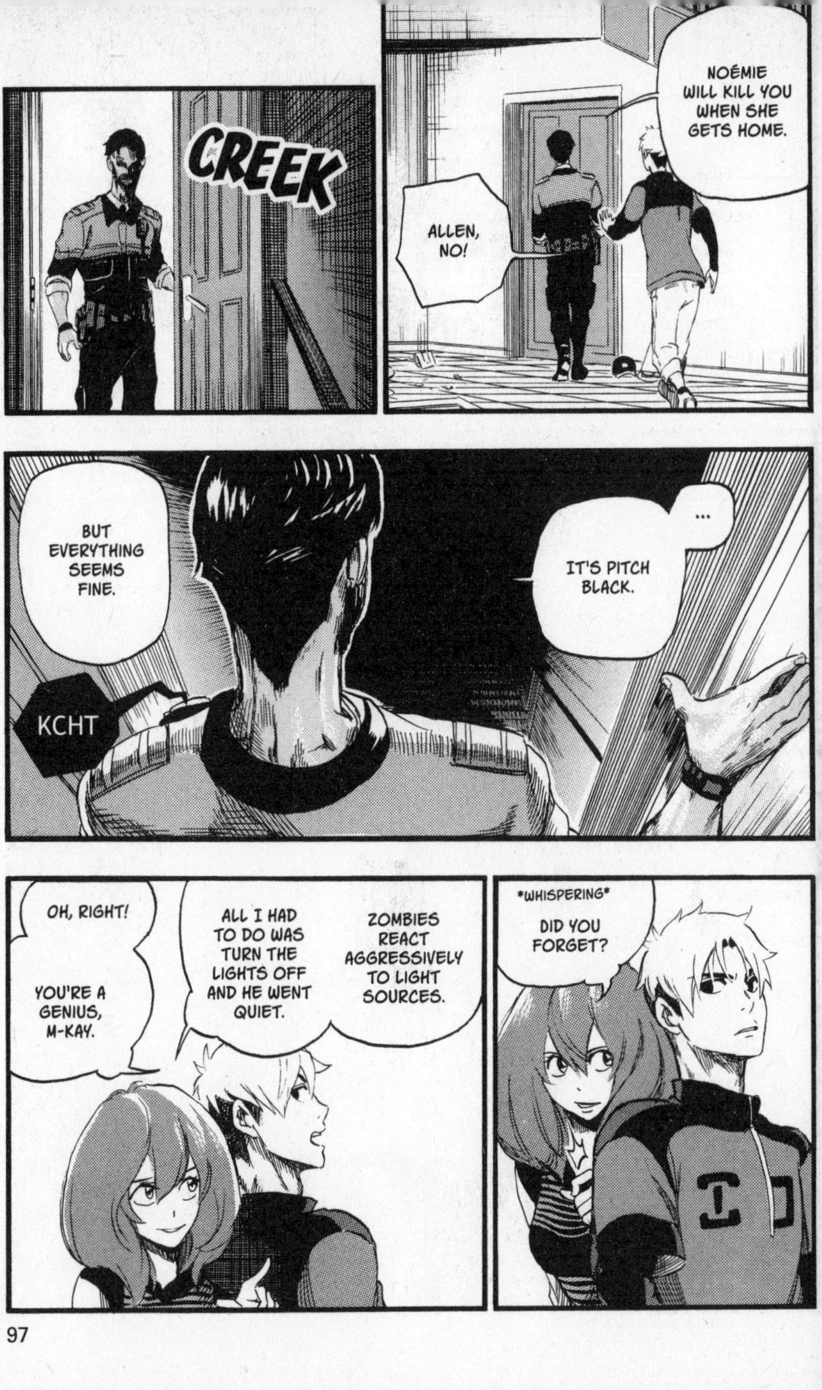
NOÉMIE WILL KILL YOU WHEN SHE GETS HOME.
ALLEN, NO!
CREEK
...
IT'S PITCH BLACK.
BUT EVERYTHING SEEMS FINE.
KCHT
WHISPERING
DID YOU FORGET?
ZOMBIES REACT AGGRESSIVELY TO LIGHT SOURCES.
ALL I HAD TO DO WAS TURN THE LIGHTS OFF AND HE WENT QUIET.
OH, RIGHT!
YOU'RE A GENIUS, M-KAY.

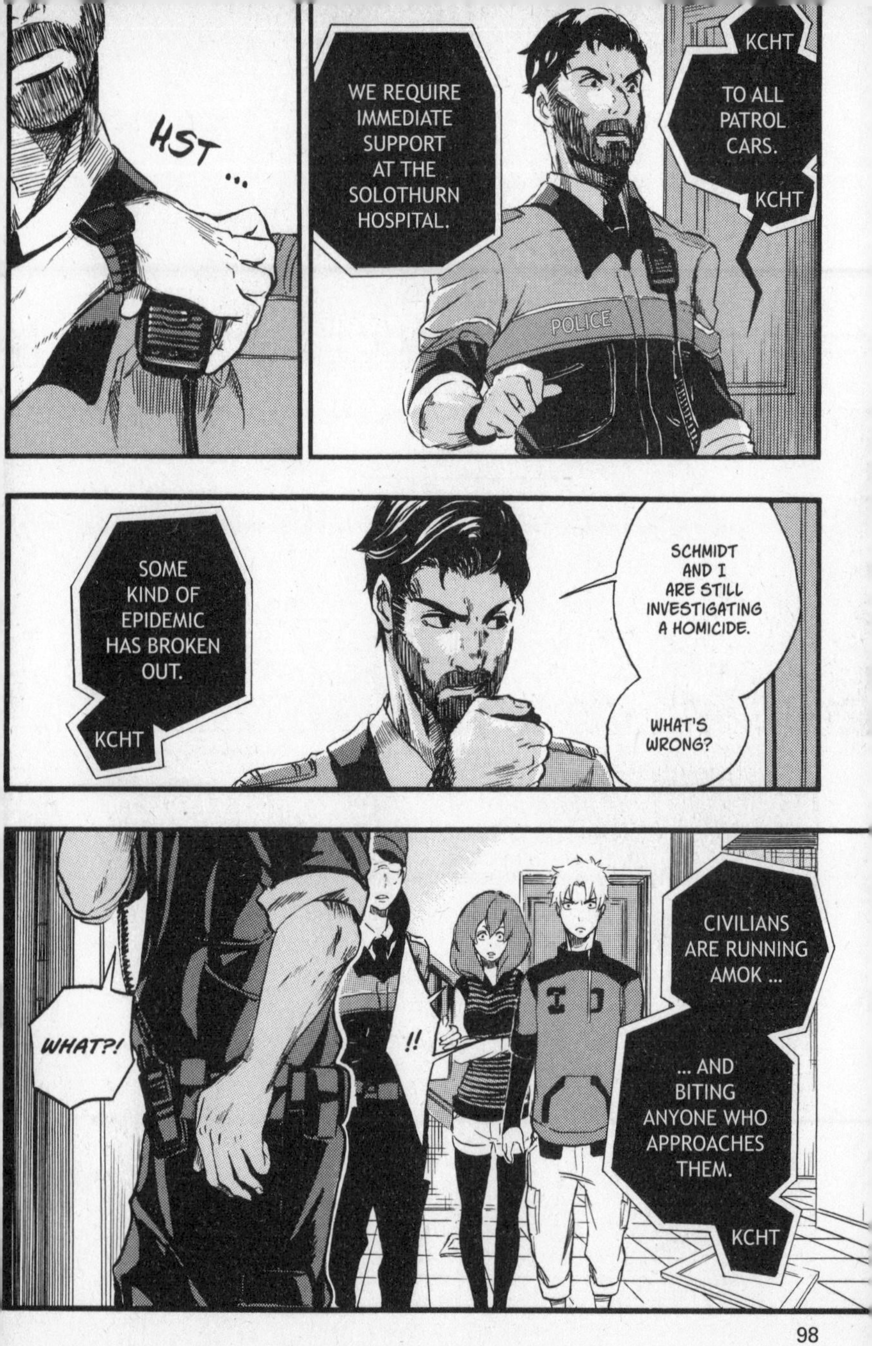
KCHT
TO ALL PATROL CARS.
KCHT
WE REQUIRE IMMEDIATE SUPPORT AT THE SOLOTHURN HOSPITAL.
HST ...
SCHMIDT AND I ARE STILL INVESTIGATING A HOMICIDE.
WHAT'S WRONG?
SOME KIND OF EPIDEMIC HAS BROKEN OUT.
KCHT
CIVILIANS ARE RUNNING AMOK ...
... AND BITING ANYONE WHO APPROACHES THEM.
KCHT
!!
WHAT?!

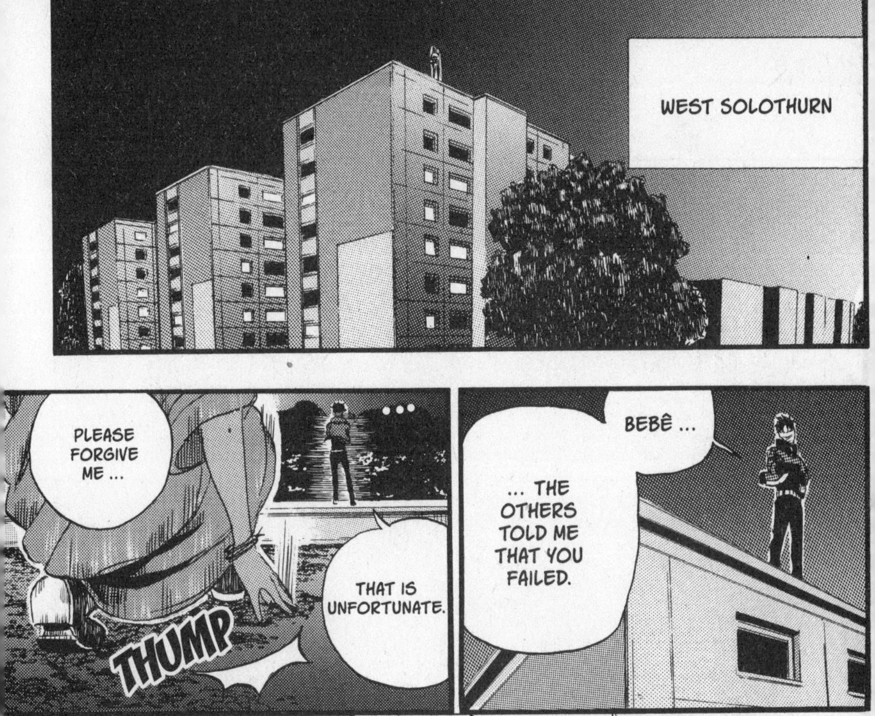
WEST SOLOTHURN
BEBÊ ...
... THE OTHERS TOLD ME THAT YOU FAILED.
PLEASE FORGIVE ME ...
THAT IS UNFORTUNATE.
THUMP

* PORTUGUESE: MASTER

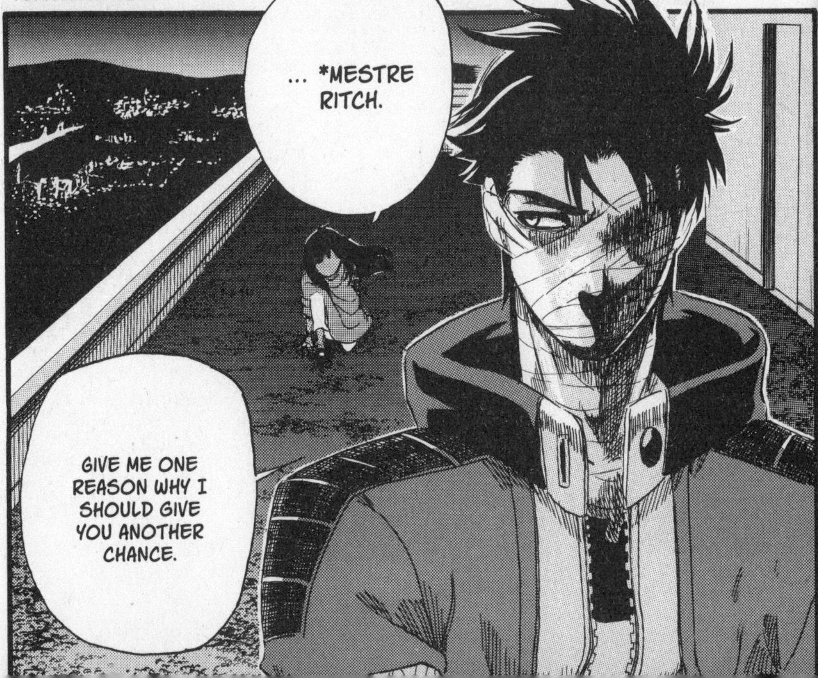
... *MESTRE RITCH.
GIVE ME ONE REASON WHY I SHOULD GIVE YOU ANOTHER CHANCE.

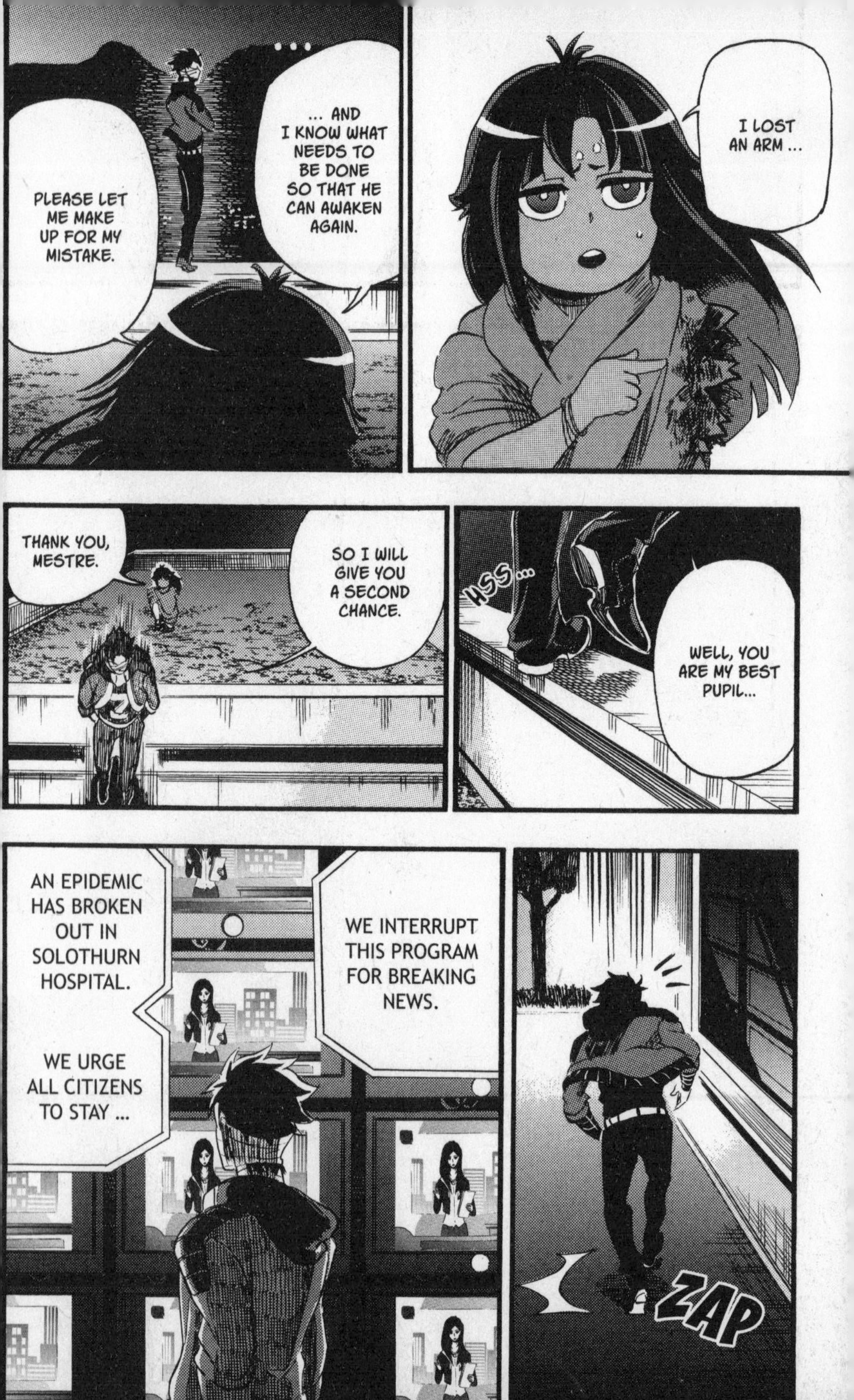
I LOST AN ARM ...
... AND I KNOW WHAT NEEDS TO BE DONE SO THAT HE CAN AWAKEN AGAIN.
PLEASE LET ME MAKE UP FOR MY MISTAKE.
HSS...
WELL, YOU ARE MY BEST PUPIL...
SO I WILL GIVE YOU A SECOND CHANCE.
THANK YOU, MESTRE.
ZAP
WE INTERRUPT THIS PROGRAM FOR BREAKING NEWS.
AN EPIDEMIC HAS BROKEN OUT IN SOLOTHURN HOSPITAL.
WE URGE ALL CITIZENS TO STAY ...

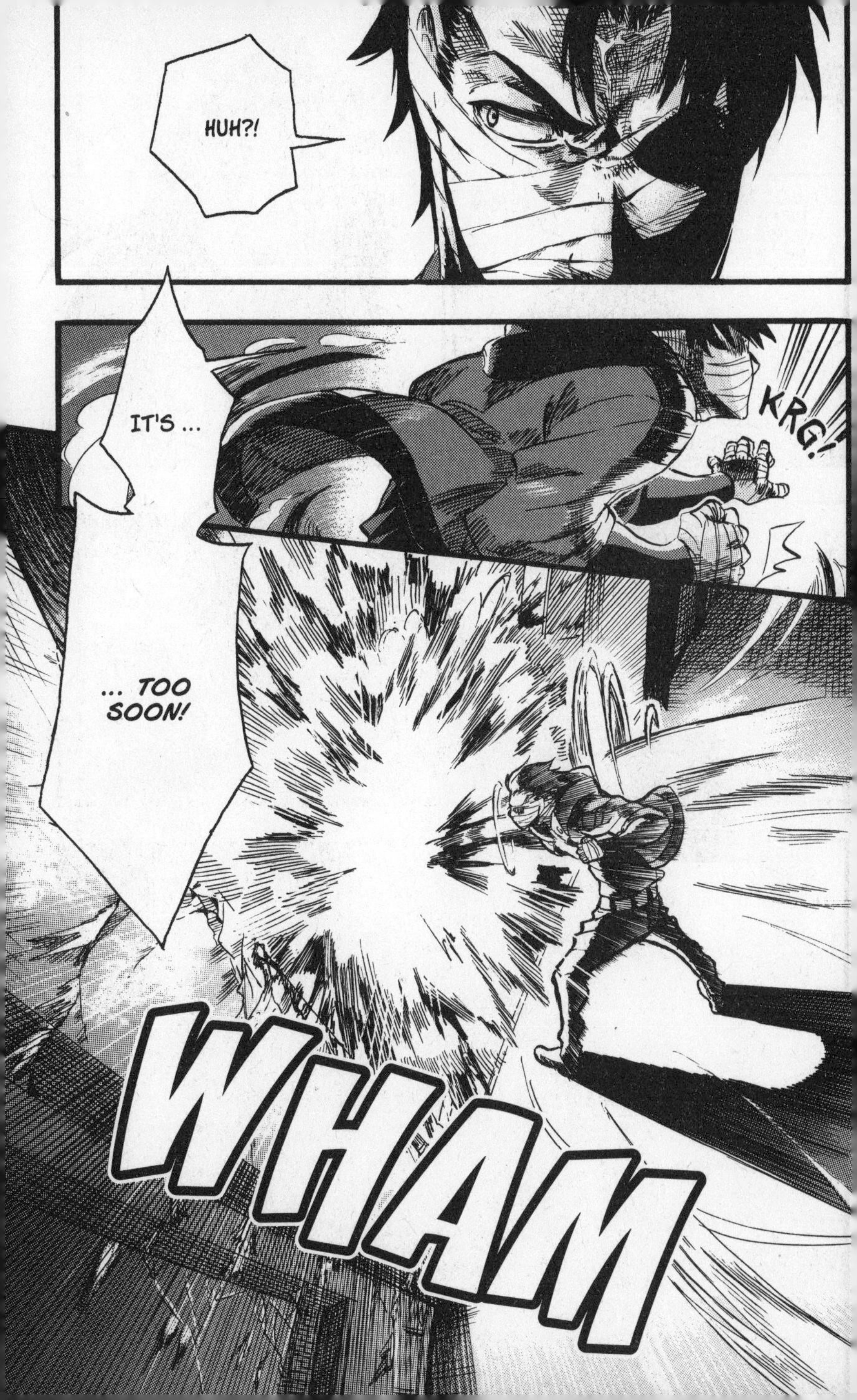
HUH?!
KRG!
IT'S ...
... TOO SOON!
WHAM

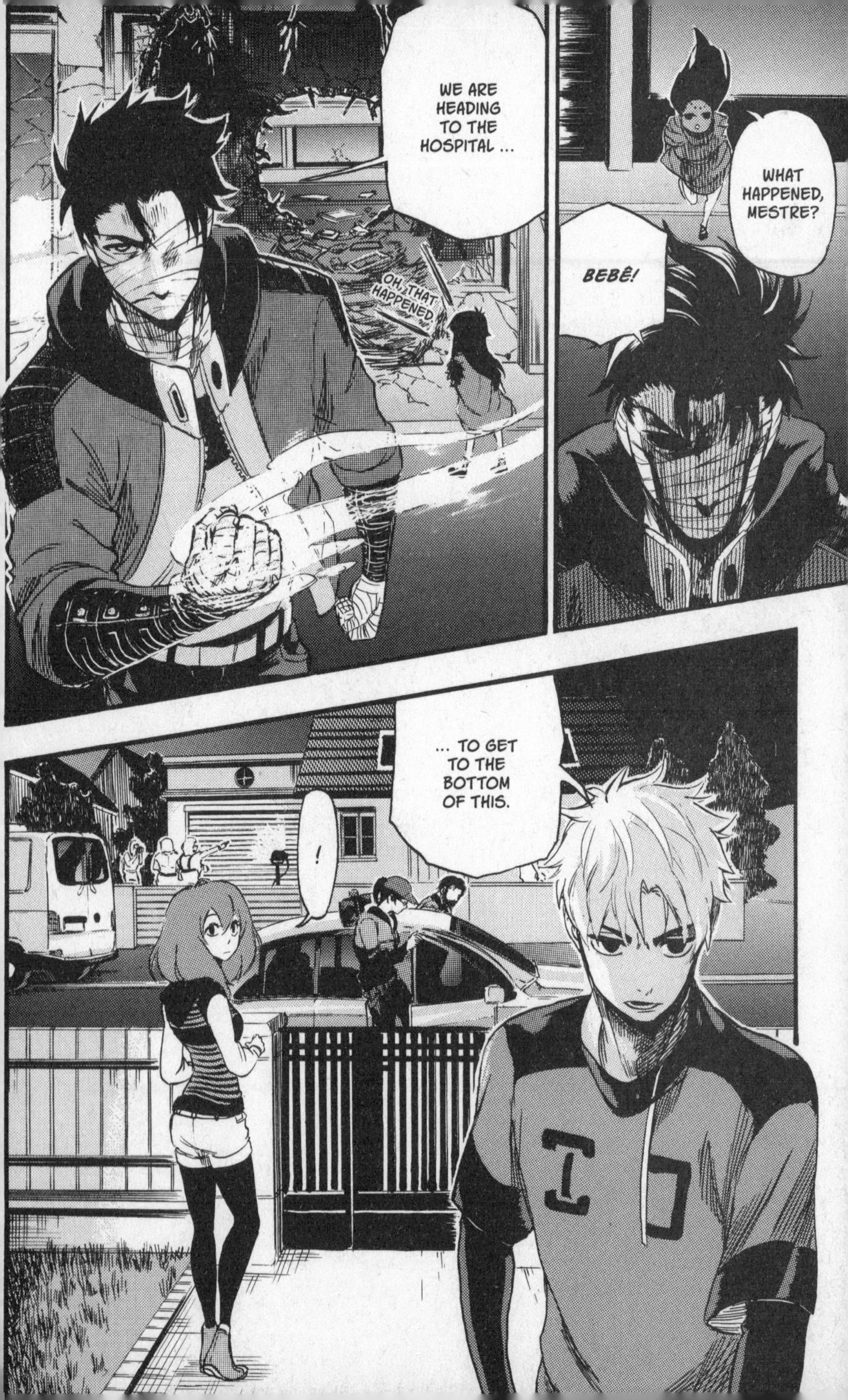
WHAT HAPPENED, MESTRE?
BEBÊ!
WE ARE HEADING TO THE HOSPITAL ...
OH, THAT HAPPENED.
... TO GET TO THE BOTTOM OF THIS.
!

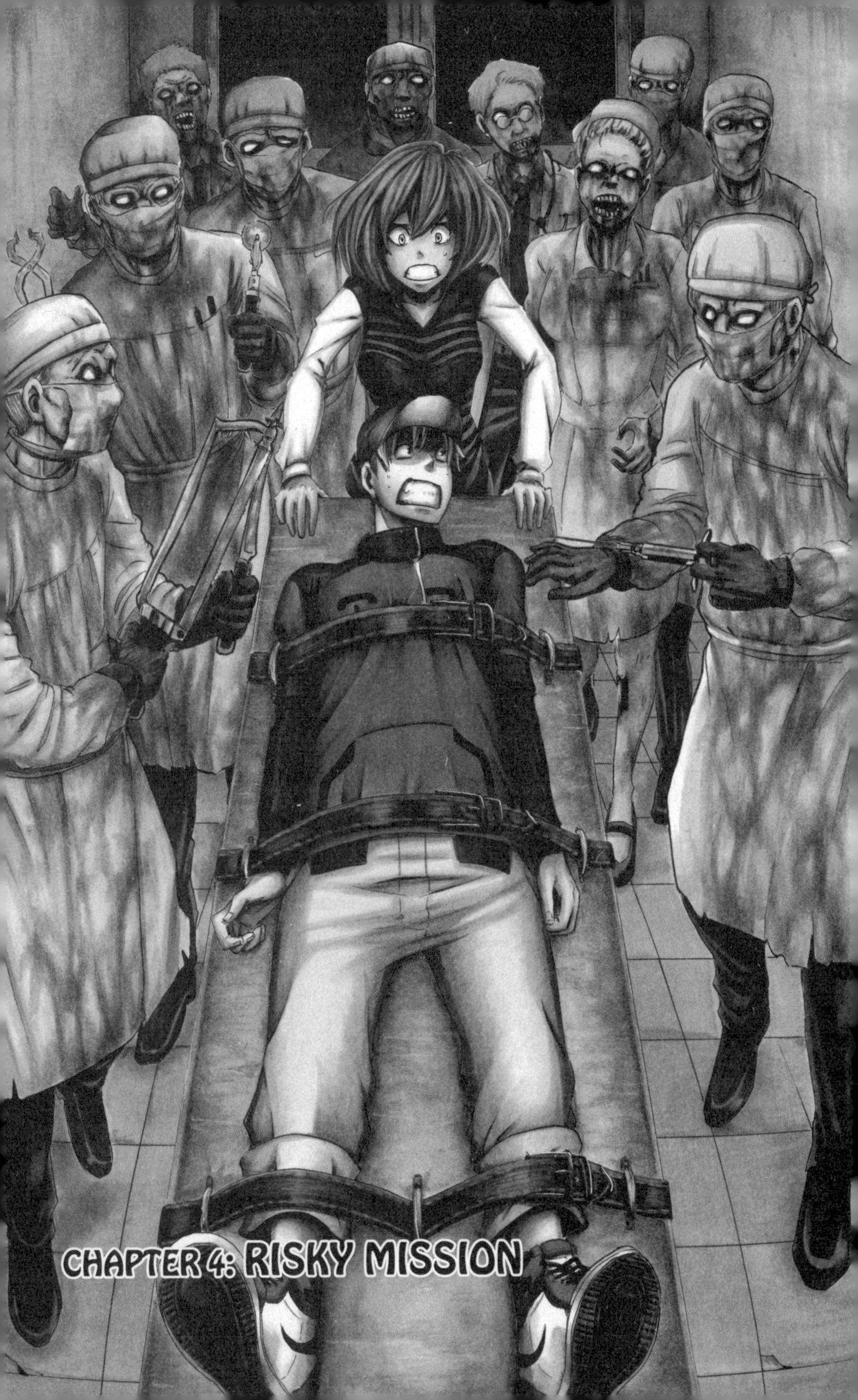
CHAPTER 4: RISKY MISSION

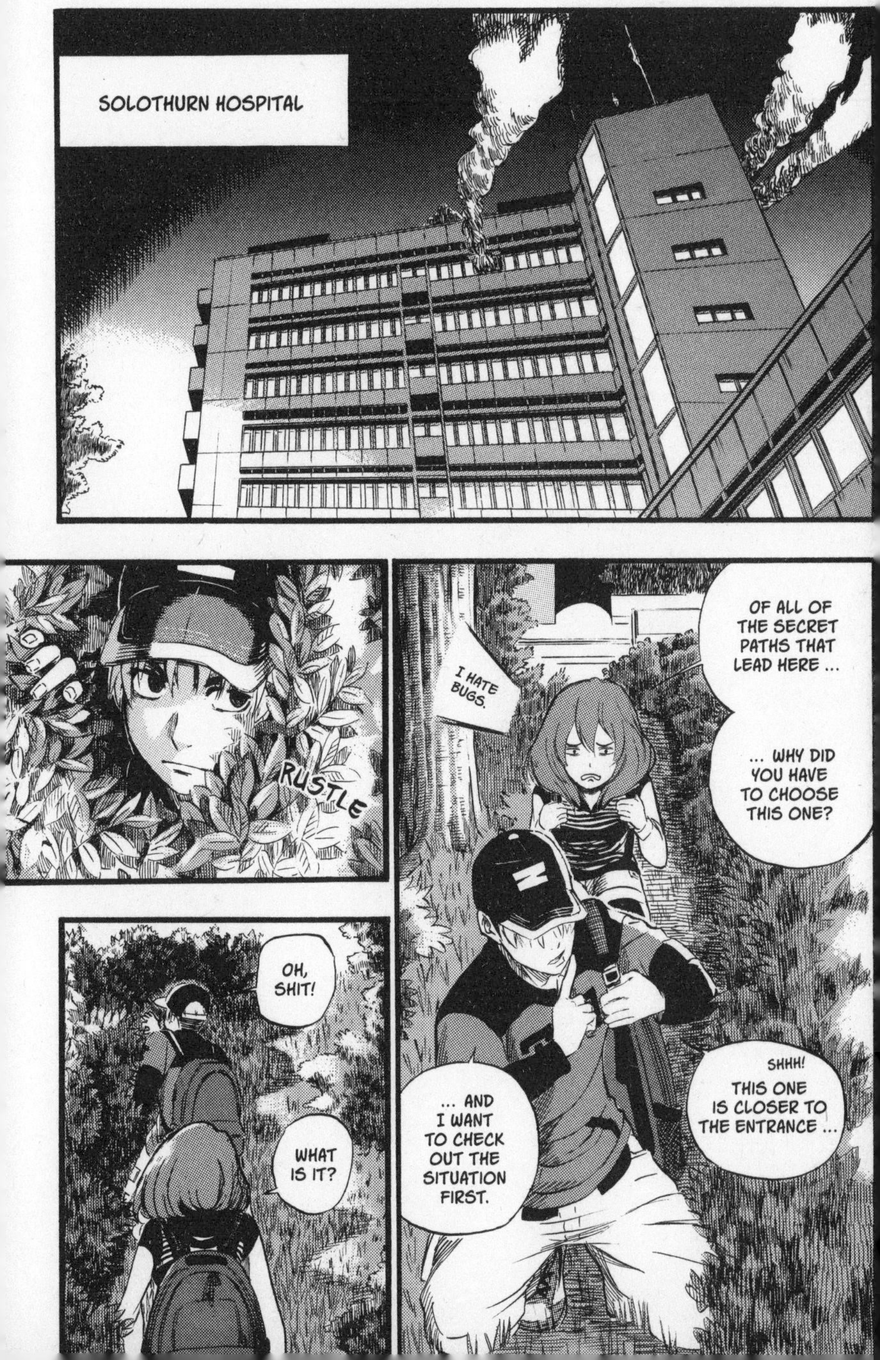
SOLOTHURN HOSPITAL
OF ALL OF THE SECRET PATHS THAT LEAD HERE ...
... WHY DID YOU HAVE TO CHOOSE THIS ONE?
I HATE BUGS.
SHHH! THIS ONE IS CLOSER TO THE ENTRANCE ...
... AND I WANT TO CHECK OUT THE SITUATION FIRST.
RUSTLE
OH, SHIT!
WHAT IS IT?

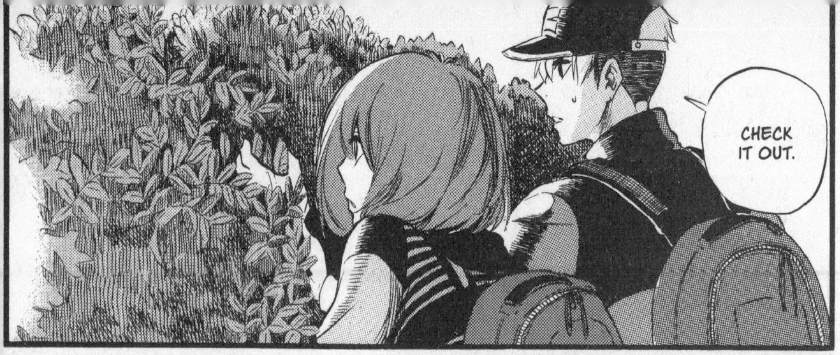
CHECK IT OUT.

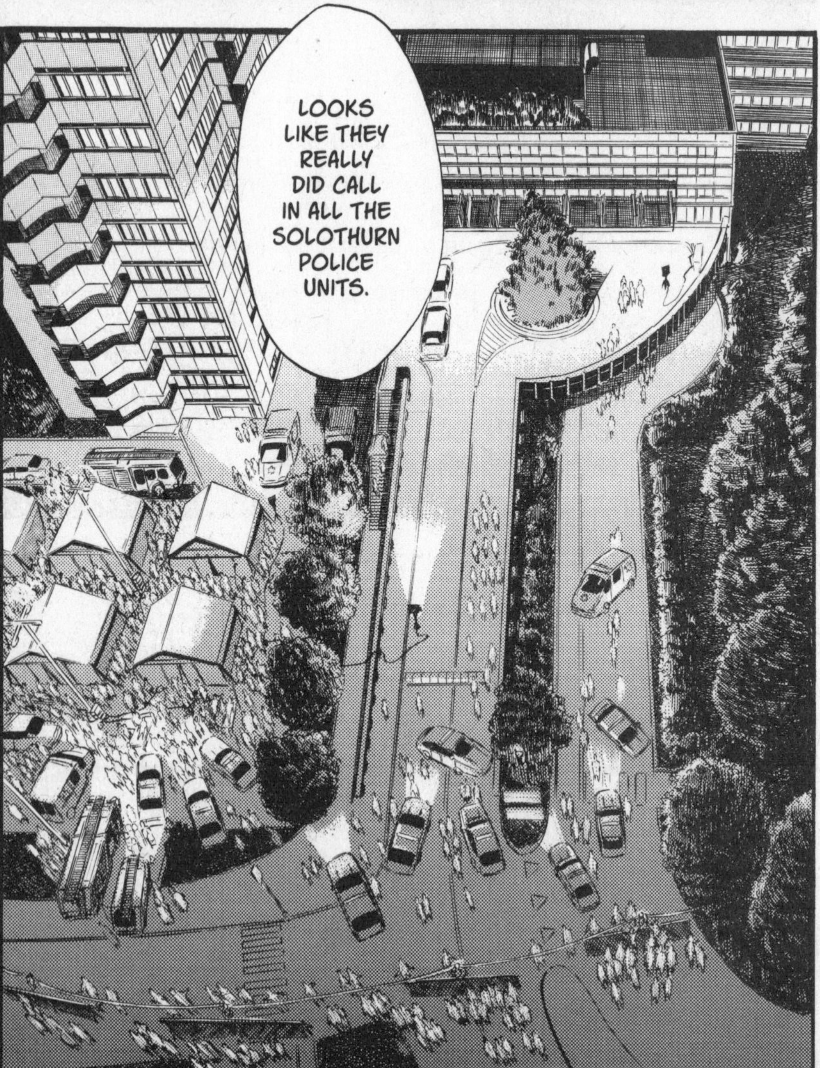
LOOKS LIKE THEY REALLY DID CALL IN ALL THE SOLOTHURN POLICE UNITS.

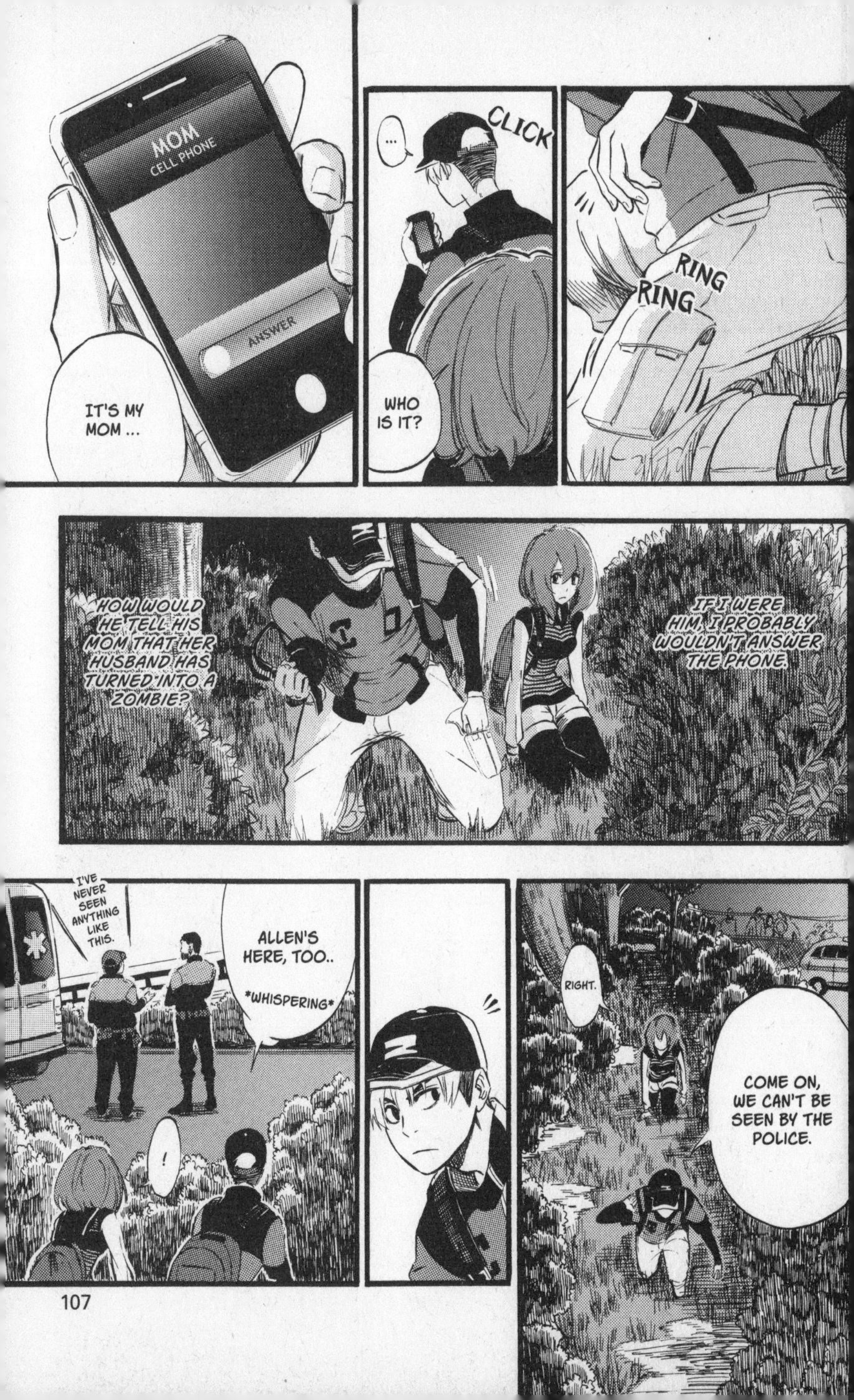
RING
RING
CLICK
...
WHO IS IT?
MOM
CELL PHONE
ANSWER
IT'S MY MOM ...
IF I WERE HIM, I PROBABLY WOULDN'T ANSWER THE PHONE.
HOW WOULD HE TELL HIS MOM THAT HER HUSBAND HAS TURNED INTO A ZOMBIE?
COME ON, WE CAN'T BE SEEN BY THE POLICE.
RIGHT.
I'VE NEVER SEEN ANYTHING LIKE THIS.
ALLEN'S HERE, TOO..
WHISPERING
!

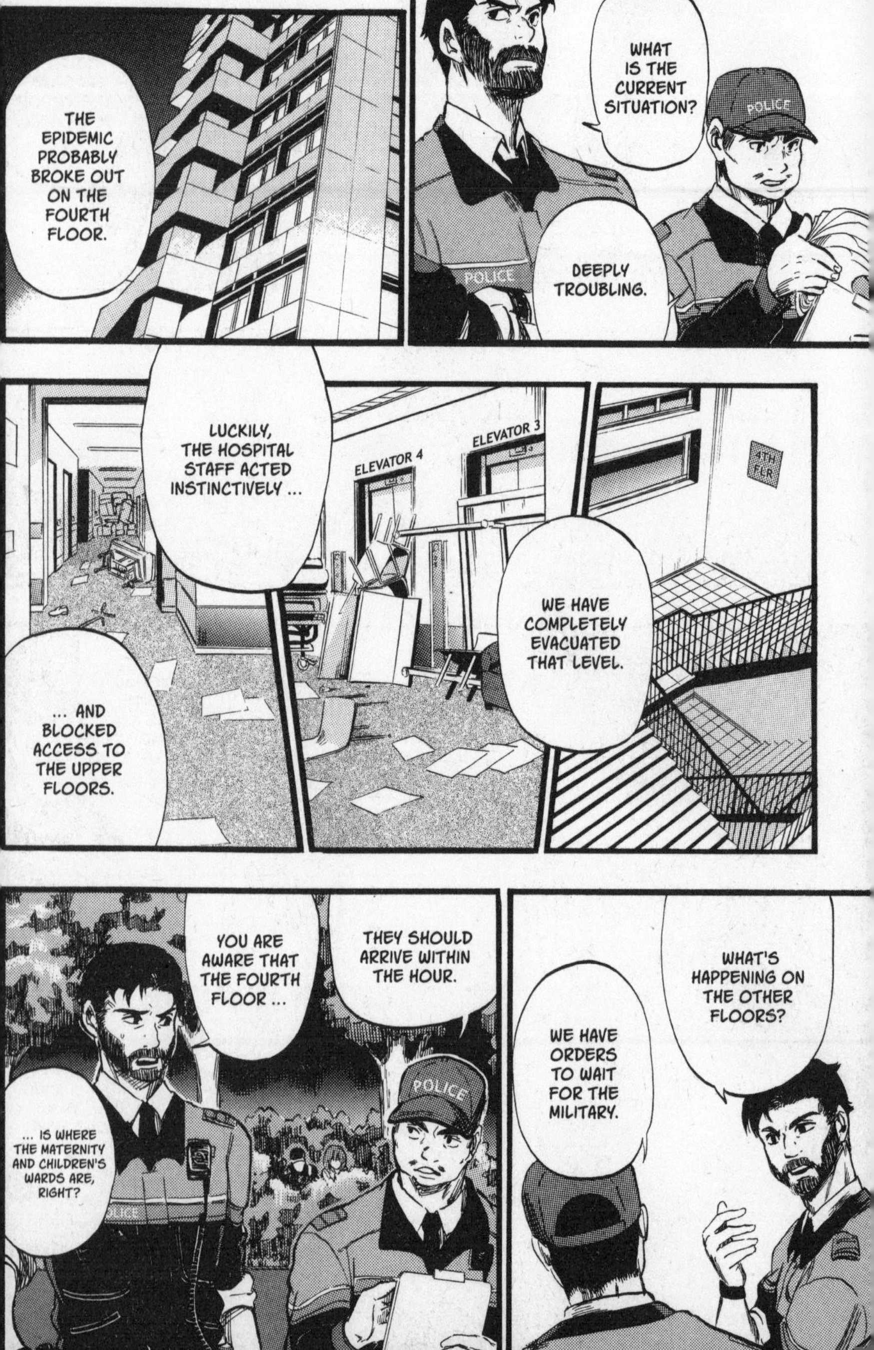
WHAT IS THE CURRENT SITUATION?
DEEPLY TROUBLING.
THE EPIDEMIC PROBABLY BROKE OUT ON THE FOURTH FLOOR.
4TH FLR
WE HAVE COMPLETELY EVACUATED THAT LEVEL.
ELEVATOR 3
ELEVATOR 4
LUCKILY, THE HOSPITAL STAFF ACTED INSTINCTIVELY ...
... AND BLOCKED ACCESS TO THE UPPER FLOORS.
WHAT'S HAPPENING ON THE OTHER FLOORS?
WE HAVE ORDERS TO WAIT FOR THE MILITARY.
THEY SHOULD ARRIVE WITHIN THE HOUR.
YOU ARE AWARE THAT THE FOURTH FLOOR ...
... IS WHERE THE MATERNITY AND CHILDREN'S WARDS ARE, RIGHT?

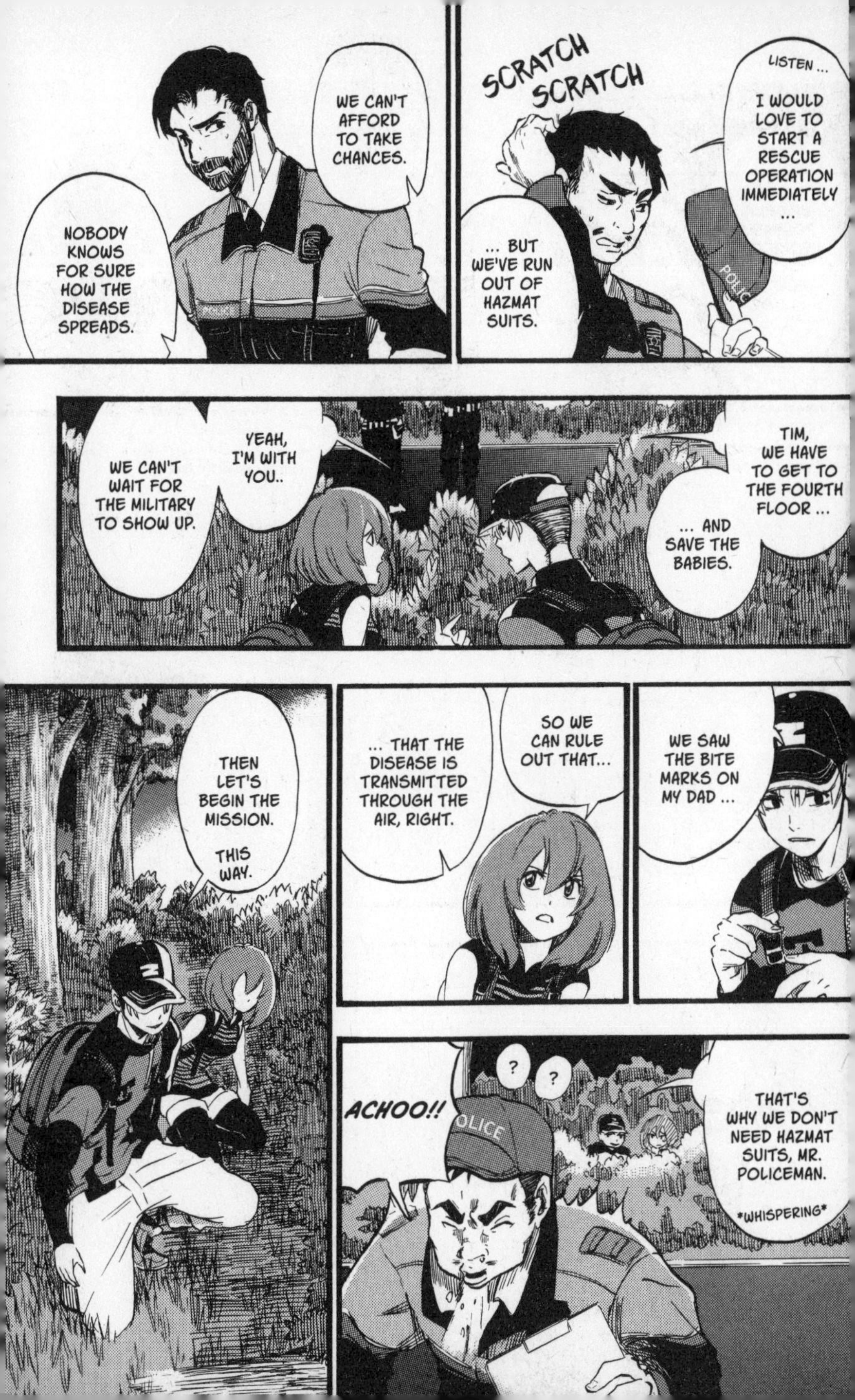
LISTEN ... I WOULD LOVE TO START A RESCUE OPERATION IMMEDIATELY ...
SCRATCH SCRATCH
... BUT WE'VE RUN OUT OF HAZMAT SUITS.
WE CAN'T AFFORD TO TAKE CHANCES.
NOBODY KNOWS FOR SURE HOW THE DISEASE SPREADS.
TIM, WE HAVE TO GET TO THE FOURTH FLOOR ...
... AND SAVE THE BABIES.
YEAH, I'M WITH YOU..
WE CAN'T WAIT FOR THE MILITARY TO SHOW UP.
WE SAW THE BITE MARKS ON MY DAD ...
SO WE CAN RULE OUT THAT...
... THAT THE DISEASE IS TRANSMITTED THROUGH THE AIR, RIGHT.
THAT'S WHY WE DON'T NEED HAZMAT SUITS, MR. POLICEMAN.
WHISPERING
?
?
ACHOO!!
THEN LET'S BEGIN THE MISSION.
THIS WAY.

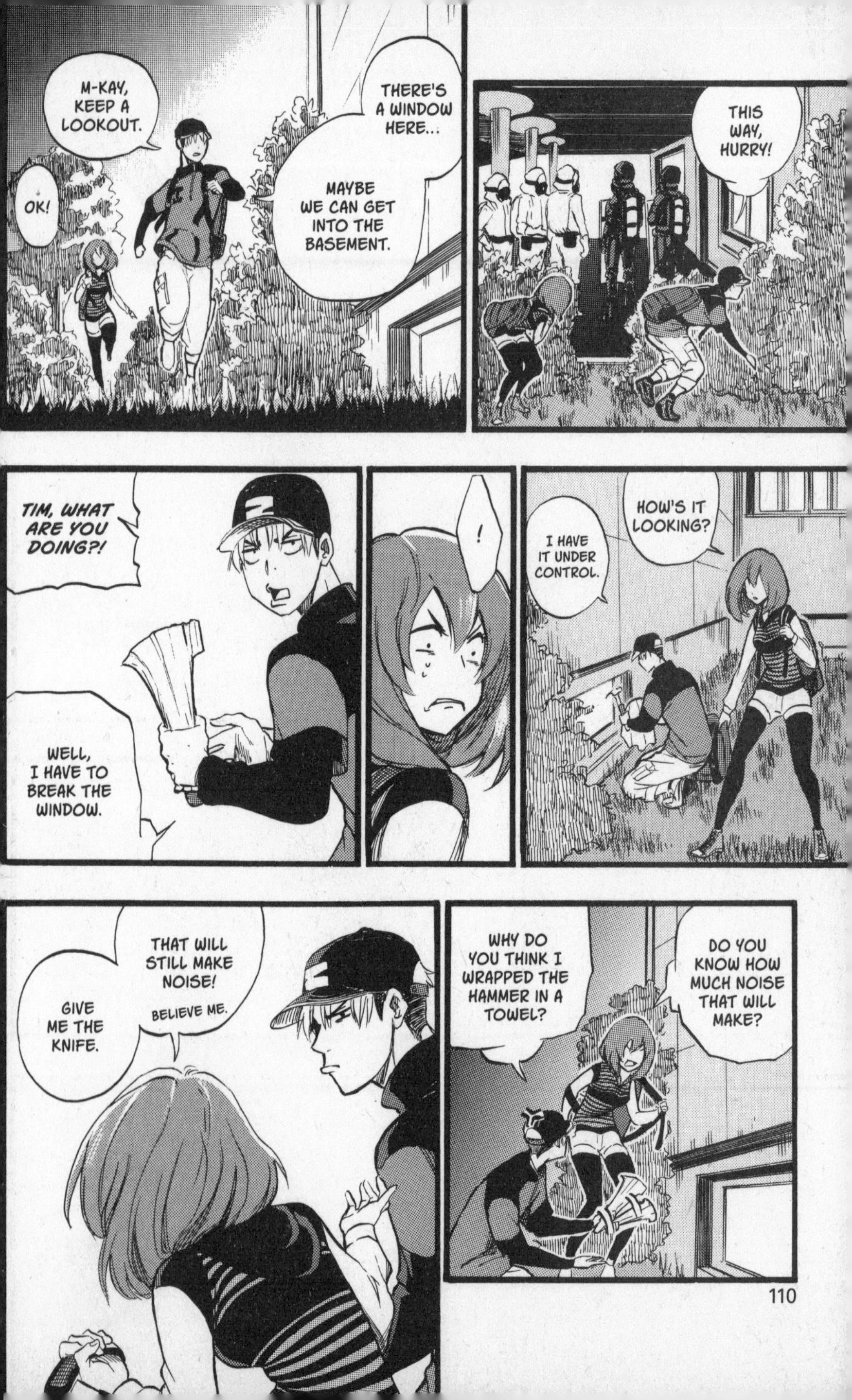
THIS WAY, HURRY!
THERE'S A WINDOW HERE...
MAYBE WE CAN GET INTO THE BASEMENT.
M-KAY, KEEP A LOOKOUT.
OK!
HOW'S IT LOOKING?
I HAVE IT UNDER CONTROL.
!
TIM, WHAT ARE YOU DOING?!
WELL, I HAVE TO BREAK THE WINDOW.
DO YOU KNOW HOW MUCH NOISE THAT WILL MAKE?
WHY DO YOU THINK I WRAPPED THE HAMMER IN A TOWEL?
THAT WILL STILL MAKE NOISE!
BELIEVE ME.
GIVE ME THE KNIFE.

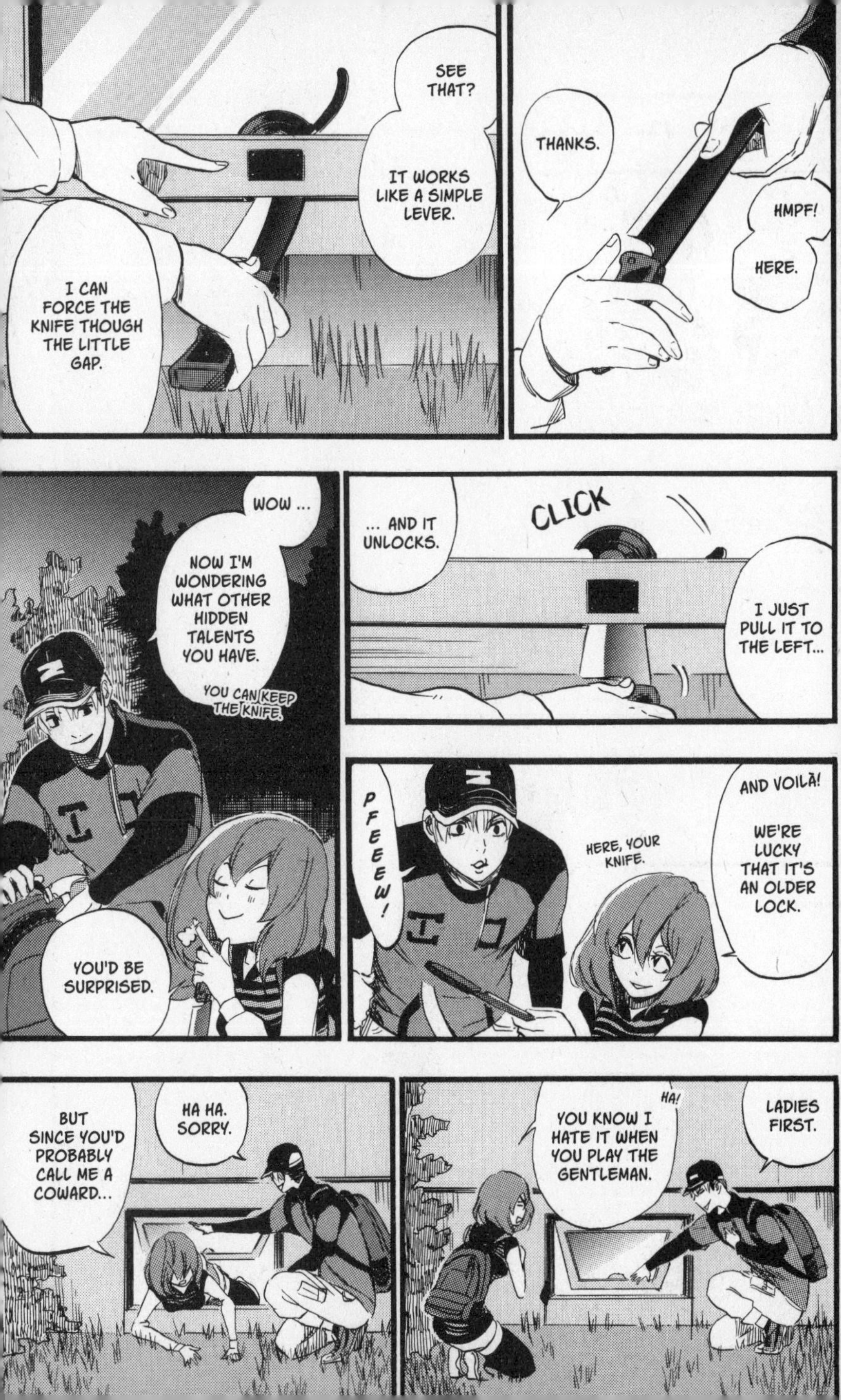
HMPF!
HERE.
THANKS.
SEE THAT?
IT WORKS LIKE A SIMPLE LEVER.
I CAN FORCE THE KNIFE THOUGH THE LITTLE GAP.
I JUST PULL IT TO THE LEFT...
CLICK
... AND IT UNLOCKS.
AND VOILÀ!
WE'RE LUCKY THAT IT'S AN OLDER LOCK.
HERE, YOUR KNIFE.
PFEEEW!
WOW ...
NOW I'M WONDERING WHAT OTHER HIDDEN TALENTS YOU HAVE.
YOU CAN KEEP THE KNIFE.
YOU'D BE SURPRISED.
LADIES FIRST.
HA!
YOU KNOW I HATE IT WHEN YOU PLAY THE GENTLEMAN.
HA HA. SORRY.
BUT SINCE YOU'D PROBABLY CALL ME A COWARD...

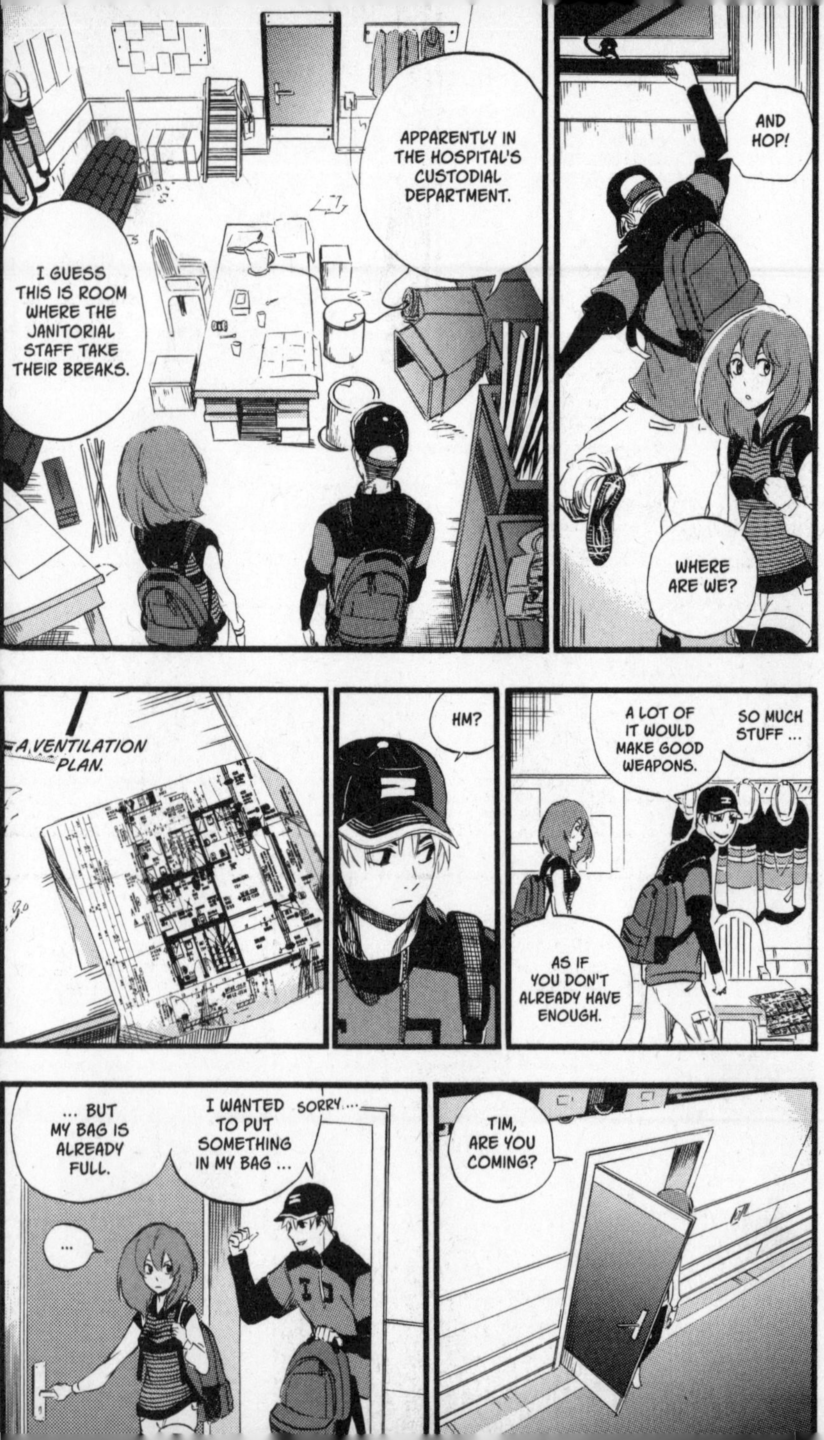
AND HOP!
WHERE ARE WE?
APPARENTLY IN THE HOSPITAL'S CUSTODIAL DEPARTMENT.
I GUESS THIS IS ROOM WHERE THE JANITORIAL STAFF TAKE THEIR BREAKS.
SO MUCH STUFF ...
A LOT OF IT WOULD MAKE GOOD WEAPONS.
AS IF YOU DON'T ALREADY HAVE ENOUGH.
HM?
A VENTILATION PLAN.
TIM, ARE YOU COMING?
SORRY....
I WANTED TO PUT SOMETHING IN MY BAG ...
... BUT MY BAG IS ALREADY FULL.
...

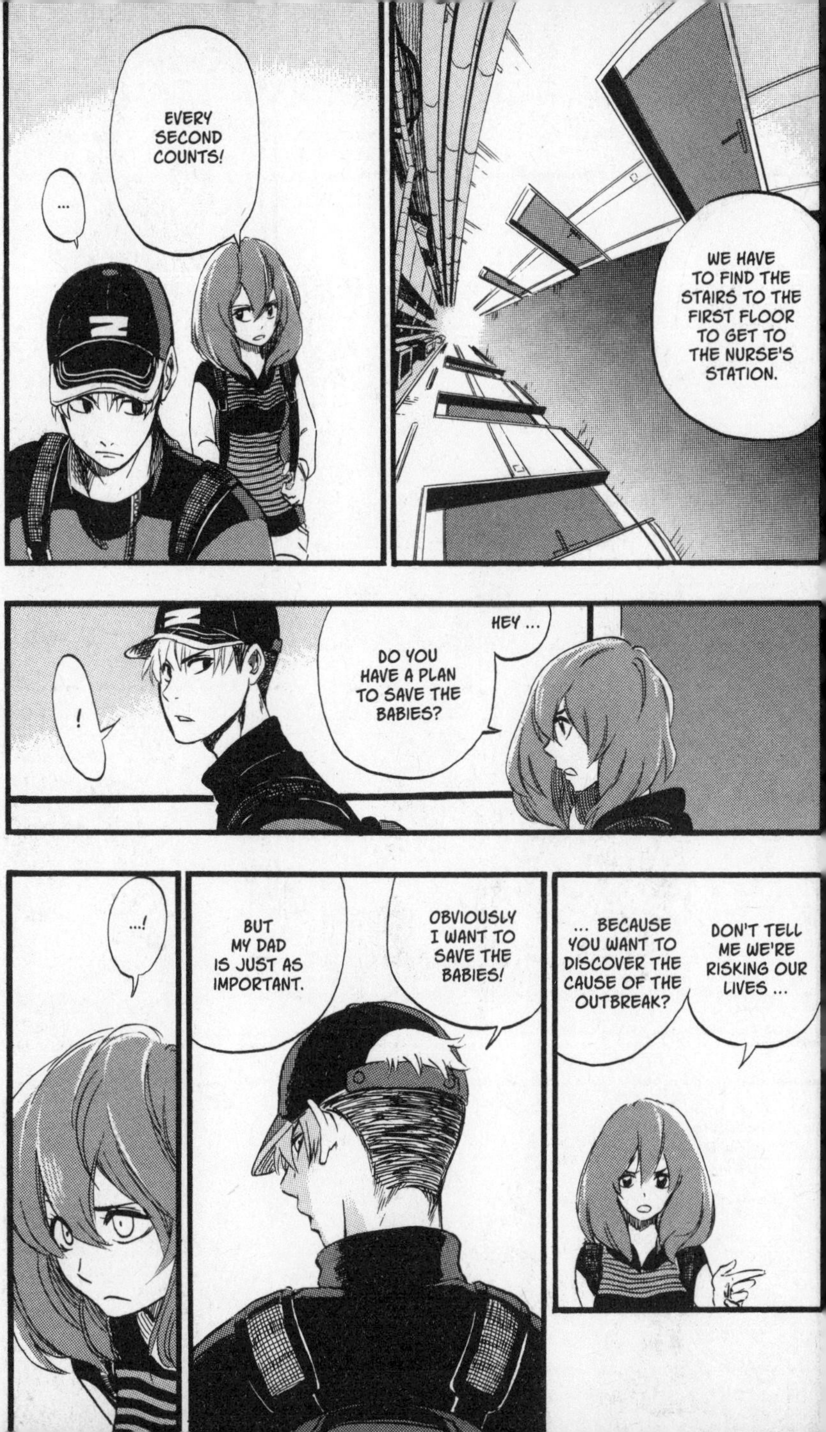
WE HAVE TO FIND THE STAIRS TO THE FIRST FLOOR TO GET TO THE NURSE'S STATION.
EVERY SECOND COUNTS!
...
HEY ...
DO YOU HAVE A PLAN TO SAVE THE BABIES?
!
DON'T TELL ME WE'RE RISKING OUR LIVES ...
... BECAUSE YOU WANT TO DISCOVER THE CAUSE OF THE OUTBREAK?
OBVIOUSLY I WANT TO SAVE THE BABIES!
BUT MY DAD IS JUST AS IMPORTANT.
...!

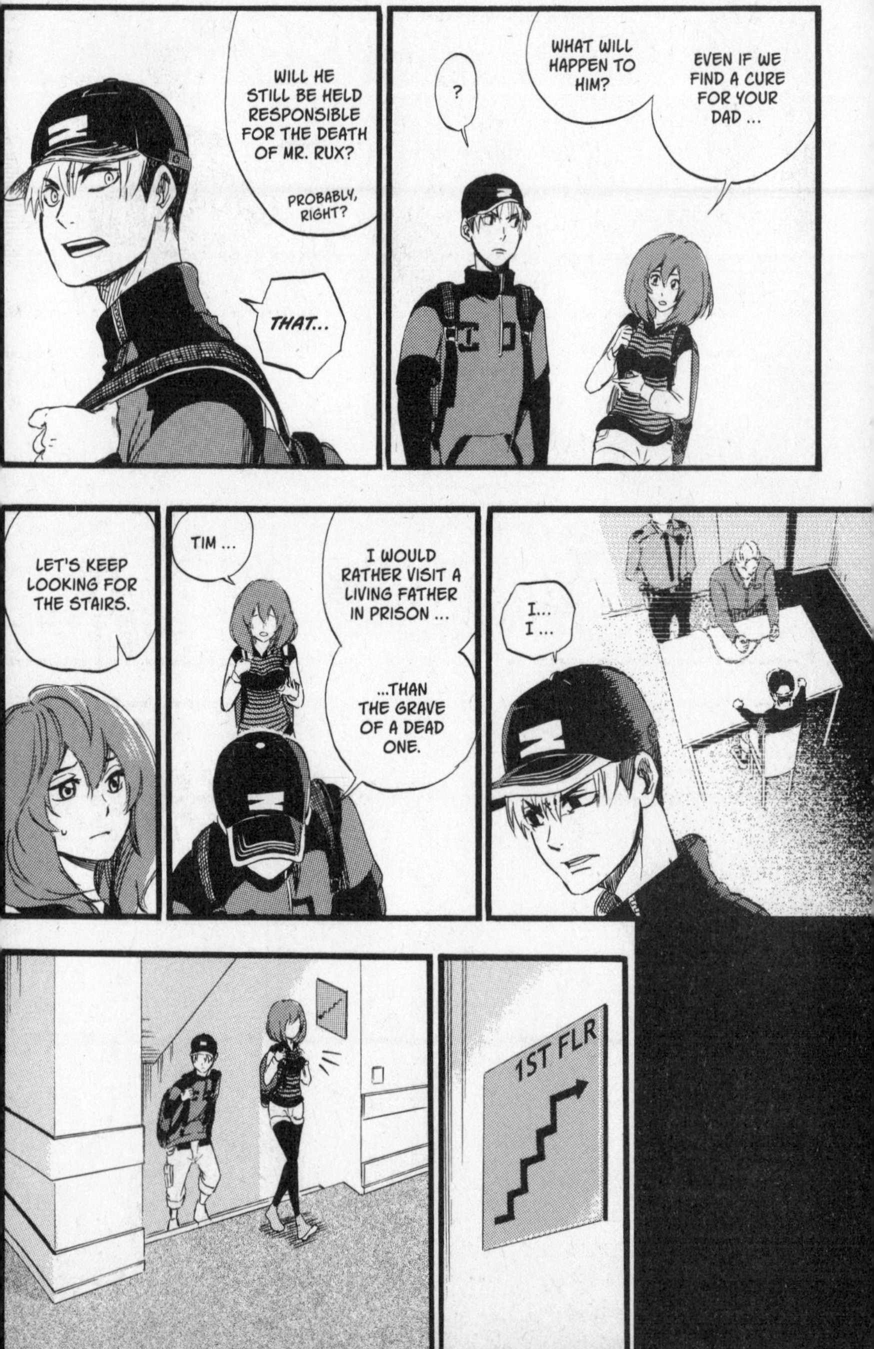
EVEN IF WE FIND A CURE FOR YOUR DAD ...
WHAT WILL HAPPEN TO HIM?
?
WILL HE STILL BE HELD RESPONSIBLE FOR THE DEATH OF MR. RUX?
PROBABLY, RIGHT?
THAT...
I... I ...
I WOULD RATHER VISIT A LIVING FATHER IN PRISON ...
...THAN THE GRAVE OF A DEAD ONE.
TIM ...
LET'S KEEP LOOKING FOR THE STAIRS.
1ST FLR

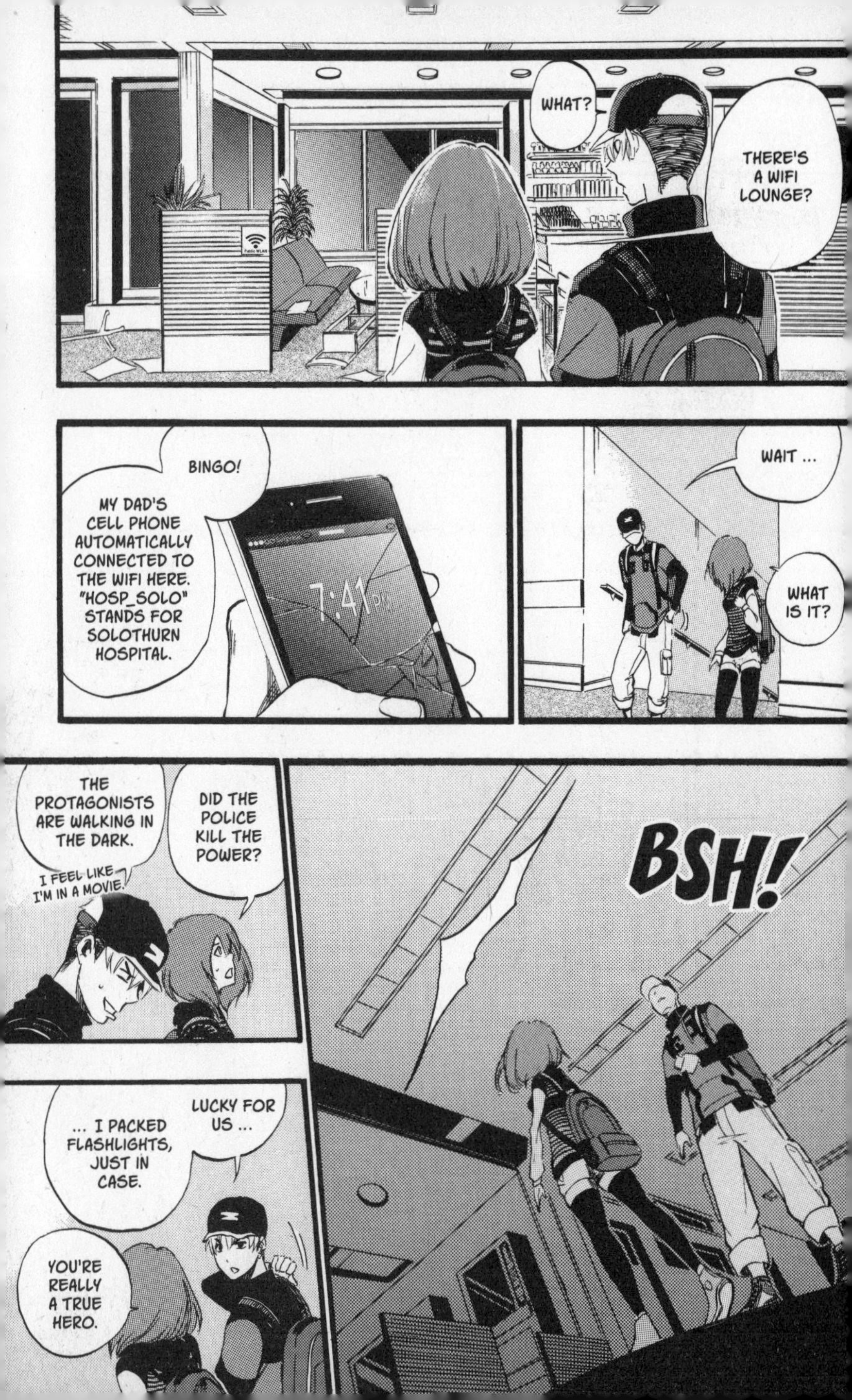
WHAT?
THERE'S A WIFI LOUNGE?
WAIT ...
WHAT IS IT?
BINGO!
MY DAD'S CELL PHONE AUTOMATICALLY CONNECTED TO THE WIFI HERE. "HOSP_SOLO" STANDS FOR SOLOTHURN HOSPITAL.
7:41 PM
BSH!
DID THE POLICE KILL THE POWER?
THE PROTAGONISTS ARE WALKING IN THE DARK.
I FEEL LIKE I'M IN A MOVIE.
LUCKY FOR US ...
... I PACKED FLASHLIGHTS, JUST IN CASE.
YOU'RE REALLY A TRUE HERO.

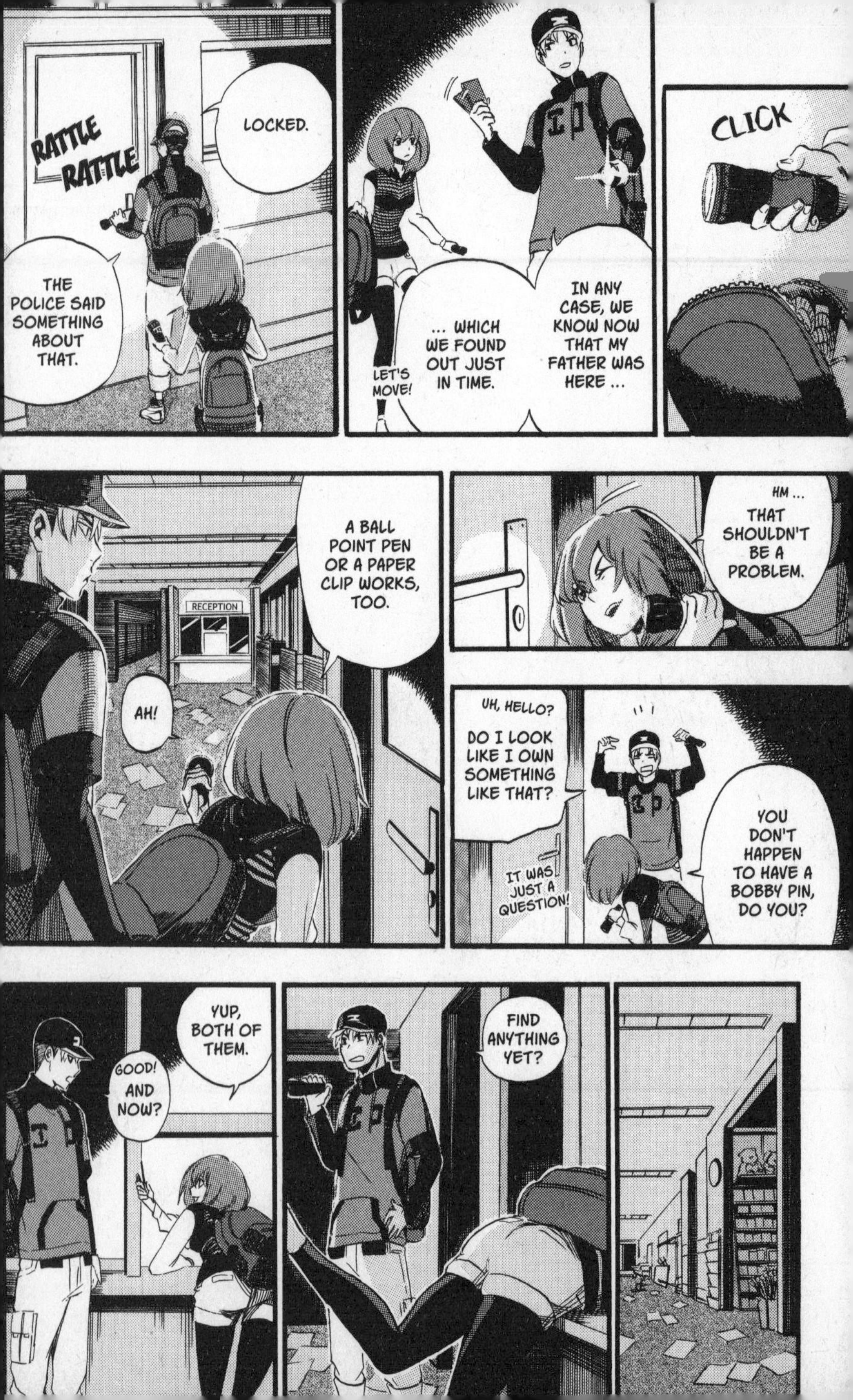
CLICK
IN ANY CASE, WE KNOW NOW THAT MY FATHER WAS HERE ...
... WHICH WE FOUND OUT JUST IN TIME.
LET'S MOVE!
LOCKED.
RATTLE RATTLE
THE POLICE SAID SOMETHING ABOUT THAT.
HM ... THAT SHOULDN'T BE A PROBLEM.
YOU DON'T HAPPEN TO HAVE A BOBBY PIN, DO YOU?
UH, HELLO? DO I LOOK LIKE I OWN SOMETHING LIKE THAT?
IT WAS JUST A QUESTION!
A BALL POINT PEN OR A PAPER CLIP WORKS, TOO.
RECEPTION
AH!
FIND ANYTHING YET?
YUP, BOTH OF THEM.
GOOD! AND NOW?

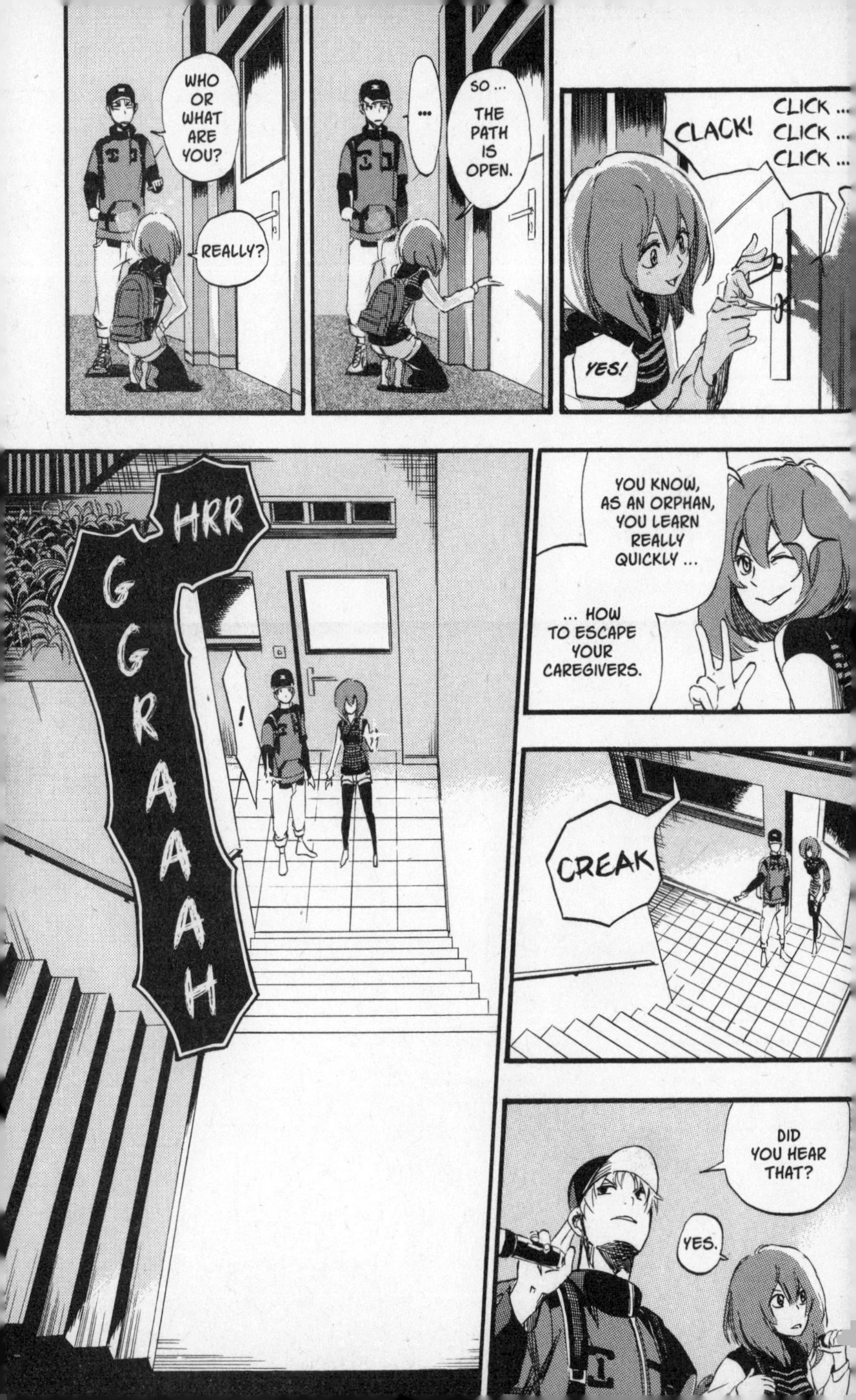

CLICK ... CLICK ... CLICK ...
CLACK!
YES!
SO ... THE PATH IS OPEN.
...
WHO OR WHAT ARE YOU?
REALLY?
YOU KNOW, AS AN ORPHAN, YOU LEARN REALLY QUICKLY ...
... HOW TO ESCAPE YOUR CAREGIVERS.
CREAK
DID YOU HEAR THAT?
YES.
HRR GGRAAAAH
!

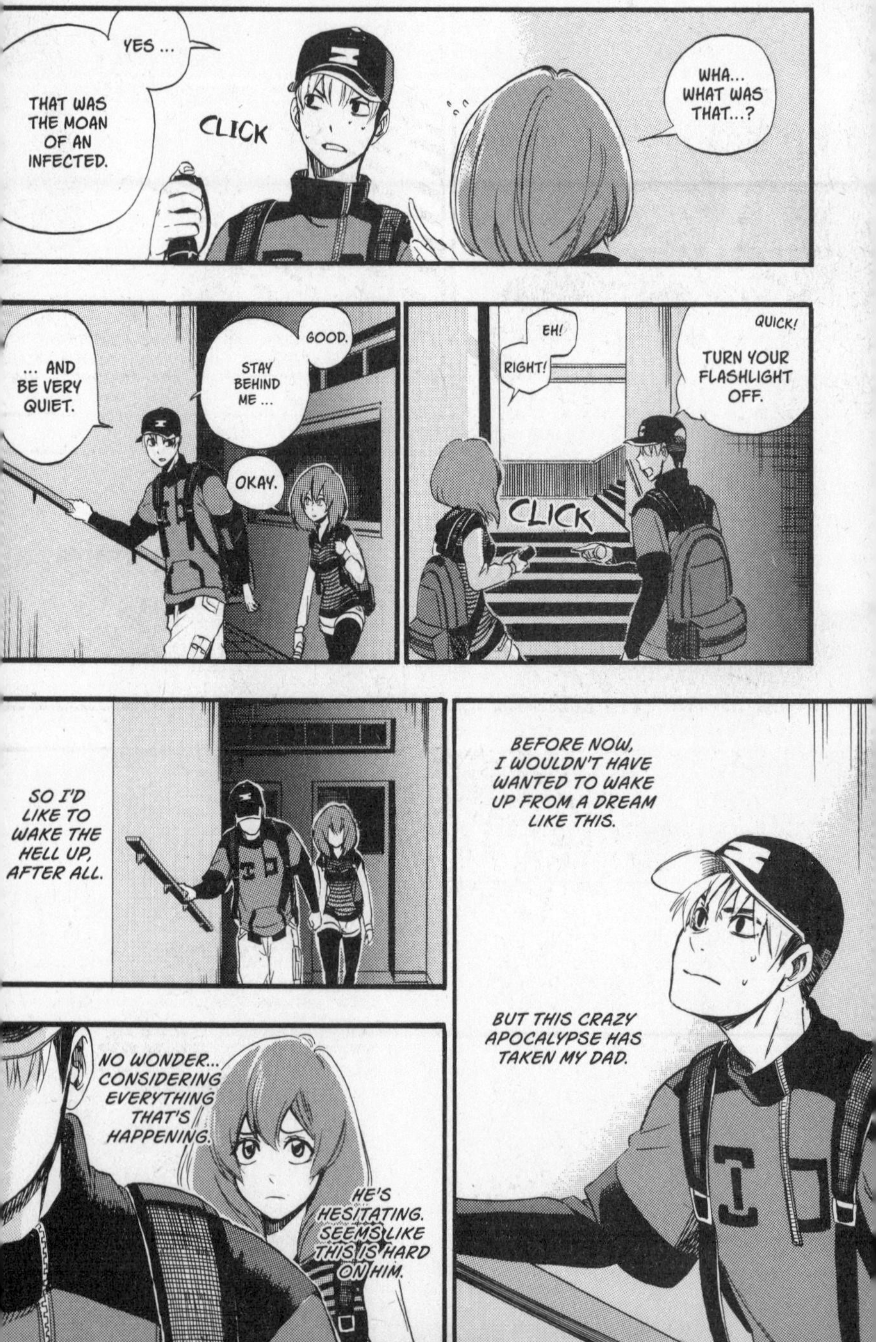
WHA... WHAT WAS THAT...?
YES ...
THAT WAS THE MOAN OF AN INFECTED.
CLICK
QUICK!
TURN YOUR FLASHLIGHT OFF.
EH!
RIGHT!
CLICK
GOOD.
STAY BEHIND ME ...
... AND BE VERY QUIET.
OKAY.
BEFORE NOW, I WOULDN'T HAVE WANTED TO WAKE UP FROM A DREAM LIKE THIS.
BUT THIS CRAZY APOCALYPSE HAS TAKEN MY DAD.
SO I'D LIKE TO WAKE THE HELL UP, AFTER ALL.
NO WONDER... CONSIDERING EVERYTHING THAT'S HAPPENING.
HE'S HESITATING. SEEMS LIKE THIS IS HARD ON HIM.

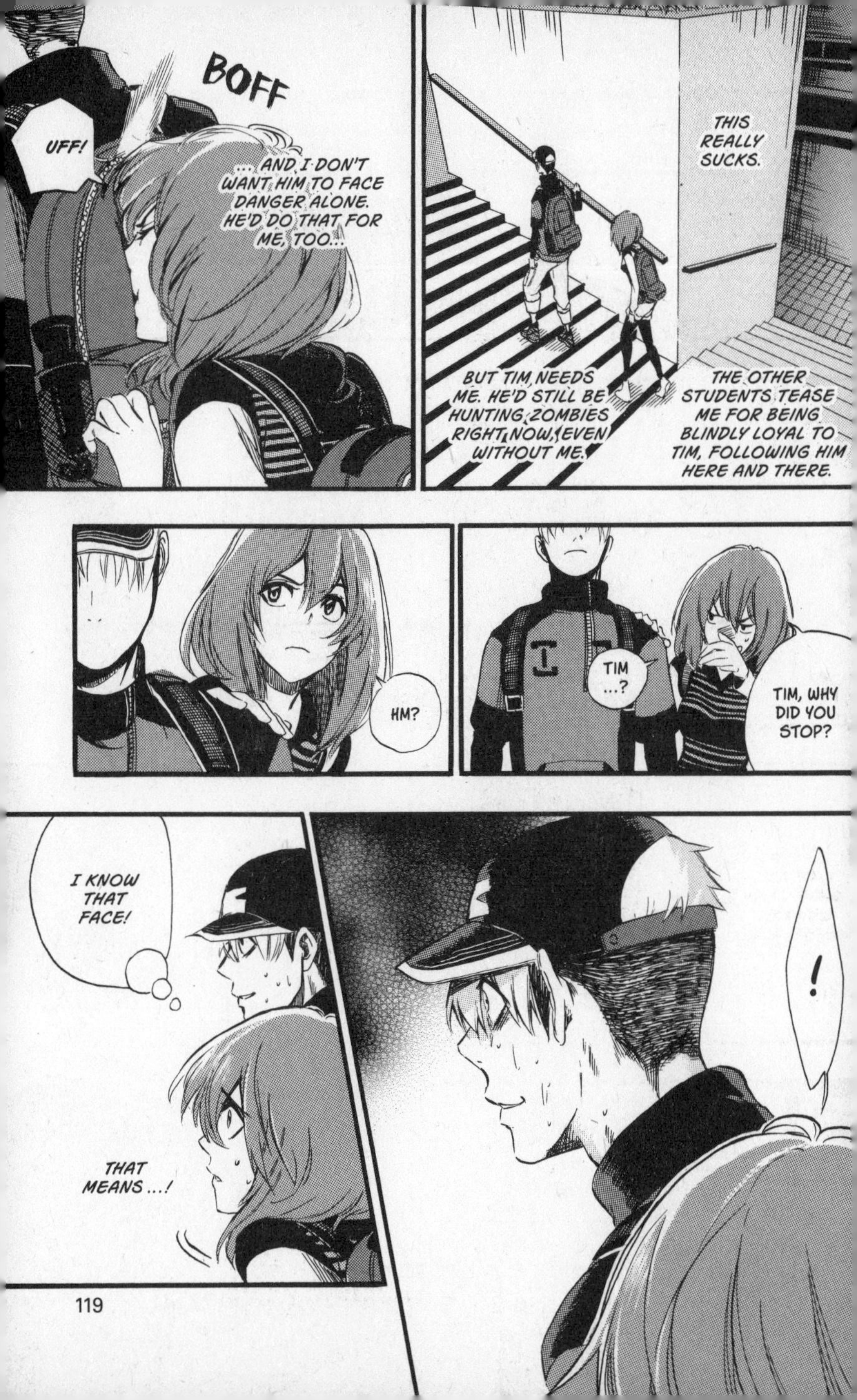
THIS REALLY SUCKS.
THE OTHER STUDENTS TEASE ME FOR BEING BLINDLY LOYAL TO TIM, FOLLOWING HIM HERE AND THERE.
BUT TIM NEEDS ME. HE'D STILL BE HUNTING ZOMBIES RIGHT NOW, EVEN WITHOUT ME.
BOFF
... AND I DON'T WANT HIM TO FACE DANGER ALONE. HE'D DO THAT FOR ME, TOO...
UFF!
TIM, WHY DID YOU STOP?
TIM ...?
HM?
!
I KNOW THAT FACE!
THAT MEANS ...!

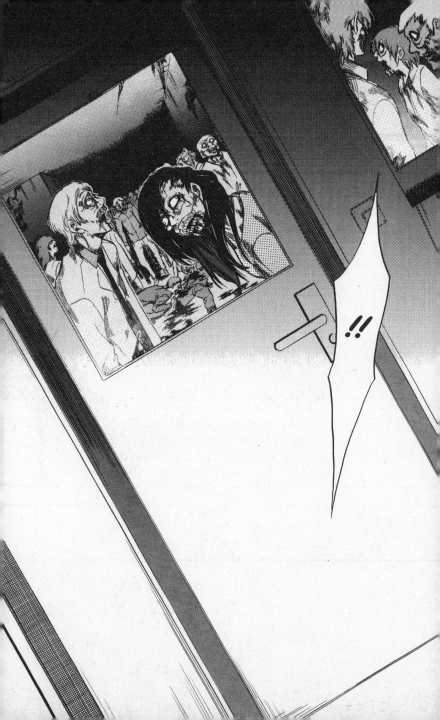

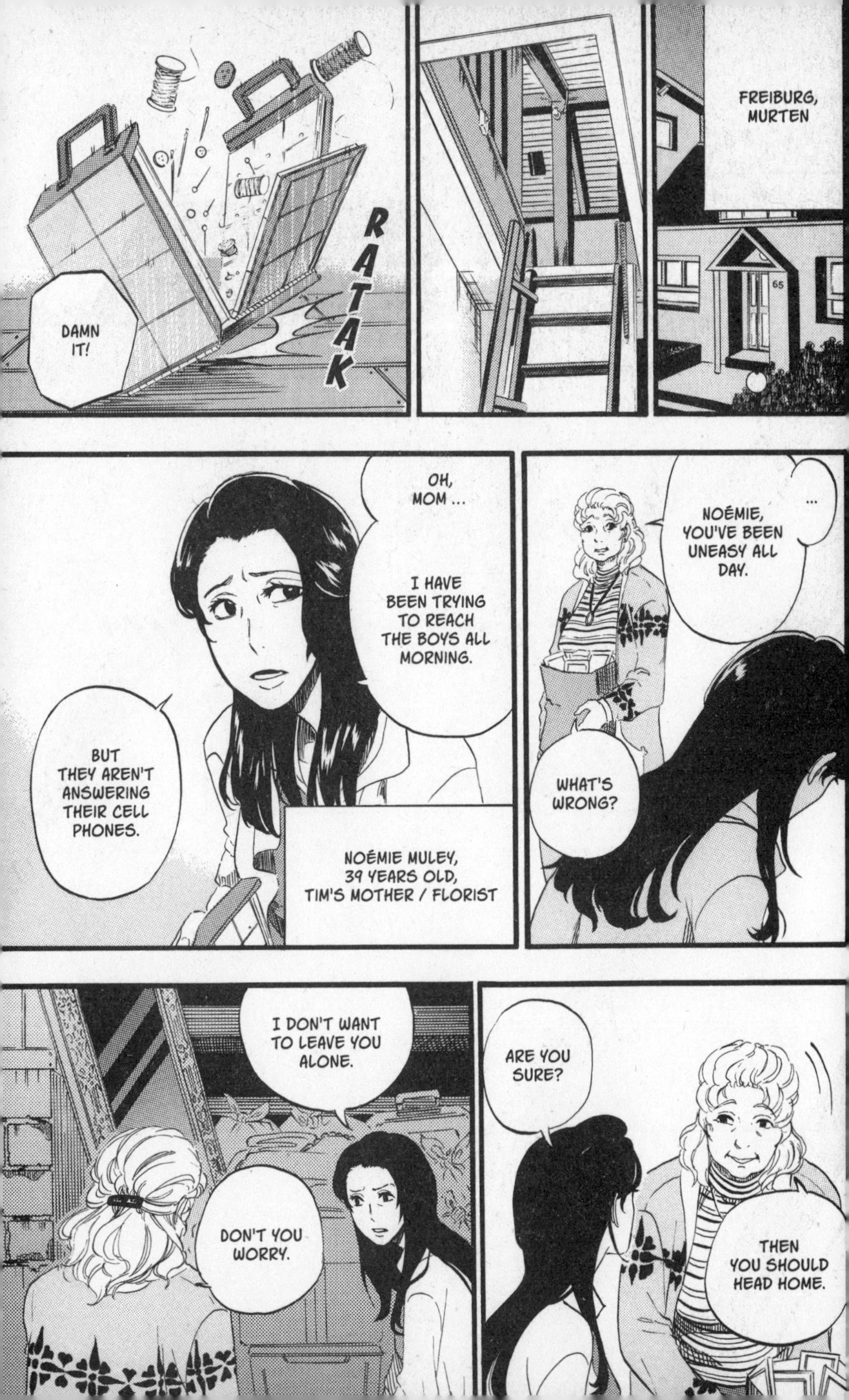
FREIBURG, MURTEN
RATAK
DAMN IT!
...
NOÉMIE, YOU'VE BEEN UNEASY ALL DAY.
WHAT'S WRONG?
OH, MOM ...
I HAVE BEEN TRYING TO REACH THE BOYS ALL MORNING.
BUT THEY AREN'T ANSWERING THEIR CELL PHONES.
NOÉMIE MULEY, 39 YEARS OLD, TIM'S MOTHER / FLORIST
ARE YOU SURE?
THEN YOU SHOULD HEAD HOME.
I DON'T WANT TO LEAVE YOU ALONE.
DON'T YOU WORRY.

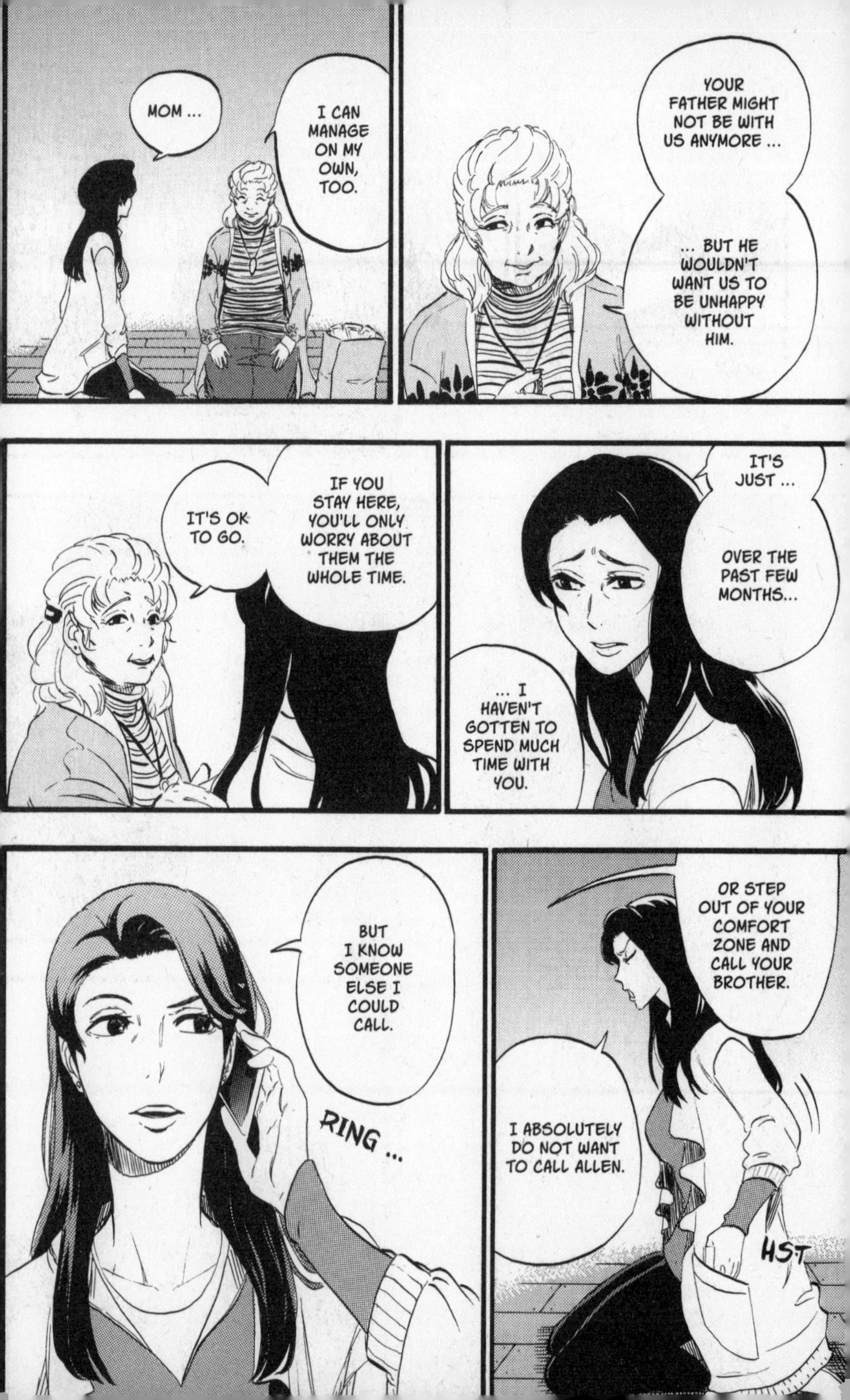
YOUR FATHER MIGHT NOT BE WITH US ANYMORE ...
... BUT HE WOULDN'T WANT US TO BE UNHAPPY WITHOUT HIM.
I CAN MANAGE ON MY OWN, TOO.
MOM ...
IT'S JUST ...
OVER THE PAST FEW MONTHS...
... I HAVEN'T GOTTEN TO SPEND MUCH TIME WITH YOU.
IF YOU STAY HERE, YOU'LL ONLY WORRY ABOUT THEM THE WHOLE TIME.
IT'S OK TO GO.
OR STEP OUT OF YOUR COMFORT ZONE AND CALL YOUR BROTHER.
I ABSOLUTELY DO NOT WANT TO CALL ALLEN.
HST
BUT I KNOW SOMEONE ELSE I COULD CALL.
RING ...

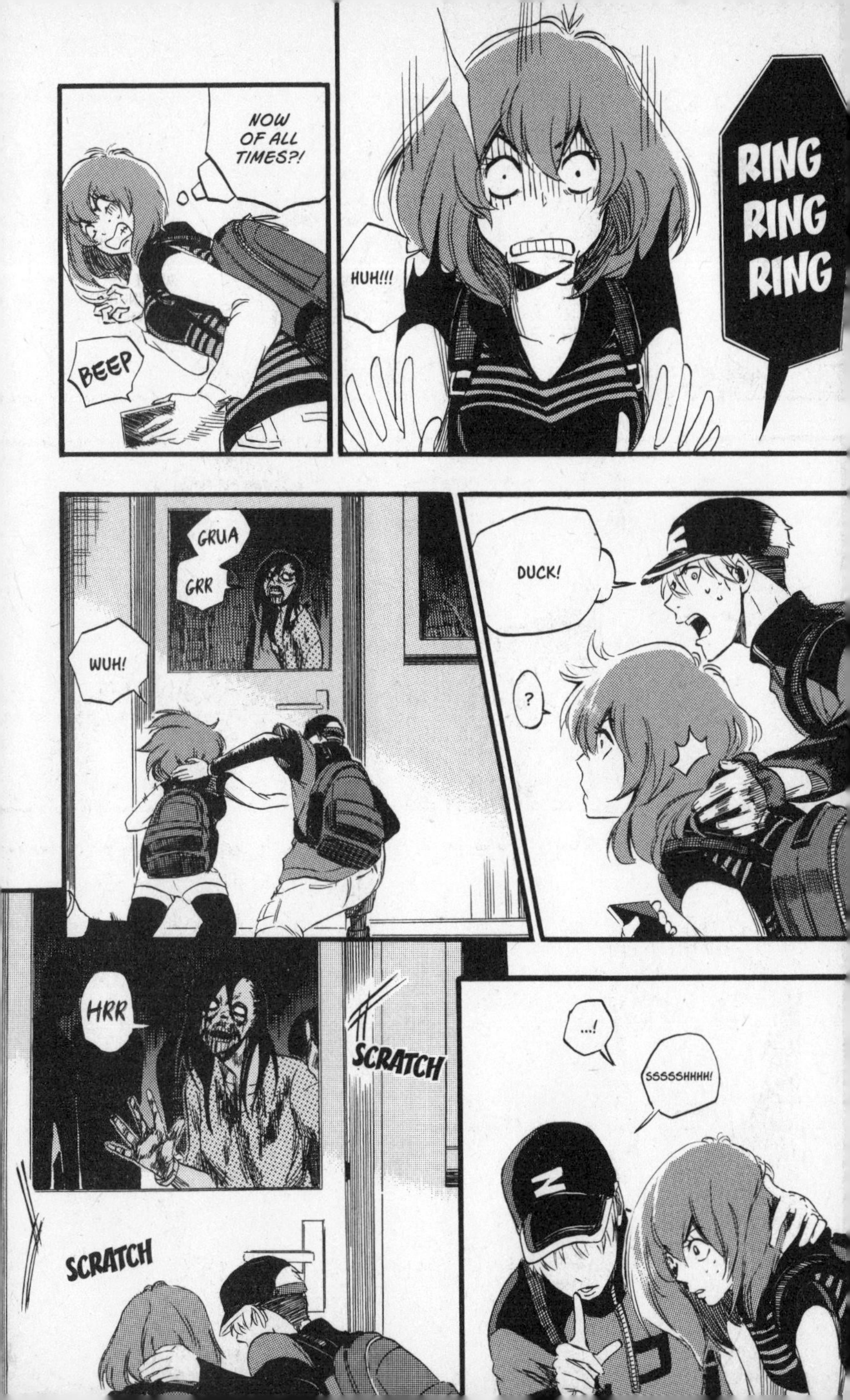
RING RING RING
HUH!!!
NOW OF ALL TIMES?!
BEEP
DUCK!
?
GRUA
GRR
WUH!
...!
SSSSSHHHH!
HRR
SCRATCH
SCRATCH

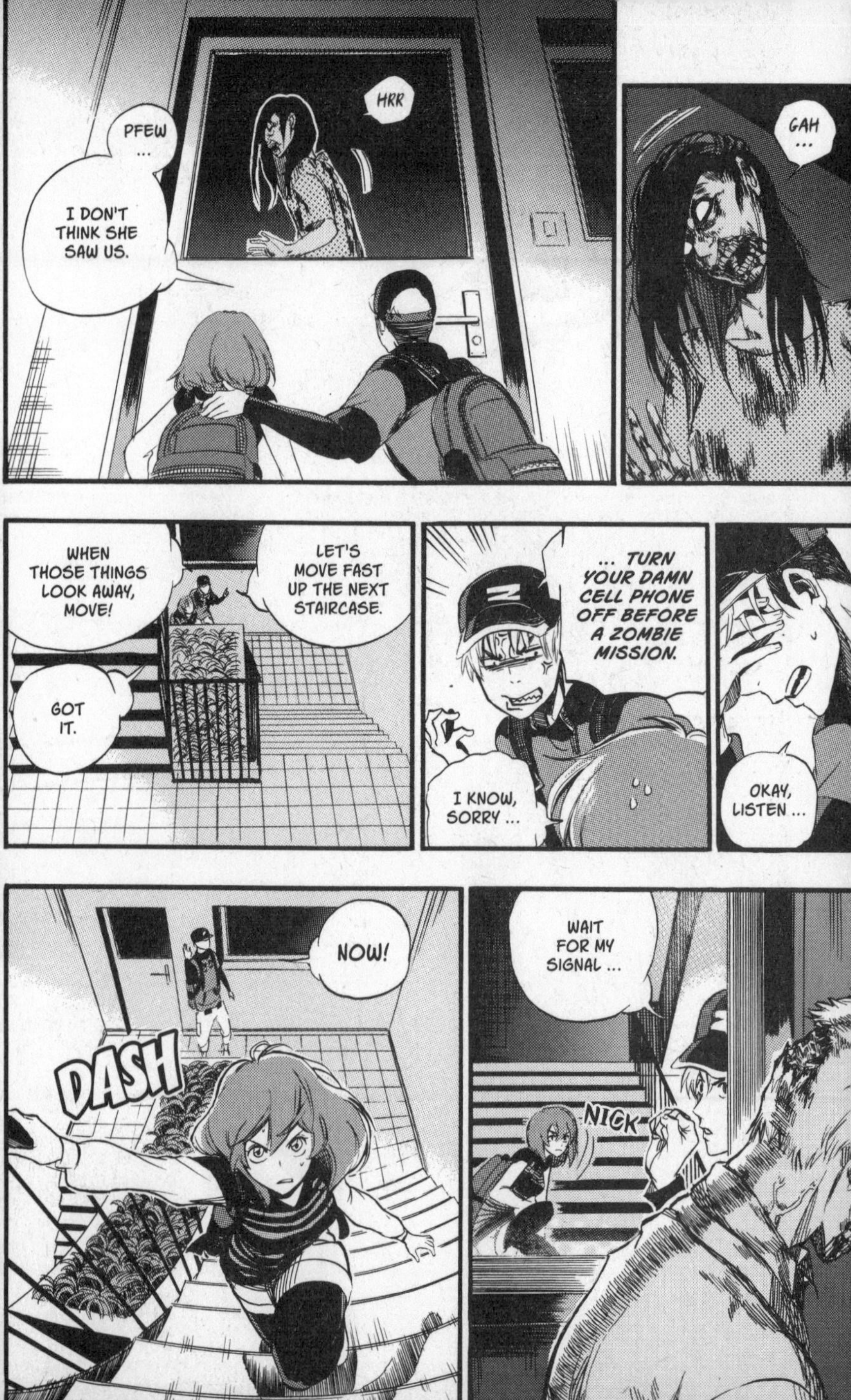
GAH ...
HRR
PFEW ...
I DON'T THINK SHE SAW US.
OKAY, LISTEN ...
... TURN YOUR DAMN CELL PHONE OFF BEFORE A ZOMBIE MISSION.
I KNOW, SORRY ...
LET'S MOVE FAST UP THE NEXT STAIRCASE.
WHEN THOSE THINGS LOOK AWAY, MOVE!
GOT IT.
WAIT FOR MY SIGNAL ...
NICK
NOW!
DASH

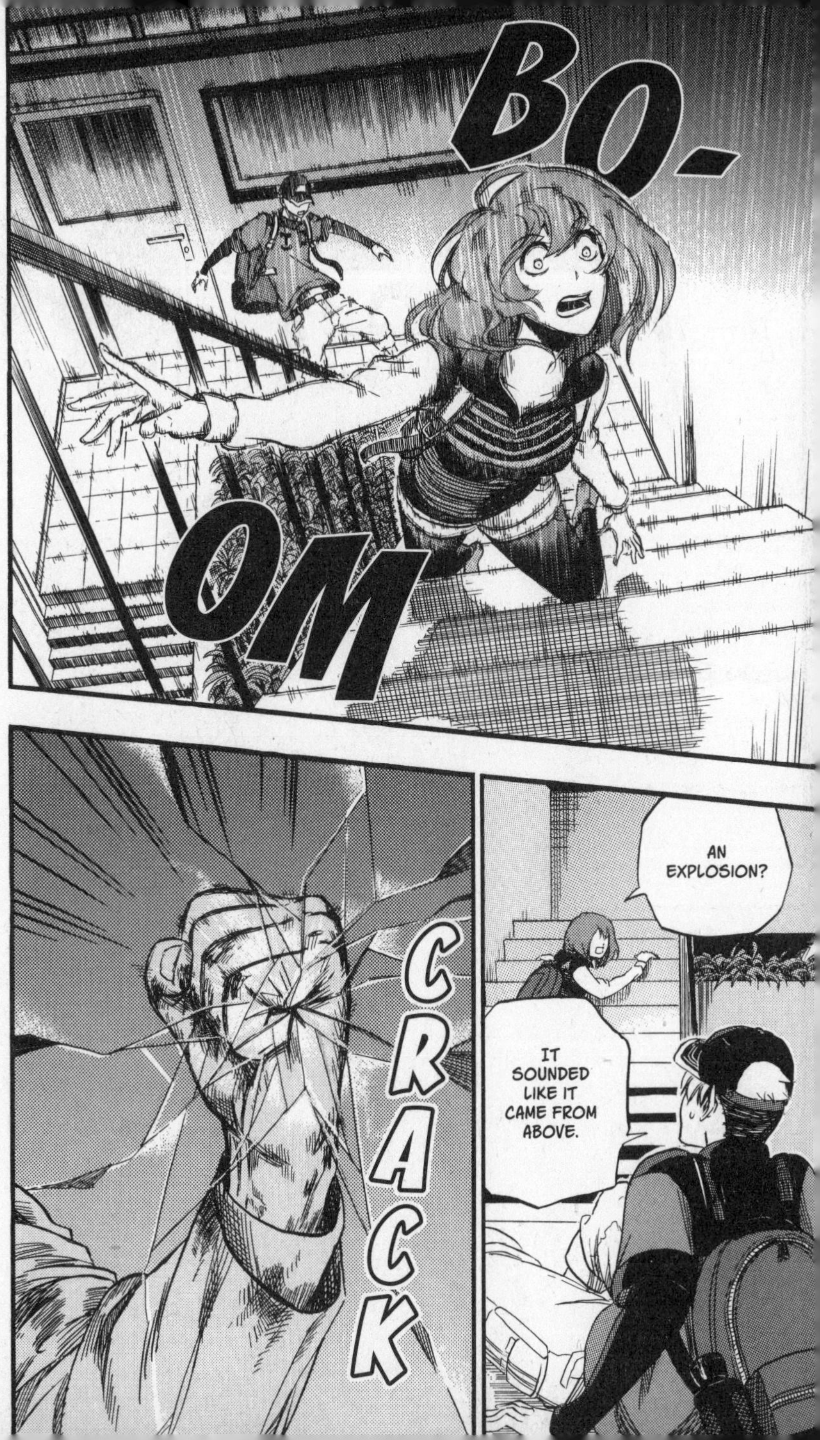
BO-
OM
AN EXPLOSION?
IT SOUNDED LIKE IT CAME FROM ABOVE.
CRACK

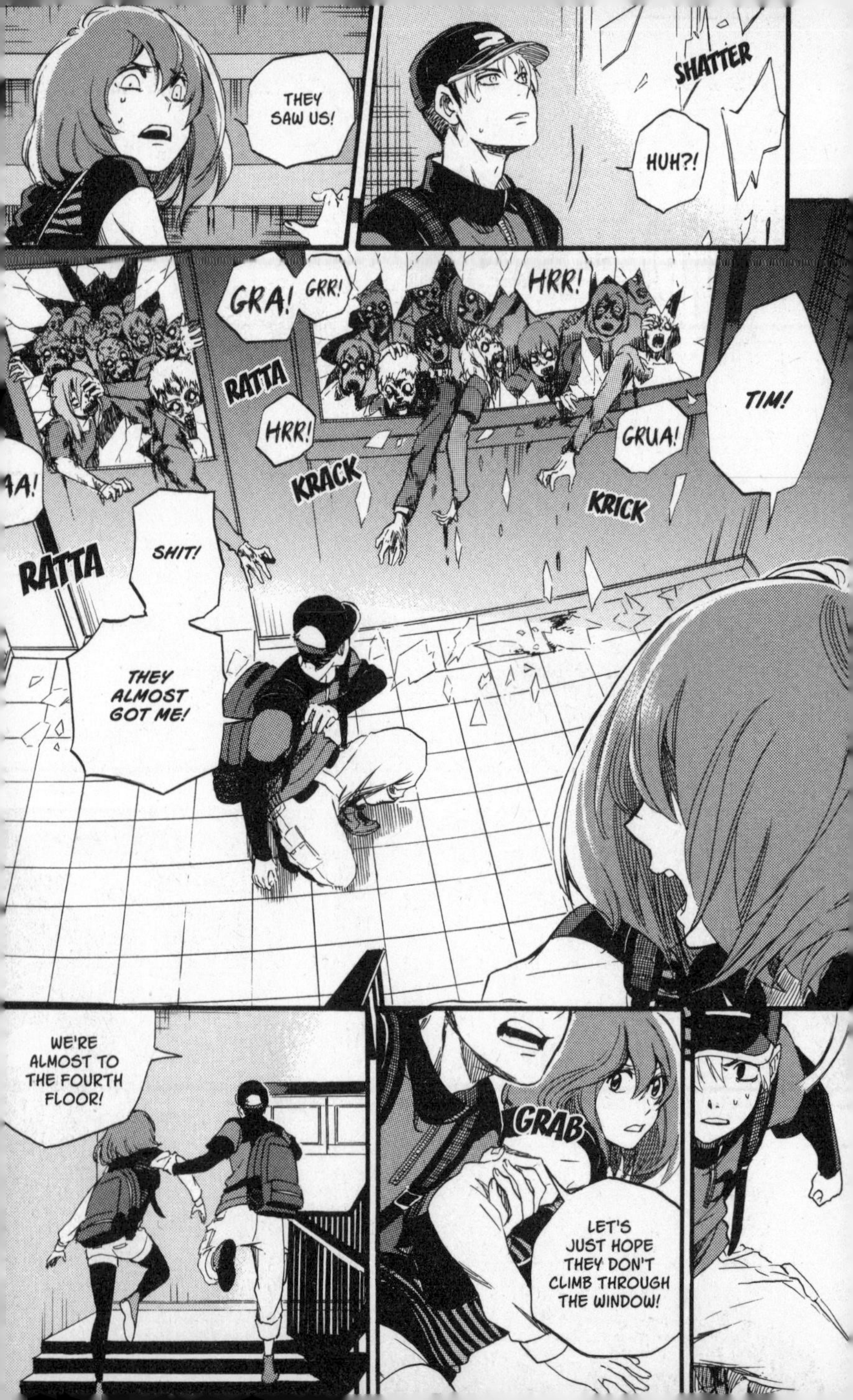
SHATTER
HUH?!
THEY SAW US!
TIM!
HRR!
GRUA!
GRR!
GRA!
RATTA
HRR!
KRACK
KRICK
SHIT!
RATTA
THEY ALMOST GOT ME!
GRAB
LET'S JUST HOPE THEY DON'T CLIMB THROUGH THE WINDOW!
WE'RE ALMOST TO THE FOURTH FLOOR!

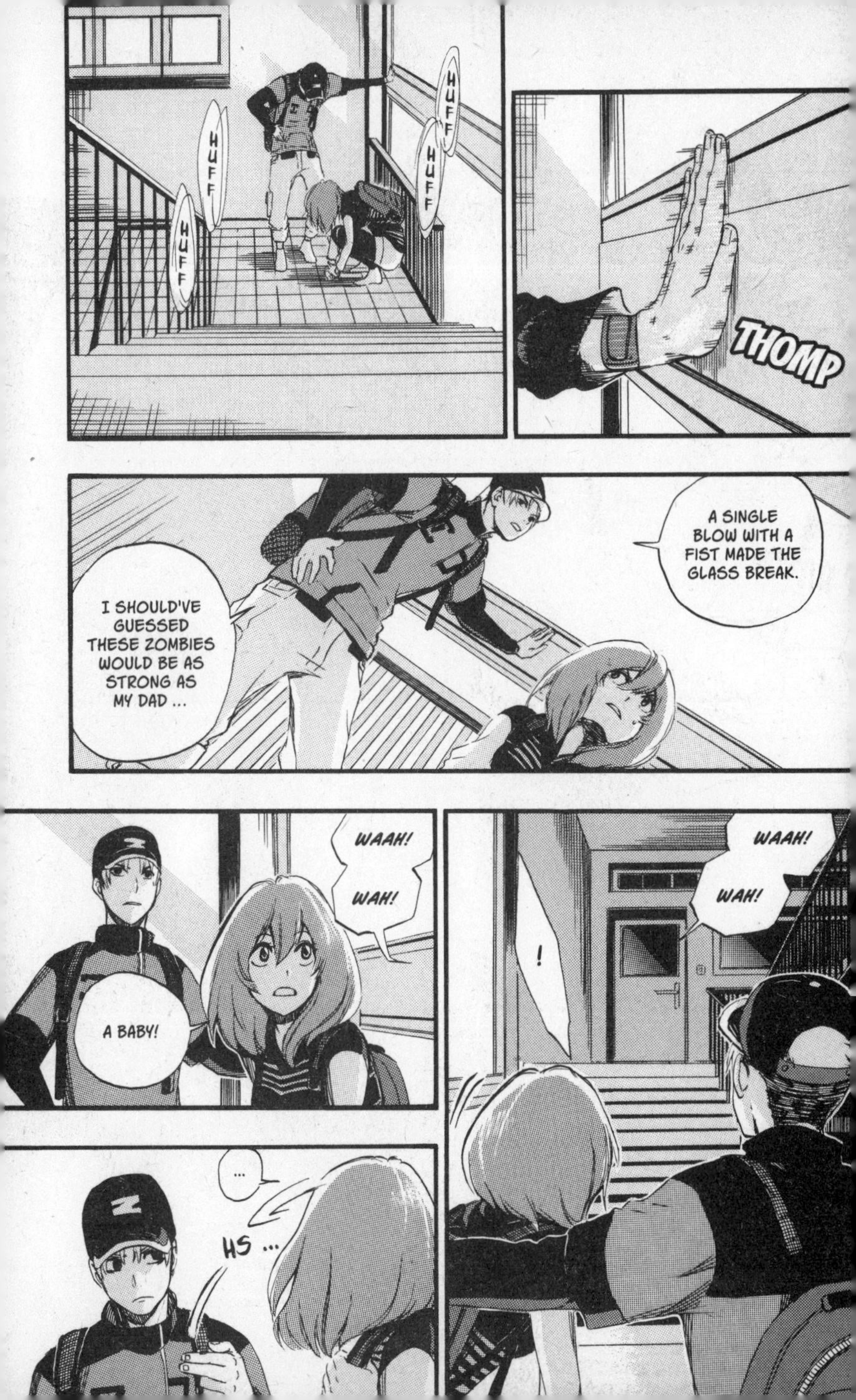
THOMP
HUFF
HUFF
HUFF
HUFF
A SINGLE BLOW WITH A FIST MADE THE GLASS BREAK.
I SHOULD'VE GUESSED THESE ZOMBIES WOULD BE AS STRONG AS MY DAD ...
WAAH!
WAH!
!
WAAH!
WAH!
A BABY!
...
HS ...

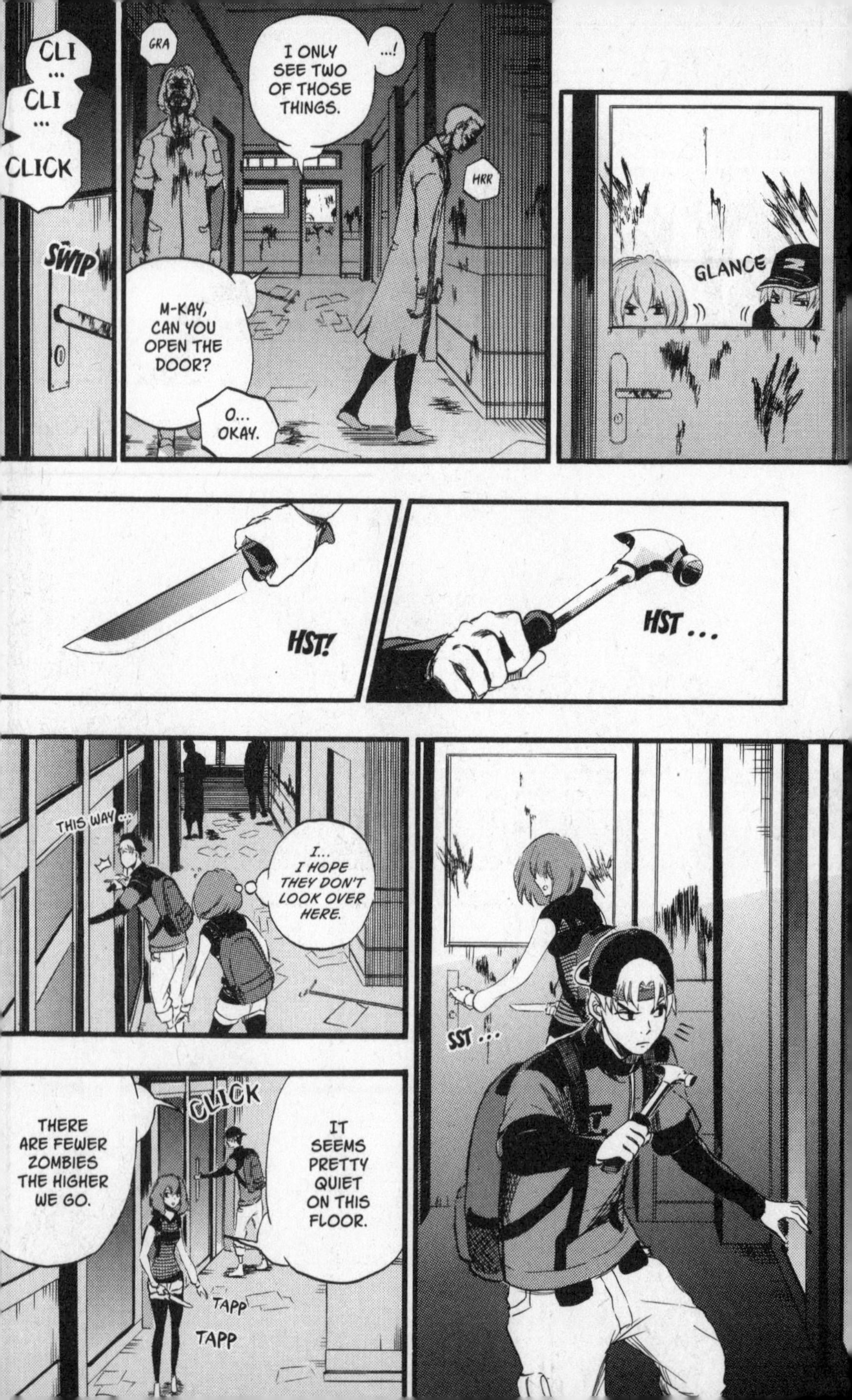
GLANCE
...!
I ONLY SEE TWO OF THOSE THINGS.
HRR
GRA
M-KAY, CAN YOU OPEN THE DOOR?
O... OKAY.
CLI ... CLI ... CLICK
SWIP
HST ...
HST!
SST ...
I... I HOPE THEY DON'T LOOK OVER HERE.
THIS WAY ...
IT SEEMS PRETTY QUIET ON THIS FLOOR.
CLICK
THERE ARE FEWER ZOMBIES THE HIGHER WE GO.
TAPP
TAPP

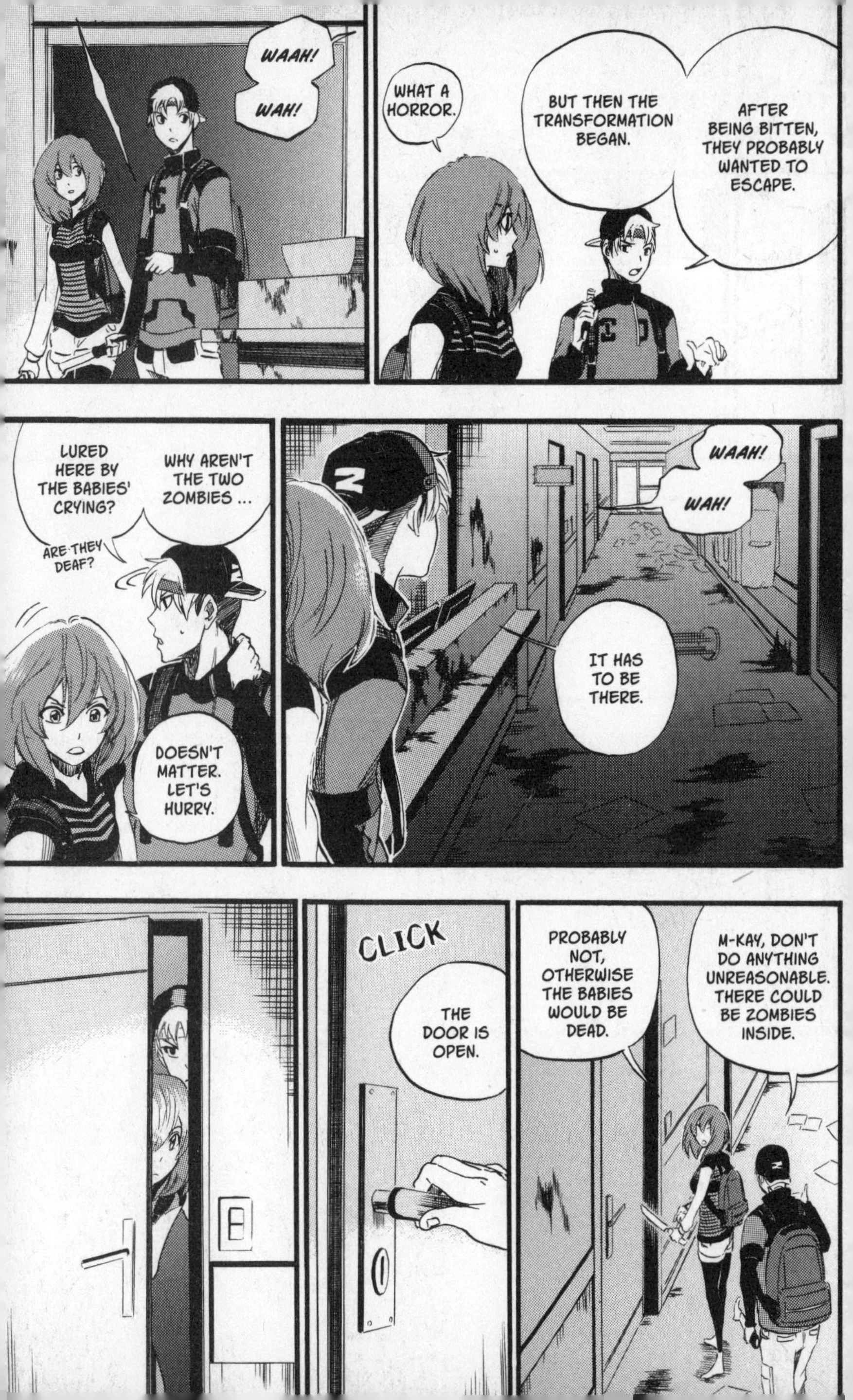
AFTER BEING BITTEN, THEY PROBABLY WANTED TO ESCAPE.
BUT THEN THE TRANSFORMATION BEGAN.
WHAT A HORROR.
WAAH!
WAH!
WAAH!
WAH!
IT HAS TO BE THERE.
WHY AREN'T THE TWO ZOMBIES ...
LURED HERE BY THE BABIES' CRYING?
ARE THEY DEAF?
DOESN'T MATTER. LET'S HURRY.
M-KAY, DON'T DO ANYTHING UNREASONABLE. THERE COULD BE ZOMBIES INSIDE.
PROBABLY NOT, OTHERWISE THE BABIES WOULD BE DEAD.
CLICK
THE DOOR IS OPEN.

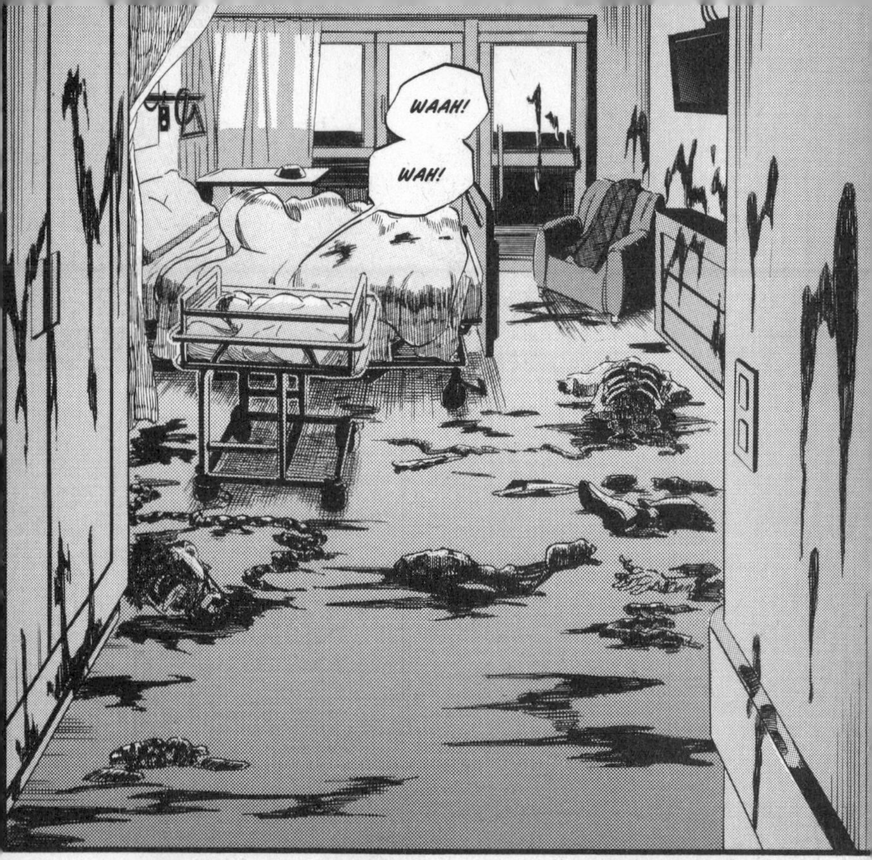
WAAH!
WAH!

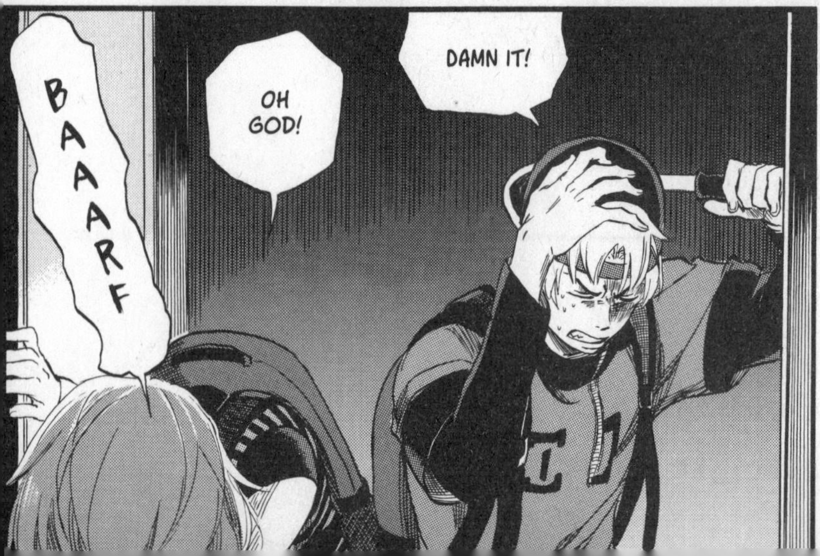
DAMN IT!
OH GOD!
BAAARF

UGH...

IT'S JUST LIKE WHAT HAPPENED YESTERDAY.

TIM?

WAAH!

WAH!

WAH!

...

EWW! THE HEAD!

CREETCH!

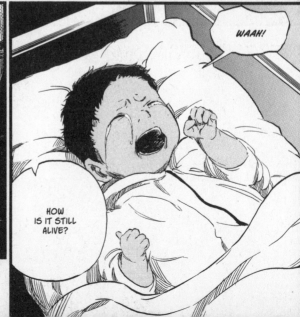

WAAH!

HOW IS IT STILL ALIVE?

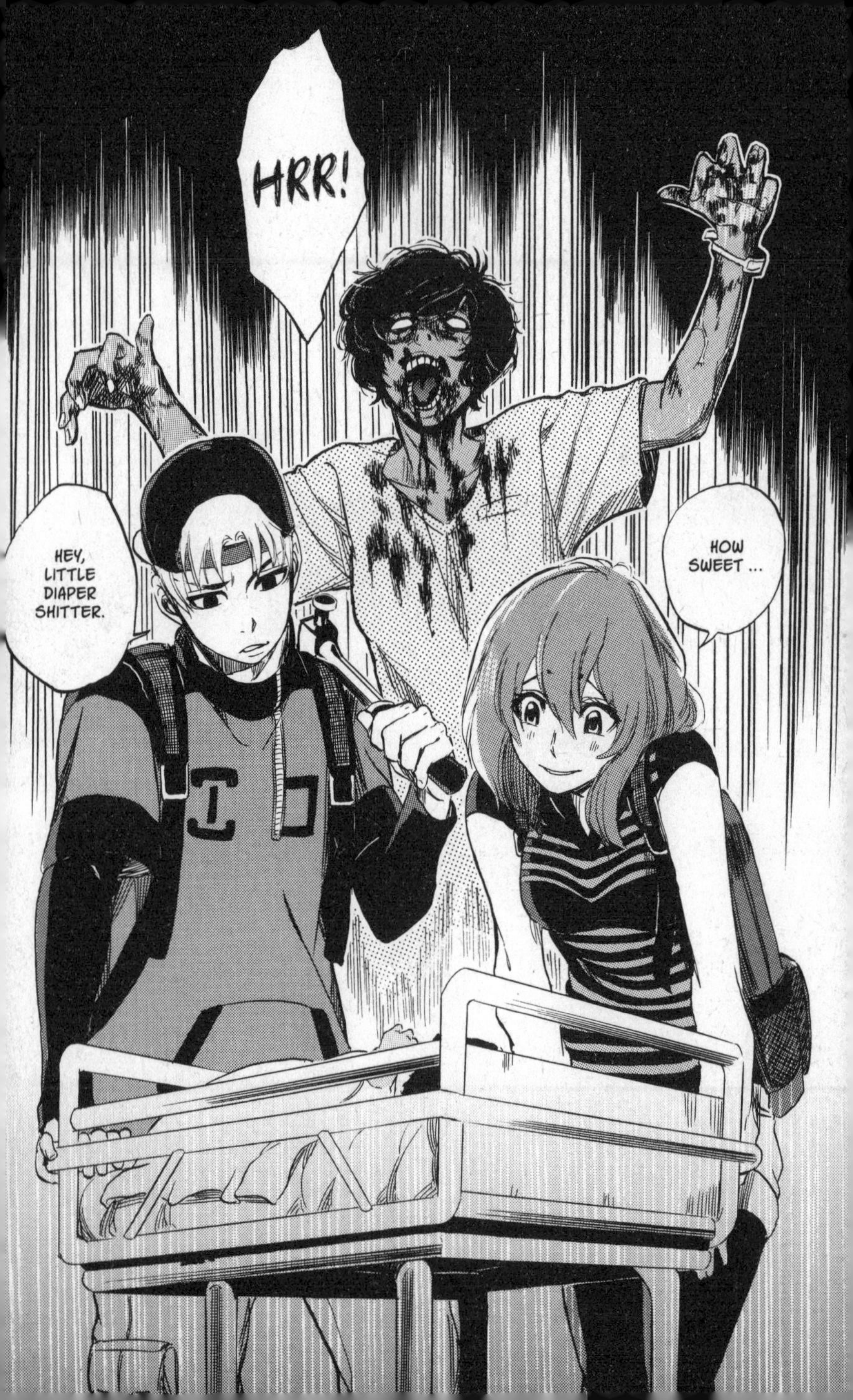
HRR!
HOW SWEET ...
HEY, LITTLE DIAPER SHITTER.

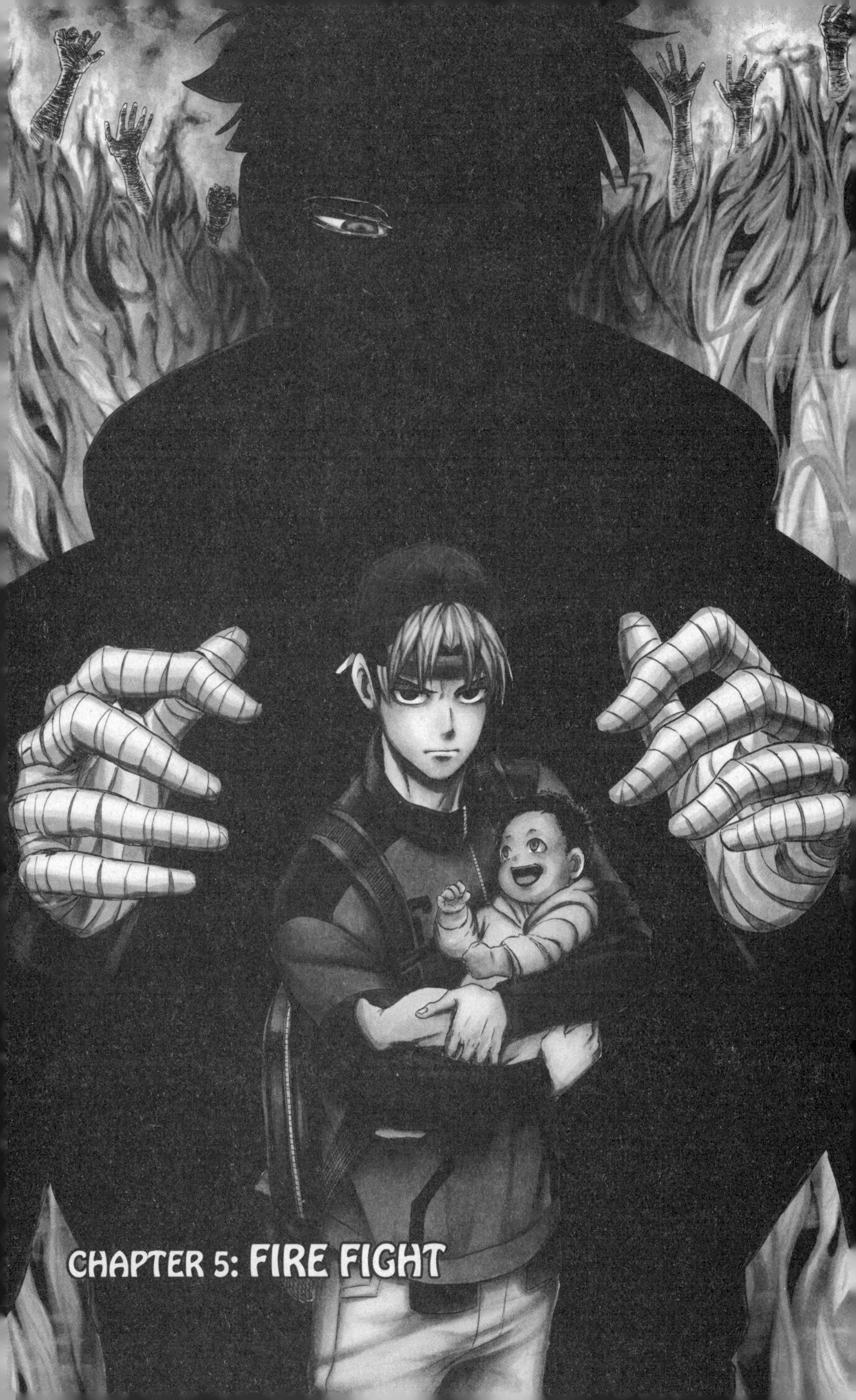
CHAPTER 5: FIRE FIGHT

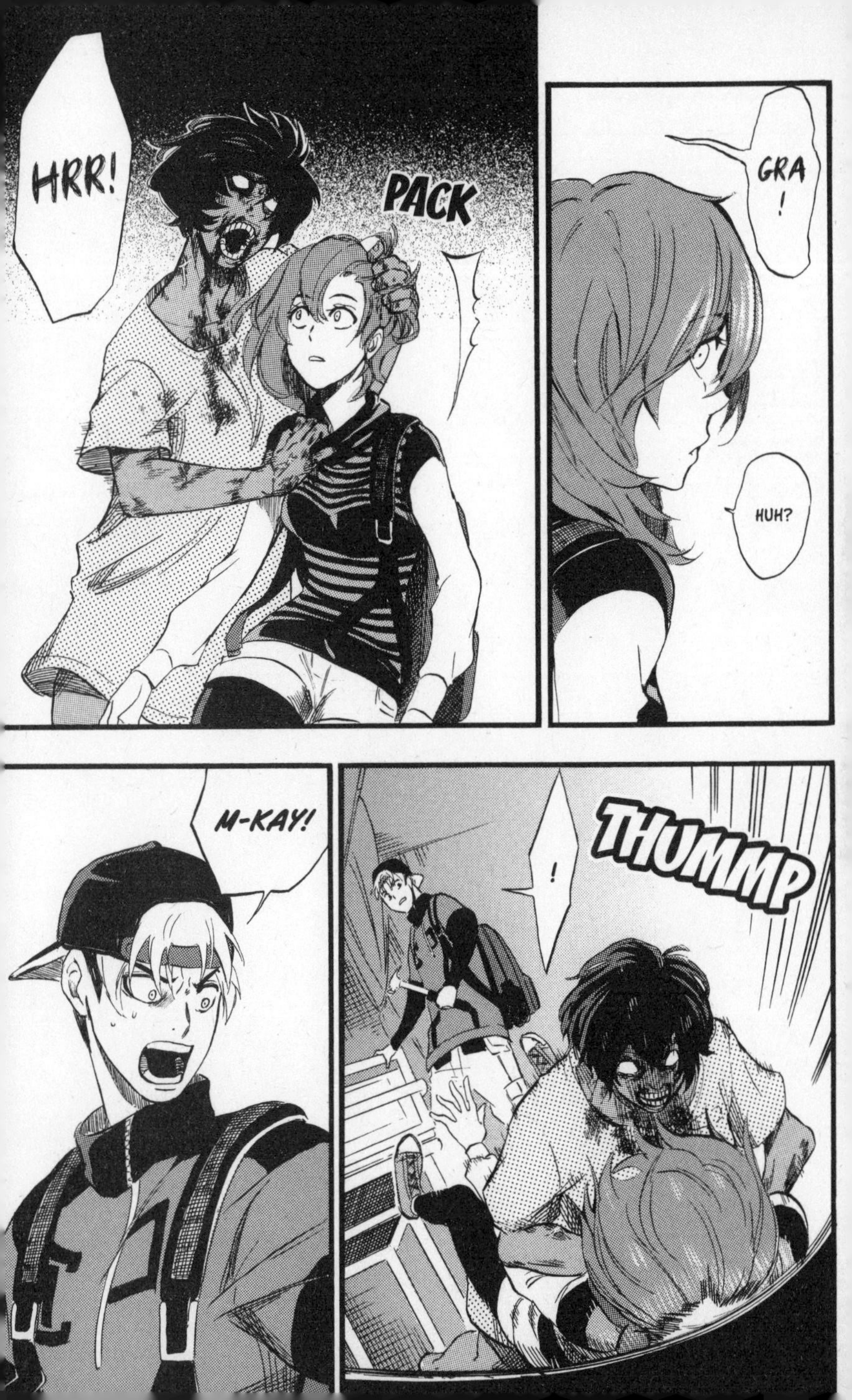
GRA!
HUH?
PACK
HRR!
THUMMP
!
M-KAY!

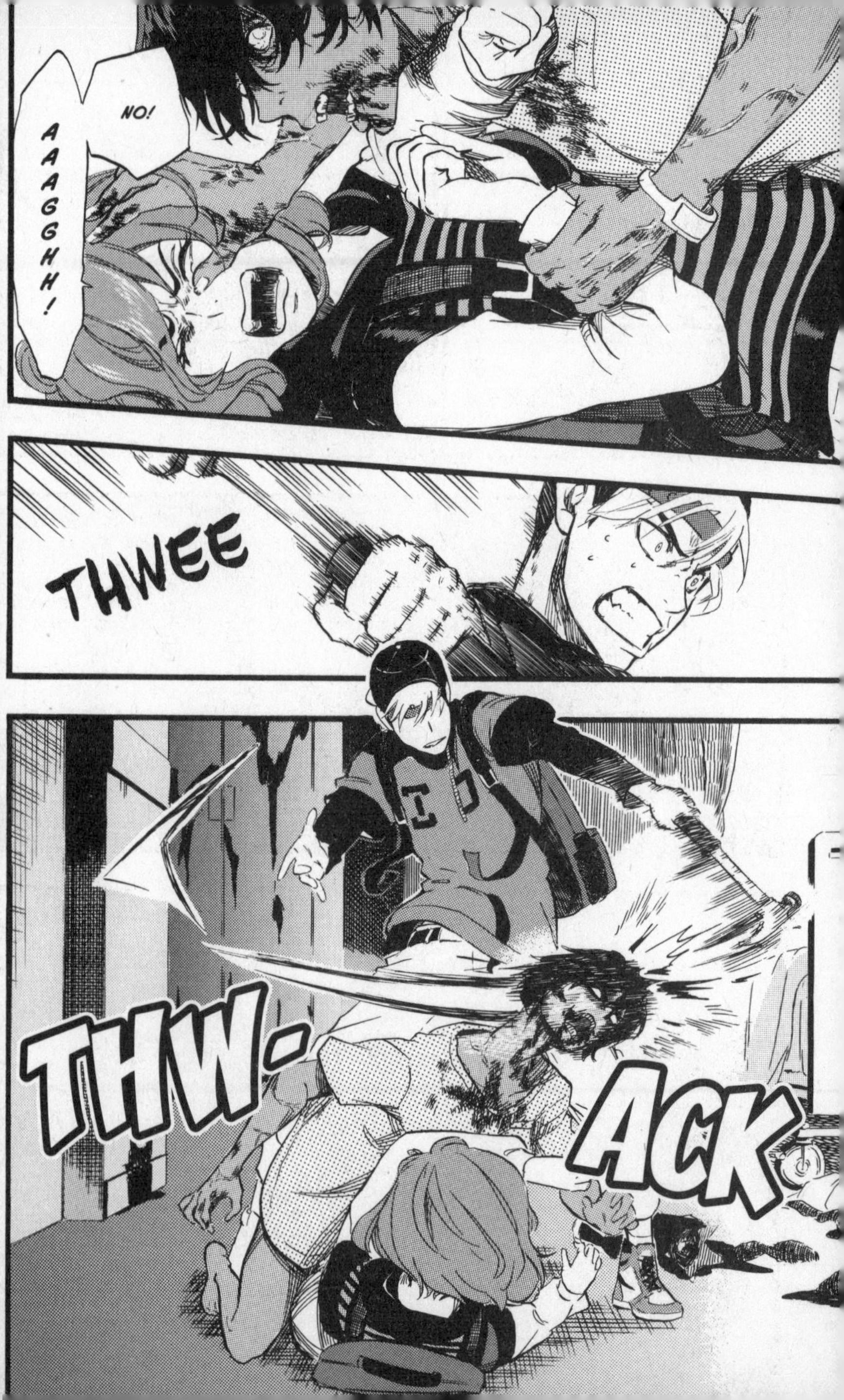
NO!
AAAAGGHH!
THWEE
THW-
ACK

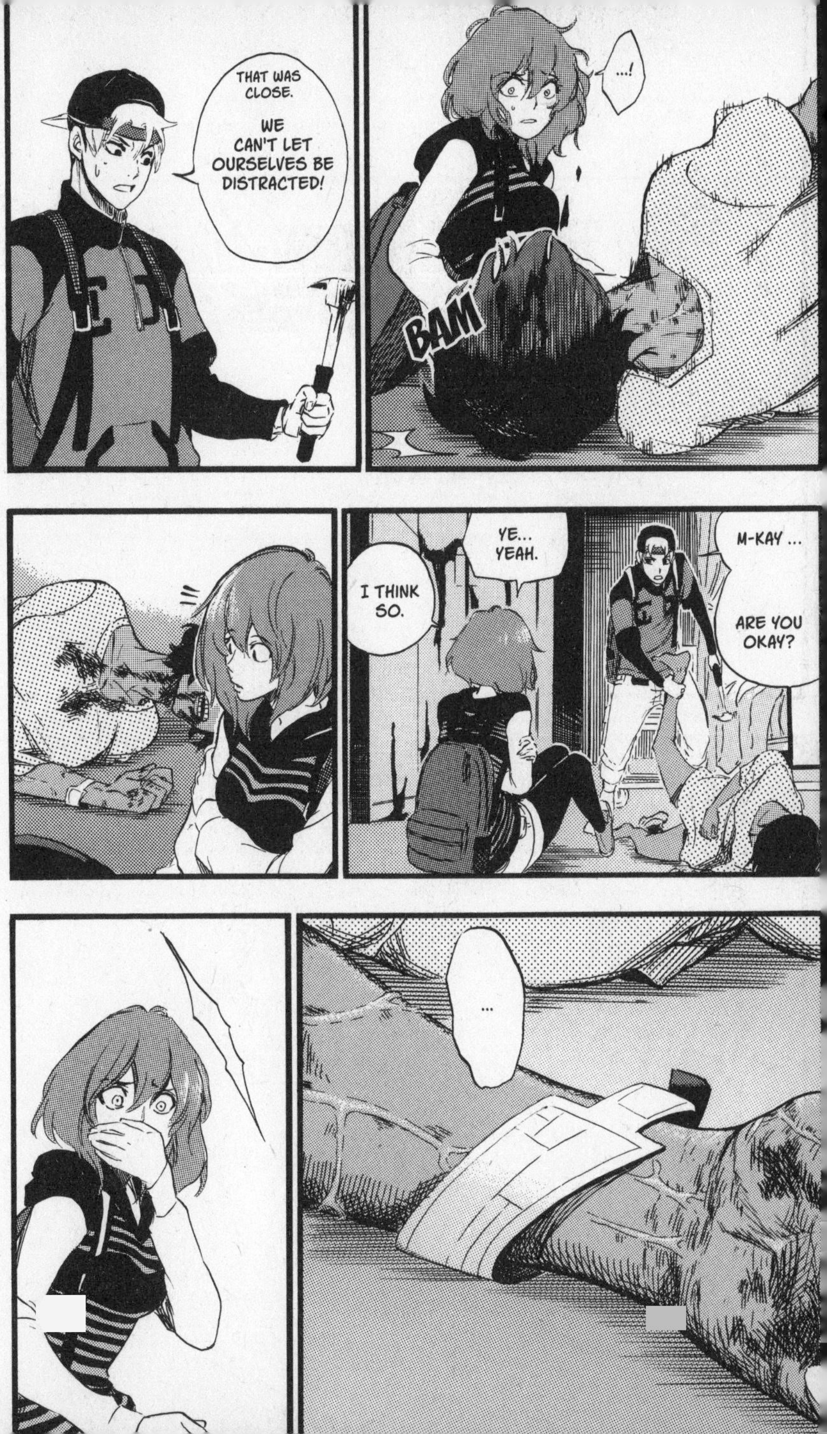
...!
THAT WAS CLOSE.
WE CAN'T LET OURSELVES BE DISTRACTED!
BAM
M-KAY ...
ARE YOU OKAY?
YE... YEAH.
I THINK SO.
...

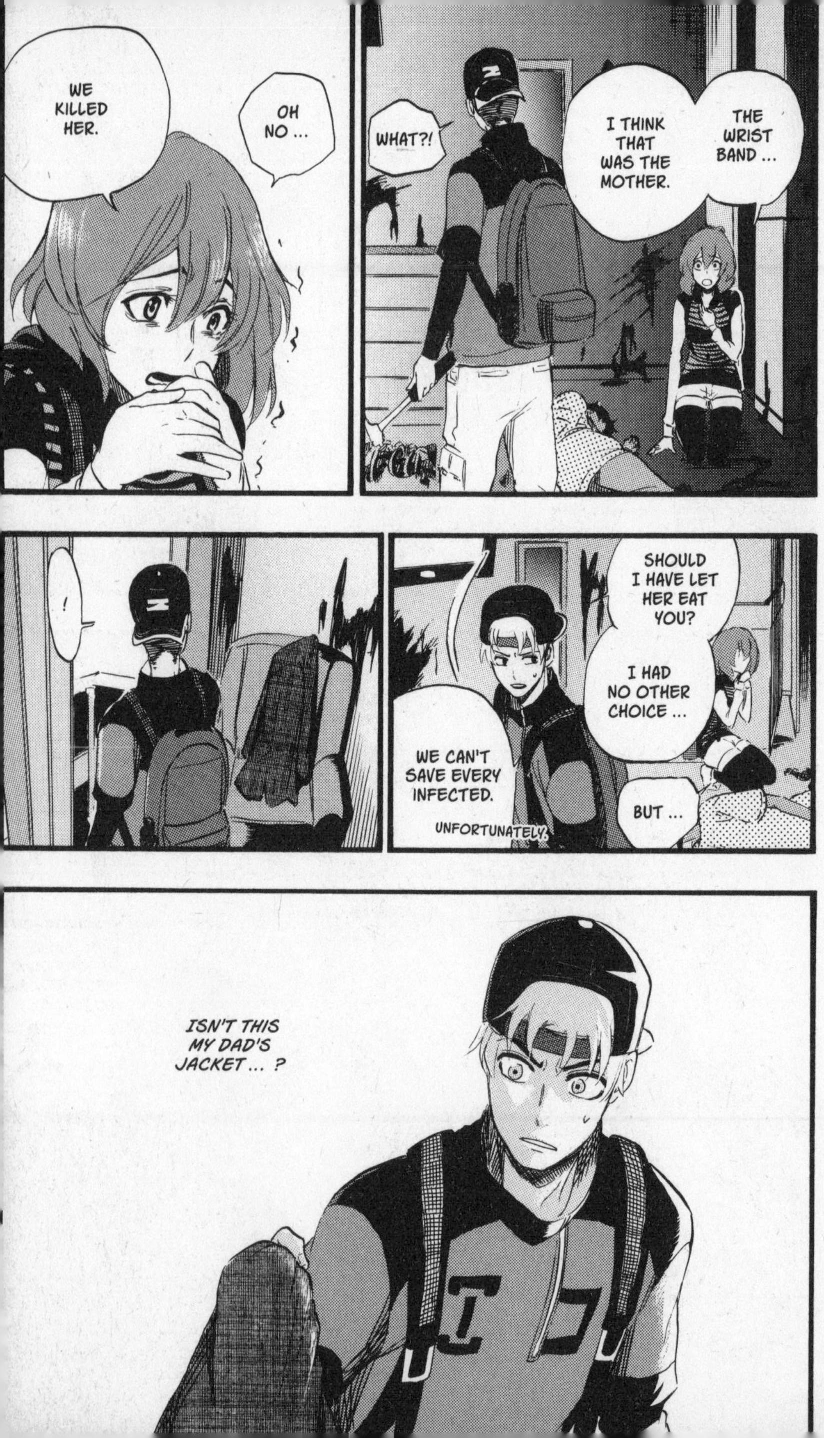
THE WRIST BAND ...
I THINK THAT WAS THE MOTHER.
WHAT?!
OH NO ...
WE KILLED HER.
SHOULD I HAVE LET HER EAT YOU?
I HAD NO OTHER CHOICE ...
BUT ...
WE CAN'T SAVE EVERY INFECTED.
UNFORTUNATELY.
!
ISN'T THIS MY DAD'S JACKET ... ?

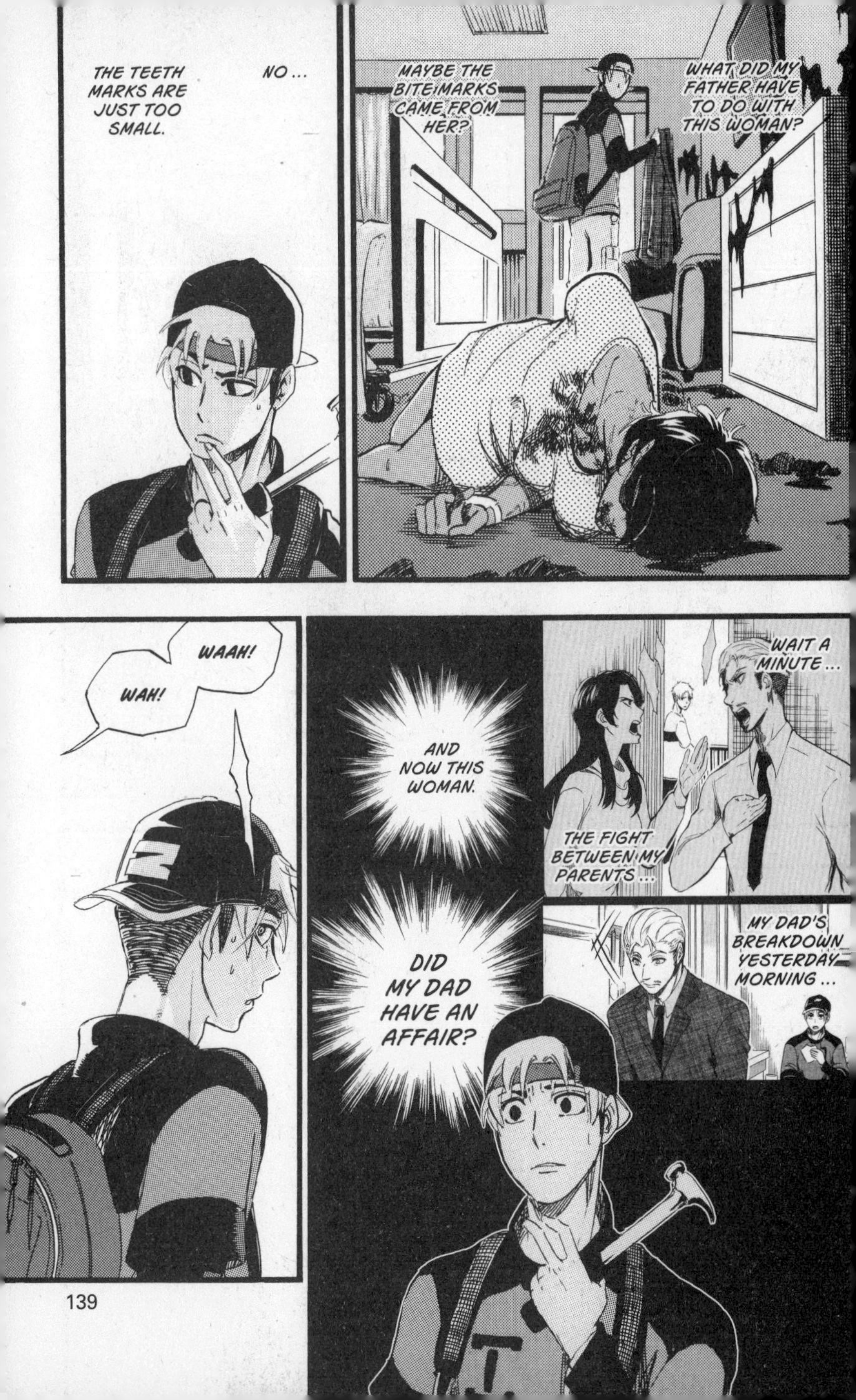
WHAT DID MY FATHER HAVE TO DO WITH THIS WOMAN?
MAYBE THE BITE MARKS CAME FROM HER?
NO ...
THE TEETH MARKS ARE JUST TOO SMALL.
WAIT A MINUTE ...
THE FIGHT BETWEEN MY PARENTS ...
MY DAD'S BREAKDOWN YESTERDAY MORNING ...
AND NOW THIS WOMAN.
DID MY DAD HAVE AN AFFAIR?
WAAH!
WAH!

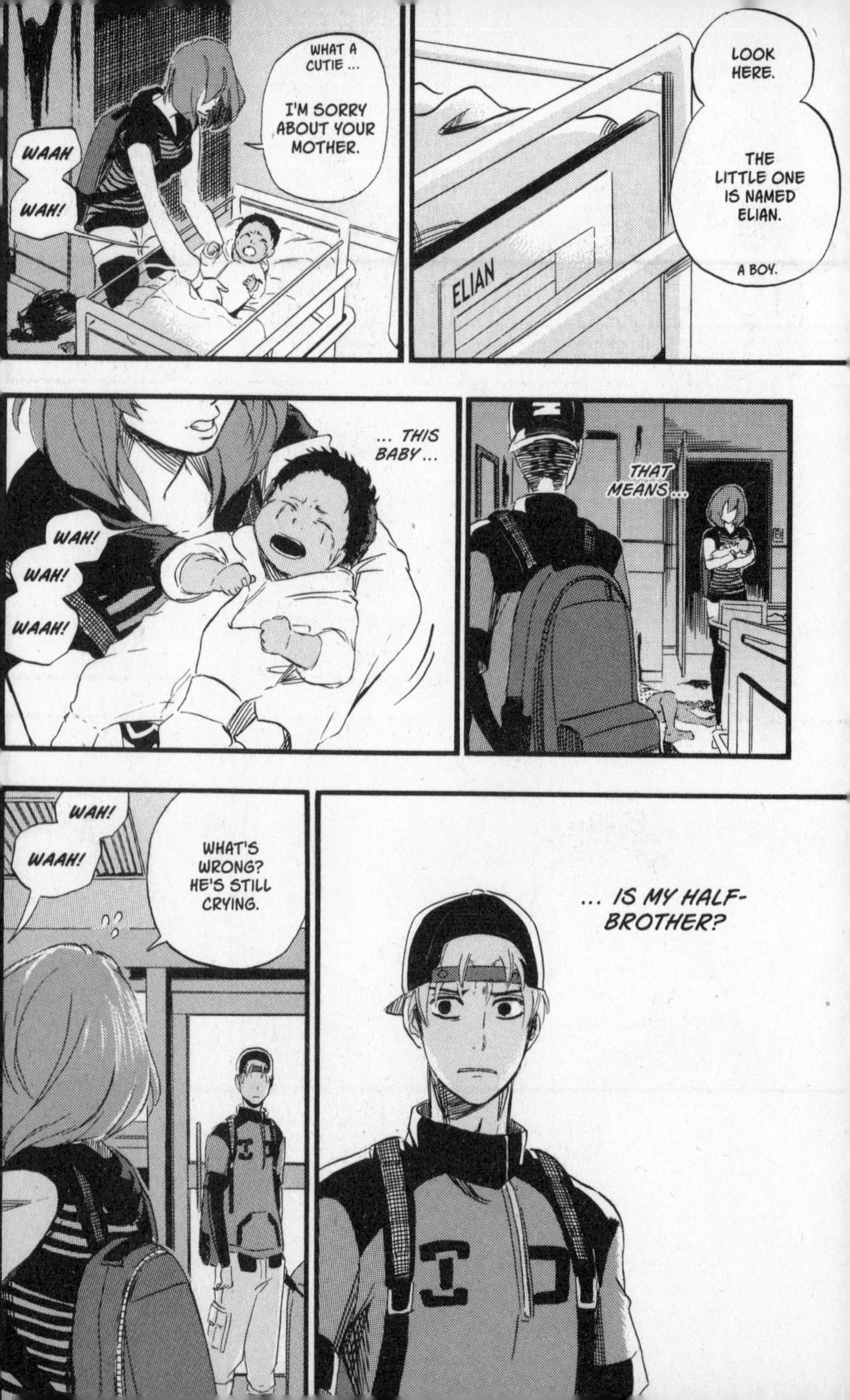
LOOK HERE.
THE LITTLE ONE IS NAMED ELIAN.
A BOY.
ELIAN
WHAT A CUTIE ...
I'M SORRY ABOUT YOUR MOTHER.
WAAH
WAH!
THAT MEANS ...
... THIS BABY ...
WAH!
WAH!
WAAH!
... IS MY HALF-BROTHER?
WAH!
WAAH!
WHAT'S WRONG? HE'S STILL CRYING.

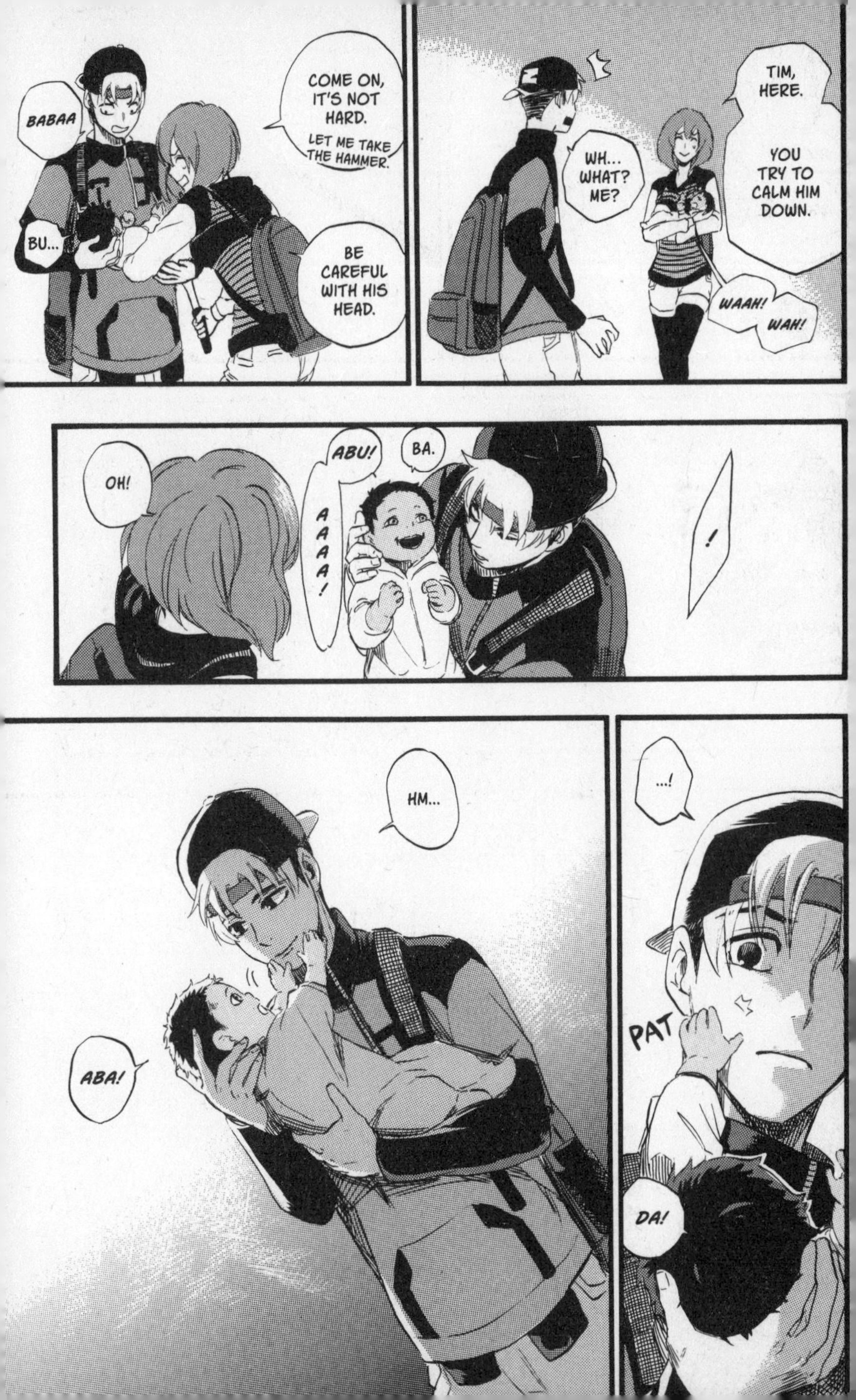
TIM, HERE.
YOU TRY TO CALM HIM DOWN.
WH... WHAT? ME?
WAAH!
WAH!
COME ON, IT'S NOT HARD.
LET ME TAKE THE HAMMER.
BABAA
BE CAREFUL WITH HIS HEAD.
BU...
!
BA.
ABU!
AAAAA!
OH!
...!
PAT
DA!
HM...
ABA!

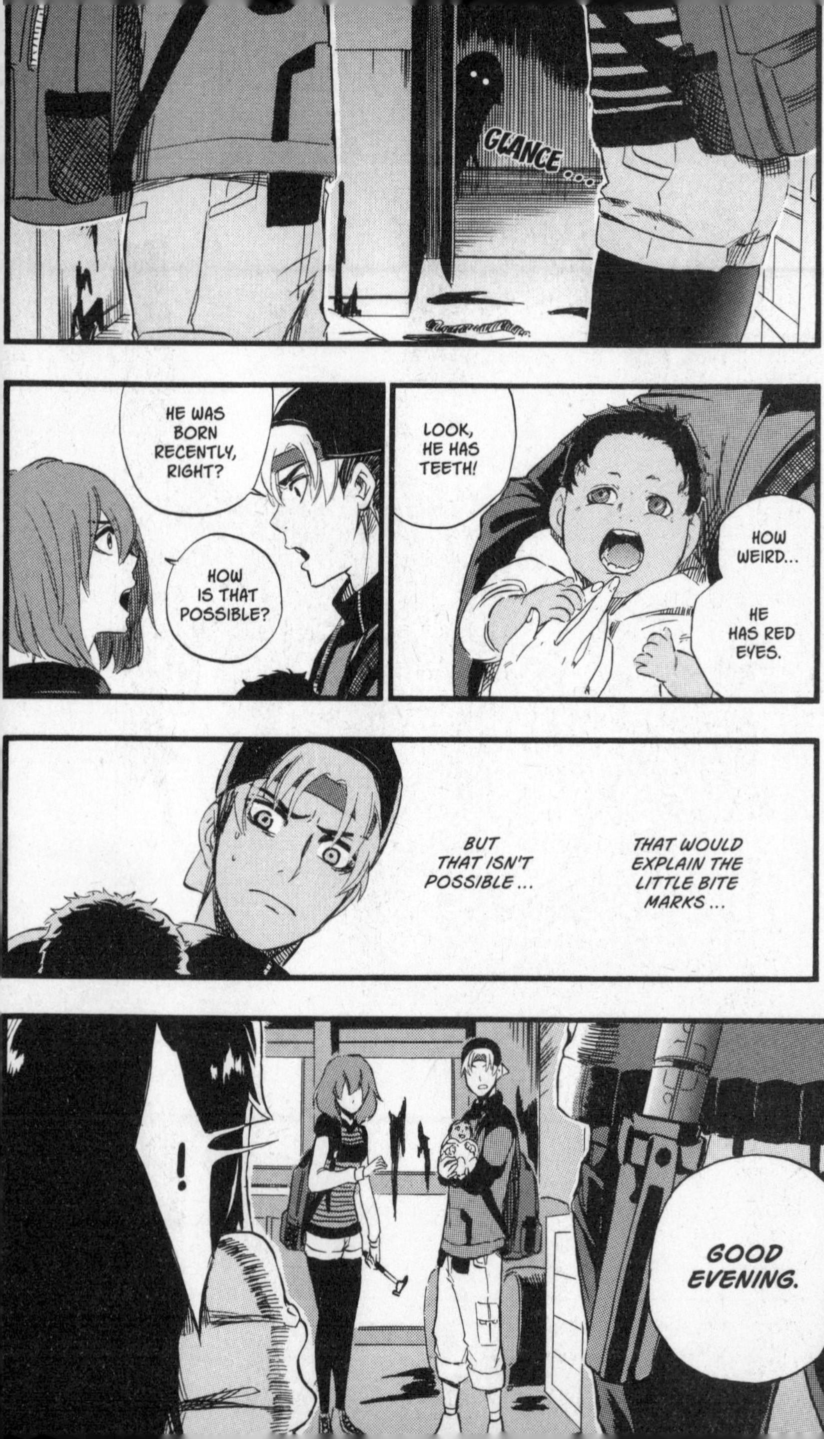
GLANCE...
LOOK, HE HAS TEETH!
HOW WEIRD...
HE HAS RED EYES.
HE WAS BORN RECENTLY, RIGHT?
HOW IS THAT POSSIBLE?
THAT WOULD EXPLAIN THE LITTLE BITE MARKS ...
BUT THAT ISN'T POSSIBLE ...
GOOD EVENING.
!

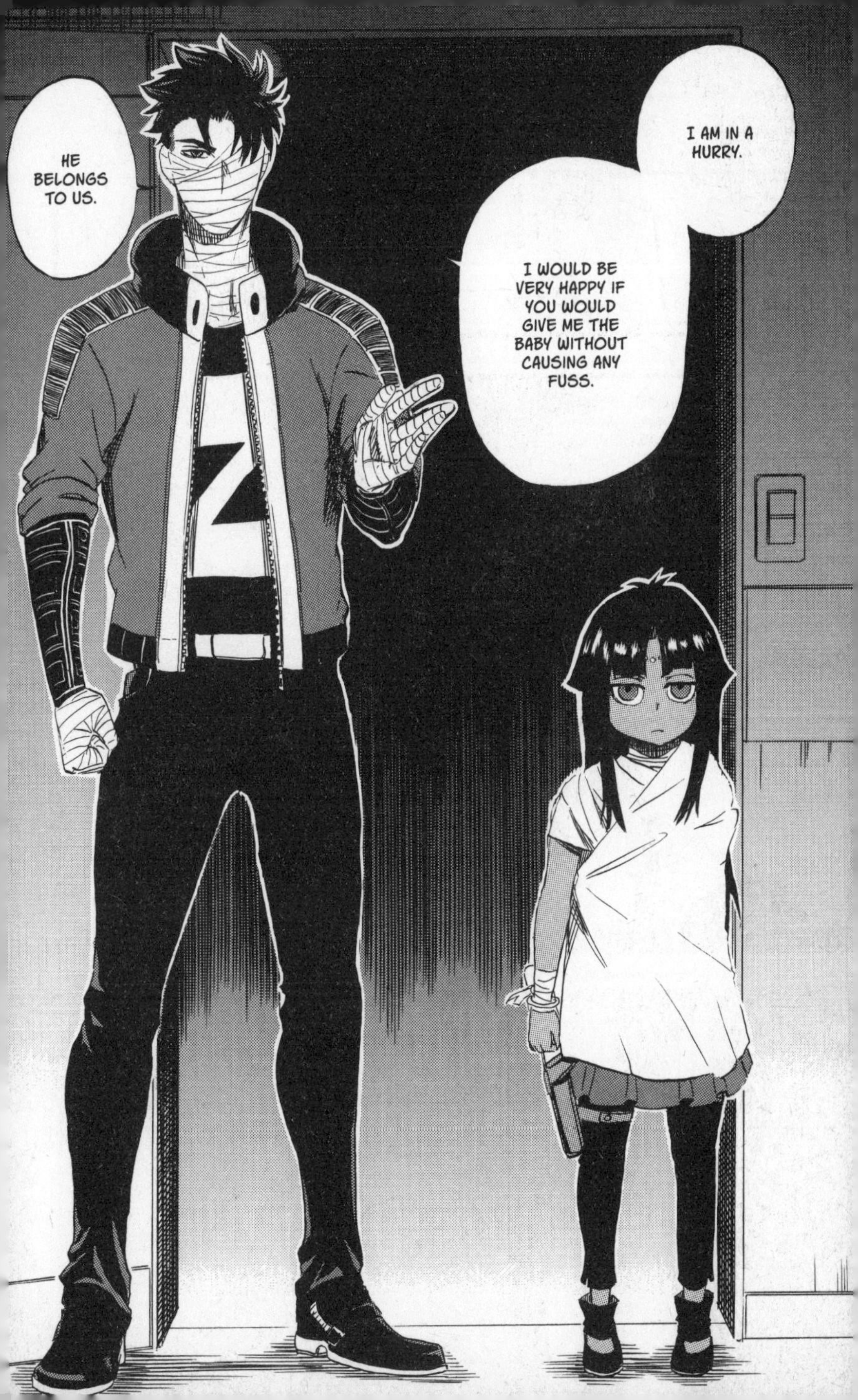
I AM IN A HURRY.
I WOULD BE VERY HAPPY IF YOU WOULD GIVE ME THE BABY WITHOUT CAUSING ANY FUSS.
HE BELONGS TO US.

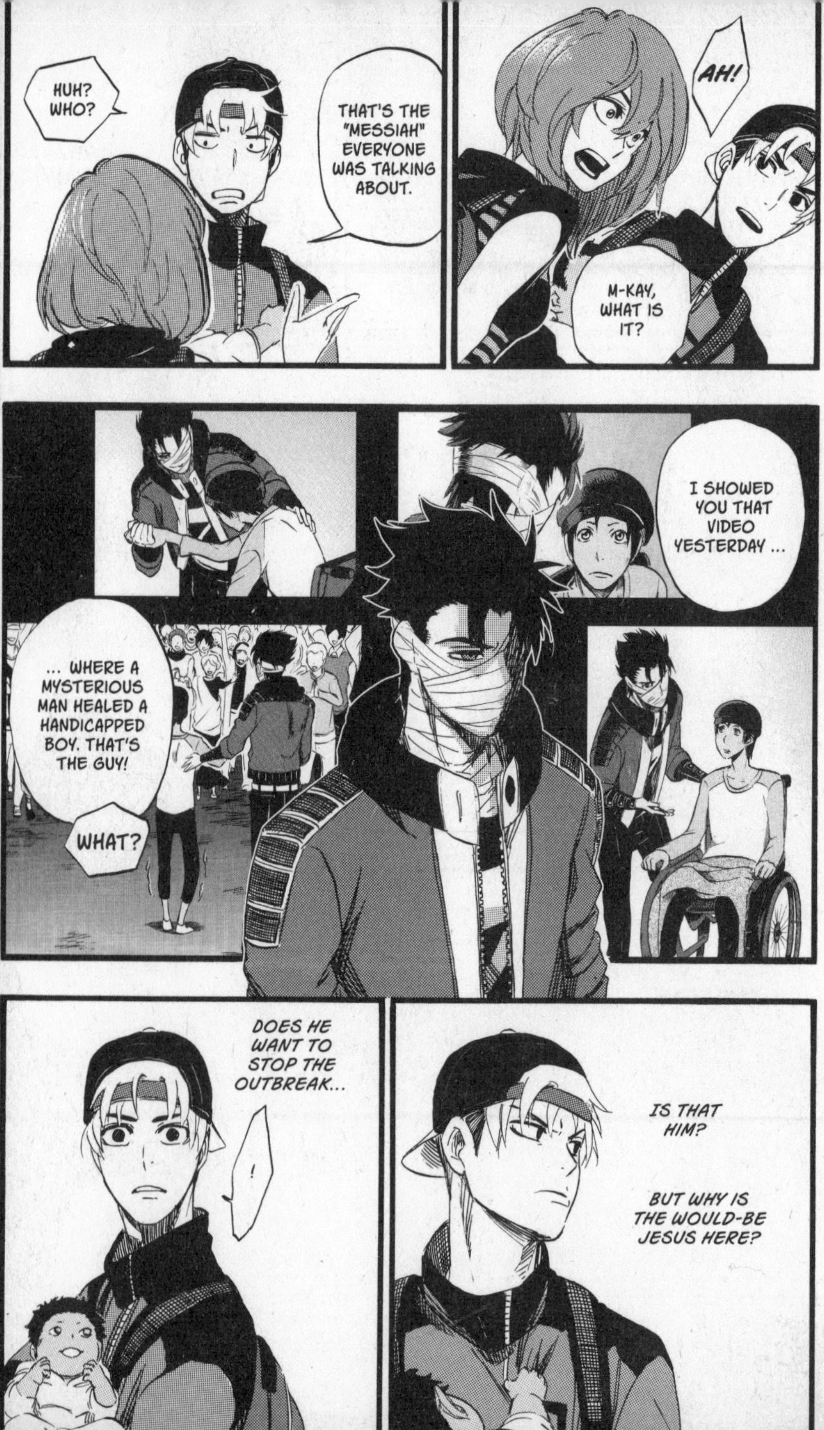
AH!
M-KAY, WHAT IS IT?
THAT'S THE "MESSIAH" EVERYONE WAS TALKING ABOUT.
HUH? WHO?
I SHOWED YOU THAT VIDEO YESTERDAY ...
... WHERE A MYSTERIOUS MAN HEALED A HANDICAPPED BOY. THAT'S THE GUY!
WHAT?
IS THAT HIM?
BUT WHY IS THE WOULD-BE JESUS HERE?
DOES HE WANT TO STOP THE OUTBREAK...
!

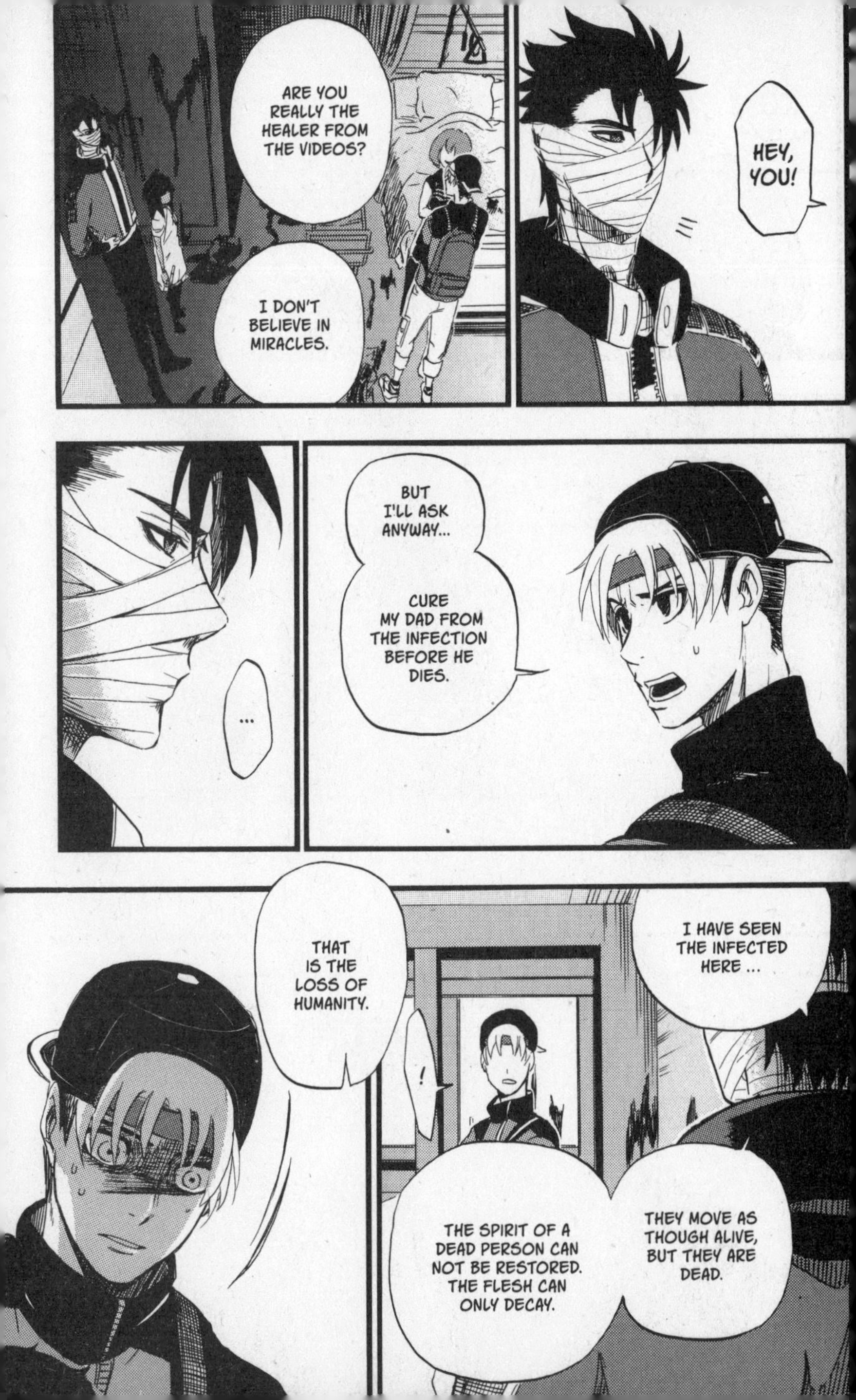
HEY, YOU!
ARE YOU REALLY THE HEALER FROM THE VIDEOS?
I DON'T BELIEVE IN MIRACLES.
BUT I'LL ASK ANYWAY...
CURE MY DAD FROM THE INFECTION BEFORE HE DIES.
...
I HAVE SEEN THE INFECTED HERE ...
THEY MOVE AS THOUGH ALIVE, BUT THEY ARE DEAD.
THE SPIRIT OF A DEAD PERSON CAN NOT BE RESTORED. THE FLESH CAN ONLY DECAY.
THAT IS THE LOSS OF HUMANITY.
!

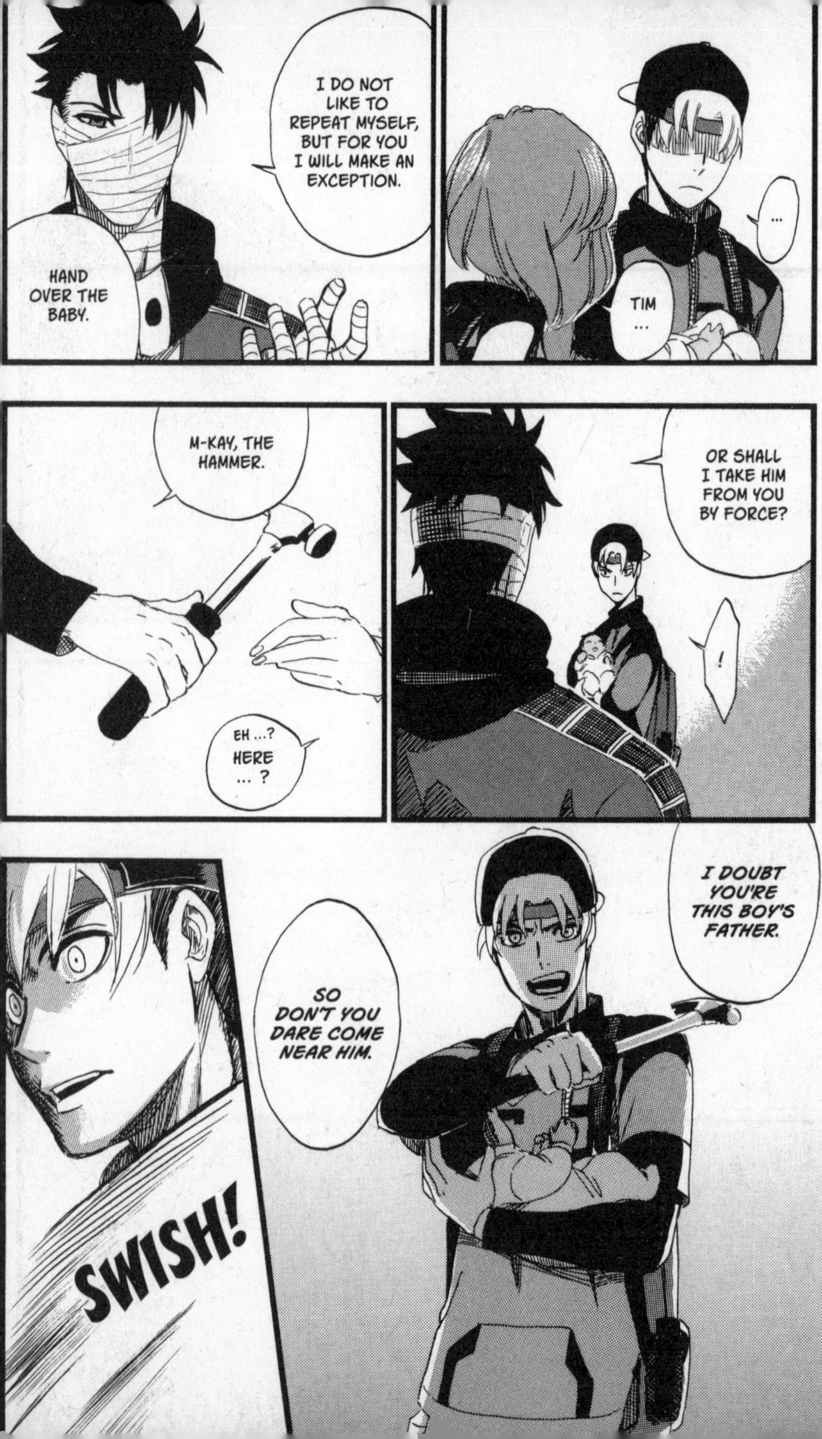
...
TIM ...
I DO NOT LIKE TO REPEAT MYSELF, BUT FOR YOU I WILL MAKE AN EXCEPTION.
HAND OVER THE BABY.
OR SHALL I TAKE HIM FROM YOU BY FORCE?
!
M-KAY, THE HAMMER.
EH ...? HERE ... ?
I DOUBT YOU'RE THIS BOY'S FATHER.
SO DON'T YOU DARE COME NEAR HIM.
SWISH!

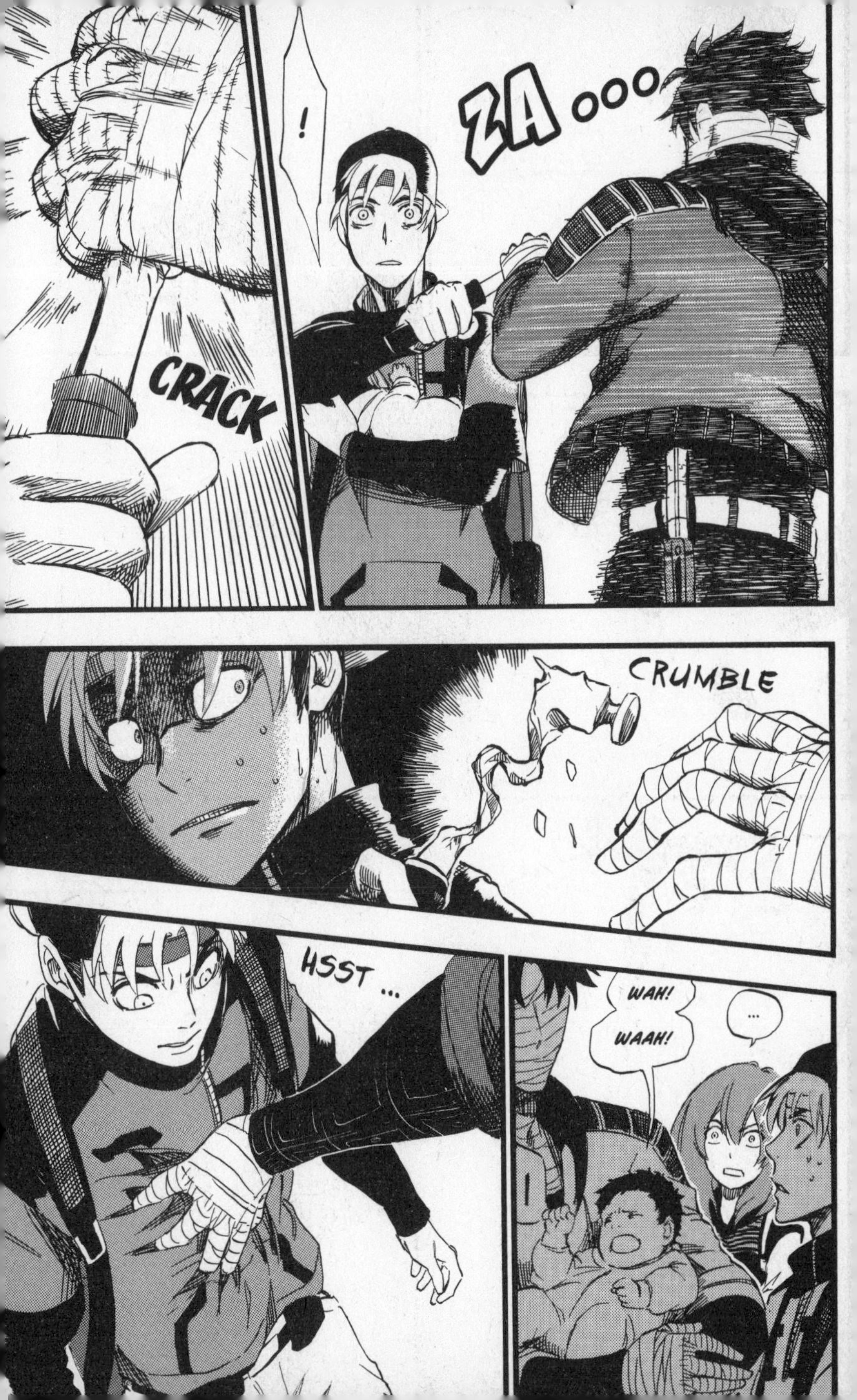
ZA ooo
!
CRACK
CRUMBLE
...
WAH!
WAAH!
HSST ...

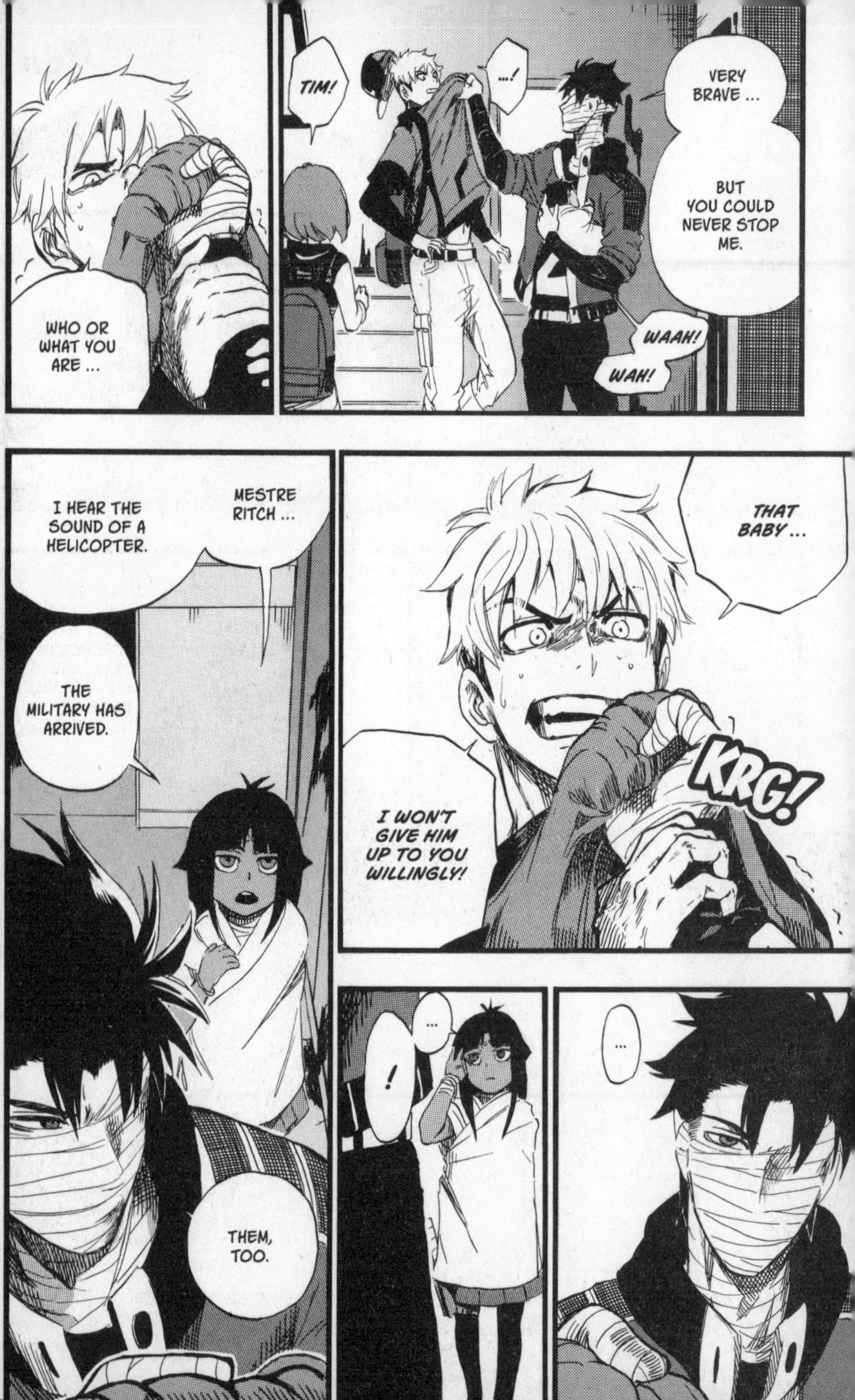
VERY BRAVE ...
BUT YOU COULD NEVER STOP ME.
...!
TIM!
WAAH!
WAH!
WHO OR WHAT YOU ARE ...
THAT BABY ...
KRG!
I WON'T GIVE HIM UP TO YOU WILLINGLY!
...
...
!
MESTRE RITCH ...
I HEAR THE SOUND OF A HELICOPTER.
THE MILITARY HAS ARRIVED.
THEM, TOO.

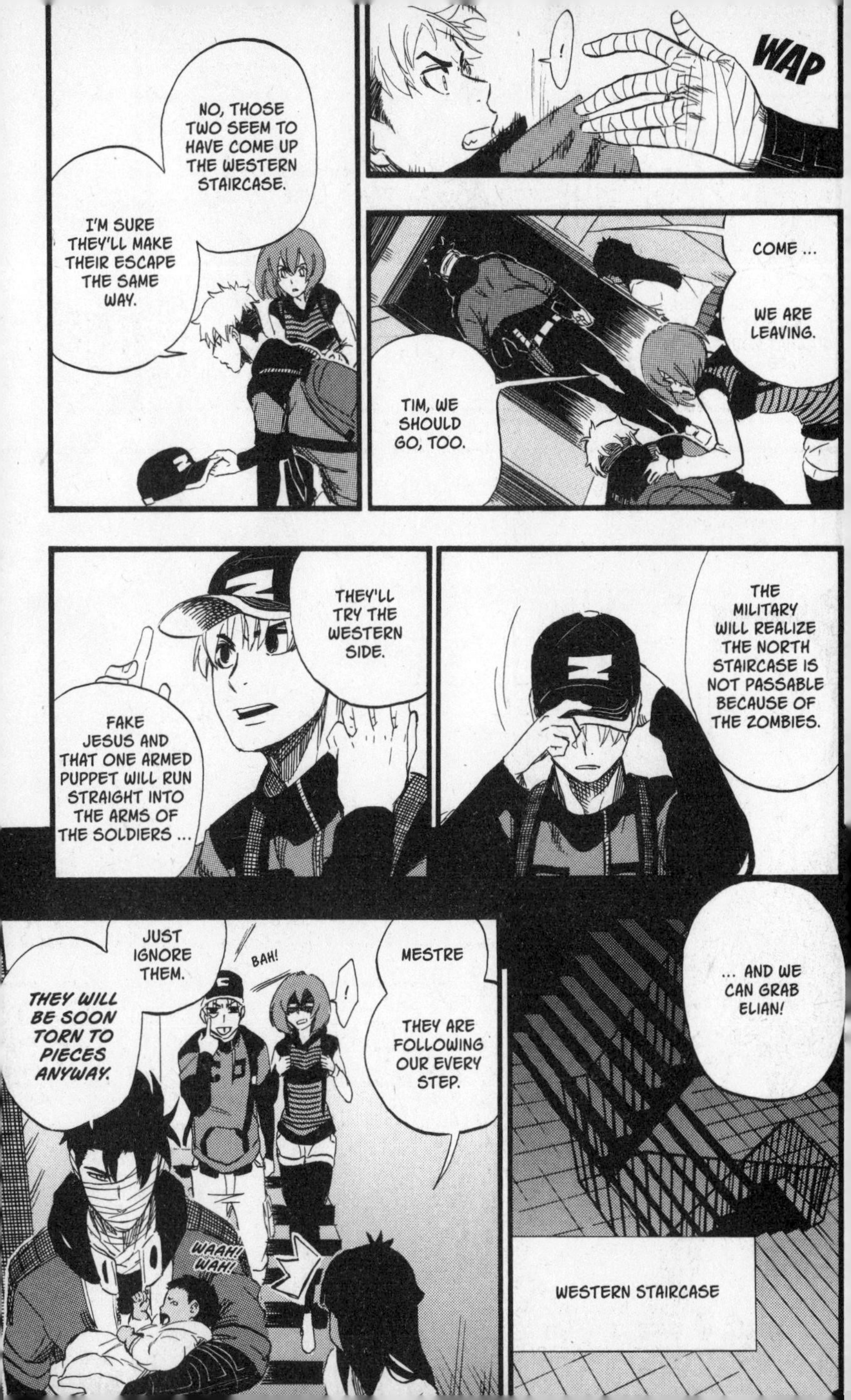
!
WAP
COME ...
WE ARE LEAVING.
TIM, WE SHOULD GO, TOO.
NO, THOSE TWO SEEM TO HAVE COME UP THE WESTERN STAIRCASE.
I'M SURE THEY'LL MAKE THEIR ESCAPE THE SAME WAY.
THE MILITARY WILL REALIZE THE NORTH STAIRCASE IS NOT PASSABLE BECAUSE OF THE ZOMBIES.
THEY'LL TRY THE WESTERN SIDE.
FAKE JESUS AND THAT ONE ARMED PUPPET WILL RUN STRAIGHT INTO THE ARMS OF THE SOLDIERS ...
... AND WE CAN GRAB ELIAN!
WESTERN STAIRCASE
MESTRE
THEY ARE FOLLOWING OUR EVERY STEP.
!
BAH!
JUST IGNORE THEM.
THEY WILL BE SOON TORN TO PIECES ANYWAY.
WAAH! WAH!

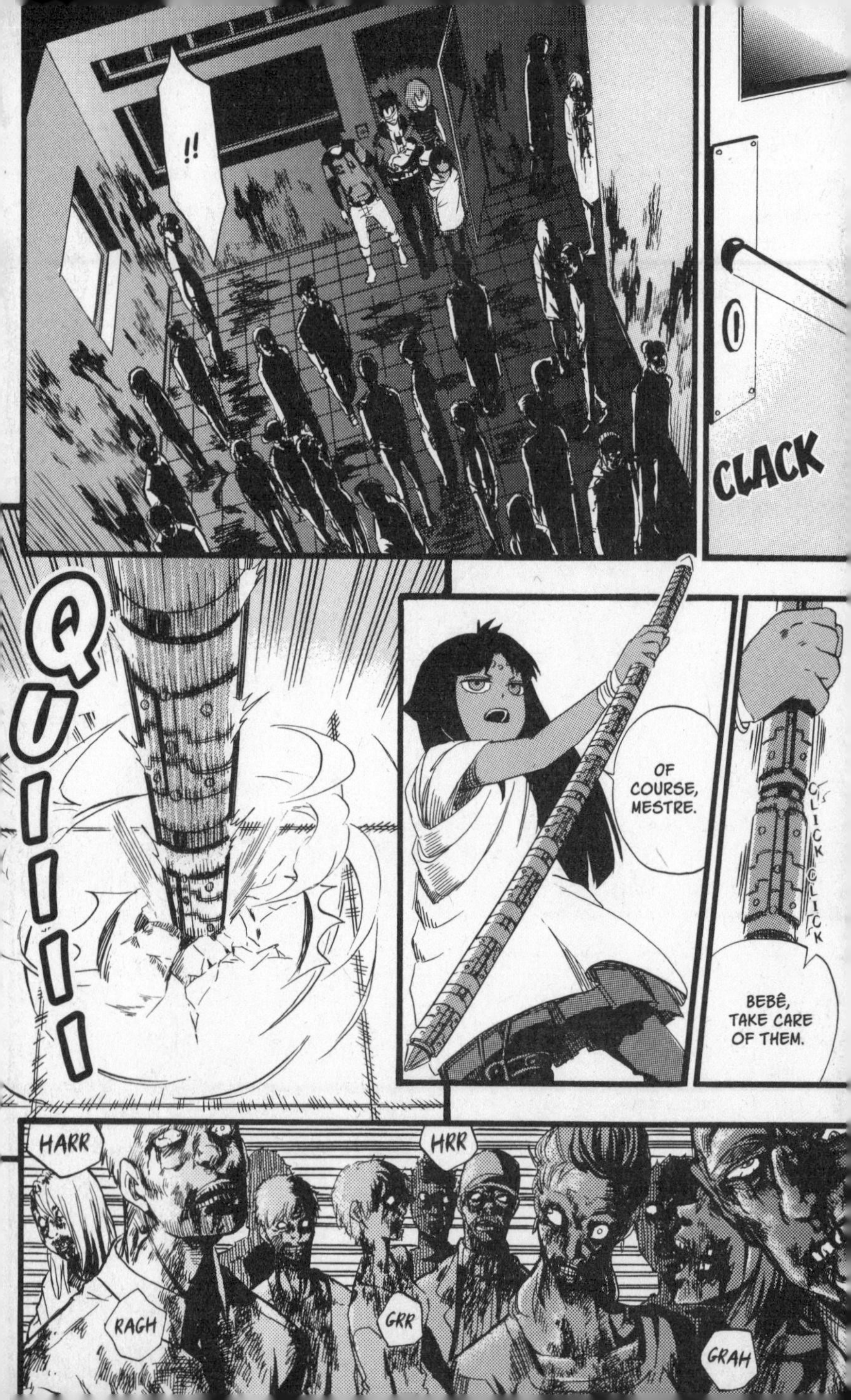
CLACK
!!
CLICK CLICK
BEBÊ, TAKE CARE OF THEM.
OF COURSE, MESTRE.
AQUIIIII
HRR
HARR
GRAH
GRR
RAGH

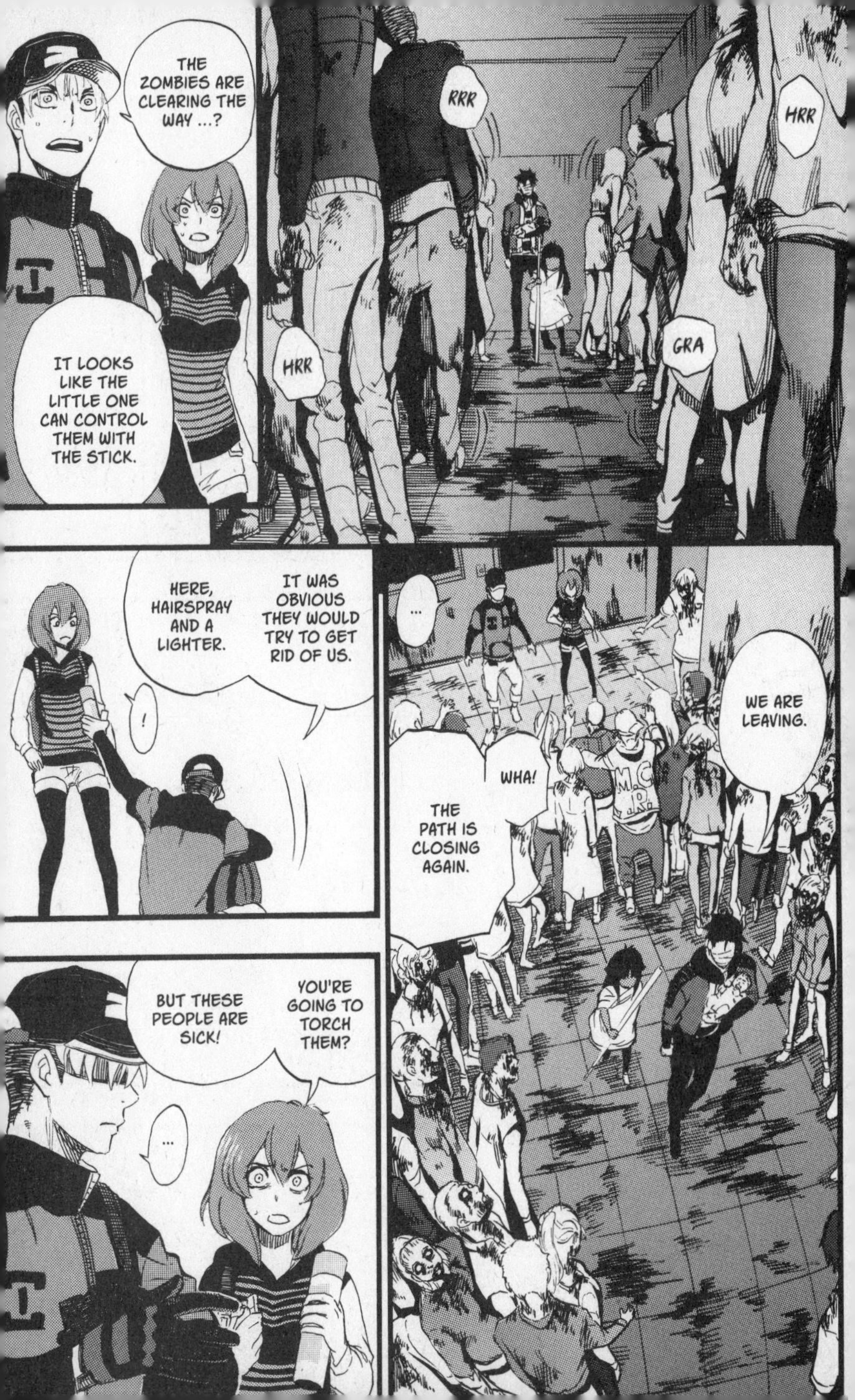
HRR
RRR
GRA
HRR
THE ZOMBIES ARE CLEARING THE WAY ...?
IT LOOKS LIKE THE LITTLE ONE CAN CONTROL THEM WITH THE STICK.
...
WE ARE LEAVING.
WHA!
THE PATH IS CLOSING AGAIN.
IT WAS OBVIOUS THEY WOULD TRY TO GET RID OF US.
HERE, HAIRSPRAY AND A LIGHTER.
!
YOU'RE GOING TO TORCH THEM?
BUT THESE PEOPLE ARE SICK!
...

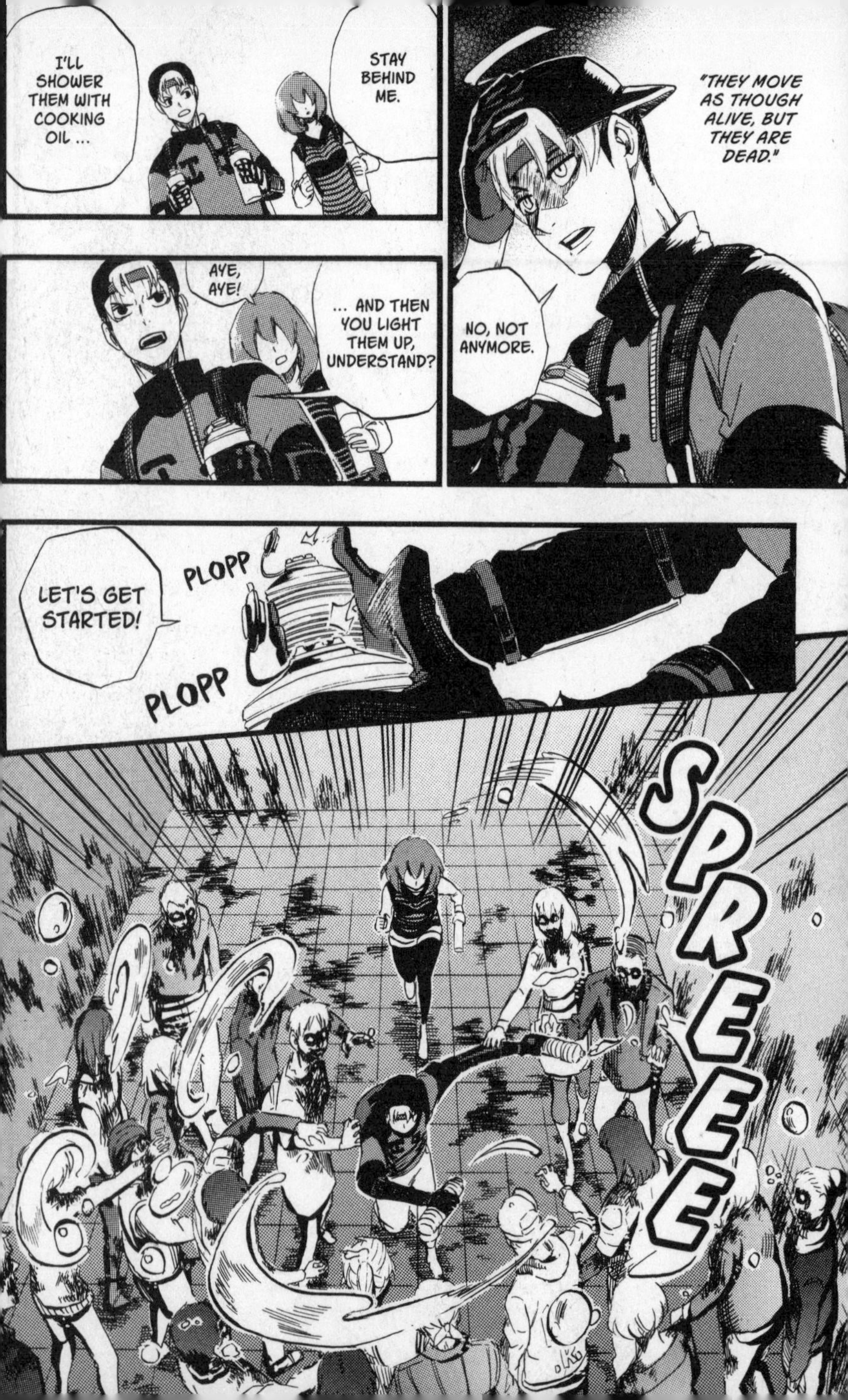
"THEY MOVE AS THOUGH ALIVE, BUT THEY ARE DEAD."
NO, NOT ANYMORE.
STAY BEHIND ME.
I'LL SHOWER THEM WITH COOKING OIL ...
... AND THEN YOU LIGHT THEM UP, UNDERSTAND?
AYE, AYE!
PLOPP
PLOPP
LET'S GET STARTED!
SPREEEE

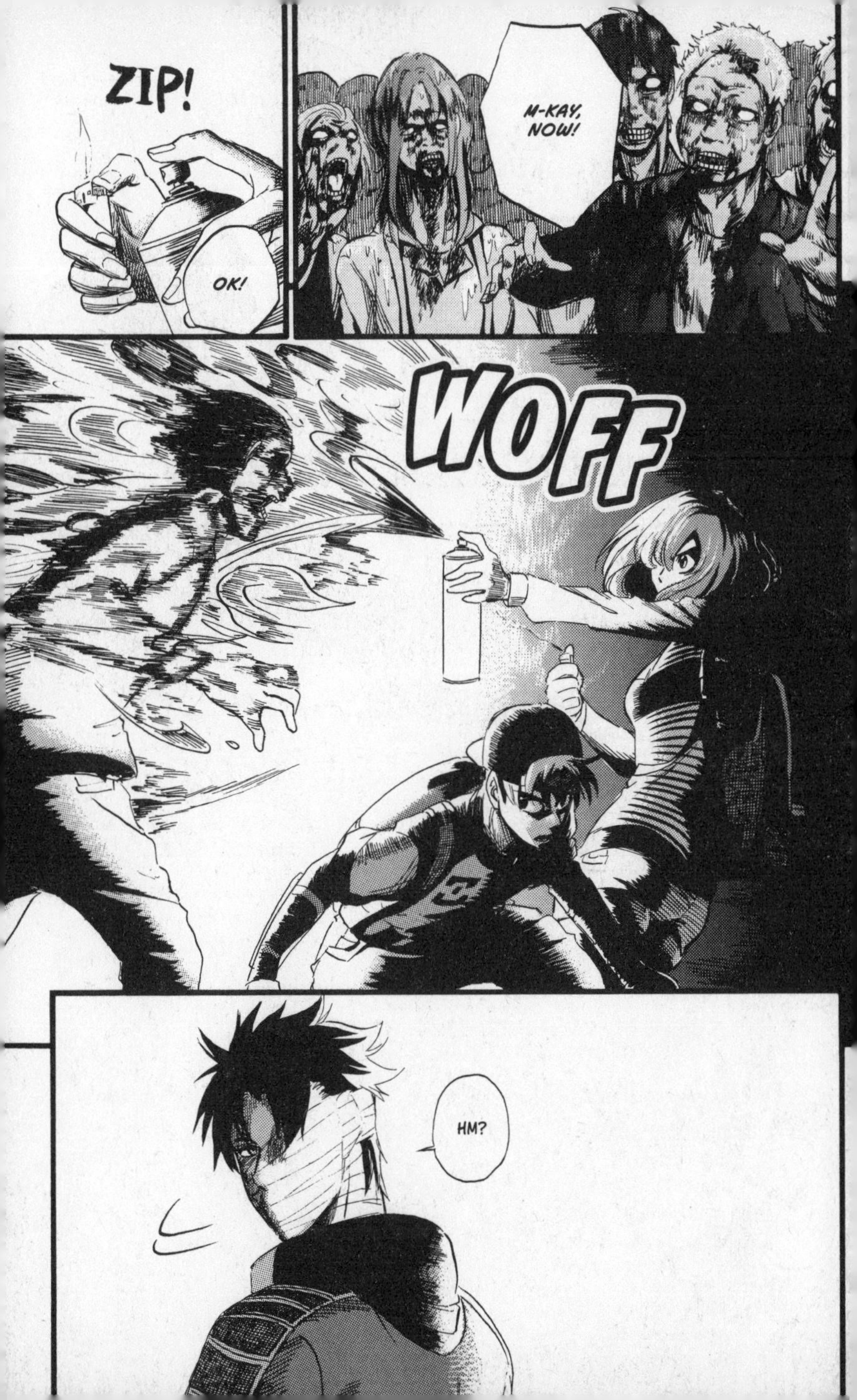
M-KAY, NOW!
ZIP!
OK!
WOFF
HM?

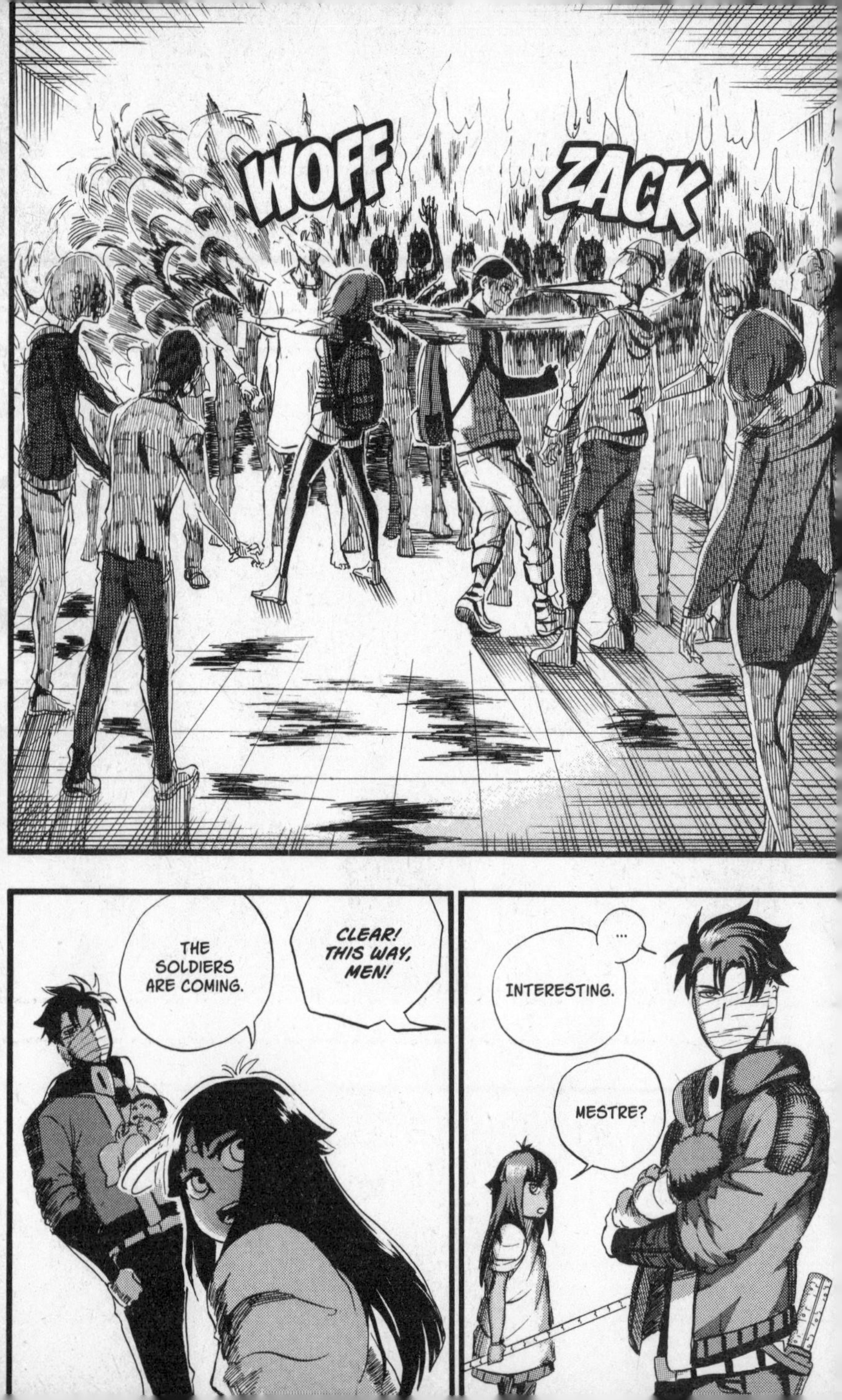
ZACK
WOFF
...
INTERESTING.
MESTRE?
CLEAR! THIS WAY, MEN!
THE SOLDIERS ARE COMING.

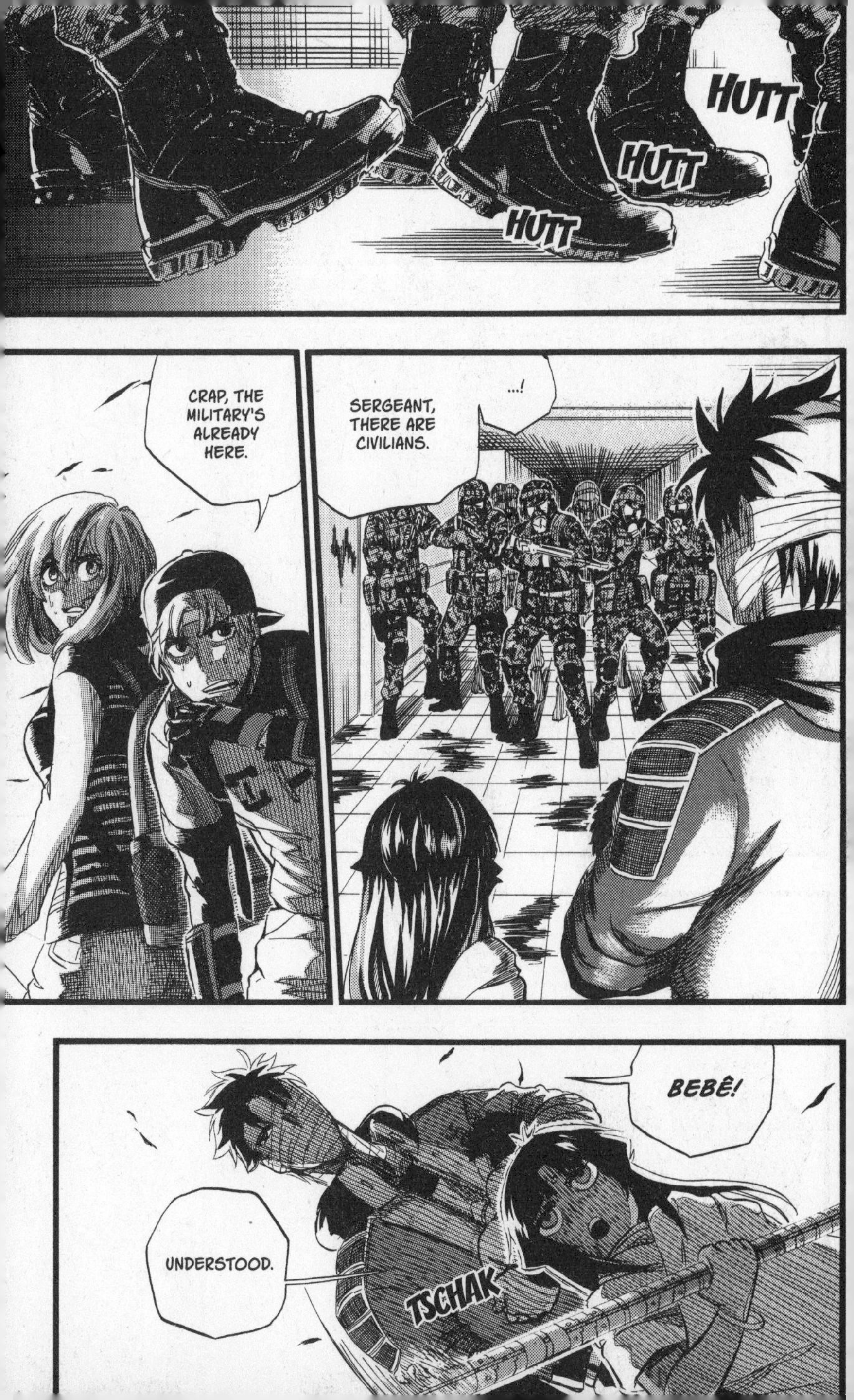
HUTT
HUTT
HUTT
...!
SERGEANT, THERE ARE CIVILIANS.
CRAP, THE MILITARY'S ALREADY HERE.
BEBÊ!
UNDERSTOOD.
TSCHAK

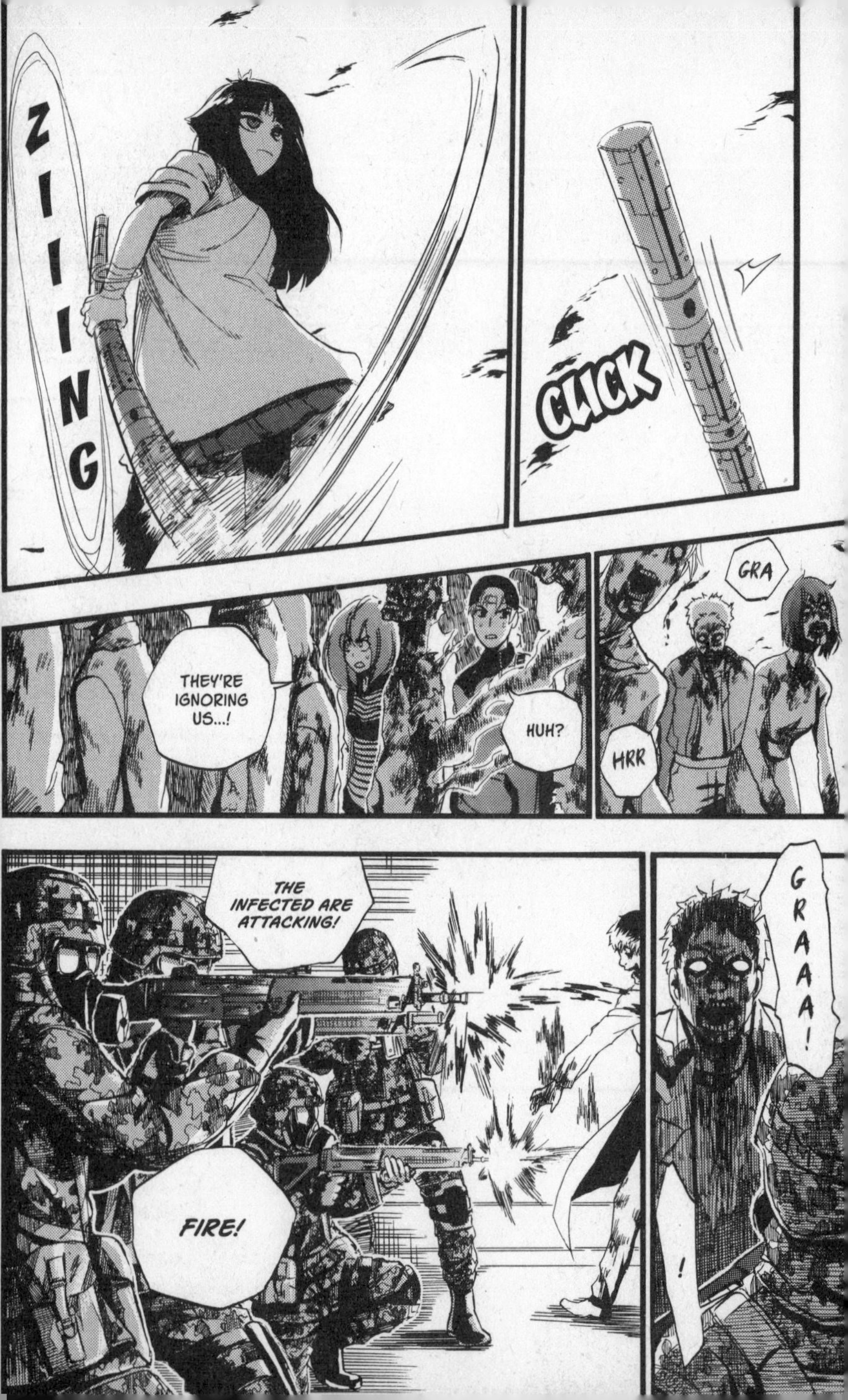
CLICK
ZIING
GRA
HRR
HUH?
THEY'RE IGNORING US...!
GRAAA!
!
THE INFECTED ARE ATTACKING!
FIRE!

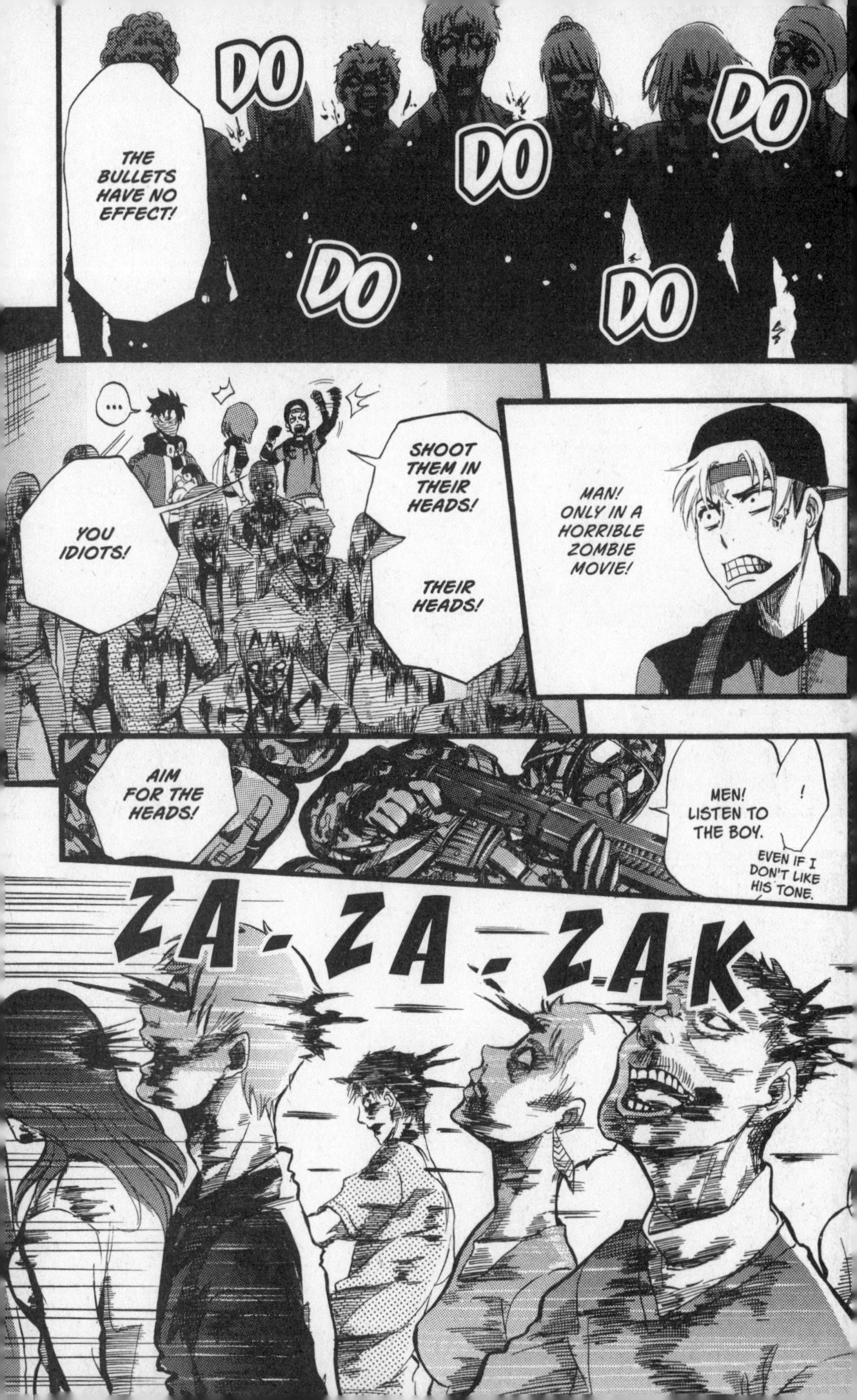
DO
DO
DO
DO
DO
THE BULLETS HAVE NO EFFECT!
MAN! ONLY IN A HORRIBLE ZOMBIE MOVIE!
SHOOT THEM IN THEIR HEADS!
THEIR HEADS!
YOU IDIOTS!
...
MEN! LISTEN TO THE BOY.
!
EVEN IF I DON'T LIKE HIS TONE.
AIM FOR THE HEADS!
ZA-ZA-ZAK

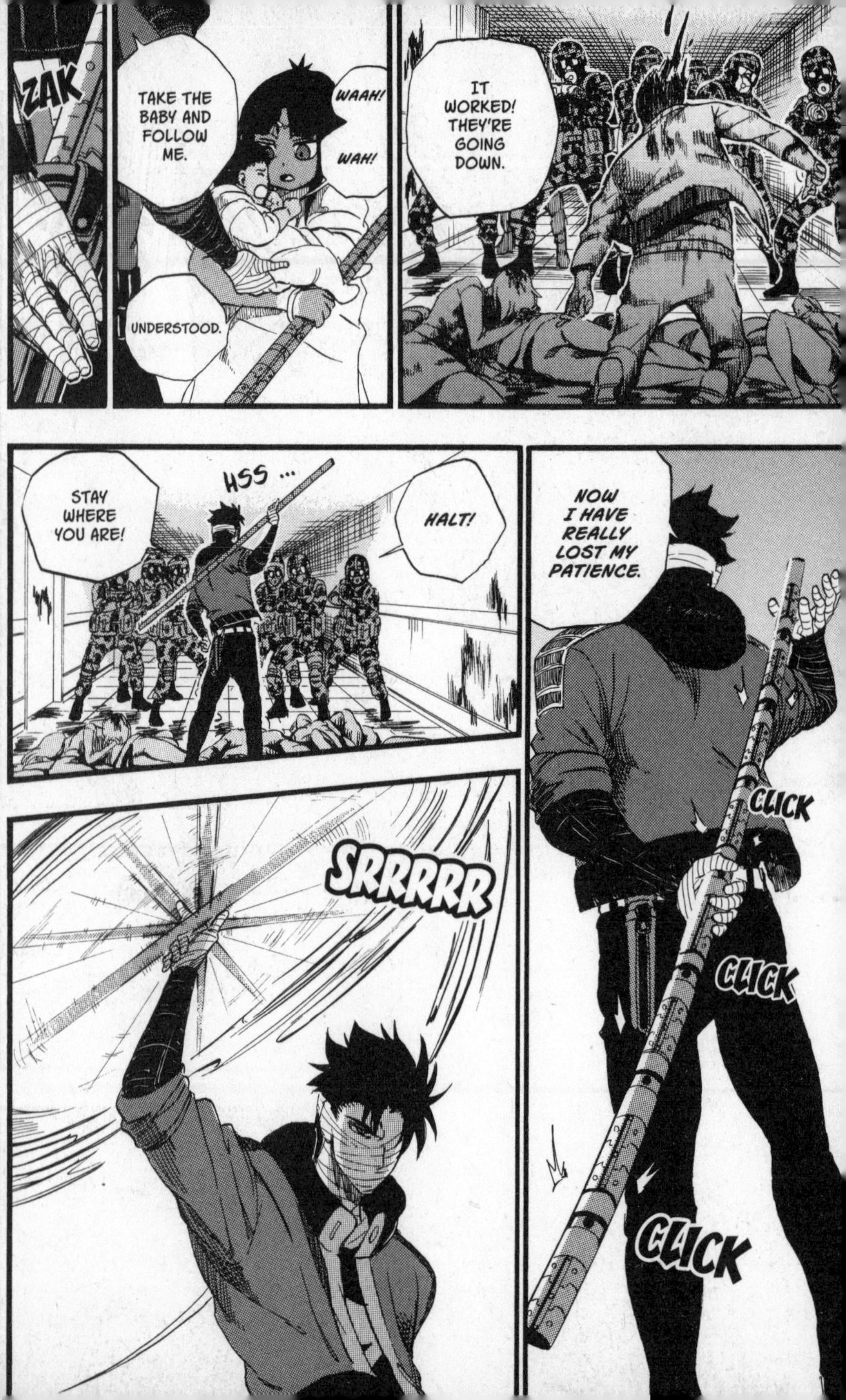
IT WORKED! THEY'RE GOING DOWN.
WAAH!
TAKE THE BABY AND FOLLOW ME.
WAH!
UNDERSTOOD.
ZAK
NOW I HAVE REALLY LOST MY PATIENCE.
CLICK
CLICK
CLICK
HALT!
HSS ...
STAY WHERE YOU ARE!
SRRRRRR

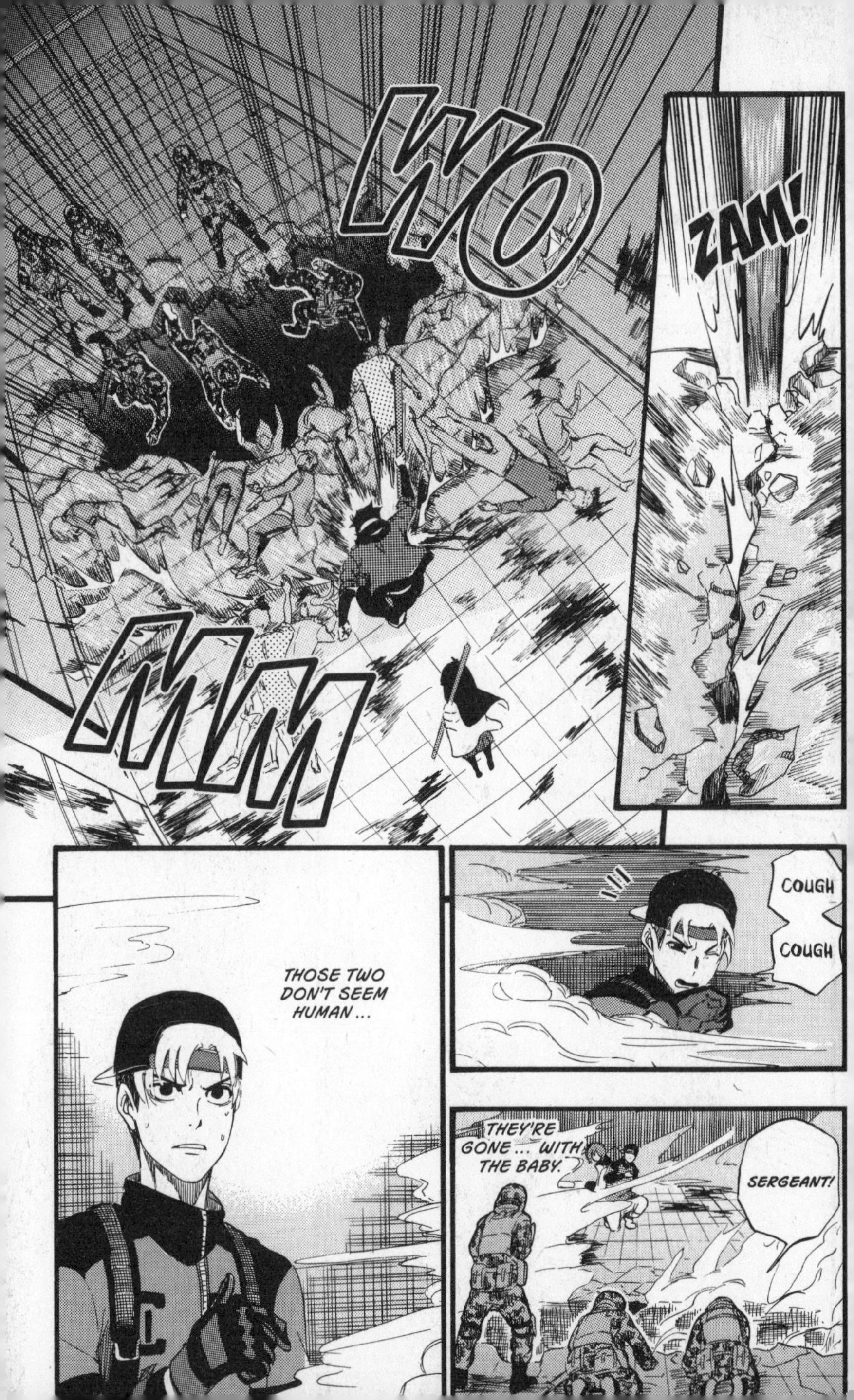
ZAM!
WO
MM
COUGH
COUGH
SERGEANT!
THEY'RE GONE... WITH THE BABY.
THOSE TWO DON'T SEEM HUMAN...

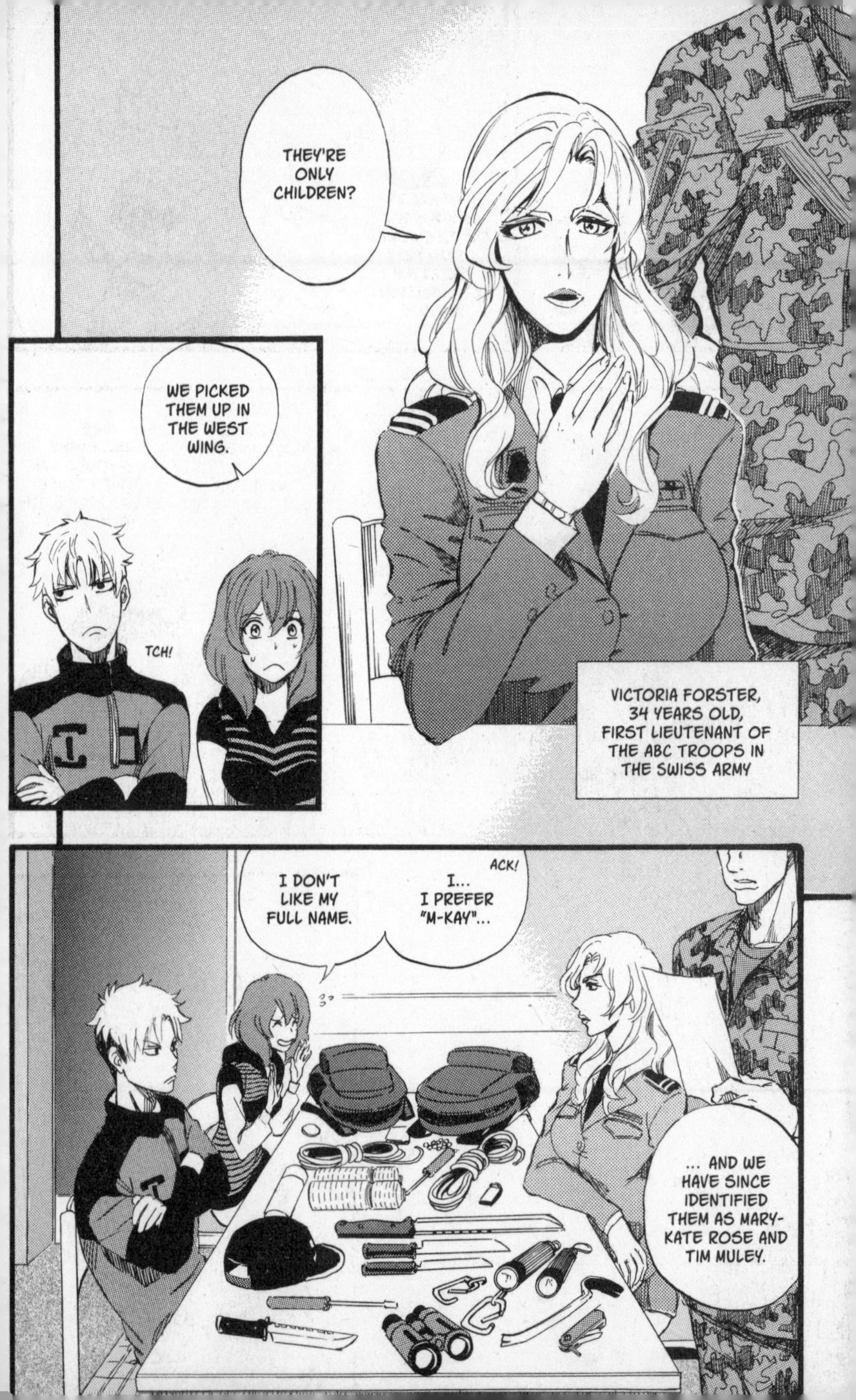
THEY'RE ONLY CHILDREN?
VICTORIA FORSTER, 34 YEARS OLD, FIRST LIEUTENANT OF THE ABC TROOPS IN THE SWISS ARMY
WE PICKED THEM UP IN THE WEST WING.
TCH!
ACK!
I... I PREFER "M-KAY"...
I DON'T LIKE MY FULL NAME.
... AND WE HAVE SINCE IDENTIFIED THEM AS MARY-KATE ROSE AND TIM MULEY.

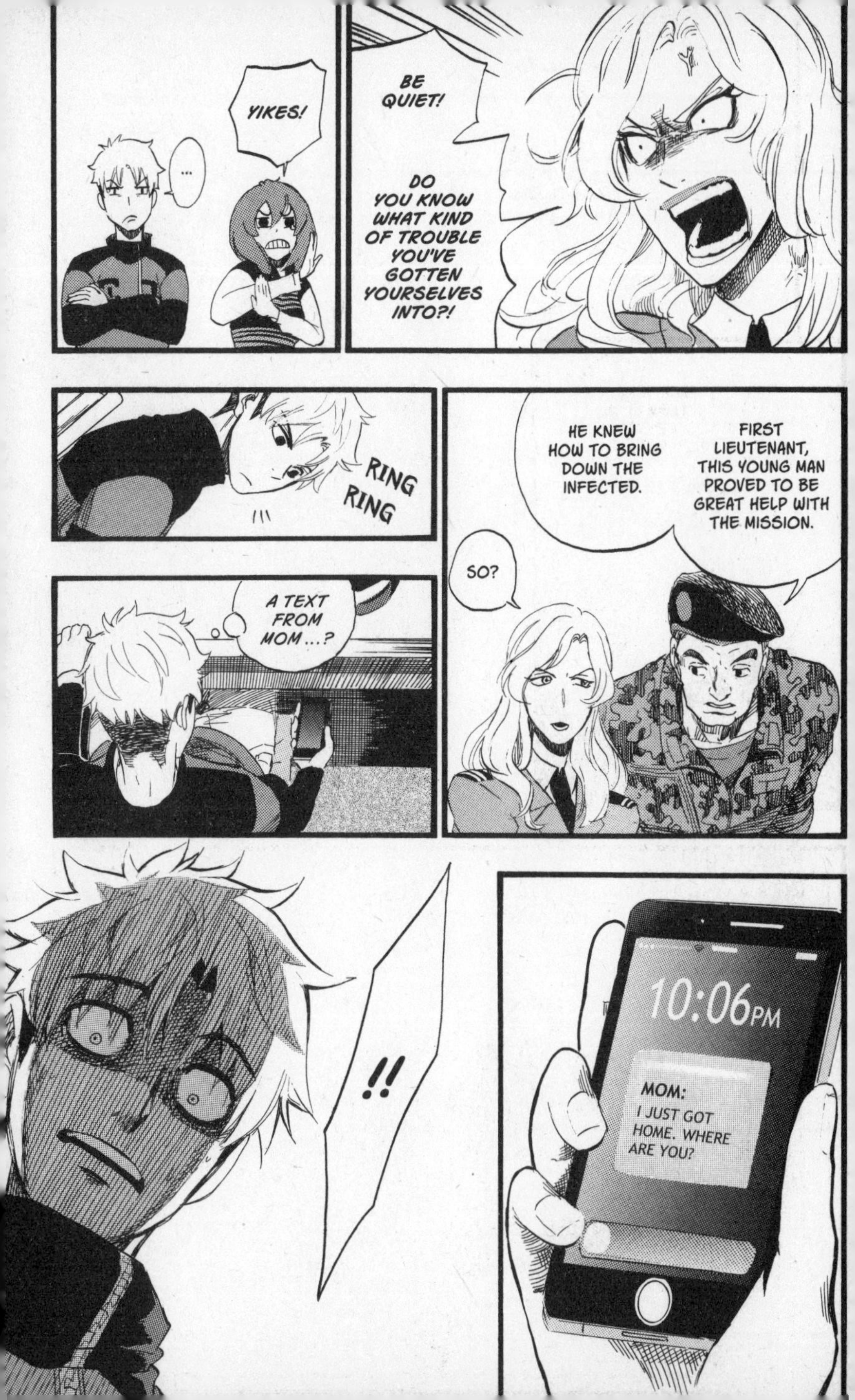
BE QUIET!
DO YOU KNOW WHAT KIND OF TROUBLE YOU'VE GOTTEN YOURSELVES INTO?!
YIKES!
...
FIRST LIEUTENANT, THIS YOUNG MAN PROVED TO BE GREAT HELP WITH THE MISSION.
HE KNEW HOW TO BRING DOWN THE INFECTED.
SO?
RING RING
A TEXT FROM MOM ...?
10:06PM
MOM:
I JUST GOT HOME. WHERE ARE YOU?
!!

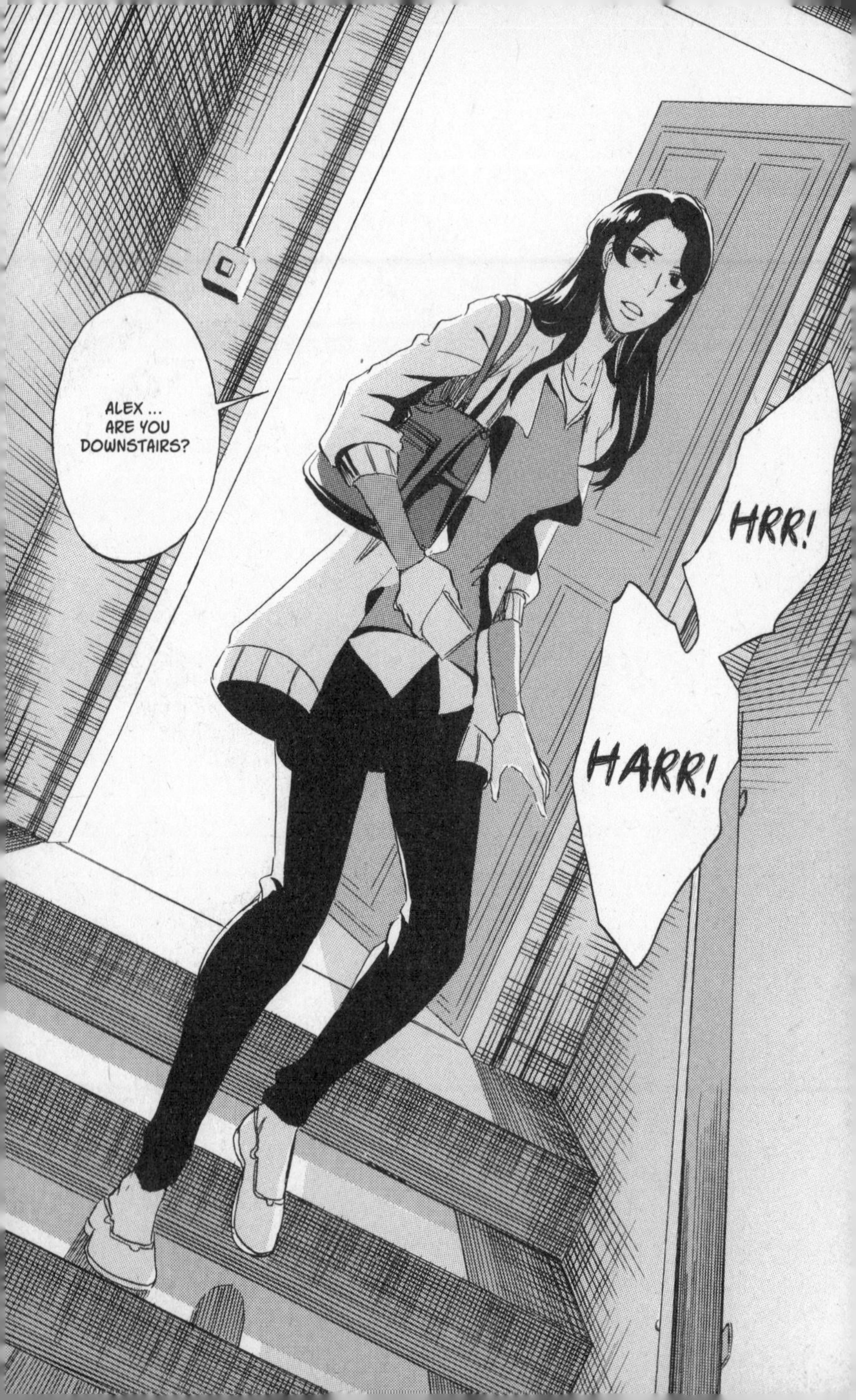
HRR!
HARR!
ALEX ... ARE YOU DOWNSTAIRS?

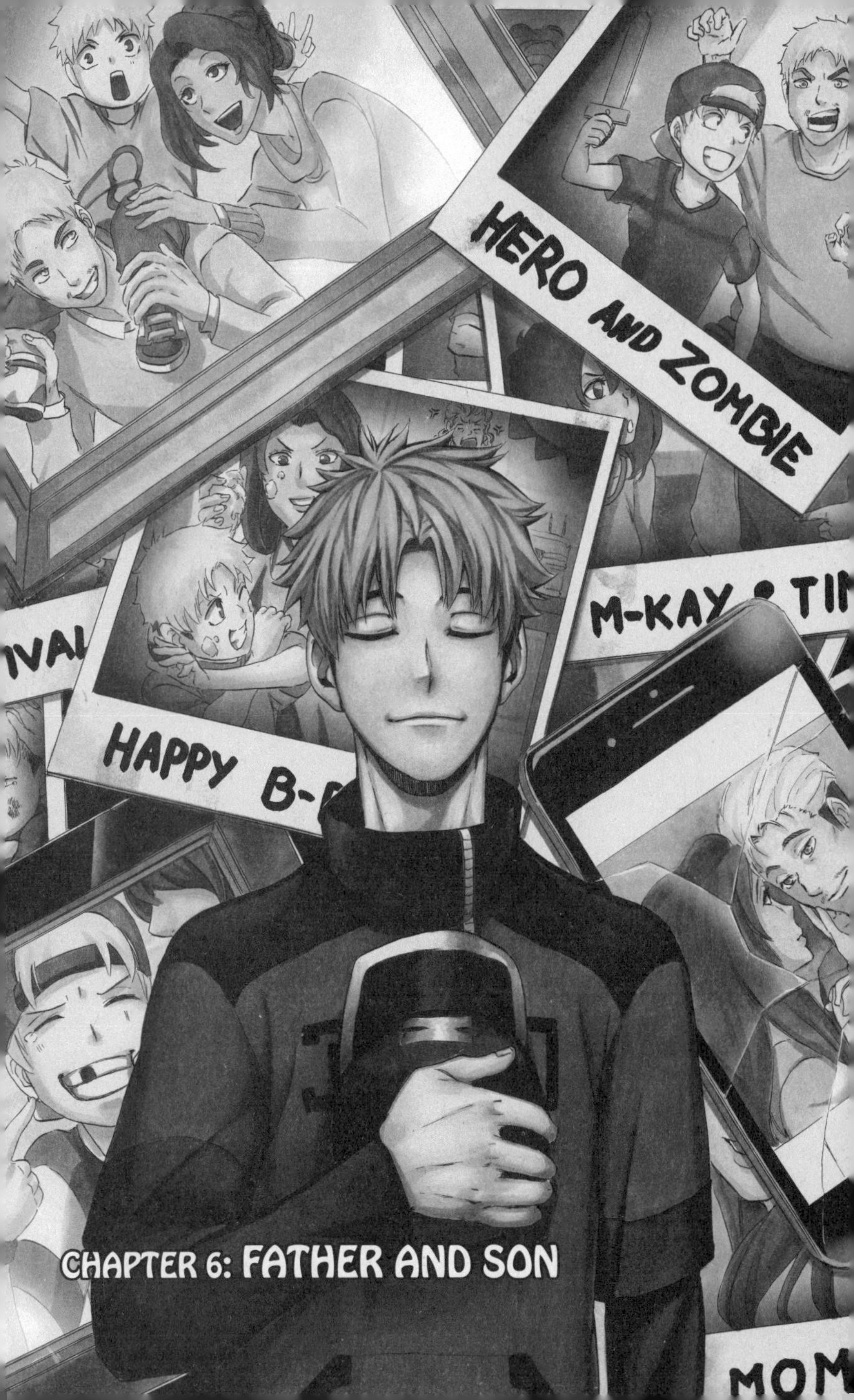
HERO AND ZOMBIE
M-KAY & TIM
IVAL
HAPPY B-
MOM
CHAPTER 6: FATHER AND SON

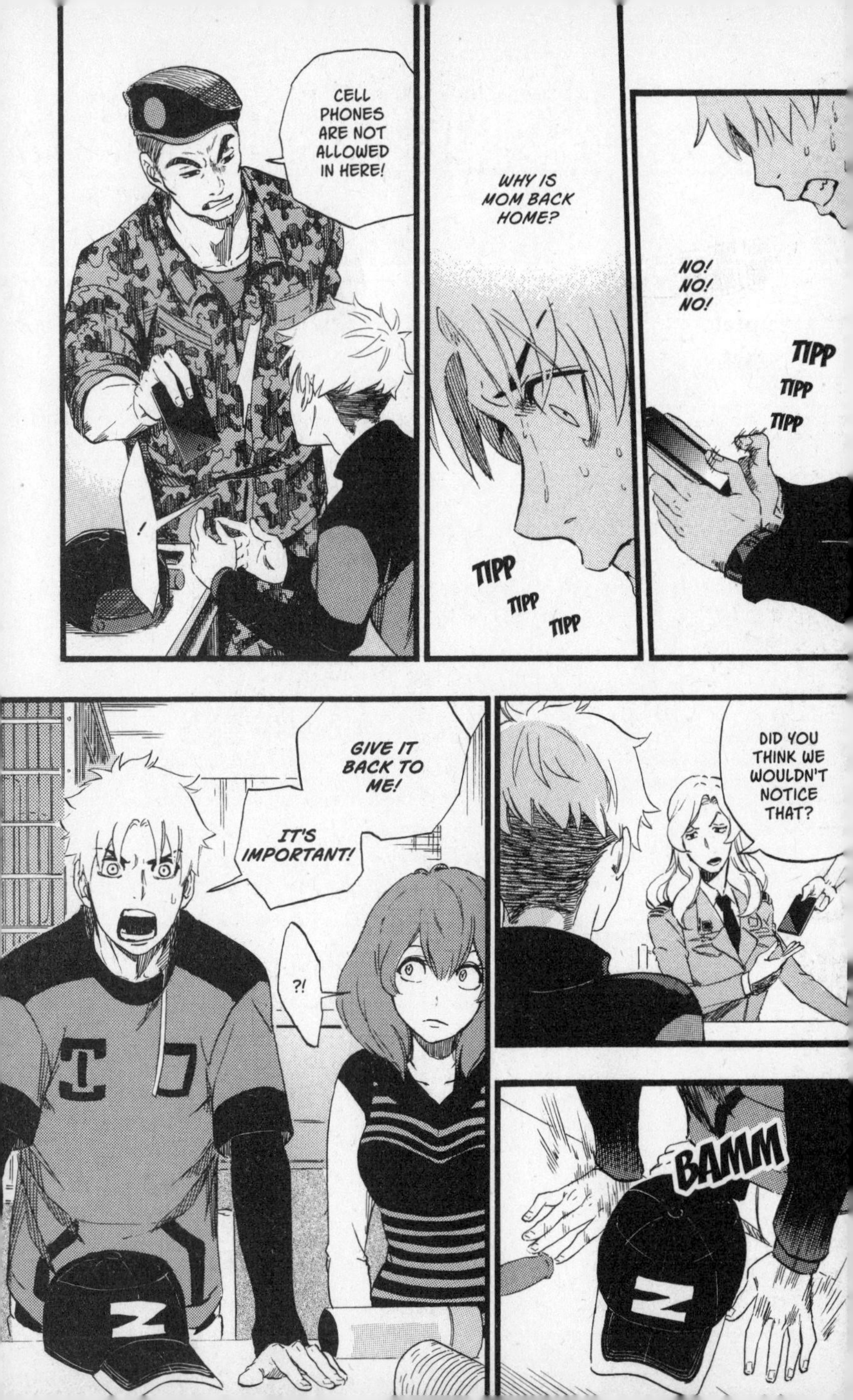
NO! NO! NO!
TIPP
TIPP
TIPP
WHY IS MOM BACK HOME?
TIPP
TIPP
TIPP
CELL PHONES ARE NOT ALLOWED IN HERE!
!
DID YOU THINK WE WOULDN'T NOTICE THAT?
BAMM
GIVE IT BACK TO ME!
IT'S IMPORTANT!
?!

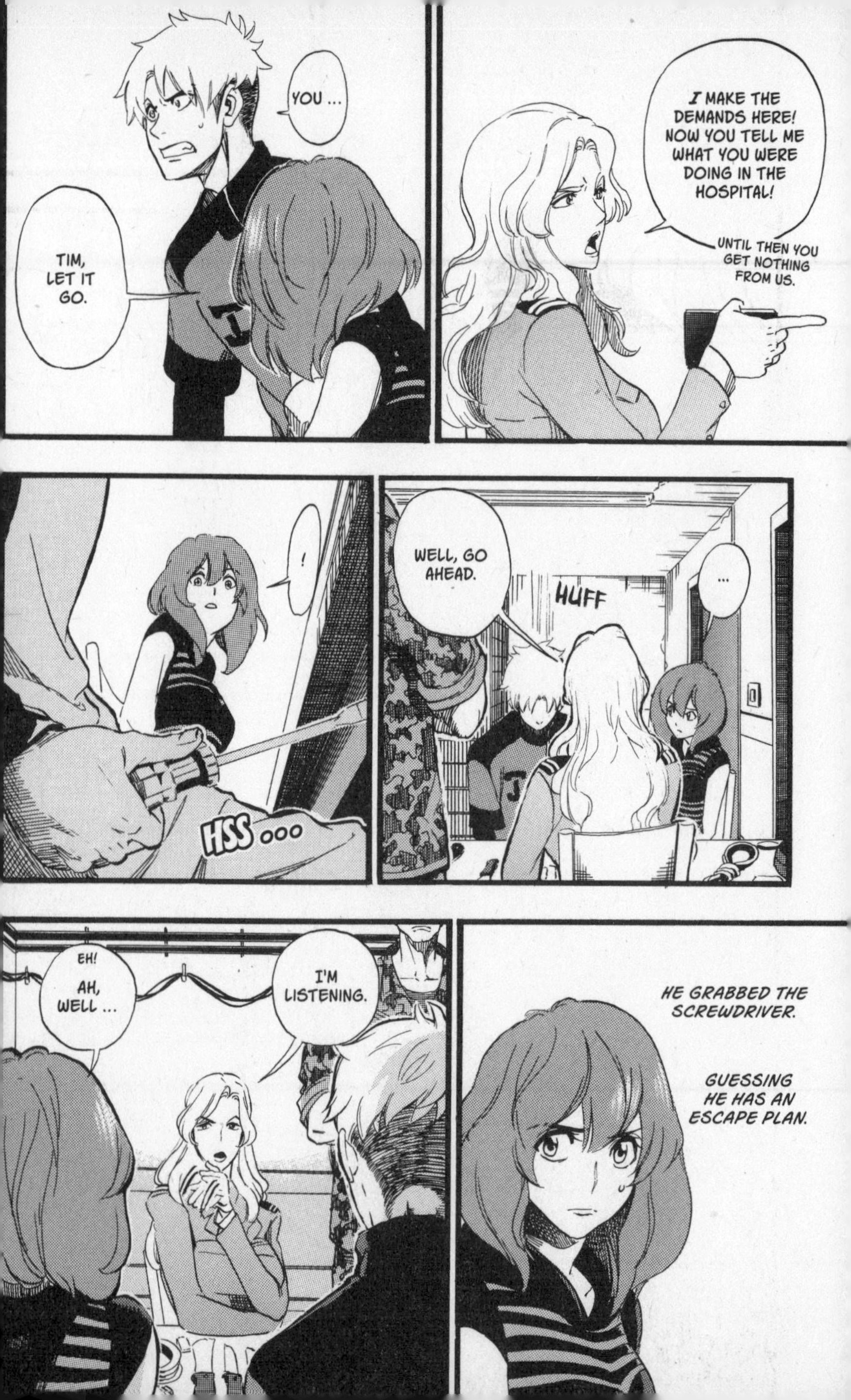
I MAKE THE DEMANDS HERE! NOW YOU TELL ME WHAT YOU WERE DOING IN THE HOSPITAL!
UNTIL THEN YOU GET NOTHING FROM US.
YOU ...
TIM, LET IT GO.
...
WELL, GO AHEAD.
HUFF
!
HSS ooo
HE GRABBED THE SCREWDRIVER.
GUESSING HE HAS AN ESCAPE PLAN.
I'M LISTENING.
EH!
AH, WELL ...

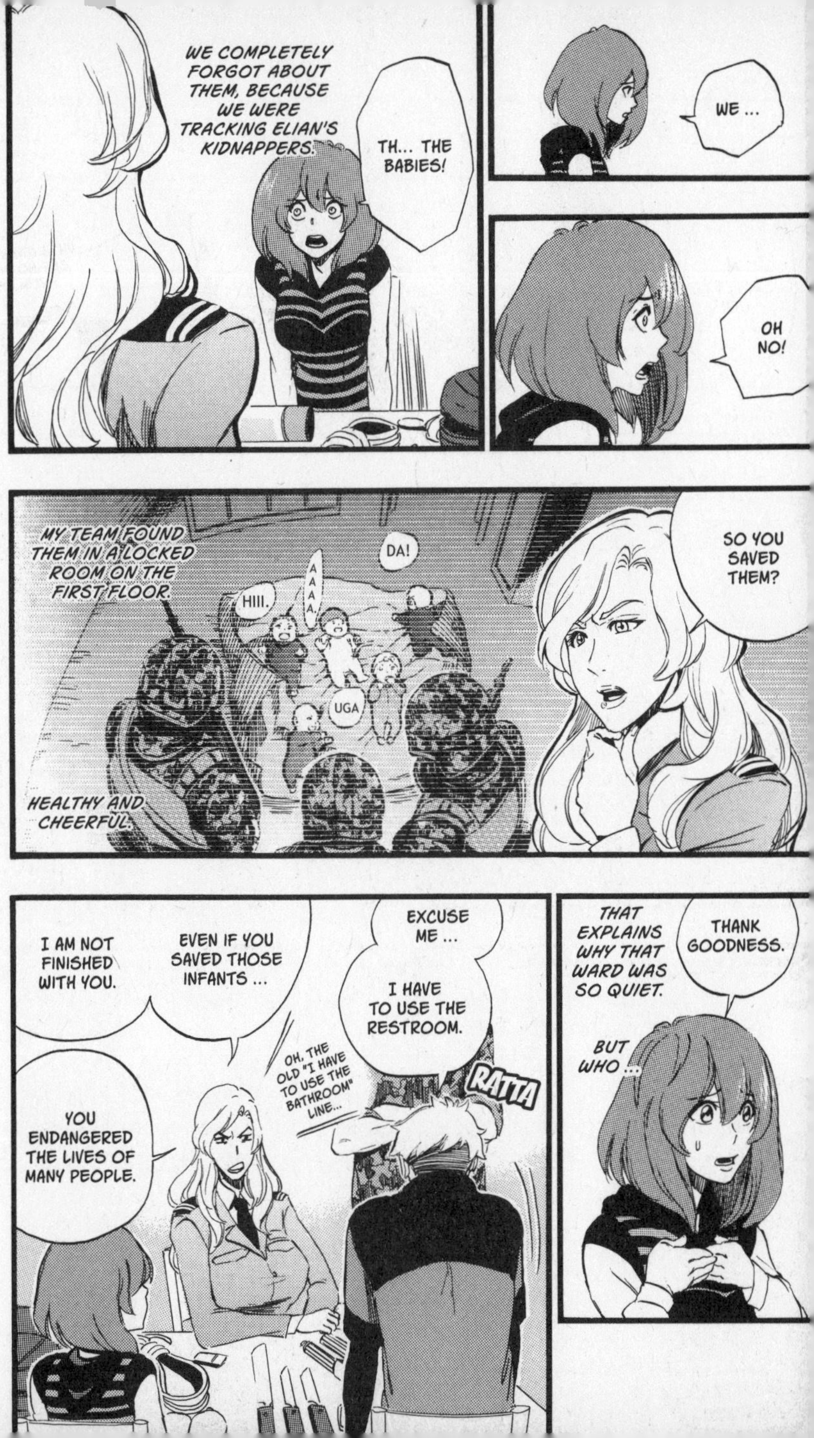

WE ...
OH NO!
TH... THE BABIES!
WE COMPLETELY FORGOT ABOUT THEM, BECAUSE WE WERE TRACKING ELIAN'S KIDNAPPERS.
SO YOU SAVED THEM?
MY TEAM FOUND THEM IN A LOCKED ROOM ON THE FIRST FLOOR.
DA!
AAAA.
HIII.
UGA
HEALTHY AND CHEERFUL.
THANK GOODNESS.
THAT EXPLAINS WHY THAT WARD WAS SO QUIET.
BUT WHO ...
EXCUSE ME ...
I HAVE TO USE THE RESTROOM.
EVEN IF YOU SAVED THOSE INFANTS ...
I AM NOT FINISHED WITH YOU.
RATTA
OH, THE OLD "I HAVE TO USE THE BATHROOM" LINE...
YOU ENDANGERED THE LIVES OF MANY PEOPLE.

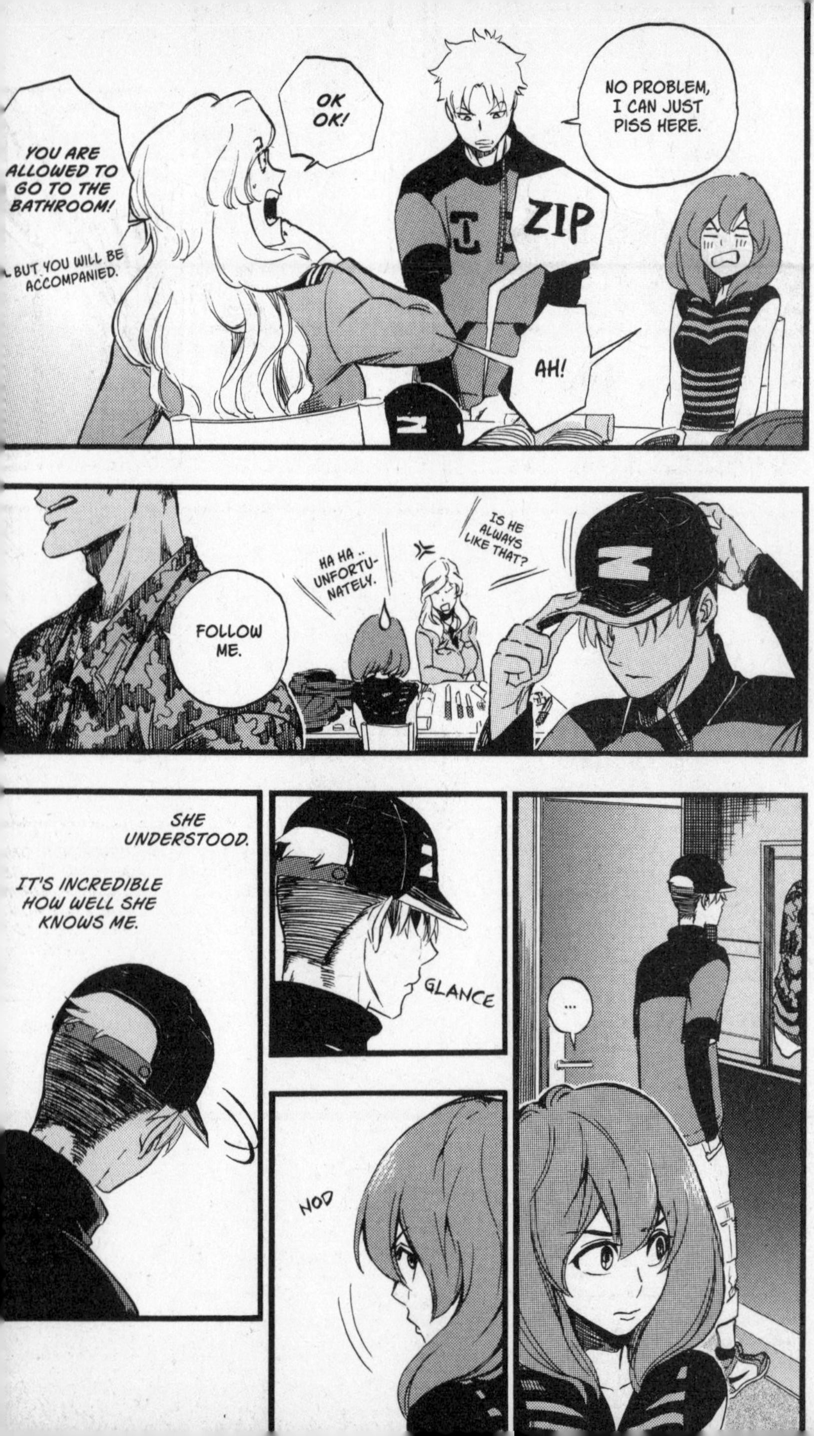
NO PROBLEM, I CAN JUST PISS HERE.
ZIP
OK OK!
YOU ARE ALLOWED TO GO TO THE BATHROOM!
BUT YOU WILL BE ACCOMPANIED.
AH!
IS HE ALWAYS LIKE THAT?
HA HA .. UNFORTU-NATELY.
FOLLOW ME.
...
GLANCE
NOD
SHE UNDERSTOOD.
IT'S INCREDIBLE HOW WELL SHE KNOWS ME.

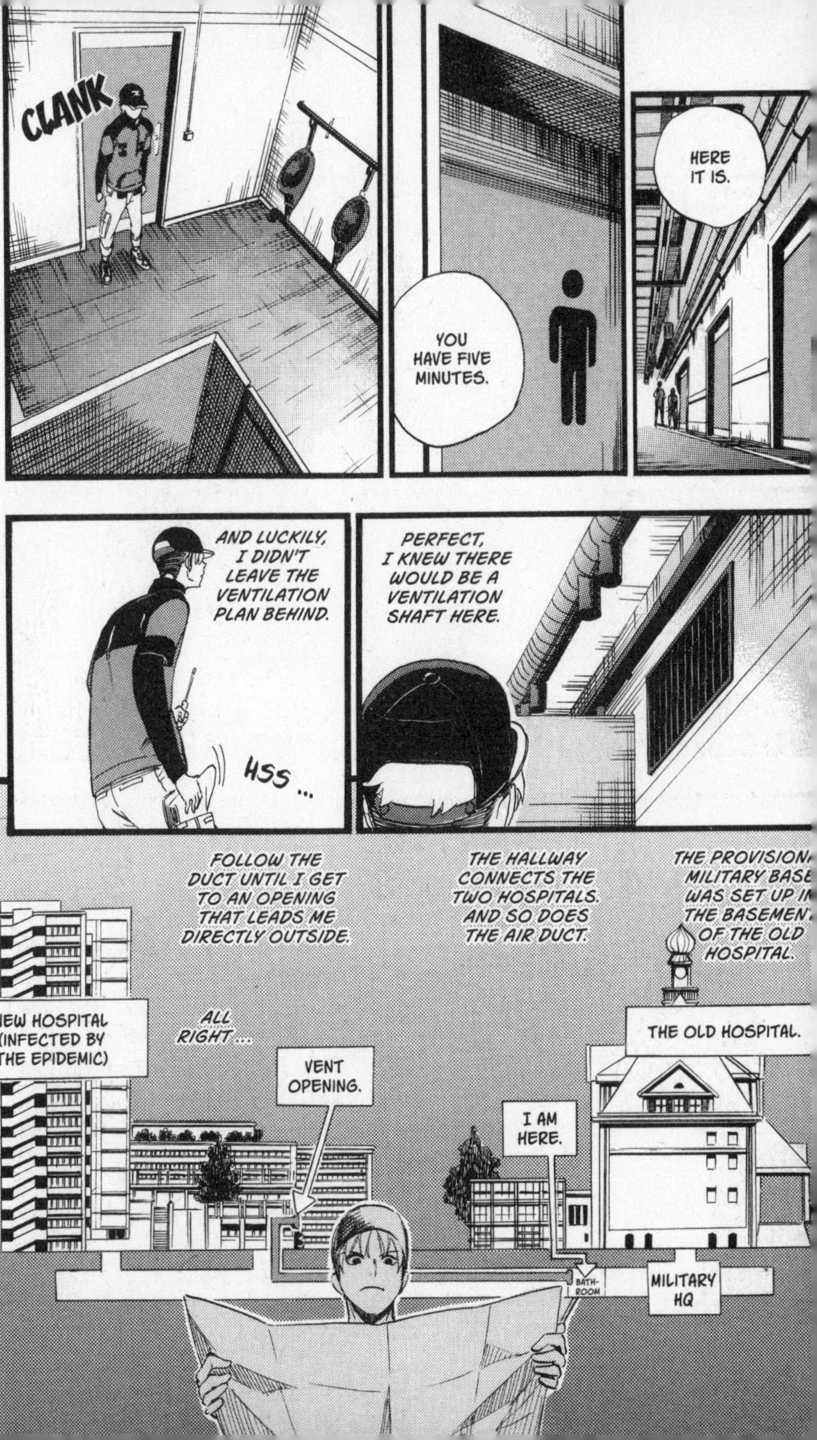
HERE IT IS.
YOU HAVE FIVE MINUTES.
CLANK
PERFECT, I KNEW THERE WOULD BE A VENTILATION SHAFT HERE.
AND LUCKILY, I DIDN'T LEAVE THE VENTILATION PLAN BEHIND.
HSS ...
THE PROVISION MILITARY BASE WAS SET UP I THE BASEMEN OF THE OLD HOSPITAL.
THE HALLWAY CONNECTS THE TWO HOSPITALS. AND SO DOES THE AIR DUCT.
FOLLOW THE DUCT UNTIL I GET TO AN OPENING THAT LEADS ME DIRECTLY OUTSIDE.
THE OLD HOSPITAL.
MILITARY HQ
I AM HERE.
BATH-ROOM
VENT OPENING.
ALL RIGHT ...
NEW HOSPITAL (INFECTED BY THE EPIDEMIC)

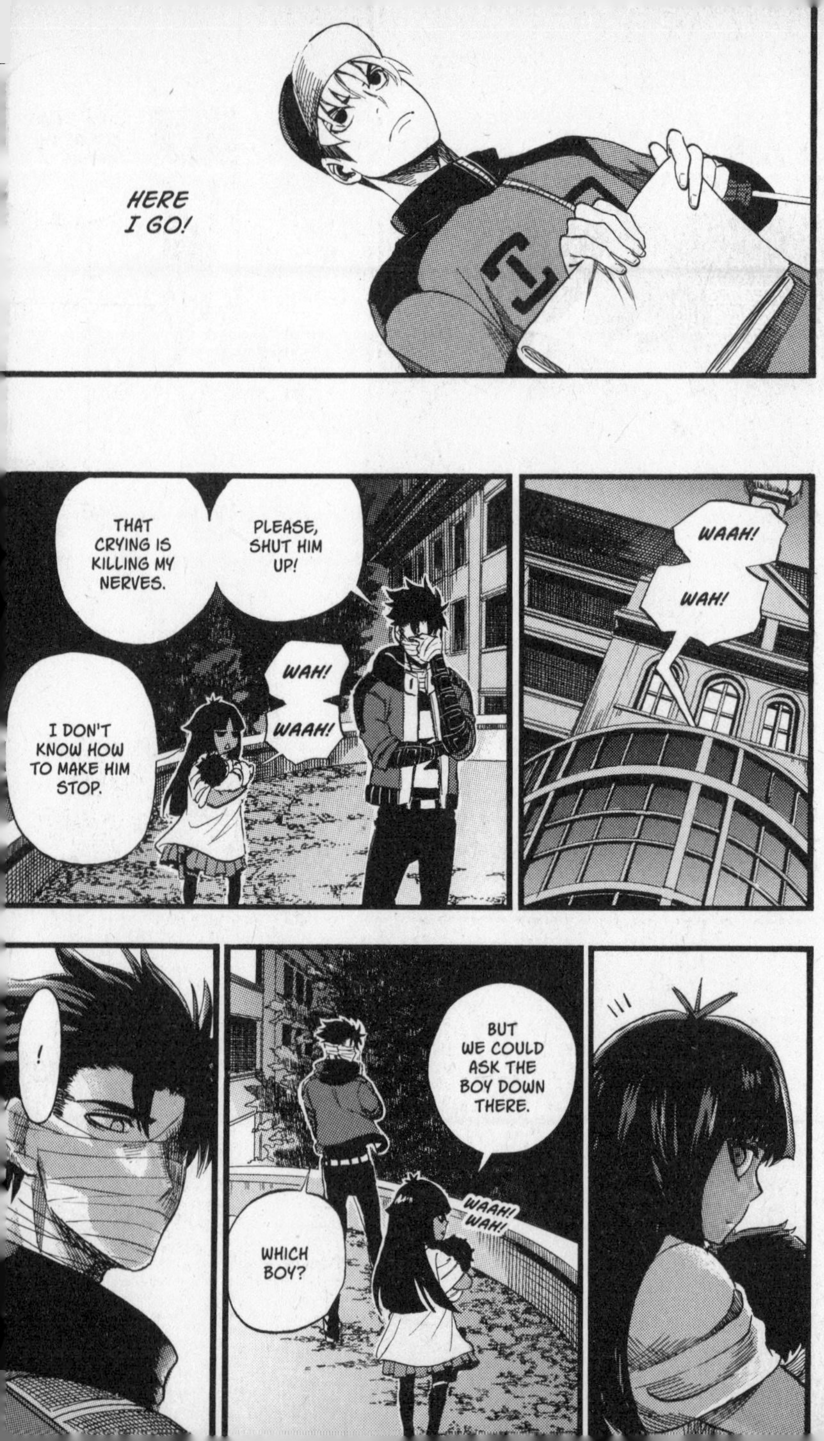
HERE I GO!
WAAH!
WAH!
PLEASE, SHUT HIM UP!
THAT CRYING IS KILLING MY NERVES.
WAH!
WAAH!
I DON'T KNOW HOW TO MAKE HIM STOP.
BUT WE COULD ASK THE BOY DOWN THERE.
WAAH! WAH!
WHICH BOY?
!

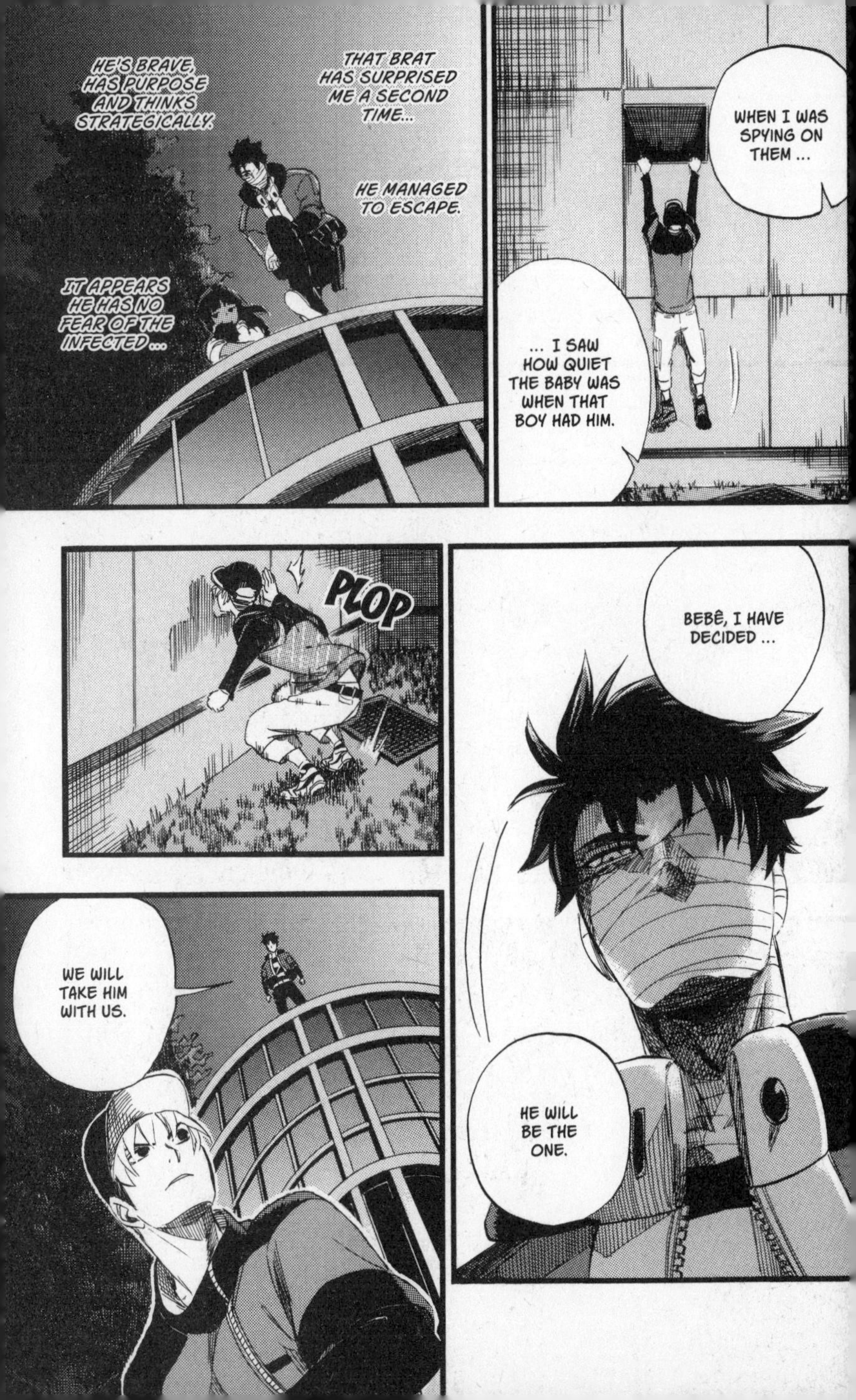
WHEN I WAS SPYING ON THEM ...
... I SAW HOW QUIET THE BABY WAS WHEN THAT BOY HAD HIM.
THAT BRAT HAS SURPRISED ME A SECOND TIME...
HE MANAGED TO ESCAPE.
HE'S BRAVE, HAS PURPOSE AND THINKS STRATEGICALLY.
IT APPEARS HE HAS NO FEAR OF THE INFECTED ...
BEBÊ, I HAVE DECIDED ...
HE WILL BE THE ONE.
PLOP
WE WILL TAKE HIM WITH US.

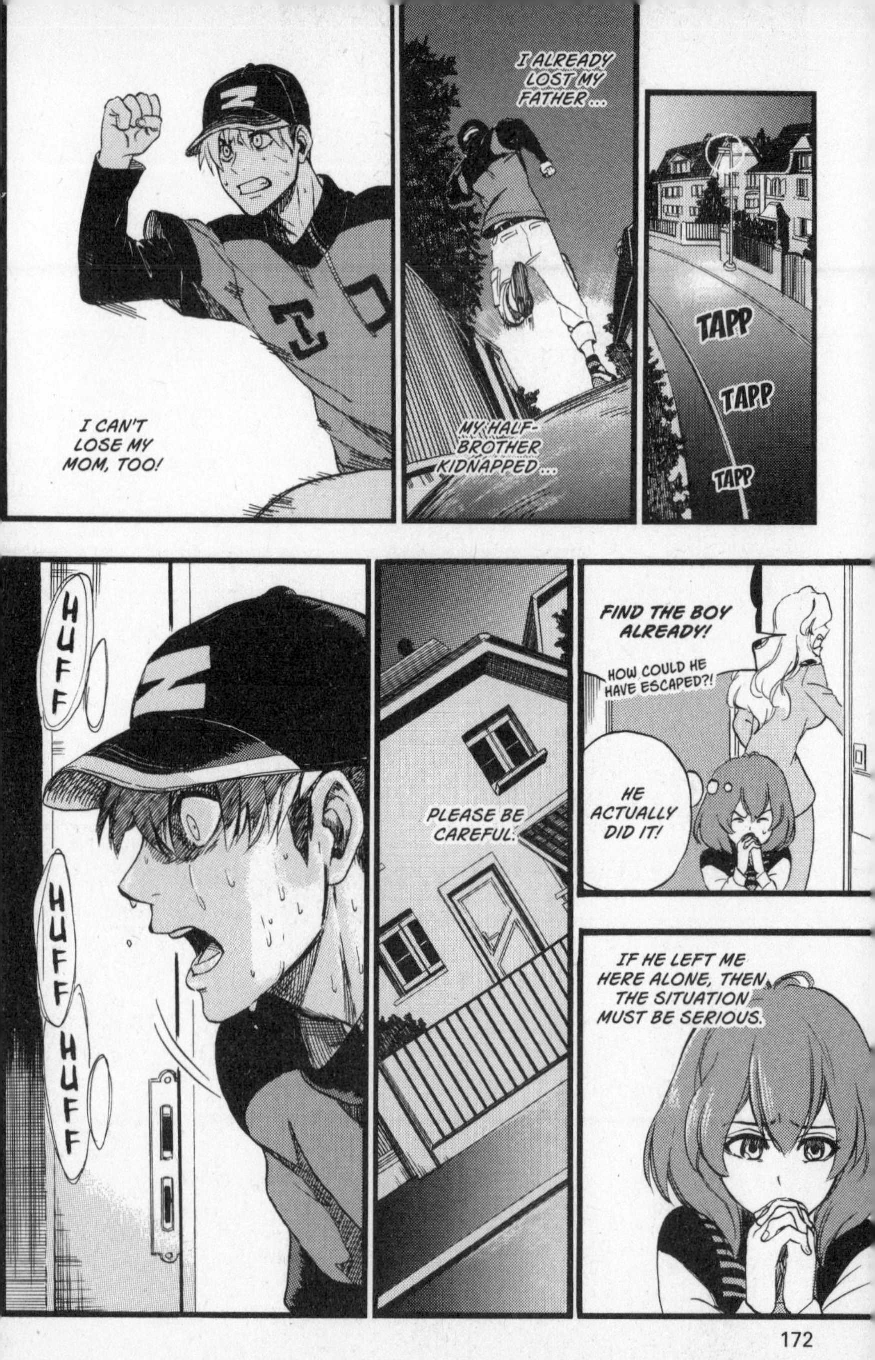
TAPP
TAPP
TAPP
I ALREADY LOST MY FATHER...
MY HALF-BROTHER KIDNAPPED...
I CAN'T LOSE MY MOM, TOO!
FIND THE BOY ALREADY!
HOW COULD HE HAVE ESCAPED?!
HE ACTUALLY DID IT!
IF HE LEFT ME HERE ALONE, THEN THE SITUATION MUST BE SERIOUS.
PLEASE BE CAREFUL.
HUFF
HUFF
HUFF
HUFF

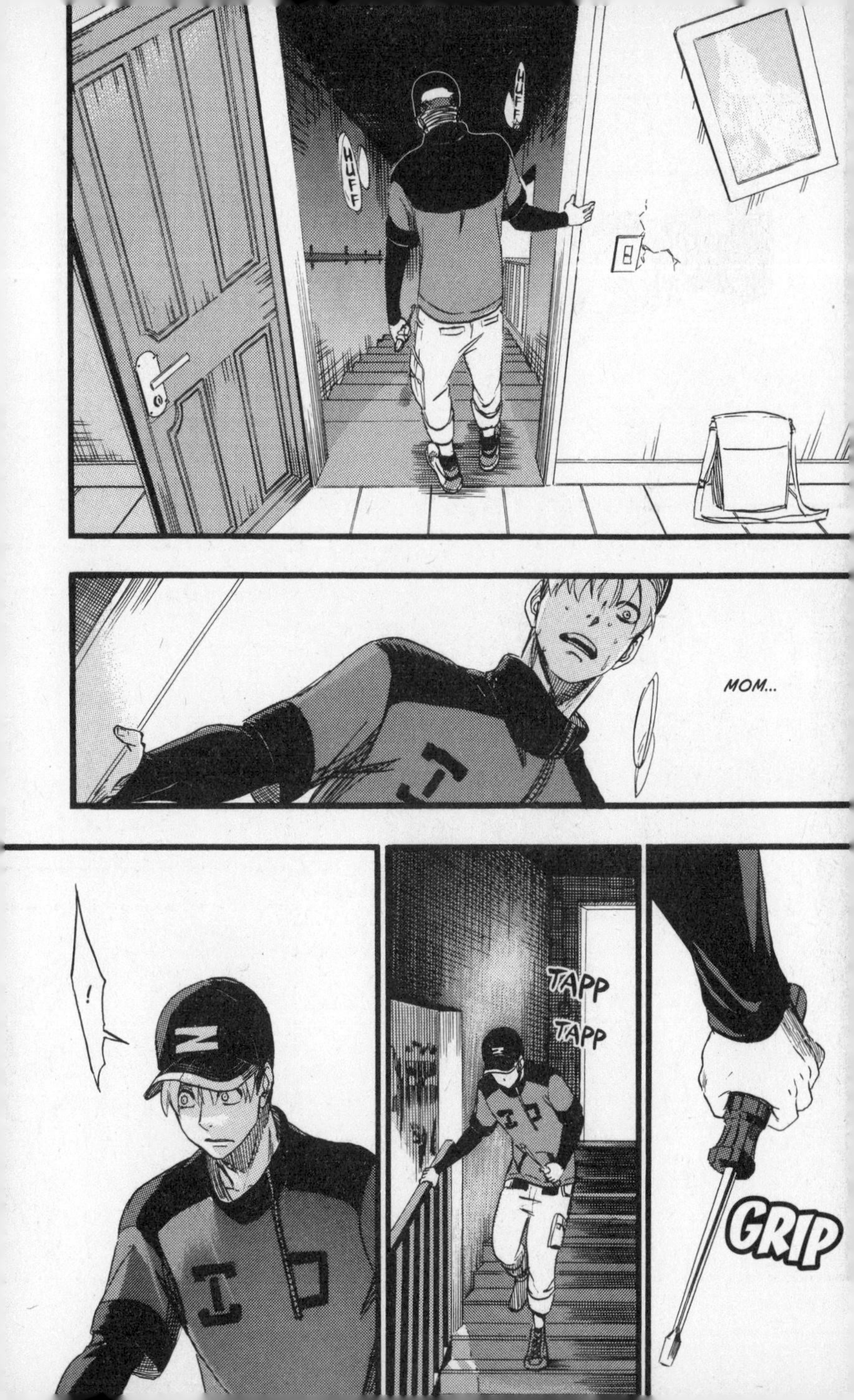
HUFF
HUFF
MOM...
GRIP
TAPP
TAPP
!

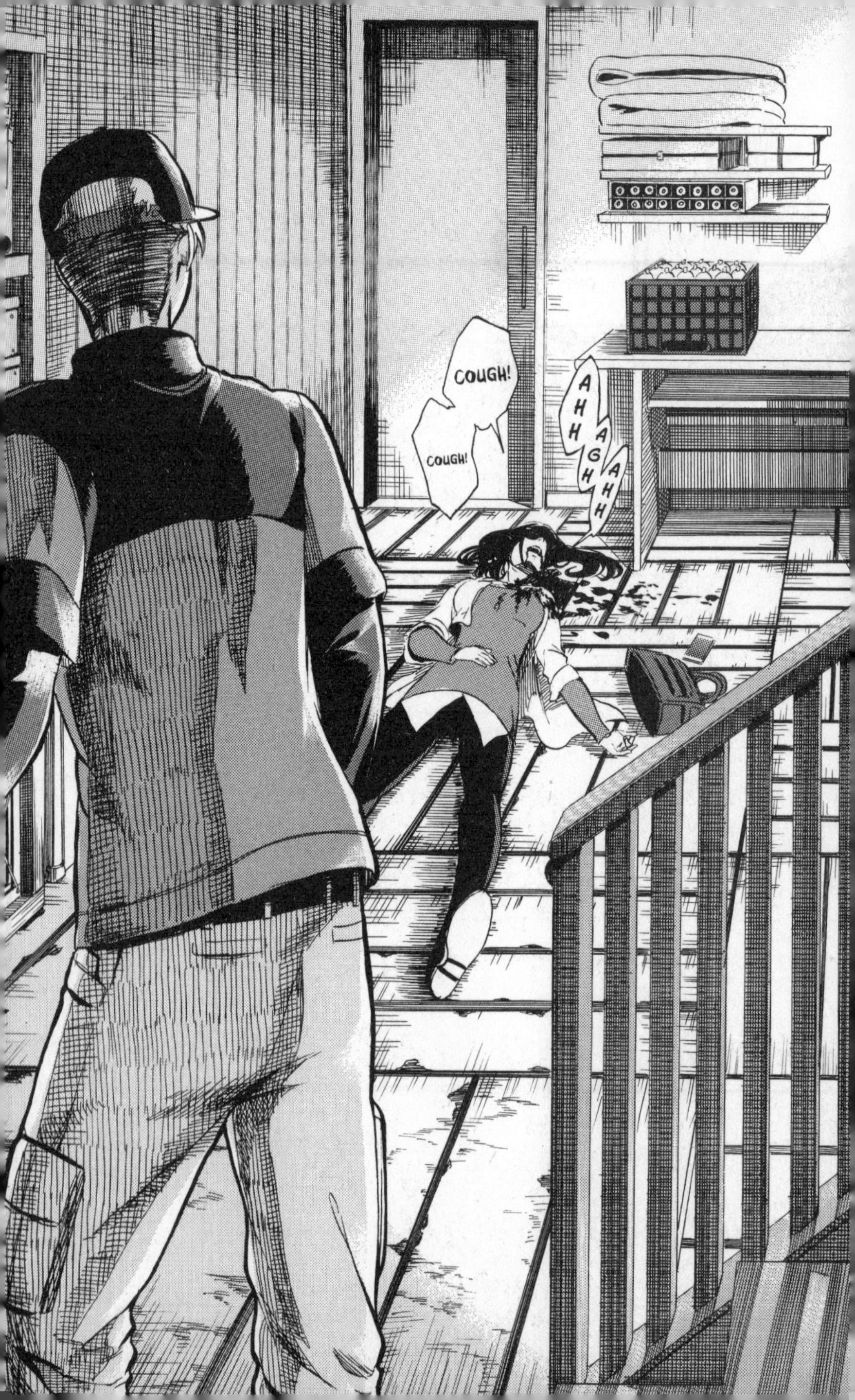
AHH
AGH
AHH
COUGH!
COUGH!

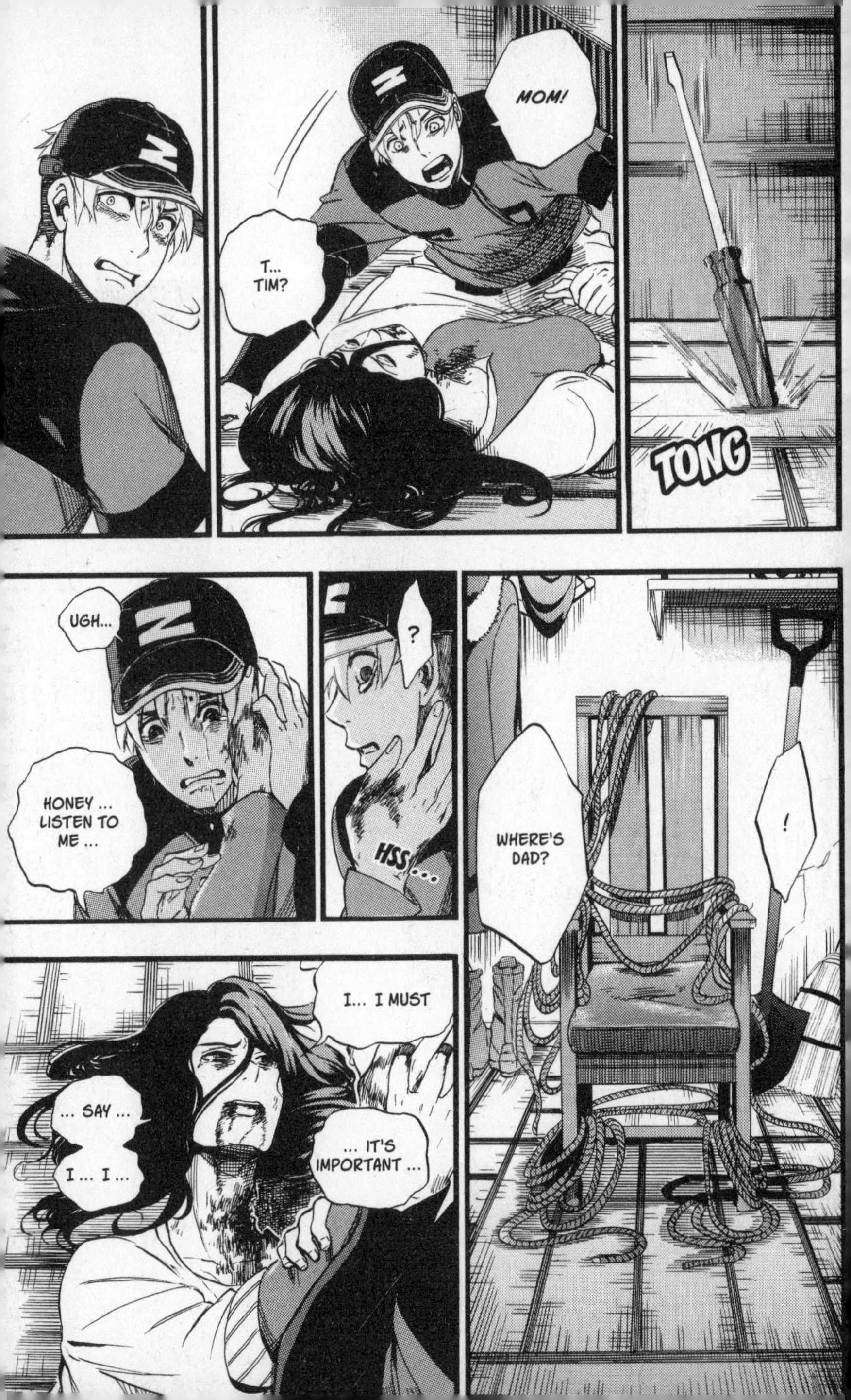
TONG
MOM!
T... TIM?
!
WHERE'S DAD?
?
HSS...
UGH...
HONEY ... LISTEN TO ME ...
I... I MUST
... IT'S IMPORTANT ...
... SAY ...
I ... I ...

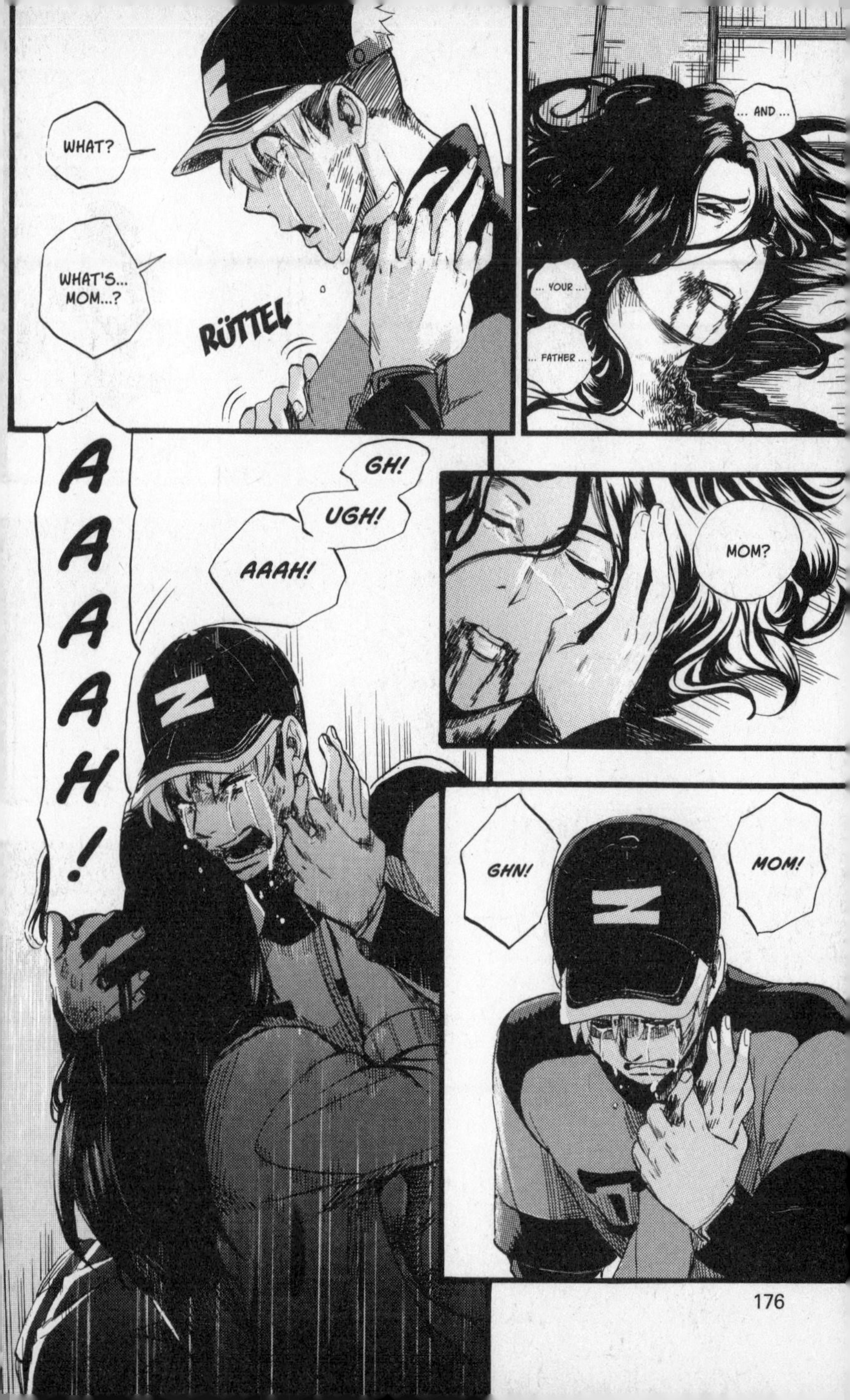
... AND ...
... YOUR ...
... FATHER ...
WHAT?
WHAT'S... MOM...?
RÜTTEL
MOM?
MOM!
GHN!
GH!
UGH!
AAAH!
AAAAAH!

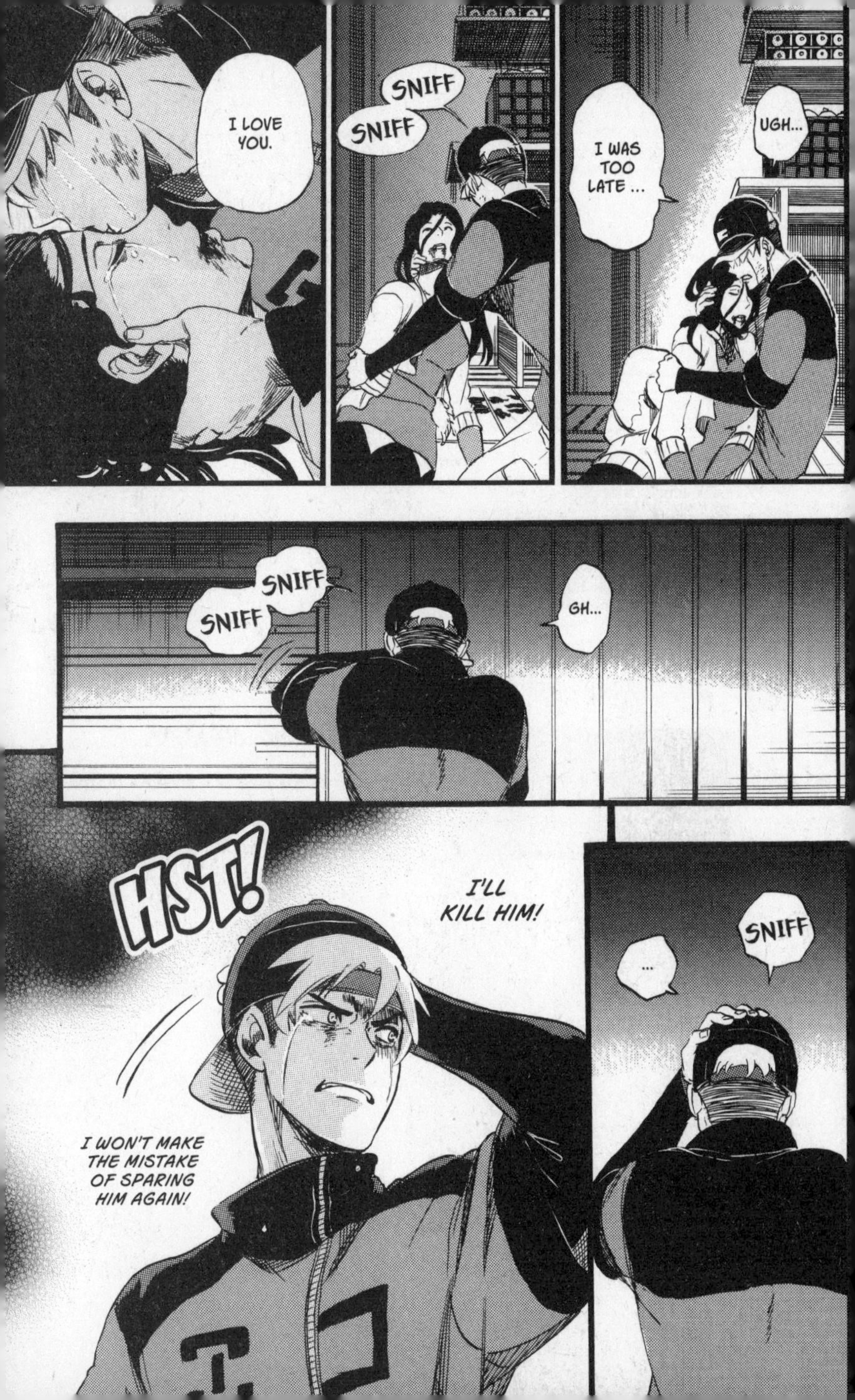
UGH...
I WAS TOO LATE ...
SNIFF
SNIFF
I LOVE YOU.
GH...
SNIFF
SNIFF
SNIFF
...
I'LL KILL HIM!
HST!
I WON'T MAKE THE MISTAKE OF SPARING HIM AGAIN!

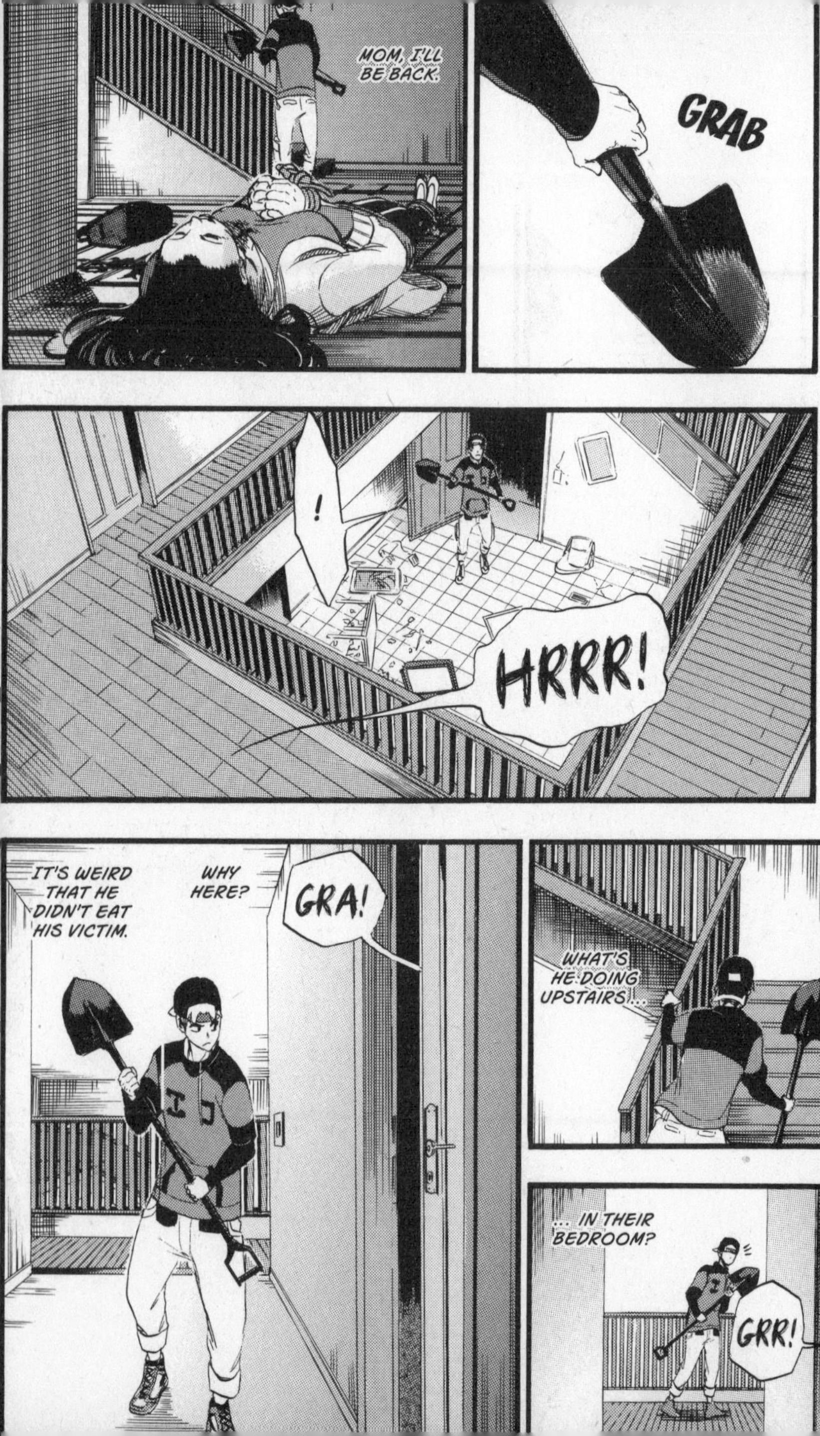
GRAB
MOM, I'LL BE BACK.
!
HRRR!
WHAT'S HE DOING UPSTAIRS...
... IN THEIR BEDROOM?
GRR!
GRA!
WHY HERE?
IT'S WEIRD THAT HE DIDN'T EAT HIS VICTIM.

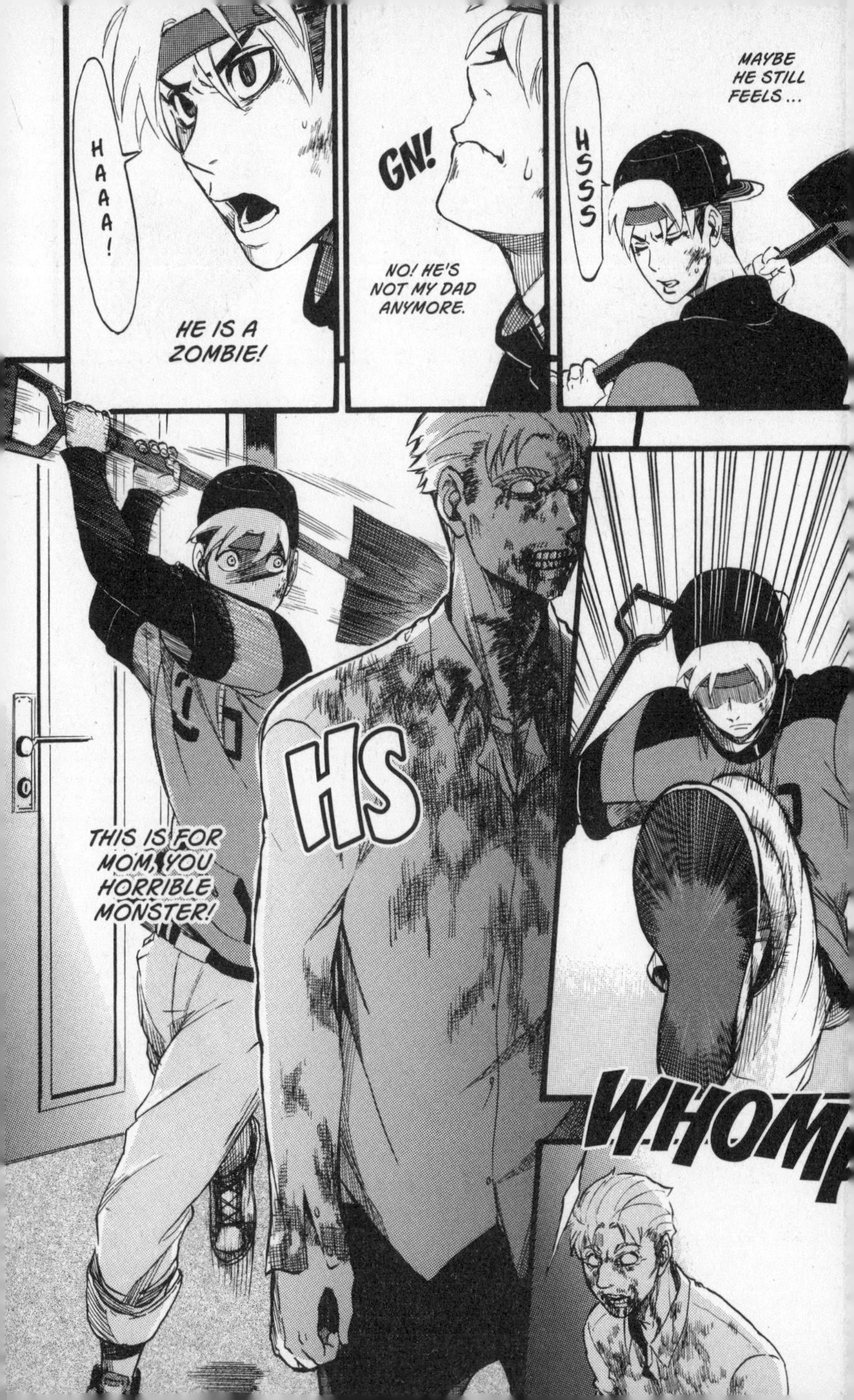
HSSS
MAYBE HE STILL FEELS ...
GN!
NO! HE'S NOT MY DAD ANYMORE.
HAAAA!
HE IS A ZOMBIE!
WHOMP
HS
THIS IS FOR MOM, YOU HORRIBLE MONSTER!

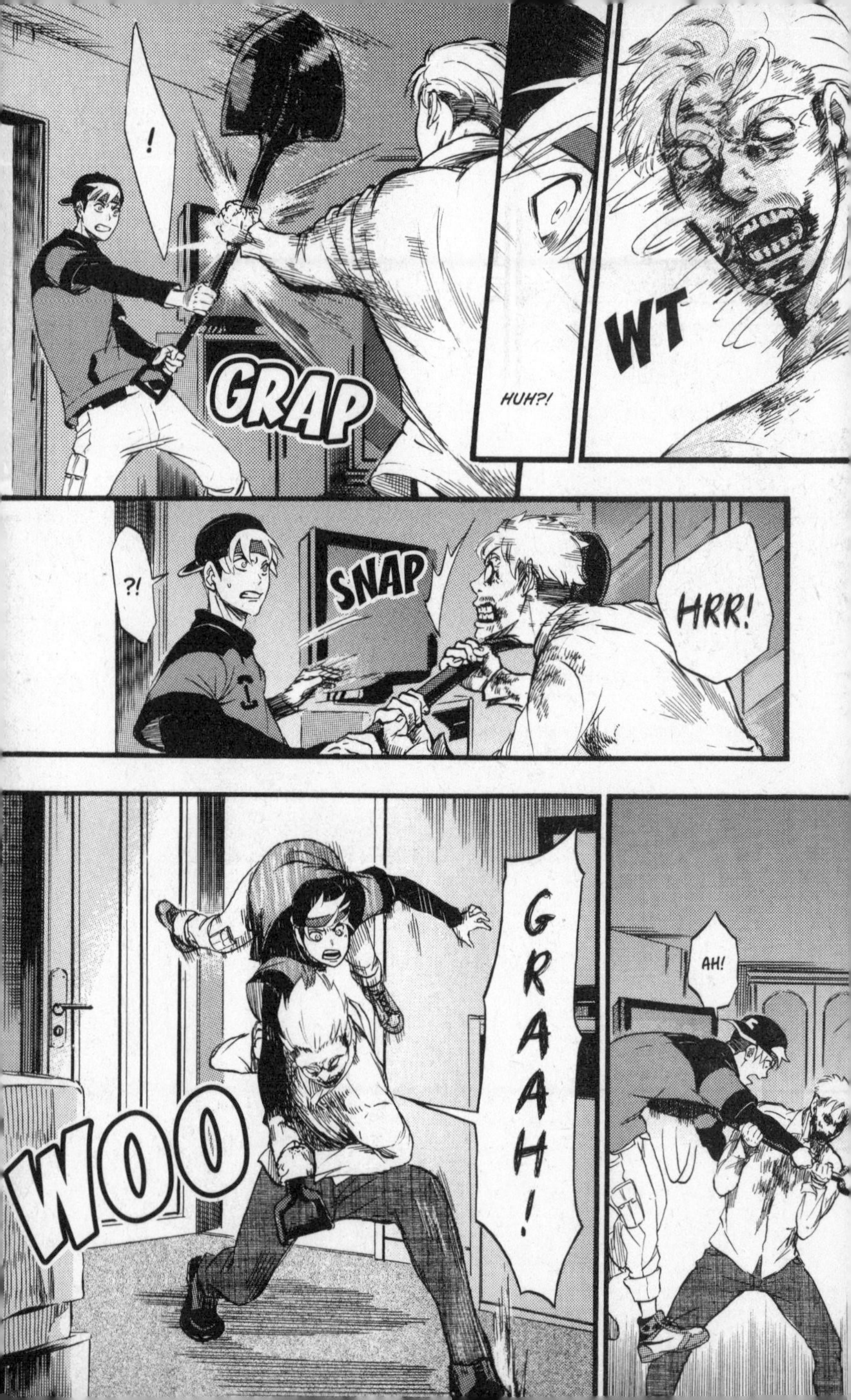
WT
HUH?!
!
GRAP
HRR!
SNAP
?!
AH!
GRAAH!
WOO

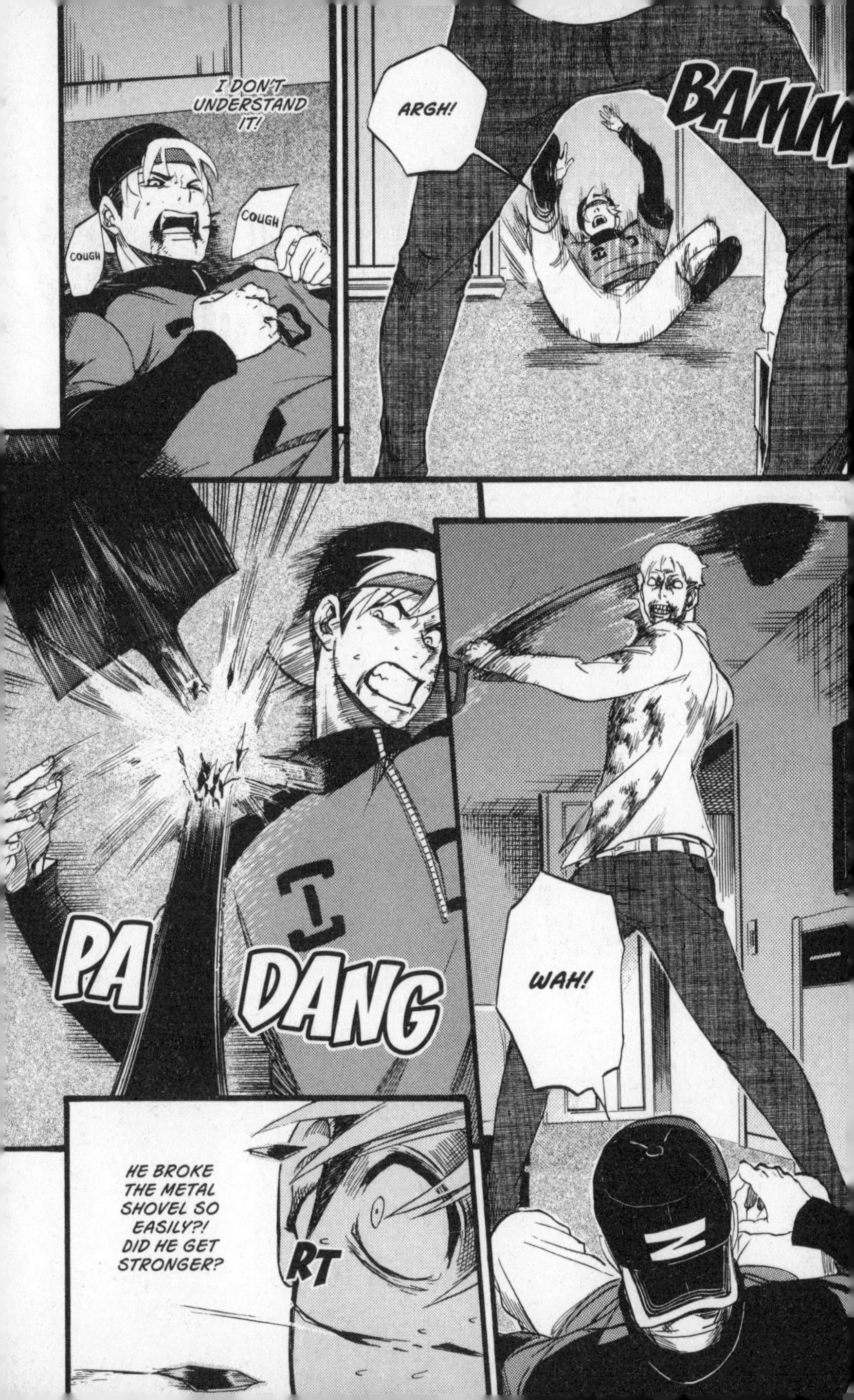
BAMM
ARGH!
I DON'T UNDERSTAND IT!
COUGH
COUGH
WAH!
PA
DANG
HE BROKE THE METAL SHOVEL SO EASILY?! DID HE GET STRONGER?
RT

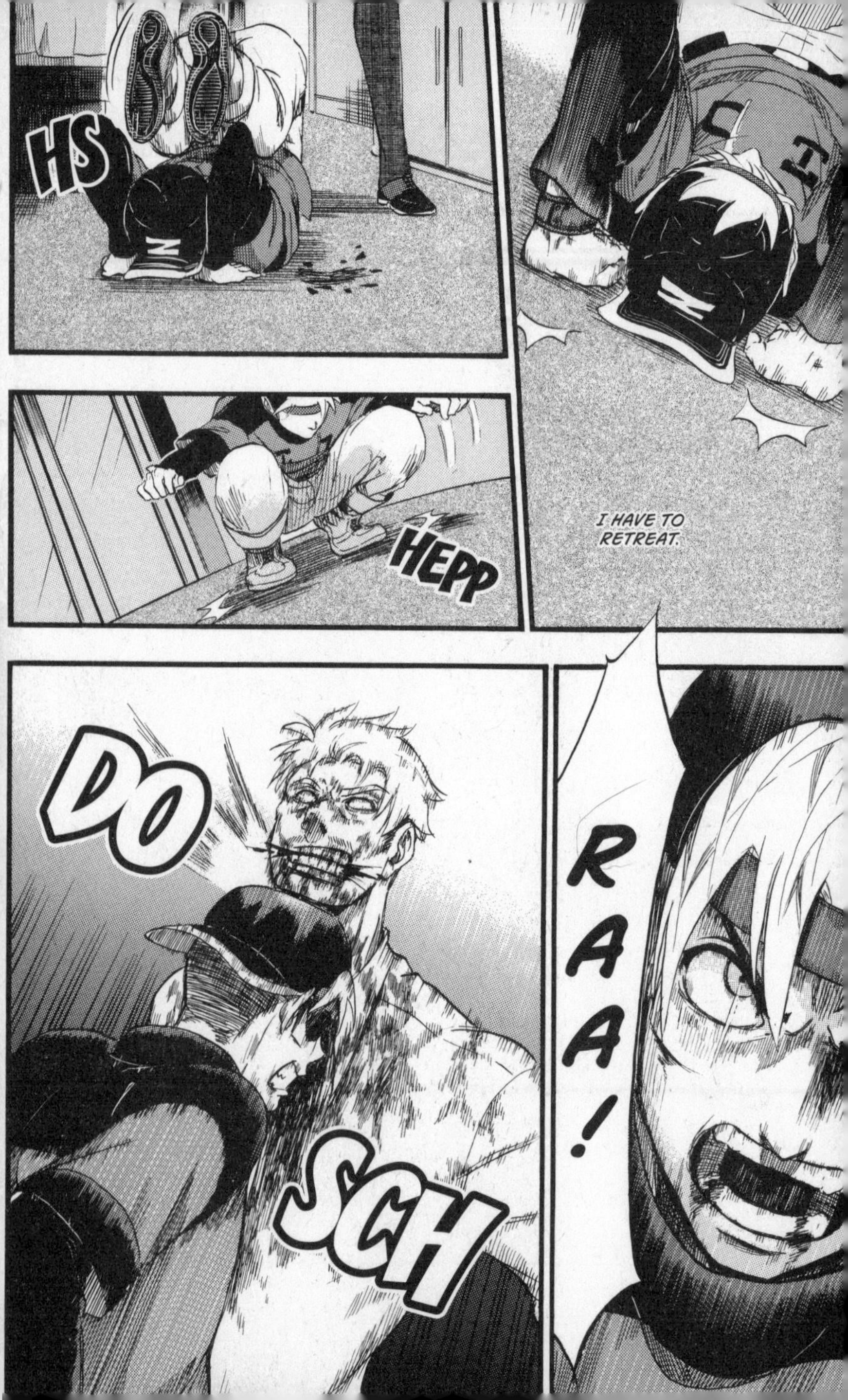
I HAVE TO RETREAT.
HS
HEPP
RAAA!
DO
SCH

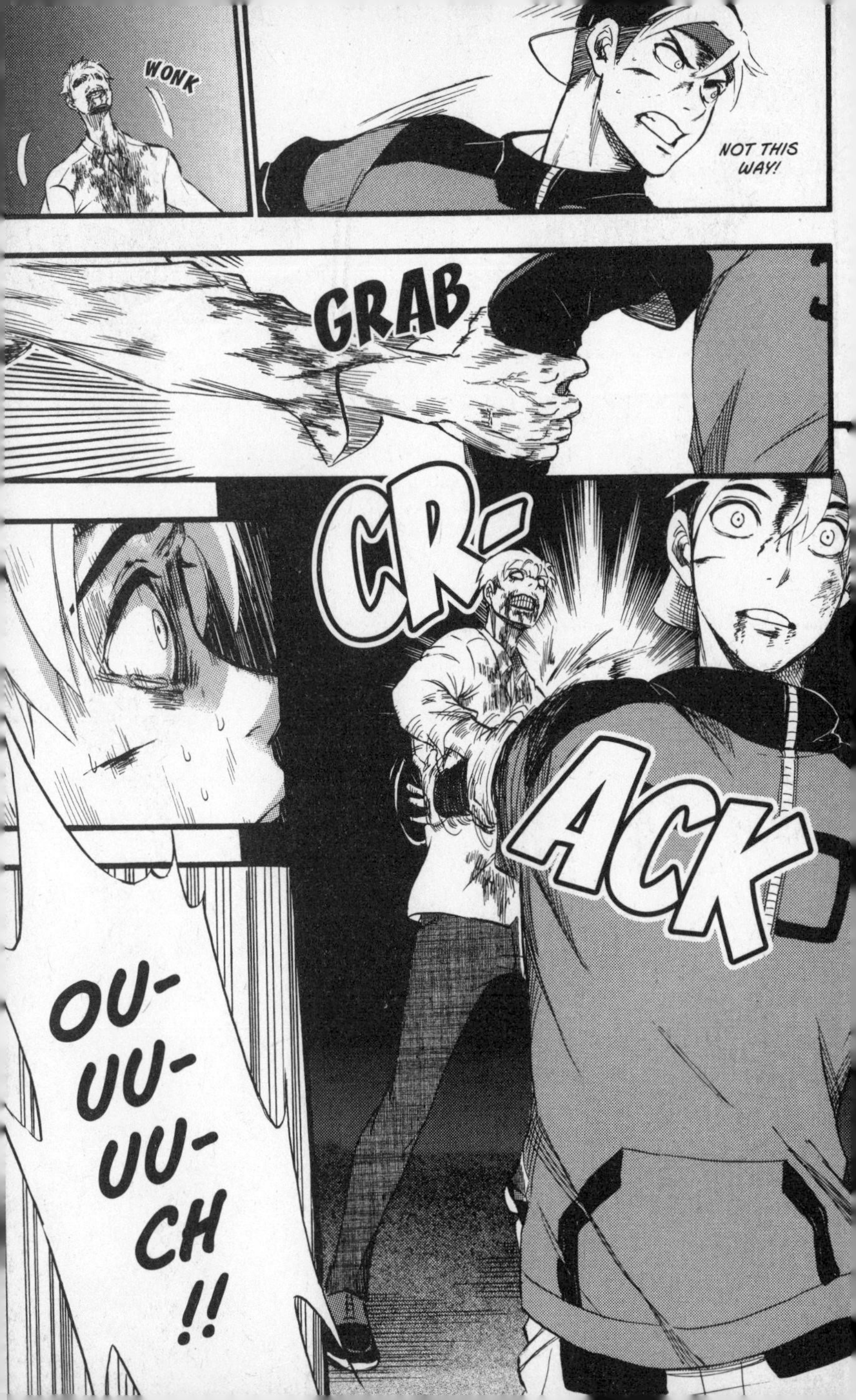
NOT THIS WAY!
WONK
GRAB
CR-
ACK
OU-UU-UU-CH!!

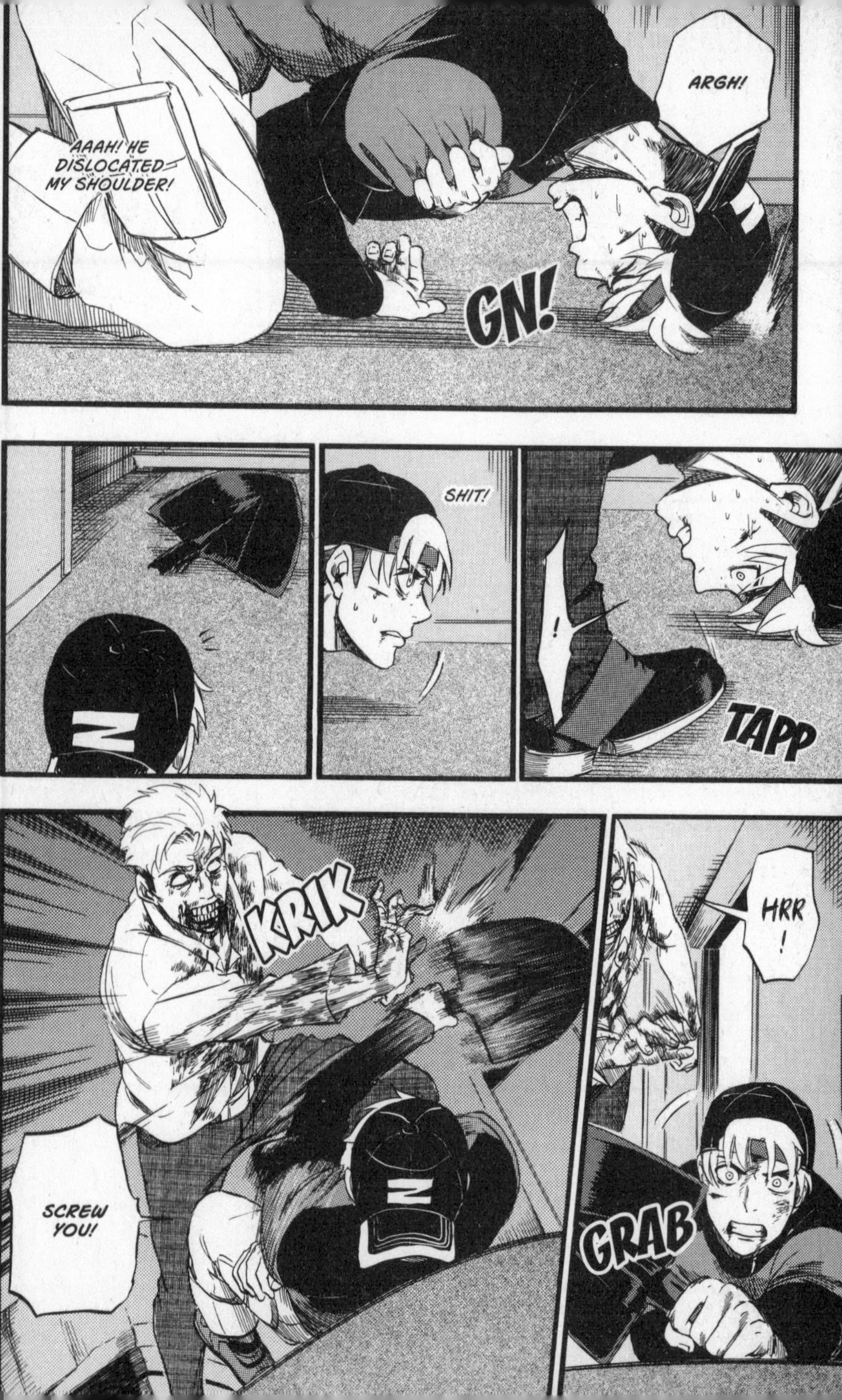
ARGH!
AAAH! HE DISLOCATED MY SHOULDER!
GN!
!
TAPP
SHIT!
HRR !
GRAB
KRIK
SCREW YOU!

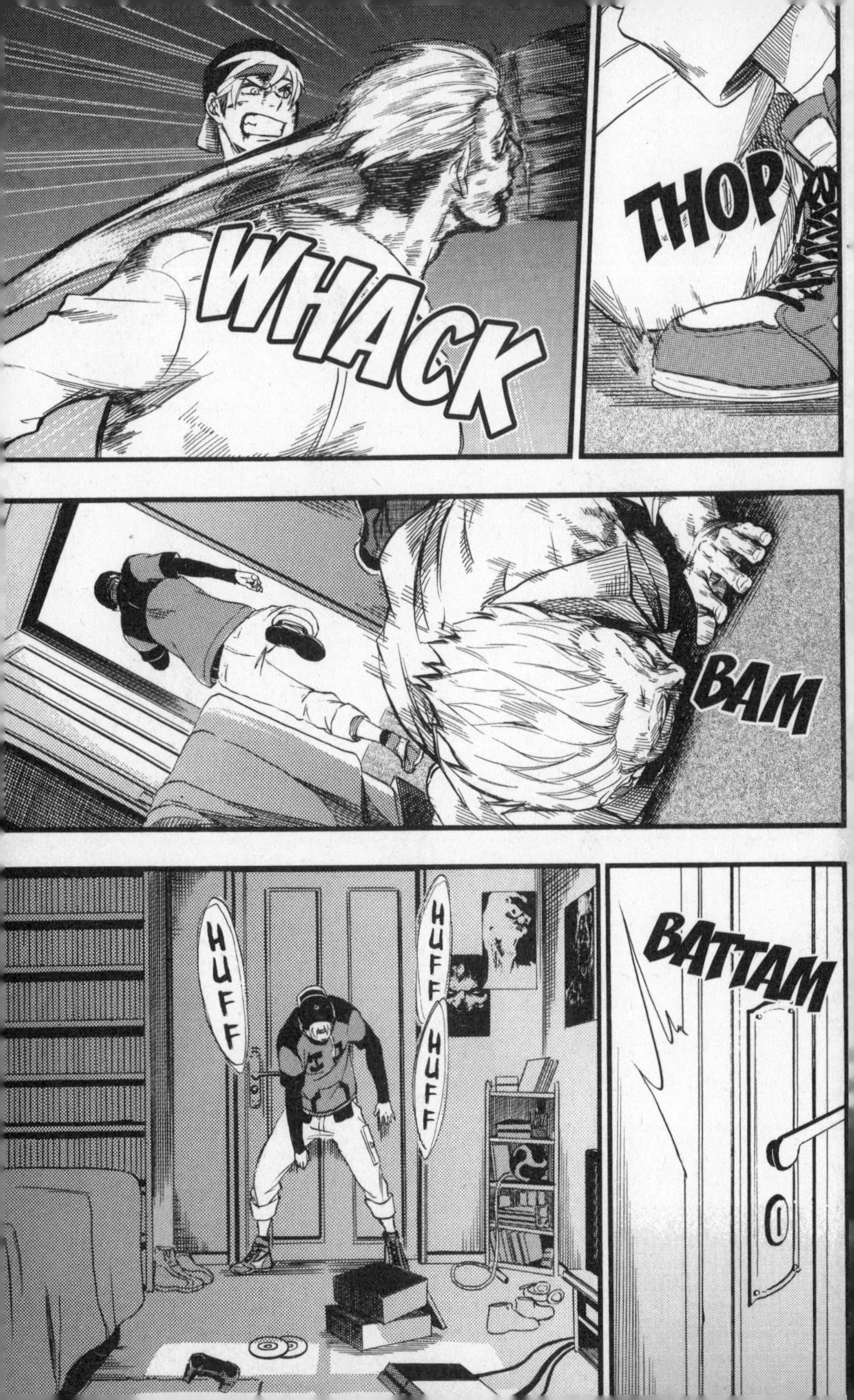
THOP
WHACK
BAM
BATTAM
HUFF HUFF
HUFF
HUFF

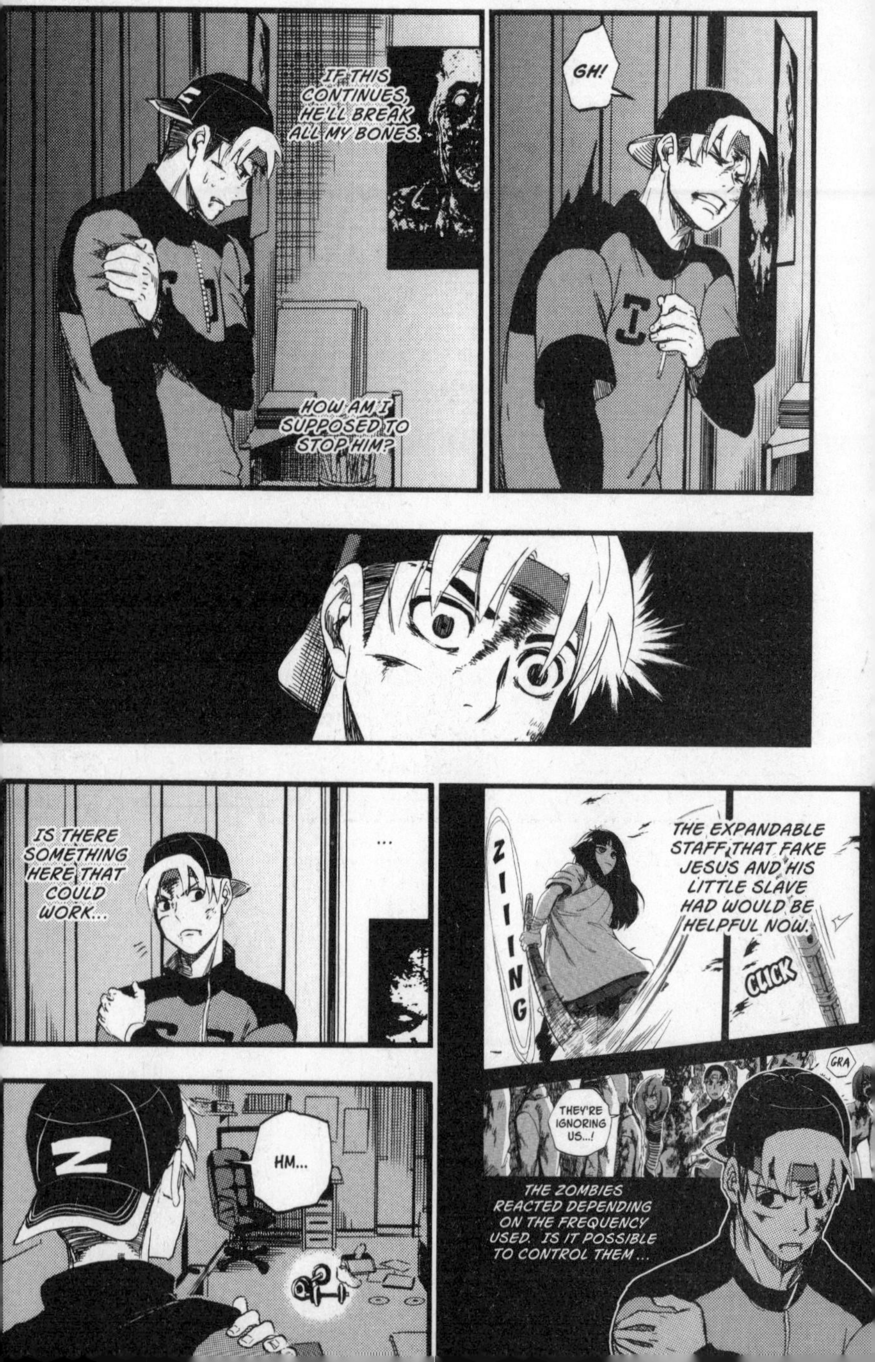
GH!
IF THIS CONTINUES, HE'LL BREAK ALL MY BONES.
HOW AM I SUPPOSED TO STOP HIM?
THE EXPANDABLE STAFF THAT FAKE JESUS AND HIS LITTLE SLAVE HAD WOULD BE HELPFUL NOW.
ZIIING
CLICK
GRA
THEY'RE IGNORING US...!
THE ZOMBIES REACTED DEPENDING ON THE FREQUENCY USED. IS IT POSSIBLE TO CONTROL THEM...
...
IS THERE SOMETHING HERE THAT COULD WORK...
HM...

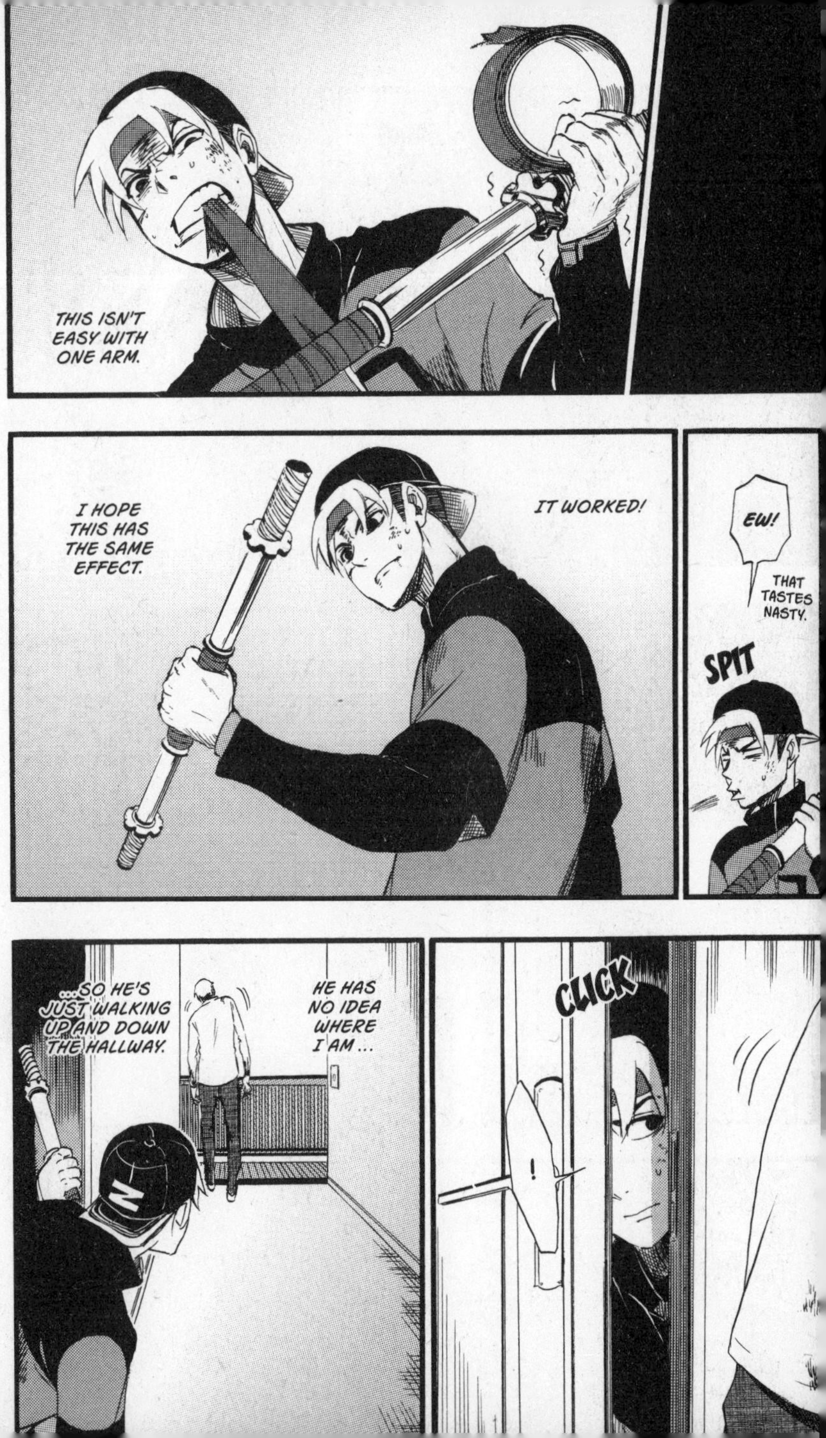
THIS ISN'T EASY WITH ONE ARM.
EW!
THAT TASTES NASTY.
SPIT
IT WORKED!
I HOPE THIS HAS THE SAME EFFECT.
CLICK
!
HE HAS NO IDEA WHERE I AM...
...SO HE'S JUST WALKING UP AND DOWN THE HALLWAY.

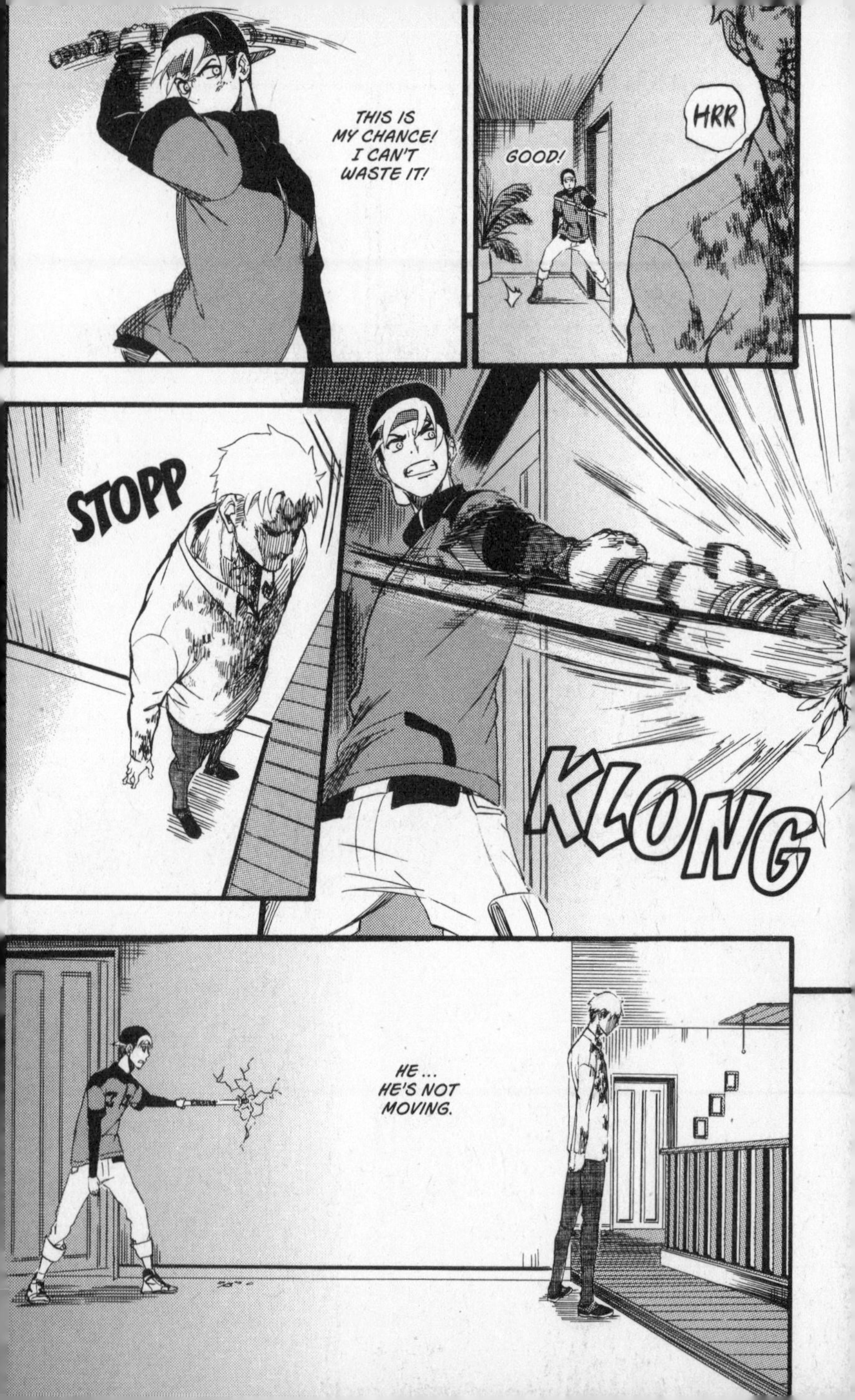
HRR
GOOD!
THIS IS MY CHANCE! I CAN'T WASTE IT!
KLONG
STOPP
HE... HE'S NOT MOVING.

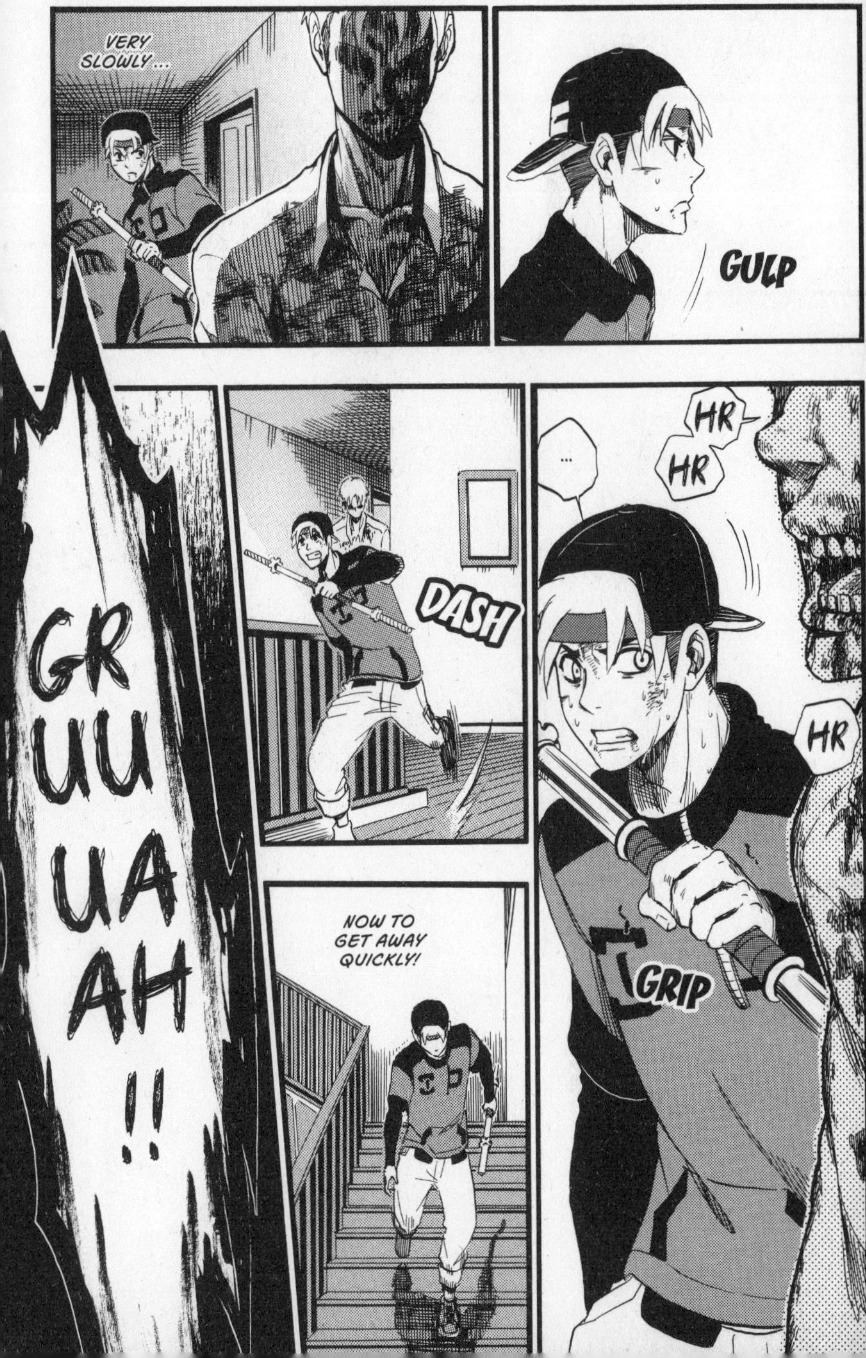
GULP
VERY SLOWLY...
...
HR
HR
HR
GRIP
DASH
NOW TO GET AWAY QUICKLY!
GRUUUAAH!!

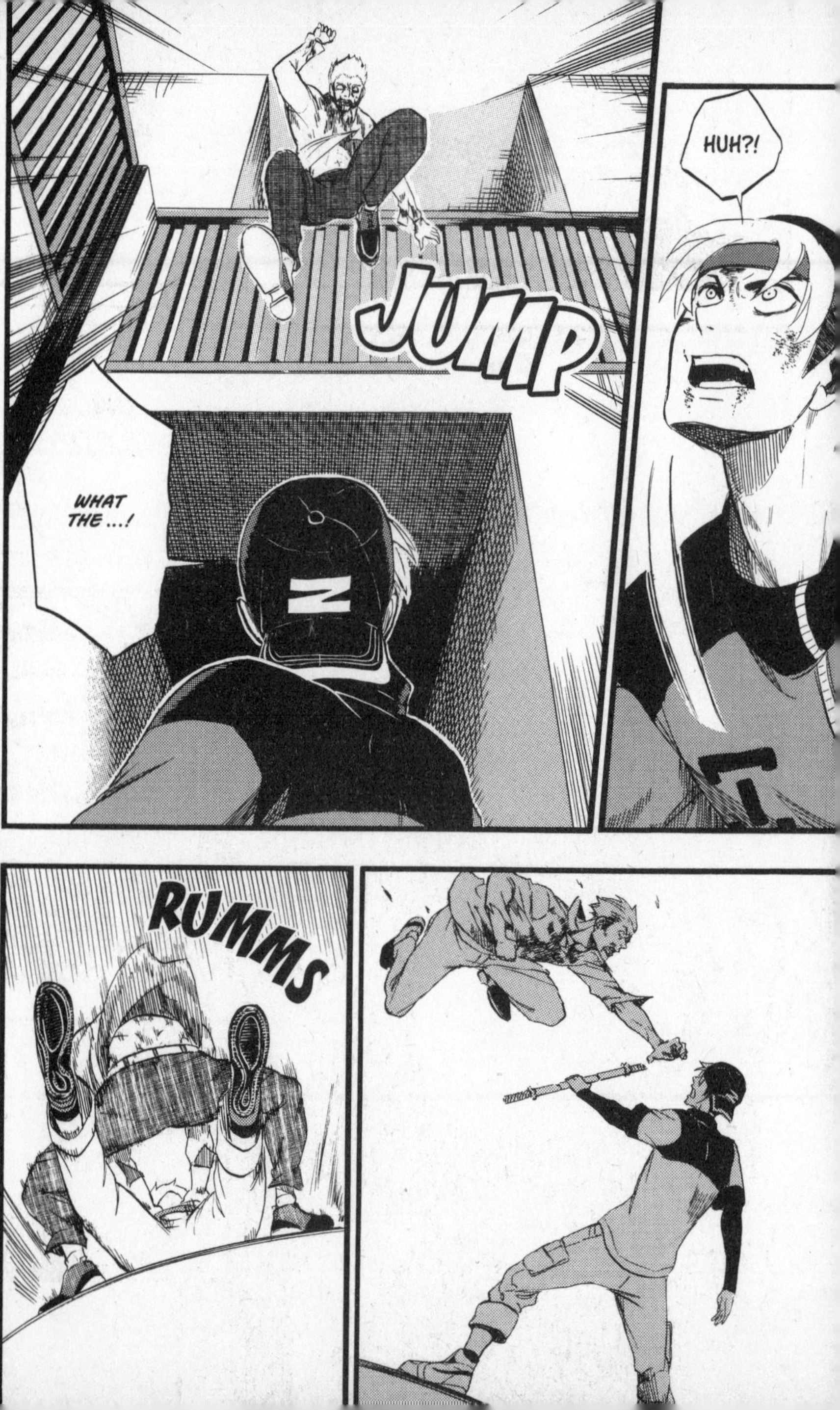
HUH?!
JUMP
WHAT THE...!
RUMMS

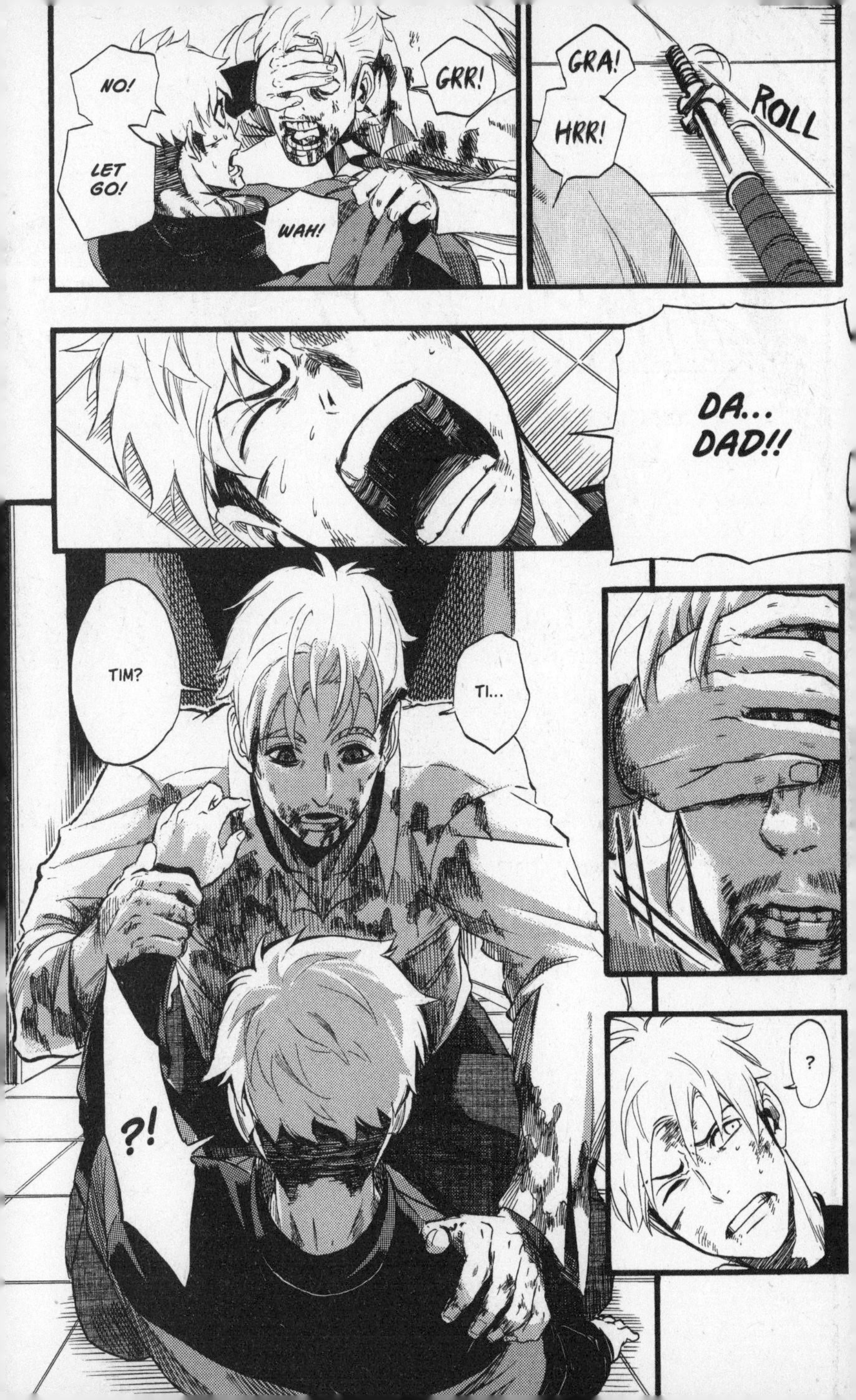
GRA!
HRR!
ROLL
GRR!
NO!
LET GO!
WAH!
DA... DAD!!
?
TI...
TIM?
?!

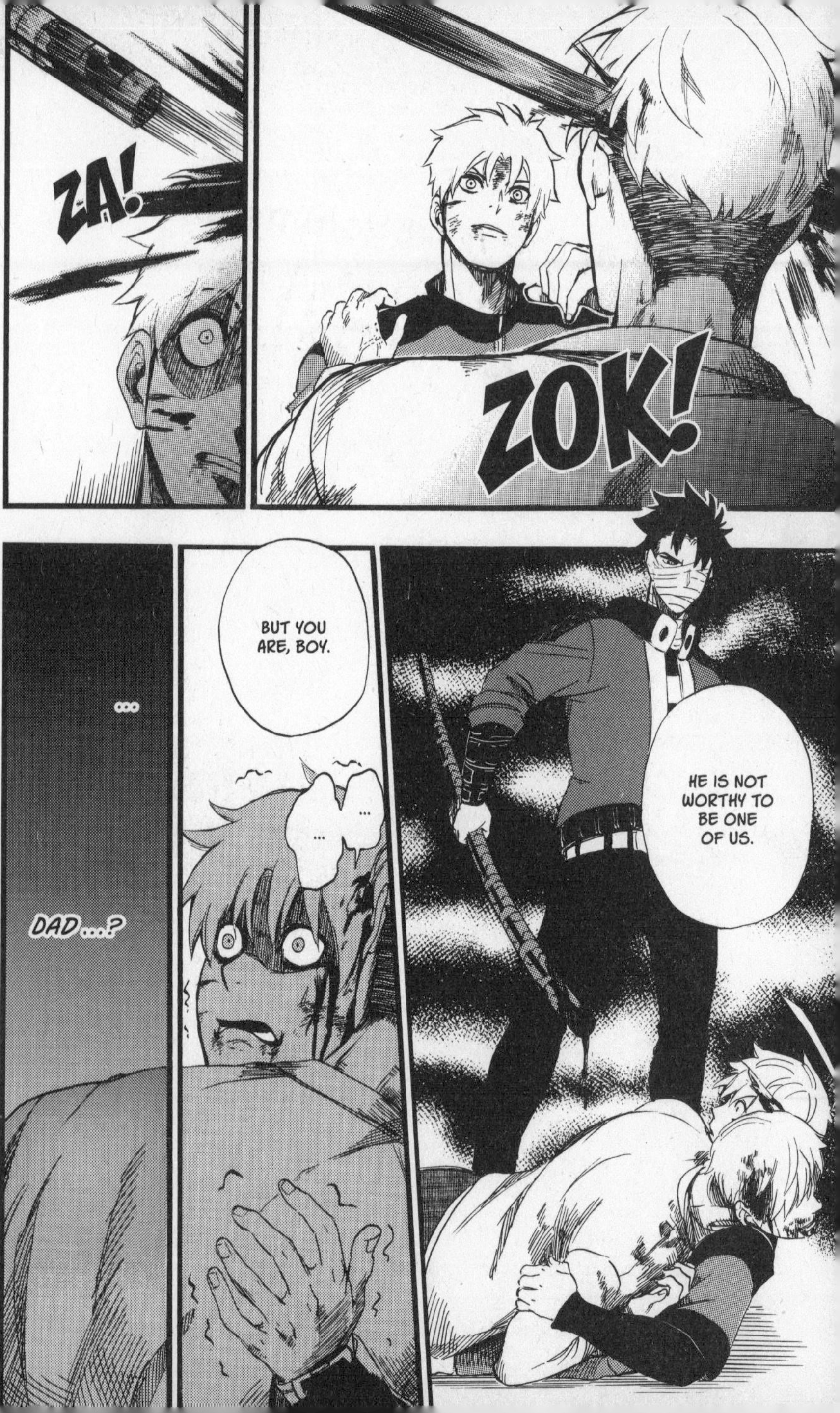
ZOK!
ZA!
HE IS NOT WORTHY TO BE ONE OF US.
BUT YOU ARE, BOY.
...
...
...
DAD...?

In the next volume of

UNDEAD MESSIAH

Tim Zachariah Muley has been recruited — against his will — into this supposed savior's bizarre organization and Tim finds himself surrounded by loyal apostles with unbelievable powers, savage zombies hungry for meat, and the kind of scientific conspiracy he could never have imagined in his wildest nightmares. Who is this secretive, bandaged antihero?

What is the truth behind the zombie virus? And what does it have to do with a fantasy-prone teenage gamer?

Find out more in volume two of *Undead Messiah*!

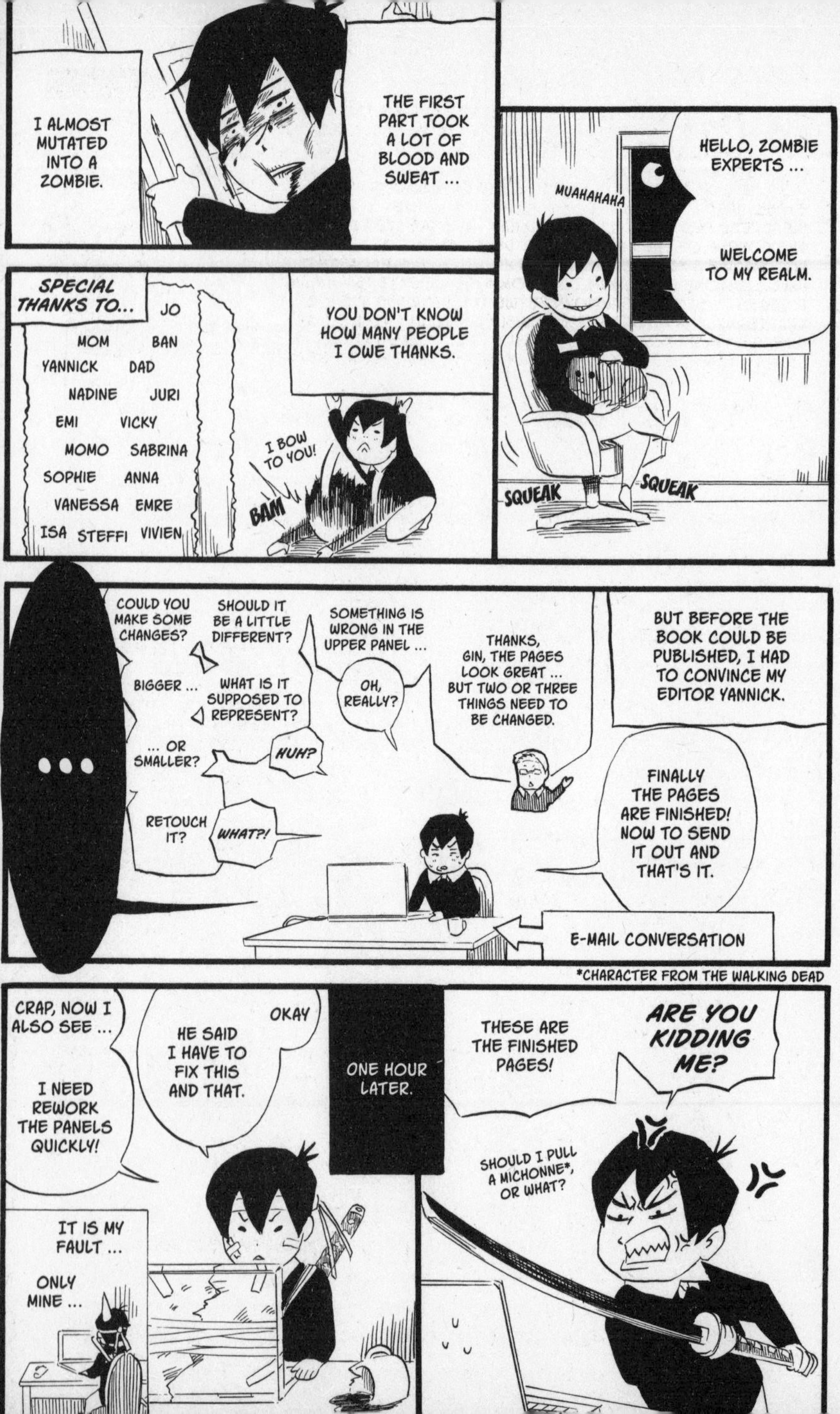
HELLO, ZOMBIE EXPERTS ...
WELCOME TO MY REALM.
MUAHAHAHA
SQUEAK
SQUEAK
THE FIRST PART TOOK A LOT OF BLOOD AND SWEAT ...
I ALMOST MUTATED INTO A ZOMBIE.
YOU DON'T KNOW HOW MANY PEOPLE I OWE THANKS.
I BOW TO YOU!
BAM
SPECIAL THANKS TO...
JO
MOM BAN
YANNICK DAD
NADINE JURI
EMI VICKY
MOMO SABRINA
SOPHIE ANNA
VANESSA EMRE
ISA STEFFI VIVIEN
BUT BEFORE THE BOOK COULD BE PUBLISHED, I HAD TO CONVINCE MY EDITOR YANNICK.
FINALLY THE PAGES ARE FINISHED! NOW TO SEND IT OUT AND THAT'S IT.
E-MAIL CONVERSATION
THANKS, GIN, THE PAGES LOOK GREAT ... BUT TWO OR THREE THINGS NEED TO BE CHANGED.
SOMETHING IS WRONG IN THE UPPER PANEL ...
OH, REALLY?
SHOULD IT BE A LITTLE DIFFERENT?
COULD YOU MAKE SOME CHANGES?
WHAT IS IT SUPPOSED TO REPRESENT?
BIGGER ...
HUH?
... OR SMALLER?
WHAT?!
RETOUCH IT?
...
ARE YOU KIDDING ME?
THESE ARE THE FINISHED PAGES!
SHOULD I PULL A MICHONNE*, OR WHAT?
ONE HOUR LATER.
OKAY
HE SAID I HAVE TO FIX THIS AND THAT.
CRAP, NOW I ALSO SEE ...
I NEED REWORK THE PANELS QUICKLY!
IT IS MY FAULT ...
ONLY MINE ...

*CHARACTER FROM THE WALKING DEAD

EPILOGUE

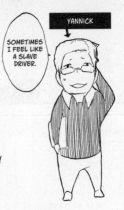

YANNICK
SOMETIMES I FEEL LIKE A SLAVE DRIVER.

HELLO AGAIN! UNFORTUNATELY, I HAVE TO KEEP THIS SHORT BECAUSE I DON'T HAVE MUCH SPACE. FIRST LET ME TELL YOU HOW HAPPY I AM WITH YANNICK AS MY EDITOR. WITH HIS HELP, I HAVE SUCCEEDED IN MAKING THE BEST VERSION OF *UNDEAD MESSIAH*. UNBELIEVABLE, THIS MANGA WOULD NOT HAVE BEEN DRAWN OR STRUCTURED IF YANNICK HAD NOT HELPED. HA HA! EVEN IF WE DISAGREED FROM TIME TO TIME AND HAD LONG DEBATES ABOUT THE COURSE OF THE STORY OR THE DEVELOPMENT OF TIM, I CAN NOT IMAGINE A BETTER EDITOR THAN HIM. I AM VERY HAPPY THAT I HAVE SOMEONE WITH WHOM I CAN COMMUNICATE EXTENSIVELY AND DISCUSS MY STORY. TEAMWORK BETWEEN EDITOR AND AUTHOR/ DRAFTSMAN IS IN MY OPINION INCREDIBLY IMPORTANT, AS WELL AS COHESION AND EXCHANGES BETWEEN THE DRAFTSMEN IN THE GERMAN MANGA SCENE. ONE CAN ONLY EVOLVE AND BECOME BETTER!

SO... THANK YOU, YANNICK FOR HAVING BEEN THERE OVER THE MONTHS AND HELPING ME DEVELOP THE STORY TOGETHER WITH ME!

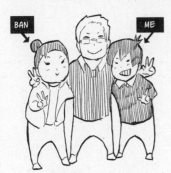

BAN
ME

SPECIAL THANKS TO MY TWIN SISTER BAN. WE HAVE ALWAYS SUPPORTED EACH OTHER. WE ARE RIVALS, COLLEAGUES AND FAMILY ALL AT THE SAME TIME.

WE ARE A TEAM!

IN ADDITION TO THE MANY PEOPLE I MENTIONED ON THE PREVIOUS PAGE, I WANT TO THANK J-STUFF.DE, MY FAVORITE MANGA ARTIST SHOP! THANK YOU! WITHOUT THEIR FIRST CLASS MATERIALS THIS MANGA WOULD NOT HAVE BEEN CREATED.

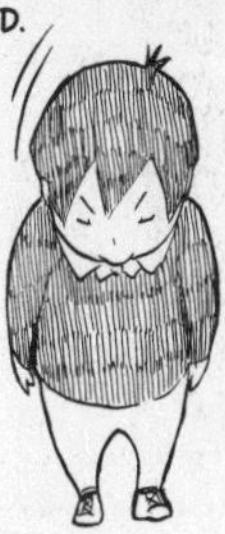

FINALLY, A BIG THANK YOU TO ALL OF YOU, MY DEAR ZOMBIE NERDS! IT REALLY MEANS A LOT TO ME THAT YOU HAVE TAKEN THIS MANGA IN YOUR HAND. YOU CAN'T IMAGINE HOW LONG I'VE BEEN WAITING FOR THIS MOMENT *SOB SOB*, SINCE IT IS ALSO MY FIRST PIECE FOR TOKYOPOP! THANKS A LOT!

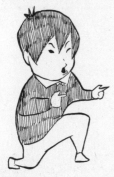

I AM CURIOUS TO SEE HOW YOU FEEL ABOUT THE MANGA AND I AM HAPPY TO HEAR CRITICISM OF ANY KIND. SO IF YOU WANT TO WRITE ME, BE IT ABOUT *UNDEAD MESSIAH* OR SOMETHING ELSE ...

... ***DON'T HESITATE! :D***

MY E-MAIL ADDRESS:

GIN.ZARBO@HOTMAIL.COM

I HOPE THAT WE MEET AGAIN IN THE NEXT BOOK!

YOUR GIN ^^

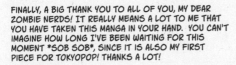

DEAR READERS,

WE WOULD ALSO LIKE TO THANK YOU FOR PURCHASING THIS FUN MANGA. WE TWO VANNESSAS HAVE HELPED GIN DIGITALLY EDIT THE PAGES, IN HOPES THAT THE PAGES WILL LOOK JUST AS GREAT IN PRINT AS THE ORIGINAL ARTWORK. WE ARE WERE SUPER-STRESSED PRODUCING THE FINAL RESULT AND KEEP YOUR FINGERS CROSSED THAT *UNDEAD MESSIAH* WILL BE A SUCCESS. SHE REALLY DESERVES IT!

GIN'S PHOTOSHOP ASSISTANTS

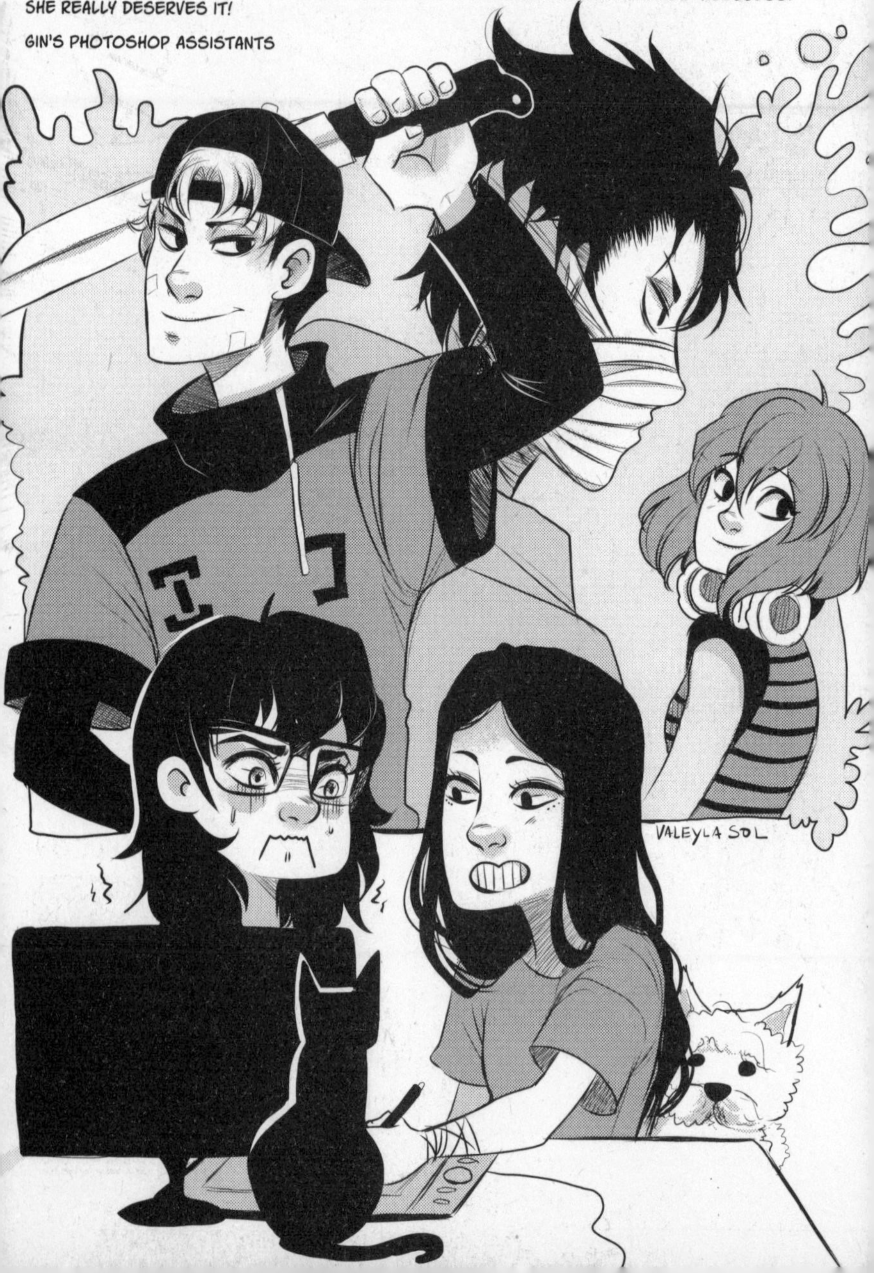
VALEYLA SOL

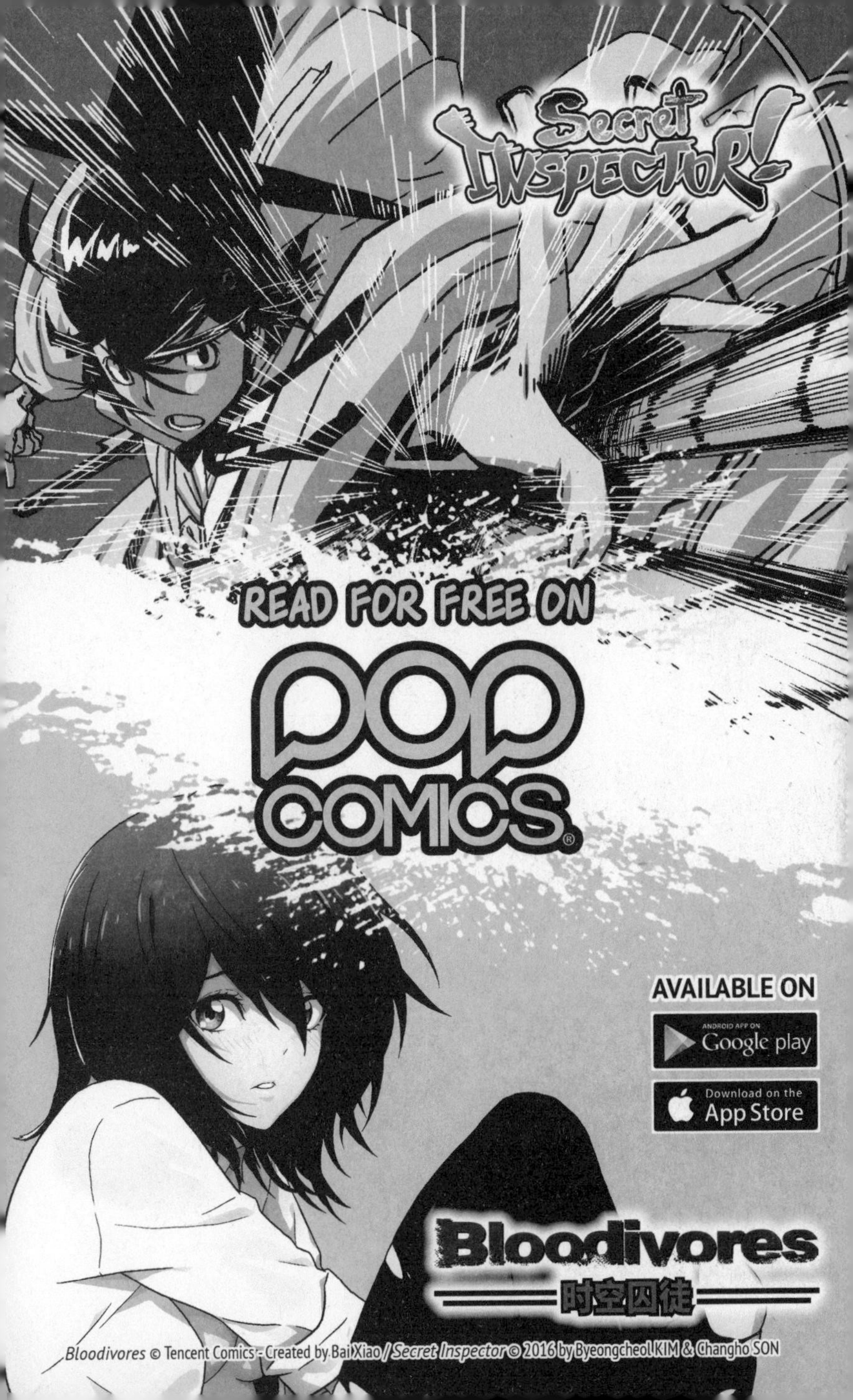
Secret INSPECTOR!
READ FOR FREE ON
POP COMICS®
AVAILABLE ON
ANDROID APP ON Google play
Download on the App Store
Bloodivores
时空囚徒
Bloodivores © Tencent Comics - Created by Bai Xiao / Secret Inspector © 2016 by Byeongcheol KIM & Changho SON

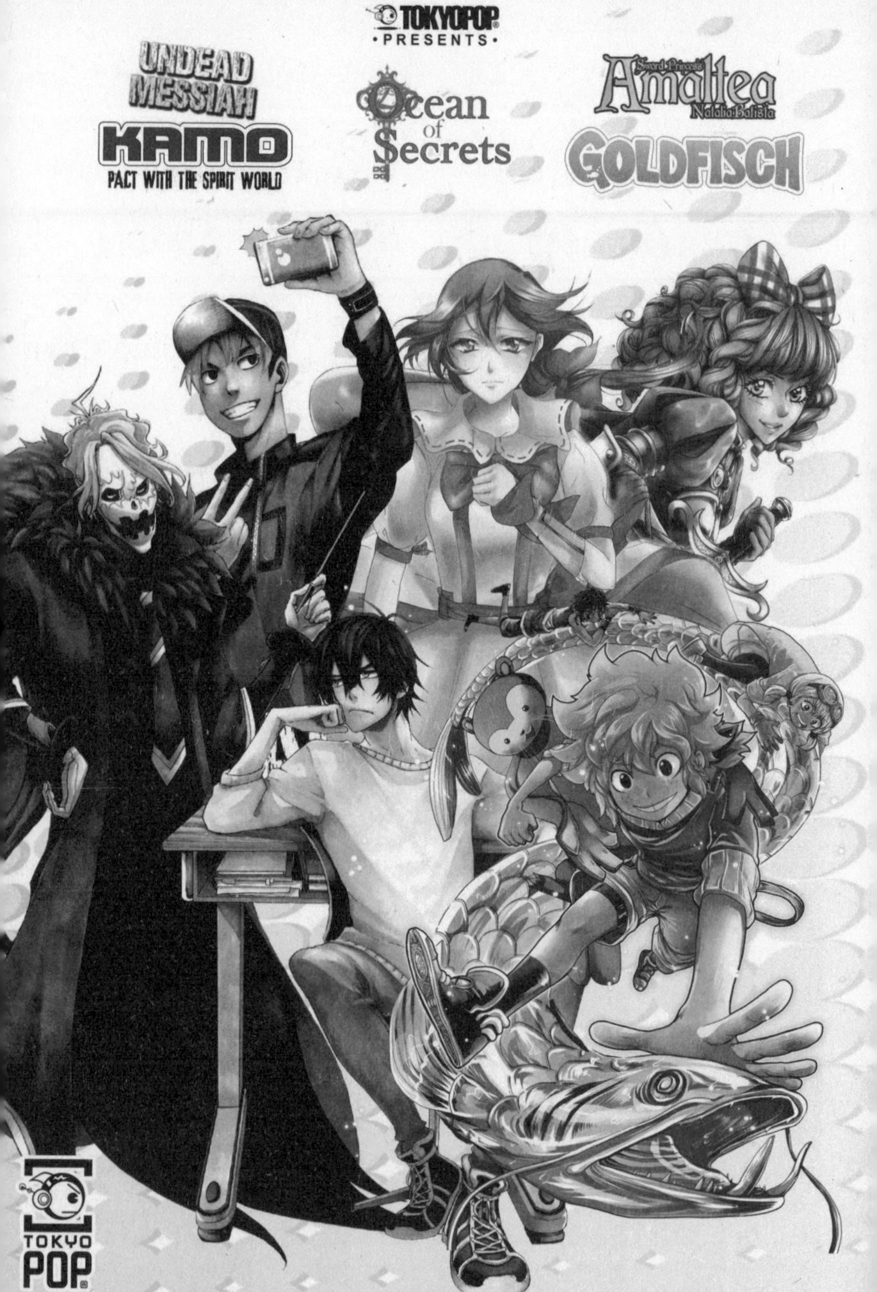
TOKYOPOP
PRESENTS
UNDEAD MESSIAH
KAMO
PACT WITH THE SPIRIT WORLD
Ocean of Secrets
Sword Princess Amaltea
Natalia Batista
GOLDFISCH
TOKYO POP

TOKYOPOP
· PRESENTS ·

INTERNATIONAL
WOMEN of MANGA

Nana Yaa

GOLDFISCH

An award-winning German manga artist with a large following for her free webcomic, *CRUSHED!!*

Sophie-Chan

Ocean of Secrets

A self-taught manga artist from the Middle East, with a huge YouTube following!

Ban Zarbo

KAMO
PACT WITH THE SPIRIT WORLD

A lifelong manga fan from Switzerland, she and her twin sister take inspiration from their Dominican roots!

Gin Zarbo

UNDEAD MESSIAH

An aspiring manga artist since she was a child, along with her twin sister she's releasing her debut title!

Natalia Batista

Sword Princess Amaltea
Natalia Batista

A Swedish creator whose popular manga has already been published in Sweden, Italy and the Czech Republic!

To Learn More Please Visit Our Website

www.TOKYOPOP.com

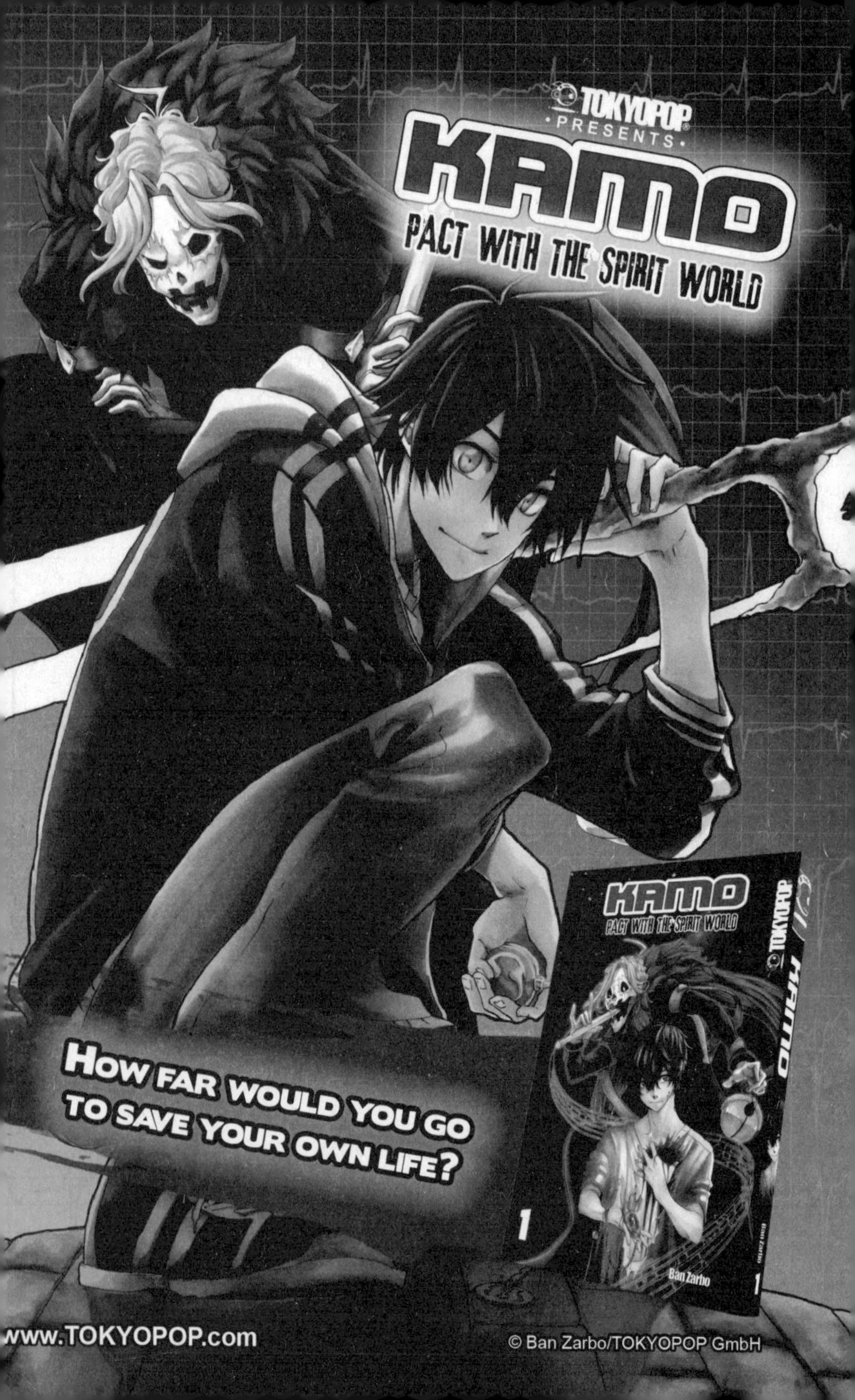

TOKYOPOP PRESENTS
KAMO
PACT WITH THE SPIRIT WORLD
HOW FAR WOULD YOU GO TO SAVE YOUR OWN LIFE?
KAMO
PACT WITH THE SPIRIT WORLD
TOKYOPOP
1
Ban Zarbo
www.TOKYOPOP.com
© Ban Zarbo/TOKYOPOP GmbH

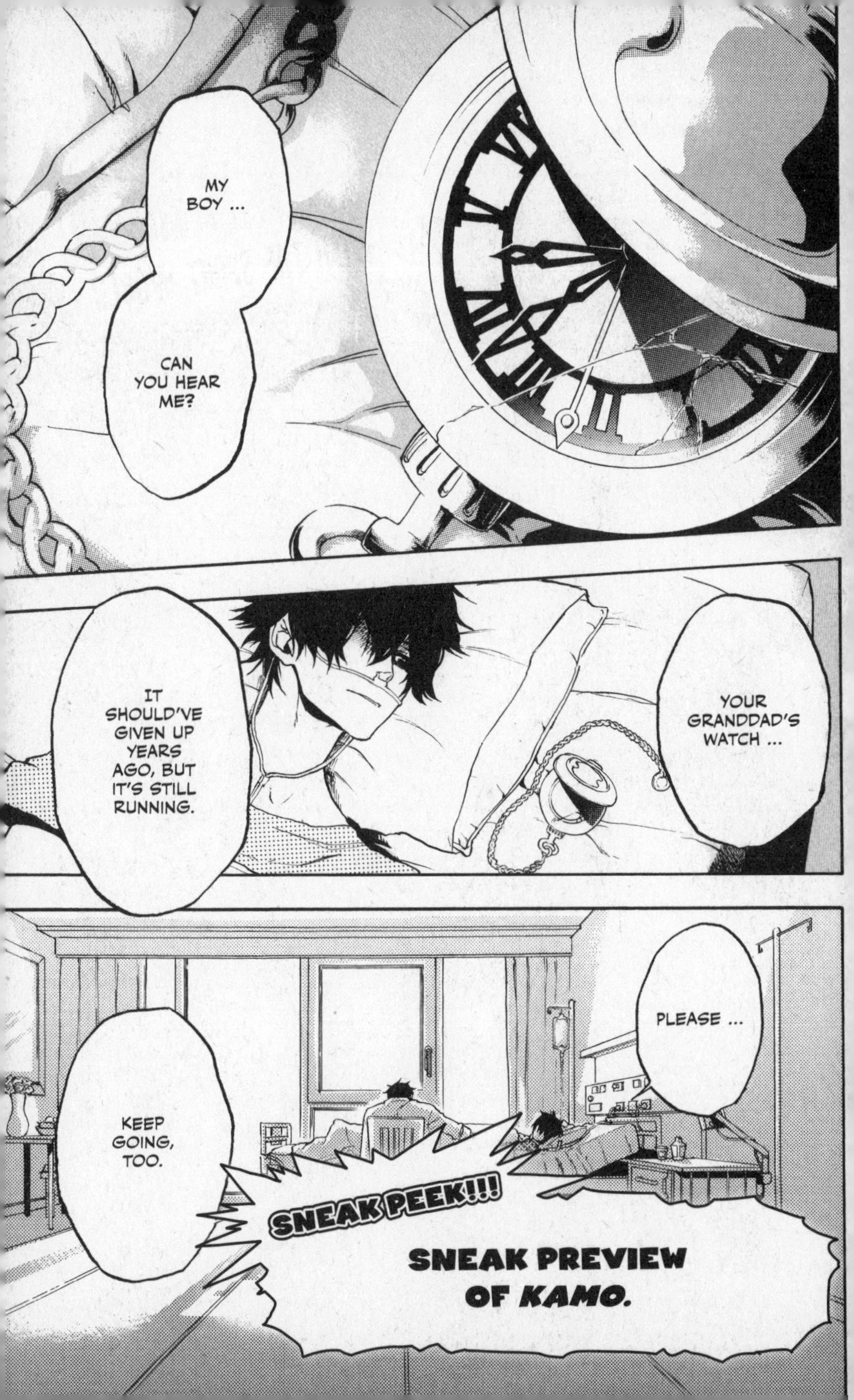
MY BOY ...
CAN YOU HEAR ME?
YOUR GRANDDAD'S WATCH ...
IT SHOULD'VE GIVEN UP YEARS AGO, BUT IT'S STILL RUNNING.
PLEASE ...
KEEP GOING, TOO.
SNEAK PEEK!!!
SNEAK PREVIEW OF *KAMO*.

YOU KNOW THERE'S NO POINT ANYMORE. YOUR TEARS BETRAY YOU.

DAD ...

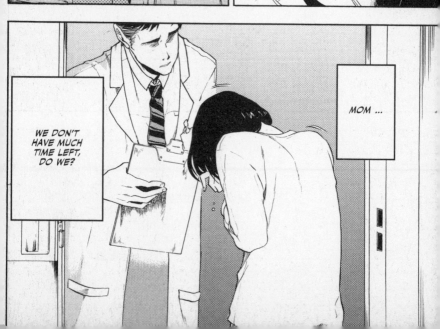

WE DON'T HAVE MUCH TIME LEFT, DO WE?

MOM ...

I ...
I DON'T WANT TO GO.

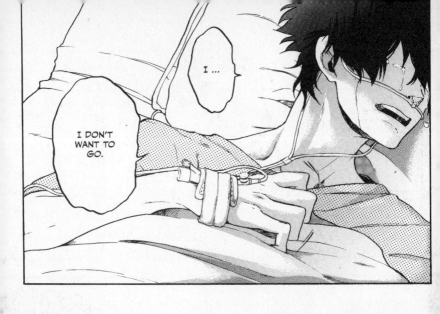

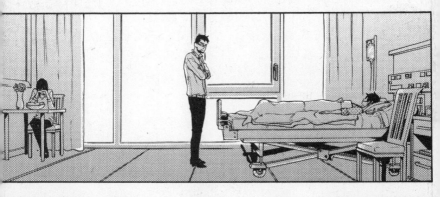

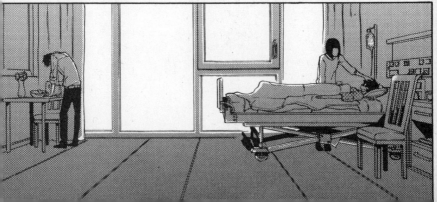

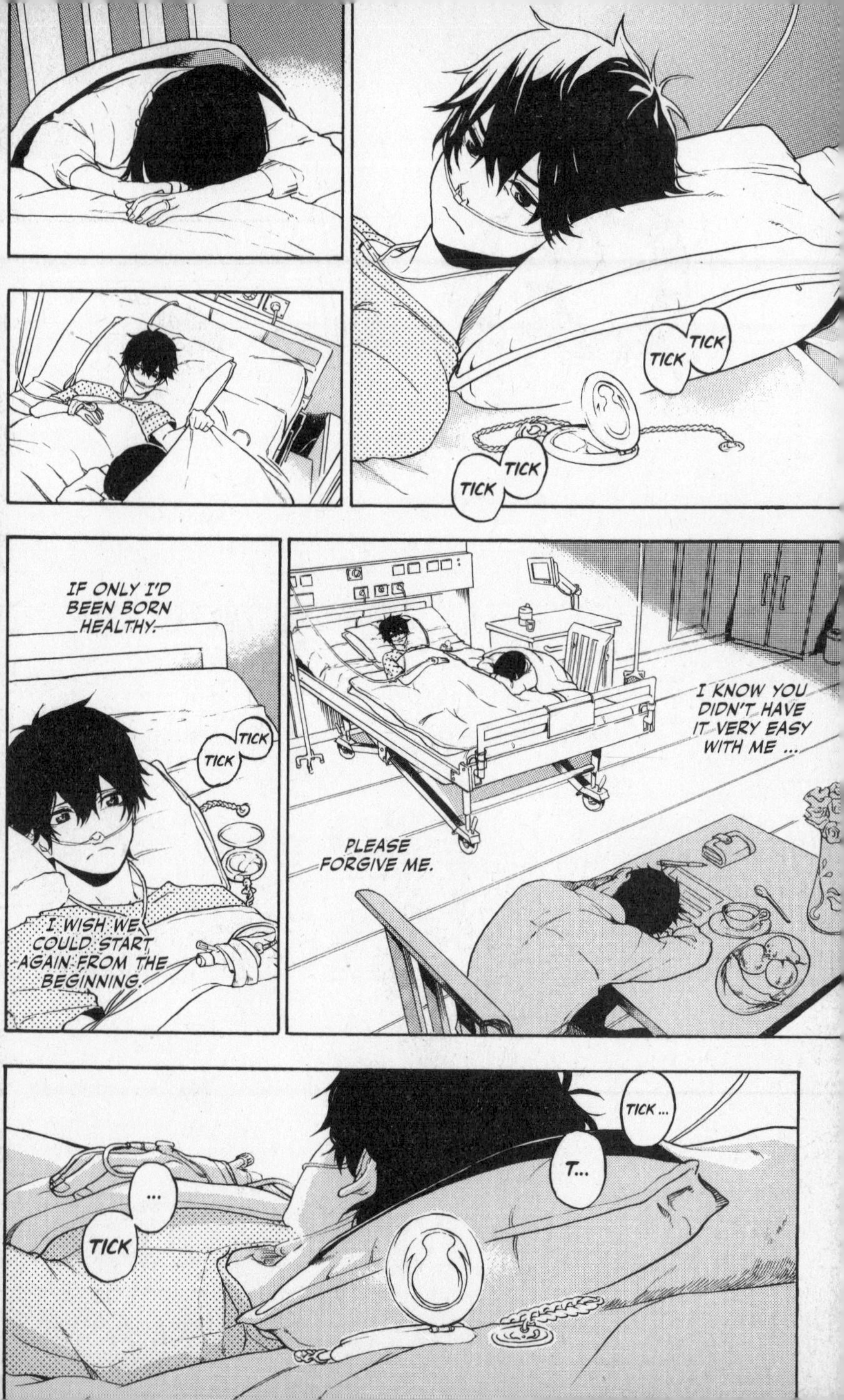
TICK
TICK
TICK
TICK
I KNOW YOU DIDN'T HAVE IT VERY EASY WITH ME ...
PLEASE FORGIVE ME.
IF ONLY I'D BEEN BORN HEALTHY.
TICK
TICK
I WISH WE COULD START AGAIN FROM THE BEGINNING.
TICK ...
T...
...
TICK

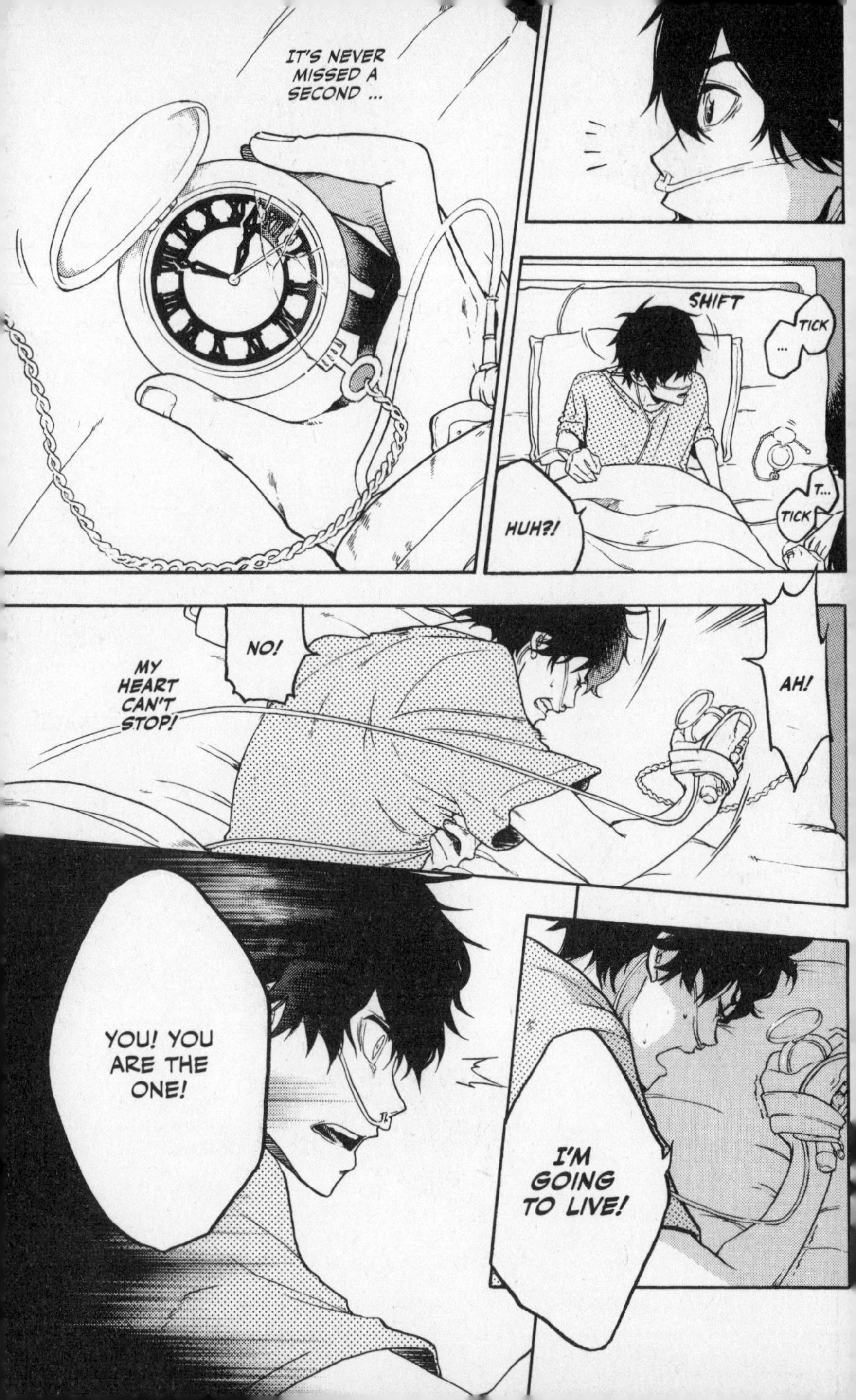
SHIFT
TICK ...
T... TICK
HUH?!
IT'S NEVER MISSED A SECOND ...
AH!
NO!
MY HEART CAN'T STOP!
I'M GOING TO LIVE!
YOU! YOU ARE THE ONE!

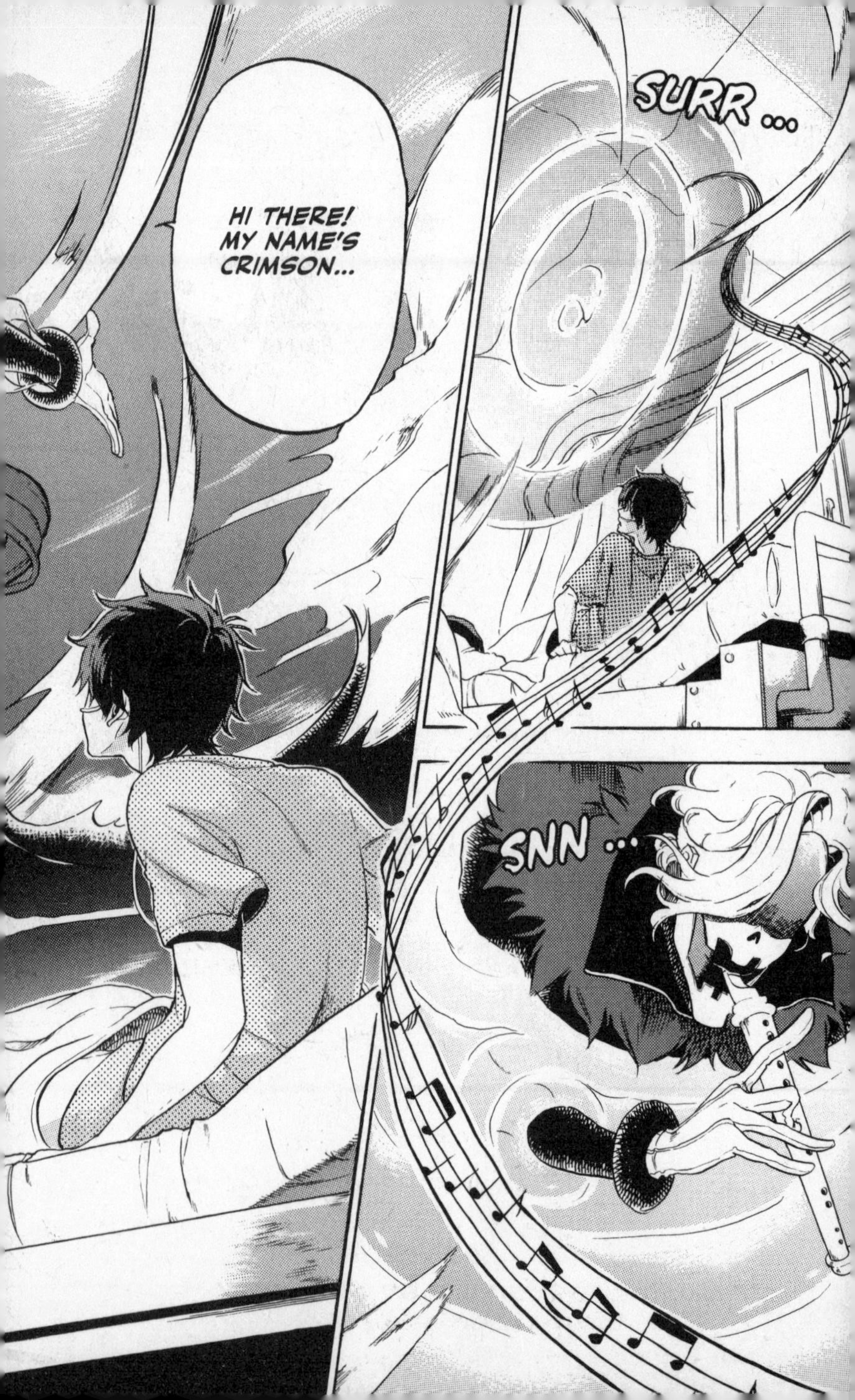
SURR...
SNN...
HI THERE! MY NAME'S CRIMSON...

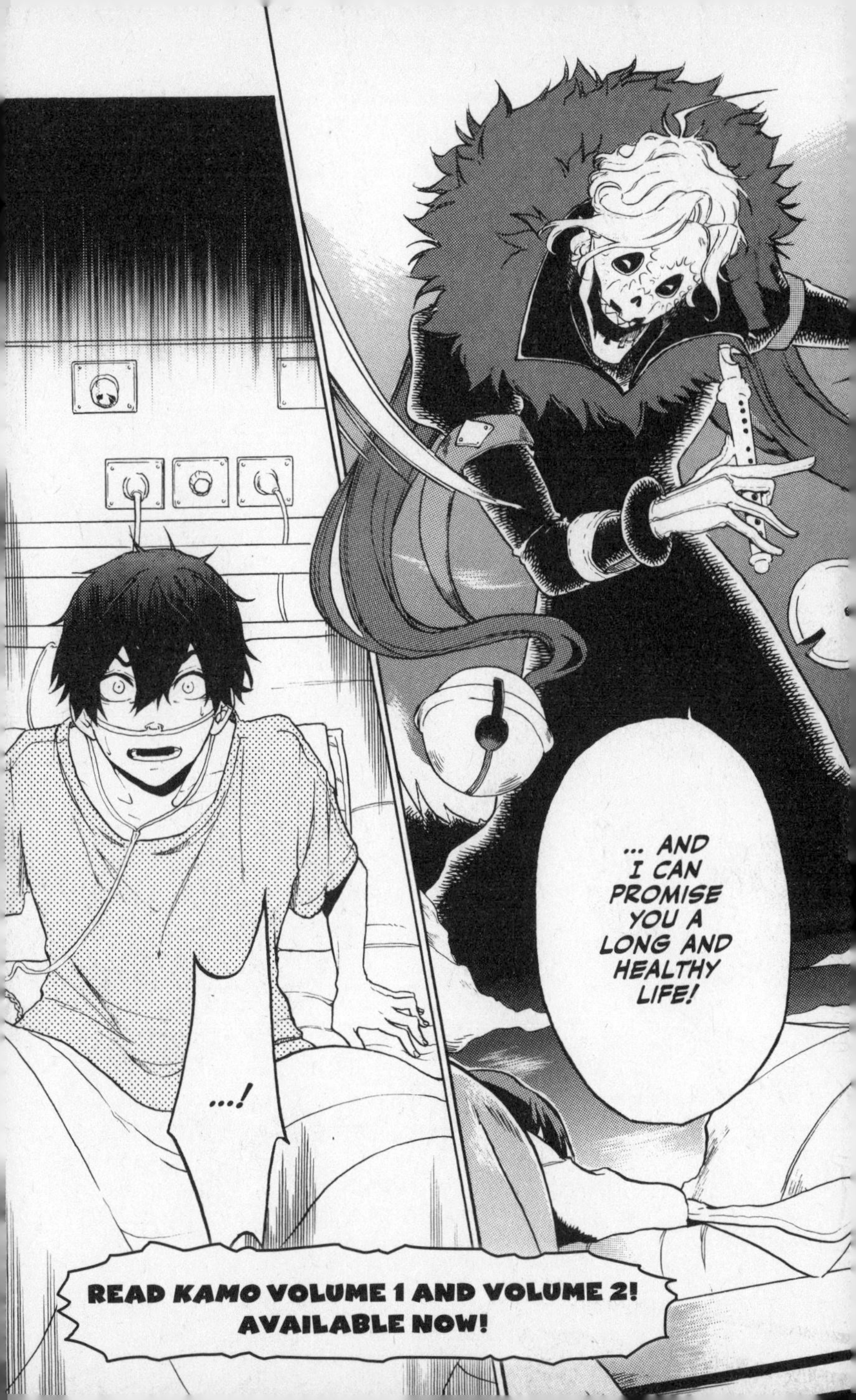
... AND I CAN PROMISE YOU A LONG AND HEALTHY LIFE!
...!
READ KAMO VOLUME 1 AND VOLUME 2! AVAILABLE NOW!

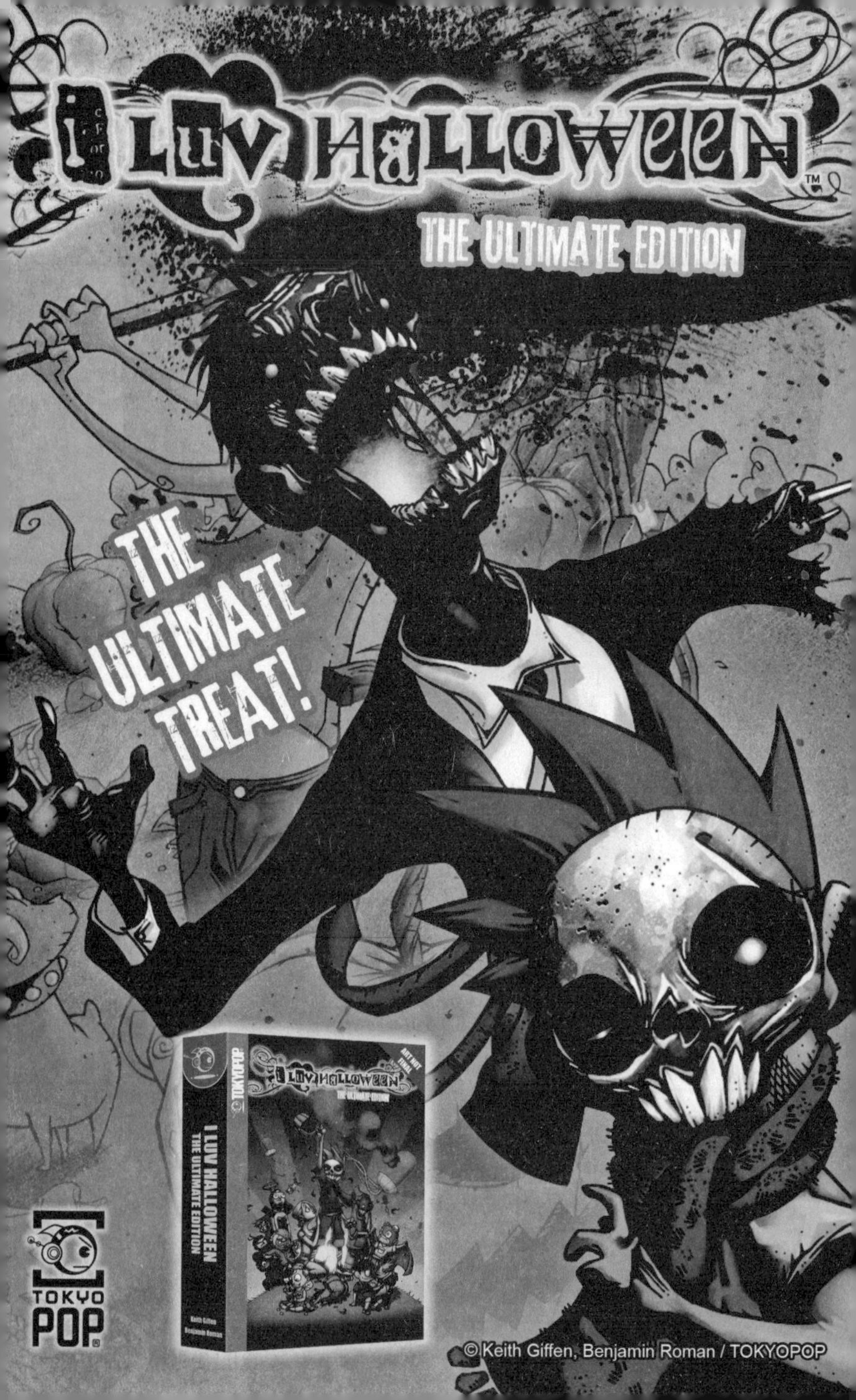

I LUV HALLOWEEN™
THE ULTIMATE EDITION
THE ULTIMATE TREAT!
I LUV HALLOWEEN
THE ULTIMATE EDITION
Keith Giffen
Benjamin Roman
TOKYOPOP
© Keith Giffen, Benjamin Roman / TOKYOPOP

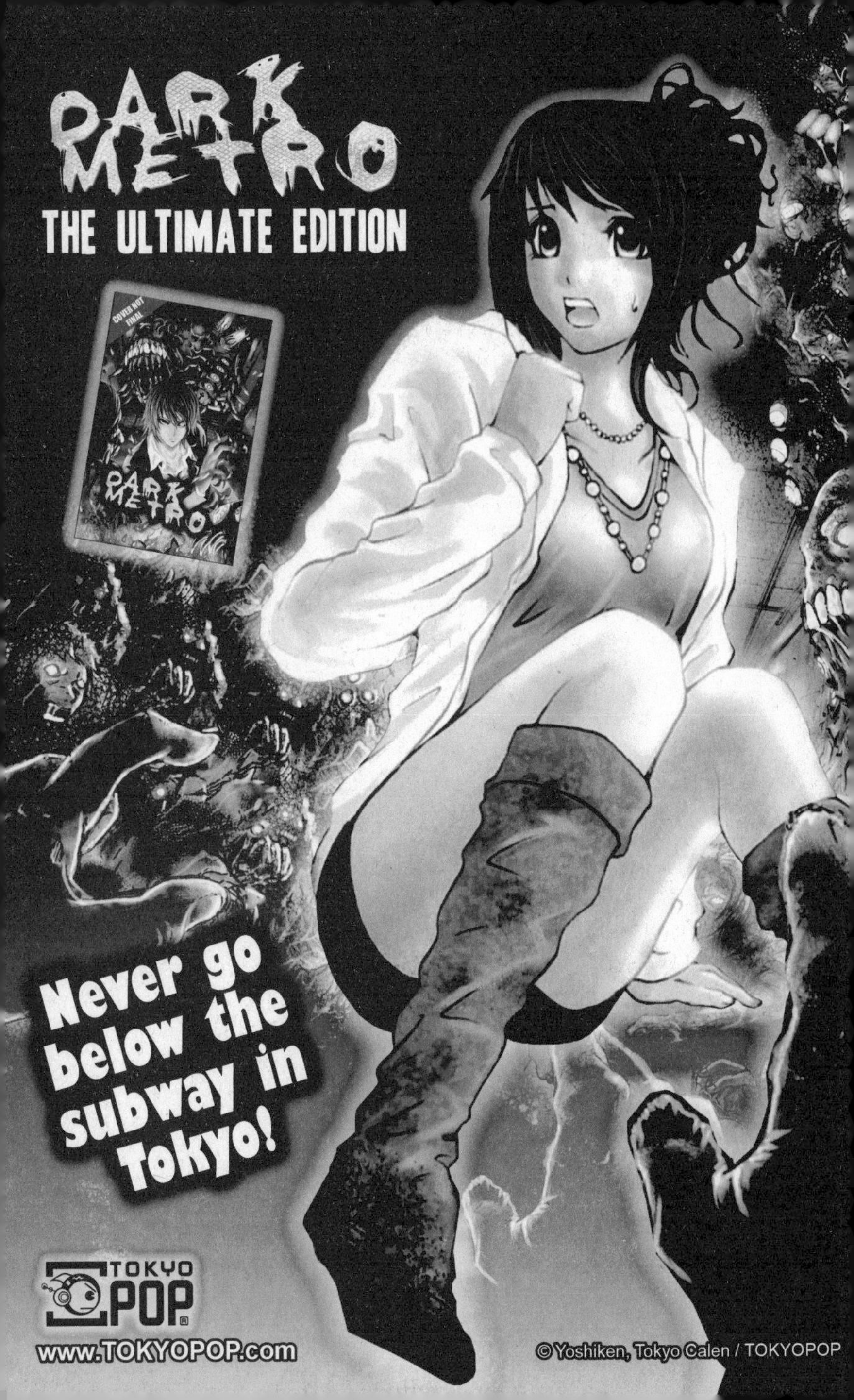
DARK METRO
THE ULTIMATE EDITION
COVER NOT FINAL
DARK METRO
Never go below the subway in Tokyo!
TOKYO POP
www.TOKYOPOP.com
© Yoshiken, Tokyo Calen / TOKYOPOP

The Author

"WHERE THERE'S A WILL THERE'S A WAY!" IS
GIN ZARBO'S CREDO, AND SINCE BEING BORN IN 1993 IN
SWITZERLAND THIS ARTIST HAS ALWAYS LOOKED FOR
NEW WAYS TO REALIZE HER DREAMS. SHE DREW HER FIRST
MANGA AT THE AGE OF 13 AND SELF-PUBLISHED HER FIRST
DOJINSHI, *COPE SOUL*. IN 2017 SHE GOT HER FIRST
PUBLISHING DEAL WHEN TOKYOPOP LICENSED *UNDEAD
MESSIAH*. GIN LOVES SHONEN MANGA AND READS SERIES
LIKE *BLEACH* (TITE KUBO) AND *TOKYO GHOUL* (SUI ISHIDA),
BUT ALSO BOYS' LOVE MANGA LIKE *TEN COUNT* (RIHITO
TAKARAI) AND *LOVE STAGE!!* (EIKI EIKI). THE IMPRESSIVE
MANGA COLLECTION IN HER STUDIO IS SHARED WITH HER
TWIN SISTER BAN, THE CREATOR BEHIND KAMO, ALSO
PUBLISHED BY TOKYOPOP. GIN'S FATHER IS ITALIAN AND
HER MOTHER COMES FROM THE DOMINICAN REPUBLIC,
SO CULTURAL DIVERSITY IS A HUGE PART OF HER
LIFE AND IS REFLECTED IN HER STORIES.

FACEBOOK: GINZARBO
TWITTER: GIN_ZARBO
INSTAGRAM: GIN.ZARBO

Undead Messiah Volume 1
Manga by: Gin Zarbo

Publishing Associate - Janae Young
Marketing Associate - Kae Winters
Technology and Digital Media Assistant - Phillip Hong
Digital Media Coordinator - Rico Brenner-Quiñonez
Licensing Specialist - Arika Yanaka
Translator - Kenneth Shinabery
Copy-editor - M. Cara Carper
Graphic Designer - Phillip Hong
Retouching and Lettering - Vibrraant Publishing Studio
Editor-in-Chief & Publisher - Stu Levy

A  Manga

TOKYOPOP and 🐸 are trademarks or registered trademarks of TOKYOPOP Inc.

TOKYOPOP inc.
5200 W Century Blvd
Suite 705
Los Angeles, CA 90045 USA

E-mail: info@TOKYOPOP.com
Come visit us online at www.TOKYOPOP.com

f www.facebook.com/TOKYOPOP
🐦 www.twitter.com/TOKYOPOP
▶ www.youtube.com/TOKYOPOPTV
📌 www.pinterest.com/TOKYOPOP
📷 www.instagram.com/TOKYOPOP

ISBN: 978-1-4278-5938-9

First TOKYOPOP Printing: June 2018
10 9 8 7 6 5 4 3 2 1
Printed in CANADA

STOP

THIS IS THE BACK OF THE BOOK!

How do you read manga-style? It's simple! Let's practice -- just start in the top right panel and follow the numbers below!

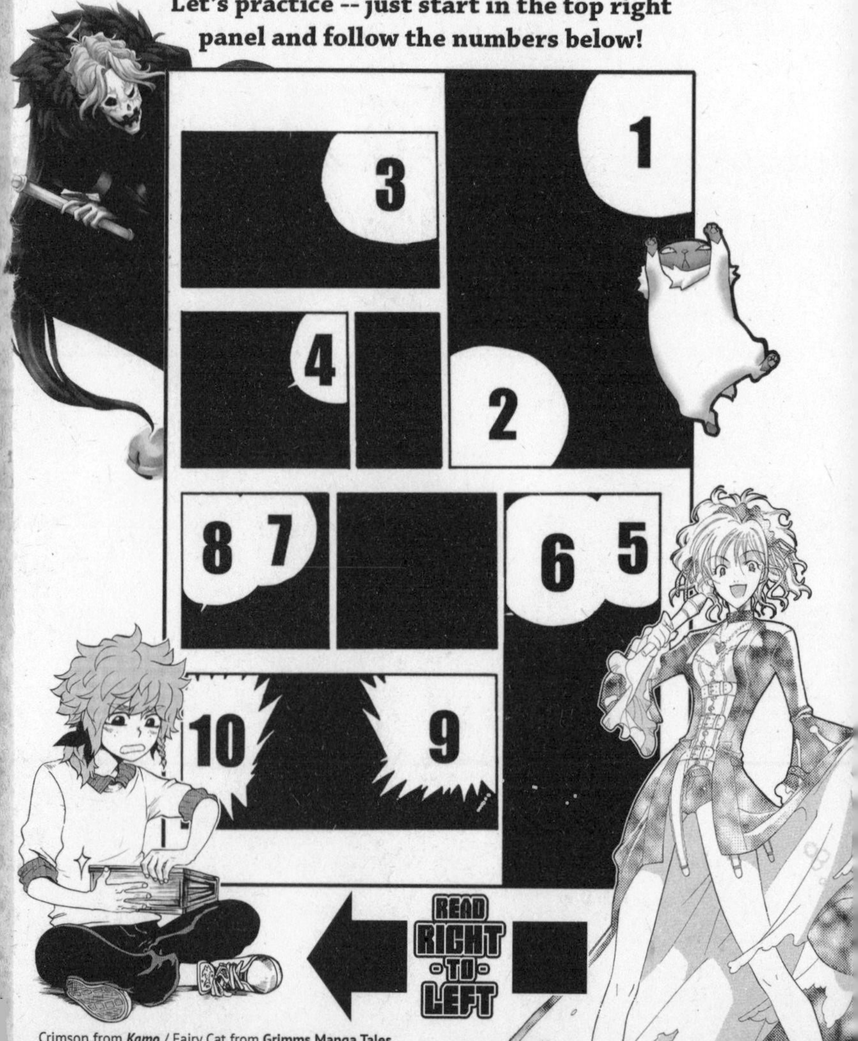
1
2
3
4
5
6
7
8
9
10
READ
RIGHT
-TO-
LEFT

Crimson from *Kamo* / Fairy Cat from **Grimms Manga Tales**
Morrey from *Goldfisch* / Princess Ai from *Princess Ai*